THE DUKES OF DUVAL COUNTY

THE DUKES OF DUVAL COUNTY

THE PARR FAMILY AND TEXAS POLITICS

ANTHONY R. CARROZZA

UNIVERSITY OF OKLAHOMA PRESS : NORMAN

LIBRARY OF CONGRESS CATALOGING-IN-PUBLICATION DATA

Names: Carrozza, Anthony R., 1942– author.

Title: Dukes of Duval County : the Parr family and Texas politics / Anthony
R. Carrozza.

Description: Norman : University of Oklahoma Press, 2017. | Includes
bibliographical references and index.

Identifiers: LCCN 2017005485 | ISBN 978-0-8061-5771-9 (hardcover) ISBN
978-0-8061-7566-9 (paper)   Subjects: LCSH: Parr family. | Parr, Archie, 1860 or 1861–
1942—Family. |

  Politicians—Texas—Duval County—Biography. | Duval County
  (Tex.)—Biography. | Duval County (Tex.)—Politics and government—20th
  century. | Elections—Texas—Duval County—History—20th century. |
  Political violence—Texas—Duval County—History—20th century. |
  Political corruption—Texas—Duval County—History—20th century. | Texas,
  South—Politics and government—20th century. | BISAC: HISTORY / United
  States / State & Local / Southwest (AZ, NM, OK, TX). | POLITICAL SCIENCE /
  Government / Local. | HISTORY / United States / 20th Century.
  Classification: LCC F392.D9 C37 2017 | DDC 976.4/4630630922 [B] —dc23
  LC record available at https://lccn.loc.gov/2017005485

The paper in this book meets the guidelines for permanence and durability of the
Committee on Production Guidelines for Book Longevity of the Council on Library
Resources, Inc. ∞

Copyright © 2017 by the University of Oklahoma Press, Norman, Publishing Division of
the University. Paperback published 2021. Manufactured in the U.S.A.

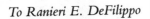

To Ranieri E. DeFilippo

CONTENTS

ILLUSTRATIONS

ACKNOWLEDGMENTS

This book would not have been possible without the help and guidance of several people. My agent, Claire Gerus, managed to get my efforts published. I am eternally grateful. University of Oklahoma Press acquisitions editor J. Kent Calder liked what I wrote and made publishing this book happen.

Throughout the years of research there were many who went out of their way to assist me. Among those to thank are Allison Ehrlich, archive coordinator for the *Corpus Christi Caller-Times*; Tim Ronk, library service supervisor, Houston Metropolitan Research Center, and his friend, Nicholas Phillips; Brandon Murray, librarian, Dallas History and Archives division, Dallas Public Library; Cathy Spitzenberger, photo collections specialist, University of Texas at Arlington; Margaret Harman, audiovisual archives, LBJ Library; Michelle Lambing, graphics coordinator, Texas State Preservation Board; the staff at the Steele Memorial Library, Elmira, New York, Owen Frank, Maria Rupp, Rose Woodard, Cola Thayer, and Pat Cuthbert; and Kathy A. Butler, of Alice, Texas, for identifying her father in a photograph.

Finally, my appreciation for those who made this book better: Sarah C. Smith, manuscript editor; Pippa Letsky, copy editor; Anna María Rodríguez, image wrangler; Julie Rushing, designer and typesetter; Anthony Roberts, jacket designer; and Susan Certo, indexer.

PART I
BIRTH OF A DYNASTY

CHAPTER 1

TEXAS POLITICS

Congressman Lyndon Baines Johnson had an opportunity to rise even higher politically in April 1941 with the sudden death of Senator John Morris Sheppard. Texas elections had long been determined by the Democratic primary; a win assured victory in November no matter who was on the Republican ticket. But this would be a special election with Democrats, Republicans, and Independents all going for the Senate seat at the same time. The official ballot listed twenty-nine names, including the formidable Governor Wilbert Lee "Pappy" O'Daniel, but only a plurality was needed to win.[1]

The special election was even more enticing to Johnson because it was being held in an off year. He could run for senator and still retain his House seat if he lost. He had already astounded political observers by coming from nowhere at the age of twenty-eight to win the House seat, and this time he had the support of President Roosevelt, who allowed Johnson to announce his senatorial candidacy on the White House steps.

As the June 28 election neared, Johnson began gaining in the polls until he passed the veteran O'Daniel. Up to this point, his campaign had been meticulously run by scrutinizing key precincts. Unfortunately, when victory seemed within his grasp, Johnson's people made a fatal error. Results from each precinct were reported to the Texas Election Bureau (an unofficial group of newspapers and radio stations), where tabulations determined the winner. John Connally, Johnson's campaign manager, kept calling bosses in key precincts they dominated to report their results as soon as possible, saying, "Get your vote in. Run it up."[2]

Election Day in Texas was Saturday, and by 1:30 on Sunday morning, the election bureau tabulated 95 percent of the votes with Johnson holding a 5,088 lead. At 5:00 P.M. on Tuesday the election bureau would issue its final report. Both the *Dallas News* and the *Houston Post* declared

Johnson the winner, and the coveted seat in the Senate was virtually his.[3] But this was Texas, and the election wasn't over until all the corrections, deletions, invalid ballots, and unreported results were in. Voting machines were being used in populous urban precincts, but rural Texas still depended on paper ballots, which took time to count, allowing for last-minute adjustment of "discrepancies" before being sent on to the Board of Elections.

With less than twenty thousand unreported votes remaining, Johnson's mistake of allowing early reporting didn't seem costly. By Monday night, "Pappy" was lagging by only one thousand votes. Before the night ended, the margin was seventy-seven votes. On Tuesday, the euphoria of becoming a U.S. senator abandoned Johnson as "corrections" whittled away more votes. By the end of the day, O'Daniel had won by 1,311 votes in a statewide election totaling 575,879 votes.[4]

After the election, President Roosevelt summoned Johnson to the White House to console him. Roosevelt told him during the meeting, "Lyndon, apparently you Texans haven't learned one of the first things we learned up in New York State, and that is that when the election is over, you have to sit on the ballot boxes."[5] The advice, a little late coming, may not have cheered the young congressman, but it was a lesson Johnson never forgot.

When O'Daniel chose not to run for reelection in 1948, Johnson decided his political career was at a turning point. If he ran for senator, he could not hold onto his House seat. The decision was even more difficult because his opponent would be former Texas governor Coke Robert Stevenson, who was even more popular than O'Daniel. For Johnson to win would require all the resources of a well-oiled political machine, including personnel to "sit on the ballot boxes." To accomplish this, Johnson enlisted the help of George Parr, a South Texas political boss who had backed Johnson in the 1941 special election.

No candidate achieved a majority in the July primary, so a special runoff primary was slated for August. Early results of the runoff primary had Stevenson leading by 800 votes, but by Monday evening it was 119. Tabulations and "correcting" continued until Friday, and Stevenson still held a slim 157-vote lead. That afternoon, six days after the election, another ballot box suddenly appeared with 200 votes for Johnson and only 2 for Stevenson. The corrected tally gave 494,104 votes to Stevenson and 494,191 to Johnson.[6] In an election with close to a million votes cast, George Parr had helped Johnson win by 87 votes.

The political power George Parr wielded was well entrenched in three southern Texas counties, and through alliances with other bosses it extended even further. His power was inherited from his father, Archer "Archie" Parr, who began the political machine and trained his son to duplicate his maneuverings in a dynasty that lasted over sixty years. Unlike urban bosses like Tom Pendergast in Kansas City and James Michael Curly in Boston, Archie's influence in South Texas was made possible by provisions in the 1875 Texas Constitution.

To decentralize government, framers of the constitution gave autonomous power to local districts. Every post—from local justice of the peace to chief justice of the Texas Supreme Court—was an elected position, leaving the governor few political appointments. Tax assessment and collection, election supervision, and control of public funds were handled by county officials. This made local governments ripe for corruption and influence by political bosses with access to public funds through officials they backed for election. Voting was controlled by doling out resources to constituents. Even the power to enforce the law rested mainly with local authorities. District judges impaneled grand juries and controlled their scope. A local political boss could easily rule by handpicking candidates. Only the federal government or the Texas Rangers could investigate criminal action, and the rangers needed a specific invitation from the locally elected district attorney.

In South Texas there was even more of an opportunity to establish a power base because of the makeup of the population. Over 90 percent of Duval County residents were of Mexican ancestry. They called themselves "Mexicans" whether or not they were U.S. citizens, and most were uneducated, illiterate, and poor. At the turn of the century, Duval ranked 253 out of 254 Texas counties in literacy, with the state ranking among the lowest nationwide. In 1930 Duval's illiteracy rate was 25.3 percent, and fewer than 7 percent of residents over twenty-five had completed high school.[7]

Since the 1880s, Anglo ranchers and businessmen controlled the vote of their Mexican laborers. The culture of Mexican peons being subjugated by wealthy hidalgo landowners remained firmly entrenched when they crossed the Rio Grande into South Texas. In Mexico they relied on their *patrónes* for guidance and direction; because of unfamiliarity with American culture and customs this domination passed to the gringo in Texas.

The son of George Berham Parr of Virginia and Sarah Pamela Givens of Kentucky, Archie was born Christmas Day 1860 on Matagorda Island, Texas. After the death of his father, he was forced to drop out of school at an early age to help earn money for the family. At the age of eleven, he became a ranch hand for the Fulton-Coleman Pasture Company, and by seventeen he was a trail boss on the famed Chisholm Trail, driving cattle from San Antonio to Abilene, Kansas. Arriving in Duval County at the age of twenty-three to work as foreman for the Lott and Nielson Pasture Company on their Sweden Ranch, he remained in the area for the next sixty years.[8] At the age of thirty, he married twenty-five-year-old Elizabeth Allen of Allendale, a graduate of the teacher's college at Huntsville. With money saved from his cowboy years, Archie purchased a ranch in Benavides for fifty cents an acre. Having no political ambitions, he was content to raise cattle and father six children.[9]

Fluent in Spanish, he became a benevolent patrón of his ranch hands and local Mexicans. A man of "even temperament and friendly manner," he was also capable of "outbursts of rage and arrogance."[10] He entered politics when elected county commissioner from Benavides in 1898 as a Democrat. Solidifying his power base, Archie was reelected in 1900, as he waited for the right opportunity. It arrived in late 1907, when John Daniel Cleary, Duval Democratic Party leader and county tax assessor, was killed in a San Diego restaurant.[11]

Cleary was also an oil property developer in the San Diego area. He owned land in the valuable Piedras Pintas oil field and was aggressive in securing properties for prospecting and development. Some felt his antagonistic manner may have been the reason for his death.[12] But there was a possible political motivation for his assassination. Against protests of Anglo ranchers, Cleary opened the Democratic Party to Mexicans and supported Mexican candidates for local public office. In 1906 his faction swept the general election, claiming every county office and all of the commissioner seats. The Republicans contested the elections, and a few days after the district court upheld the Democrats, Cleary became marked for assassination.

On December 20, 1907, Cleary joined oil man J. F. Maxwell and a bookkeeper named Stern for a late supper at a Mexican restaurant. Cleary sat on a stool with his back to the door. Halfway through their meal, a man standing on the sidewalk fired a double-barreled shotgun loaded with duck shot through the open door of the restaurant. Cleary was hit between the shoulders by eight pellets, penetrating his spinal cord and causing instant death.[13]

With no immediate suspects, wild rumors began spreading as to who was responsible. Archie Parr was mentioned as a possibility, but there was never any evidence to show he had anything to do with the killing. One newspaper speculated the killer was Mexican because "the act of shooting from a hiding place an unsuspecting and unprepared man" was typical of Mexicans, but, the article added, "if the work is that of a Mexican, a white man had a hand in it."[14]

A Texas Ranger investigation uncovered a three-man conspiracy. Former deputy sheriff Candelario Saenz was arrested as the shooter, and local merchant T. J. Lawson and his son Jeff, were accused of arranging the murder. Although Lawson was a Republican Party member, a political motive could not be established because he was also involved in a dispute with Cleary over control of the Piedras Pintas oil field. Evidence against the Lawsons was circumstantial, and the grand jury dismissed the charges. Only Saenz was indicted, but before the trial, two witnesses died of natural causes. Saenz went free but four years later was killed in a political dispute.[15]

In 2012 Saenz's grandson, named after his grandfather, told a reporter that in 1952 his father received a phone call from his uncle, the brother of Candelario. The uncle was dying and wanted to unburden a secret he had carried for years. He claimed Archie Parr was behind the murder, having hired a known assassin, Jose Estrada, to kill Cleary. Candelario Saenz, part of the conspiracy, agreed to deliver the payment to the killer, but when Saenz was arrested before the exchange could be made, Saenz's wife asked the brother to deliver the money.[16]

Archie quickly grabbed the reins and entrenched himself within the Duval Democratic Party. He was elected delegate to the Texas State Democratic Convention in May 1908 and became a member of the State Executive Committee where he formed lasting relationships with politicos who controlled nearby counties.[17] Reelected county commissioner, Archie began using the county treasury to solidify his paternalism by providing jobs for Mexican laborers on county roads and bridges. Poll taxes were added as an amendment to the state constitution in 1902 and became an established means of limiting the poor from voting (these taxes were declared unconstitutional in 1966). Needing votes of the poor to ensure political control, Archie had road crew supervisors deduct poll tax payments from wages and even provided for payment of poll taxes with his own money. By requiring all county employees to pay poll taxes, Archie padded the list with voters who would do his bidding on Election Day.

Ignoring state law, he ordered the county treasurer to issue checks to constituents without recording the purpose of the payments. Loyal voters counted on Archie to provide cash for food or funeral expenses or to tide them over between jobs. This unofficial system of welfare furthered his popularity, garnering more Mexican voters while at the same time reducing the political strength of the Duval Republican Party to a meaningless faction for the next sixty years. Furthering his dominance over local politics, Archie harassed voters by ordering the tax collector not to accept poll tax payments from anyone Archie targeted as a potential foe—Republican or Democrat. As a Duval County Democratic Executive Committee member, he eliminated precinct conventions to prevent opposition from rebelling party members and appointed precinct chairmen and the county executive committee—all of whom owed him their allegiance.

At the 1910 Texas Democratic Convention, Archie defended the bloc system of voting, saying "the Democrats of [Duval] got together and agreed to support the same candidates, and then cast their votes in accordance with the agreement." On election days he kept tight control by distributing pre-marked ballots to the mostly illiterate voters and assigned rifle-toting and pistol-packing guards to ensure compliance. Ballot box tampering was prevalent and with ballots marked in full view of his appointed election judges, Archie's candidates always won.[18]

In 1911 Archie attempted to gain control over county politics by having the county seat relocated to Benavides. The scheme met fierce opposition from Anglos in San Diego who feared that Archie's already growing power over Mexican bloc voting would increase. When this idea failed, he attacked the San Diego power base by arranging an election on May 18, 1912, to authorize San Diego to be incorporated. Both Republicans and independent Democrats vehemently opposed the plan that would allow Archie access to a new city government, which would provide him with additional funding to further his paternal handouts.

Tensions were high on Election Day as men filed into the courthouse to cast their votes. A group of Democrats suspecting fraud tried to gather affidavits from voters but were denied admission to the courthouse.[19] An argument broke out between Democratic county chairman C. M. "Neal" Robinson, who opposed the incorporation, and county clerk Pedro Eznal, who favored it. As the confrontation became heated, Constable Antonio Anguiano, a friend of Eznal's, drew his pistol and aimed it at Robinson. Three Anglos—Dr. Sam A. Roberts, a prominent San Diego physician, Charles K. Gravis, ex-sheriff and Duval County ranchman, and Frank G. Robinson, brother of Neal—drew their guns and opened fire. When the shooting ended, Anguiano lay dead on the street. Eznal, mortally wounded, died thirty minutes later. A third Mexican, Candelario Saenz, candidate for sheriff in the election scheduled two months later, heard the shots. The unarmed Saenz ran to the scene and was shot twice and killed by Gravis. Ironically, Saenz was the same man indicted four years earlier for the murder of John Cleary.[20]

Roberts, Gravis, and Frank Robinson made no attempt to escape and were all arrested by Sheriff Antonio W. Tobin. Unarmed at the time, C. M. Robinson was not arrested. As tensions in the community rose and local Mexicans geared up for a race riot, automobiles arrived loaded with sixty armed white men from nearby Alice. The shooting occurred at 9:00 A.M., but Sheriff Tobin feared a "general feud would begin before noon." To help quiet the situation, Texas Rangers were ordered to San Diego.[21] To help ease the rising tide of emotions, after putting his family on a train to Corpus Christi to get them out of harm's way, Archie headed back to San Diego. Encountering Mexicans bent on retaliation, Archie urged them, "Put up your guns, *mis amigos*, and let the law take its course."[22]

After the grand jury indicted the three men for murder, bail was set at fifteen thousand dollars each. Arguing that the "affair had gained such notoriety," Judge W. B. Hopkins transferred the case to Austin so the defendants could receive fair trials. Difficulty in having witnesses travel to Austin, plus a crowded docket, resulted in the cases being transferred again. They finally came to trial in Richmond in Fort Bend County. In his charge to members of the jury, Judge Norman G. Kittrell told them to return a verdict of not guilty. Heeding his instructions, they acquitted

Robinson. The other two defendants were tried separately, but with the same results. After the verdict Kittrell reportedly said, "Gentlemen, if I had my way I'd give you all Winchesters and tell you to go back and finish the job."[23]

The referendum voting continued the day of the shooting but failed to pass.[24] Although justice hadn't been served that day, for Archie it proved to be the catalyst forging a binding relationship with Mexicans that would steadfastly cement his rule in South Texas politics. On that fateful day, Archie was the only Anglo who stood on the side of the Mexicans and they never forgot it. Loyalty among the Hispanics was a deep-rooted value, and Archie became the trusted gringo. Without any voice in government, they took the next best thing; Archie Parr would be "El Patrón" to them and the "Duke of Duval" to the Anglos.

The Anglos in the area were a different story. Edward Cunningham Lasater, a Republican and former Progressive candidate for governor, and a wealthy rancher with over three hundred thousand acres in Duval and neighboring Starr County, was a constant thorn in Archie's side. The campaign he initiated against Archie struck at the heart of the political machine—the money that kept it oiled. With support from a group of Duval property owners, Lasater declared they would not pay county taxes until after a complete audit of the county's books. "Though the law requires an annual auditing of the accounts of any county government there has not been any such auditing in Duval County in eleven years," Lasater said.[25]

Led by Lasater, several taxpayers filed a petition in court asking for an audit. Another petition they filed asked that minutes of the Duval County Commissioner's Court be produced. They claimed that twenty-four thousand dollars had been collected by the county in 1913 for various uses, including a road and bridge fund, a jail and courthouse fund, and a general fund. Noting that the funds had been spent and there was "no public work upon which any large amount of money should have been expended," he wanted to know "for what purpose the money was expended." After swearing in a new grand jury, Judge W. B. Hopkins told jury members they had authority to appoint three citizens to examine county finances. Archie Parr was among the ten on the grand jury. Organized in 1876, Duval had never had an independent audit of its books, and Archie wasn't about to allow it to occur for the first time.[26]

After Hopkins appointed a professional accountant, the county's tax records suddenly disappeared from the courthouse. Lasater sought return of the records, as well as an injunction halting collection of a tax ostensibly levied for the creation of a county courthouse and jail. Archie Parr was called upon to testify regarding the injunction. Arrogant as well as colorful, his testimony offered a glimpse into the power he held. He was asked the condition of the county courthouse and jail, repairs made to both, access to county records, and the tax levied:

Q. *Has [the courthouse] ever had any substantial repairs of any kind since you have been there?*

A. Not to my knowledge.

Q. *Well, what is its present condition with reference to whether it is dilapidated or not?*

A. Very dilapidated, and it's kinder down on one side.

Q. *Has [the jail] ever had any repair?*

A. Not that I know of.

Q. *Now, Mr. Parr, . . . you have passed an order denying us access to the records . . . [Will you] permit us now to inspect those records, and let us have access to them?*

A. No, we are not going to let you see them.

Q. *We will have some difficulty in obtaining proof, probably, Mr. Parr, won't we?*

A. It sorter looks like it.

Q. *You levied it [the additional tax]—did you contemplate making any improvements?*

A. We did not.[27]

The court refused to lift the injunction and the battle continued.

CHAPTER 2

THE DUKE OF DUVAL

When the audit case came to court, accountant George Kidd said several county commissioners denied him access to records. N. A. Hoffman, testifying for the San Diego State Bank where tax funds were deposited, said he frequently gave out funds "over the signature of A. Parr," but he didn't know the purpose of the withdrawals. He said checks were often signed by Parr. "Some of the orders signed by Mr. Parr were written on a blank piece of paper," he said. "There was one check that came in drawn on the County Depository payable to Loftis Brothers, a diamond concern. I believe it is in Chicago." When testimony ended, Judge Hopkins issued a writ of mandamus ordering the books audited by the outside accountant and an injunction against the commissioners' court restraining them from interfering.[1]

Not foolish enough to ignore the court decree, Archie employed another tactic to prevent the audit. The court ordered District Clerk J. V. Palacios to turn over the records, but when the plaintiff's attorney tried to serve notice he was told Palacios had resigned. Furthermore, county judge S. H. Woods, Sheriff A. W. Tobin, county treasurer Alonzo Lopez, and county commissioner Archie Parr had all resigned.[2] Each one was replaced by Archie's handpicked men. Without proper names on the order, the writ and injunction could not be served.

Needing a stronger power base than the county commissioners' court, Archie had another card up his sleeve. He announced he would run for state senator from the Twenty-Third District, a seat held by John G. Willacy, who declared he was not seeking reelection. With sixteen counties, the Twenty-Third Senatorial District was one of the largest in Texas.[3]

Having resigned from the commissioners' court, Archie wasn't out of a job for long. In July 1914, he defeated Judge W. J. Perkins for state senator. Perkins received a majority in predominately white counties, but

12

Archie went ahead anyway with the $60,000 construction contract, issuing warrants paid upon submission to the county.[12]

Four months later, the temporary injunction was lifted and Archie was back in business. Always a believer in taking care of his friends, Archie passed the construction contract to one of Jim Wells's friends, L. G. Hamilton. The contract called for $67,500 to construct the building, but when completed, Hamilton had been paid over $70,000. Another $50,000 went to other "friends" and local businessmen for furnishings, plumbing, and other necessities. A review of funds spent was made by an independent contractor, and although no evidence of graft was found, the final report calculated costs had been inflated by $40,000.[13] Undaunted, the county commissioners awarded a $60,000 contract for road repair and bridge construction to Marshall White, "without advertising for, or receiving bids." A suit, settled out of court, by eight angry taxpayers reduced the contract to $25,000.[14] By simply providing two additional contracts, however, White was paid another $40,000, bringing the total to $5,000 above the original. A subsequent lawsuit to uphold the original agreement failed, and Archie pressed for an additional $100,000 bond issue to provide for improvements that the original contract had failed to correct.

Archie also faced a federal investigation. In June 1915 a federal grand jury indicted Judge Hopkins and forty-two Nueces County officials and residents for corruption in the 1914 election. Lasater, seeing an opportunity to attack Parr on the federal level, went to Washington to see U.S. attorney general Thomas Watt Gregory, a Texan who might be sympathetic to local problems. U.S. Attorney John E. Green was appointed to investigate the 1912 Duval County election but was advised by Gregory to restrict his inquiry to misconduct in the election of federal officials. After an eleven-day federal grand jury inquiry and testimony from sixty witnesses, a multitude of election fraud evidence was uncovered; however, none involved election of federal officials. The matter was quietly laid to rest, and the statute of limitations elapsed two weeks later.[15]

Based on findings of the independent audit, the anti-Parr forces persuaded Judge Taylor to convene a grand jury to further investigate. Milton Dubose, foreman of the grand jury and longtime resident of Duval County, subpoenaed several county officials, but not Archie. After Sheriff Tobin finished testifying, the grand jury refused to allow him to take back the records he had brought to court. A little later, accompanied by Tobin, Archie stormed into the grand jury room, pushed his way past the district attorney, and confronted the grand jury.

"Who is foreman of this grand jury?" he demanded. After Dubose acknowledged his position, neither the district attorney nor the grand jury foreman was prepared for Archie's next move. He ordered Tobin to gather the county records and follow him.

"I don't want this grand jury to be doing what the last one did," he stated as he left.[16] Only in Duval County could Parr violate the sanctity of a grand jury. Judge Taylor was not amused. Summoning Parr and Sheriff Tobin before the bench, he fined each man one hundred dollars for contempt of court and had them escorted by a Texas Ranger to the county jail to serve a one-hour sentence.[17]

Details of how business was conducted in Duval began emerging after accountant George Kidd testified. Road work and construction costs of the new courthouse were the main focus of funds gone astray. Nepotism was charged and backed by receipts of warrants issued to Jose Carrillo, brother of a county commissioner who received two thousand dollars for "alleged" work. One warrant read—"Jose Carrillo, road work, $50"—without specifying the work done.[18] Fred M. Percival, the engineer hired to oversee county costs, testified he made a thorough examination of Duval County roads to determine if work paid for had been done. In one instance, the commissioners paid for construction of a twenty-five-mile-long, thirty-foot-wide road out of San Diego, but Percival discovered that after one mile the road narrowed to twenty-five feet wide for the remaining distance.[19]

Ignoring the New Year's Day holiday, Judge Taylor continued the hearing. Former Duval County treasurer Crisoforo Y. Hinojosa testified that when he left office there was ten thousand dollars on the county books. The plaintiff's attorney asked, "Can you remember how the money was turned over to your successor, if it was turned over?" Hinojosa could not say whether a sum of one dollar or of ten thousand dollars was turned over. Leon Garcia, who assumed the post after Hinojosa, said that "the county books were clean and that there were no funds on hand" when he took office.[20]

Judge Givens Parr took the stand on the last day of testimony. He felt the commissioners had "acted in good faith" and nothing had been done to collect alleged monies due from former officials because the county attorney advised against such action. Givens said he "had never heard until day before yesterday" that the county books were missing.[21]

After twelve days of hearings, Judge Taylor handed down his decision. The four county commissioners were ordered to be removed from office, but he refused to take action against Givens Parr. "As to the County Judge," he said, "I have not been able to make a decision that he should be removed." Taylor also denied the injunction against constructing the new courthouse, allowing the existing contract to proceed and paid with county warrants.[22] Four new commissioners were appointed that afternoon, but in the election later that year all four ousted commissioners were restored to their previous posts.

Meanwhile, the Parr machine continued raiding county coffers as if they were its personal bank account. Six months later, Duval County voters overwhelmingly authorized $100,000 in bonds to construct a system of roads throughout the county. Duval County debt continued to soar, exceeding $315,000 by the end of 1916. No evidence of kickbacks was ever uncovered, even though only those who supported Archie were awarded bids.[23] The money kept pouring in, but there was little to show for it since funds were diverted for whatever purpose Archie decided.

Duval County was now completely under Archie's control. If anyone needed a job they went to see Archie. If anyone wanted to run for office, his endorsement was sought; without it a candidate never had a chance. In an article by Kaye Northcott in the *Texas Observer*, Archie was described as a one-man show in Duval: "Senator Parr treated the Duval County budget as his own personal bank account, but a lot of the money trickled back to Parr's faithful Mexican friends. Parr ran a one-man welfare department, and anyone who needed money for food or clothing or a doctor's bill could get it, with no strings attached."[24]

Even in the state senate, Archie proved invincible. His old adversary Ed Lasater tried going after the Duke of Duval by resurrecting an old issue—purchasing of poll tax receipts. Lasater's son Garland described his father's crusade:

In one election, Dad was incensed about Archie Parr buying poll taxes. He employed a lawyer from Fort Worth to hire detectives and get some evidence. Later the attorney stood up in the senate and read the charges and stated that he had proof Mr. Parr had paid the poll taxes. Parr was asked if he had anything to say. Parr said, "yes," and when he got to the podium, he said, "I have been accused of buying poll taxes. I have 200 right here in my pocket. We all buy them," and he swept his hand around the room. Everyone just whooped and hollered and that was the end of the whole investigation.[25]

Keeping the enemy at bay was an art form practiced daily by Archie Parr. But keeping control was not always an easy task.

Archie's toughest political battle came not on the local but on the state level, when he prepared for his 1918 reelection. His troubles stemmed from his avid support of Governor James Edward "Pa" Ferguson who had been impeached and removed from office in 1917 for malfeasance, perjury, and misuse of state funds. Ferguson always acquiesced to Archie on any Duval County appointments, and Archie stuck by his friend, being one of only four senators who voted against all twenty-one articles of impeachment.[26] The new governor, William Pettus Hobby, was not a crony of Archie and decided to back Judge D. W. Glasscock as candidate for Archie's senate seat. Hobby had his own reelection battle because he was running against the ousted Ferguson.

Glasscock was a formidable opponent with the backing of state Democratic Party leaders, Duval anti-Parr forces, and Texas Rangers. If that coalition wasn't enough, Archie also faced a group of new and potentially dangerous voters—women. The Nineteenth Amendment hadn't been ratified, but Texas anticipated it by allowing women to vote in the 1918 primary. Archie had supported every anti-suffrage vote in the senate, and women were not the type of electorate he wanted in Duval. It was a long hot summer, and the campaign provided even more heat—enough to carry the contest through the primaries, past the general election, and on to the floor of the senate with occasional stops along the way for legal battles in the courts.

During the election, the openly pro-Glasscock Texas Rangers made their presence known at polling places, intimidating Mexican voters, and in some cases driving them away. The first results in Duval gave Archie 584 votes with none for Glasscock. A revised total gave Archie 821 votes, and a subsequent tally upped his count to 1,162—still with no votes for his opponent. The *Corpus Christi Caller* cried foul, pointing out that the total in Duval County two years ago had been 816.[27]

Nominating the Democratic candidate for state senator would be made at the district convention in Corpus Christi on August 24. Archie was still 125 votes short of winning in the last count reported when he made his appearance holding the official results in his hand. Parr challenged the election on three counts: he wanted the twelve to sixteen hundred votes he held from Duval counted; votes from Brooks County should be disqualified because his name hadn't appeared on the ballot; and he challenged the right of women to vote in the primary.[28]

The Democratic Party Executive Committee accepted the 1,303 Duval vote tally from Archie (eligible voters numbered under 900). Glasscock had 23 votes, so Archie was declared the winner by 118 votes. That afternoon, delegates from eight counties in the contested district, along with three delegates from Cameron County, met in convention. They threw out the entire Duval vote total and declared Glasscock the nominee. Not to be outdone, Archie held his *own* convention, attended by delegates from seven counties and the remaining Cameron delegates, and was certified the nominee.[29] Each convention submitted its nominee to the secretary of state requesting certification. The fight was on.

Hobby had defeated Ferguson in the primary, and his faction was in control of the party's convention. At the State Democratic Convention in Waco the Credentials Committee drafted a report condemning Duval voting practices and called for "purification of the ballot" to prevent any repetition of abuses. They recommended the Duval delegation not be seated and the "alleged" vote tally submitted by Archie not counted. Amid cheers from those gathered, the convention refused to certify Archie and gave the nomination to Glasscock.[30]

Undeterred, Archie filed suit in Judge Taylor's court to set aside the convention's nomination and declare him the winner. The hearing was set for September 23, but in the meantime, the secretary of state decided to certify Glasscock as the Democratic nominee.[31] Before the court hearing took place, Archie had some backroom dealing to take care of first.

Judge Taylor presided over the Seventy-Ninth District, but a "sweetheart" arrangement was made for Judge F. G. Chambliss in the Thirty-Sixth District to handle the case. Defeated in his own reelection bid, Chambliss also had a suit contending the women's vote should be declared unconstitutional. It was agreed that Chambliss would hear Archie's case at his court in Hidalgo County, and Taylor would preside over Chambliss's case in San Patricio County.

On opening day Archie's attorney, Marshall Hicks of San Antonio, obtained a temporary injunction preventing ballots being issued with Glasscock's name on them. Glasscock's counsel, Claude Pollard of Houston, was absent because he was handling the case against Chambliss. After a one-week trial without a jury, Chambliss ruled Archie was the Democratic nominee for the general election, and it came as no surprise that Chambliss later won his lawsuit in Judge Taylor's courtroom.[32]

Glasscock refused to fold. Backed by ardent supporters and with less than two weeks before the general election, he began a write-in campaign. Claiming to be the rightful nominee, he urged voters to scratch out Parr's name on the ballot and write in his. Hobby-Glasscock Clubs sprang up overnight to rid their district of the "corrupt machine" and install "clean politics."[33]

Governor Hobby, now assured of reelection, provided services of the Texas Rangers to help Glasscock in the November election. Rangers were posted at every predominantly Mexican rural polling place, and through intimidation and outright interference (Mexicans were warned if they failed to pass illiteracy tests they would go to prison), many of Archie's usual supporters shied away from voting. In Duval County, where thirteen hundred votes had been cast in the primary, only two hundred showed up to vote on Election Day.

Early returns gave Glasscock a clear-cut victory. With half reporting complete tallies, and the remaining counties giving him the lead, uncounted votes from a few ballot boxes didn't seem to matter. As counting continued, he still held a lead of less than two hundred votes. "The elimination of Archie Parr is not certain," a *Corpus Christi Caller* editorial warned, and they were right.[34]

One month after the election, Archie made his move by releasing the final count from the stray counties. Starr County gave Archie 341 votes while Glasscock received 4. The *Corpus Christi Caller* reported that "not only the great majority of the voters were alien Mexicans, but that in many instances the presiding judges of the election could neither read nor write the English language and on sworn affidavits they said they did not know whether Archie Parr was running for constable or for president of

Mexico."[35] As predicted, Archie managed to garner enough votes to have Judge H. R. Suterland of Nueces County, who held certifying authority for the election, declare him the winner by 624 votes. But Glasscock would not concede defeat.

When the Texas Senate convened in January, Glasscock filed charges with the Privileges and Elections Committee, whose responsibility was to resolve election challenges and determine member qualification. Presiding over the senate, Lieutenant Governor William Arnold Johnson ruled that since the contested election was not officially before the senate, Archie should be sworn in.[36]

Although Glasscock wanted hearings to include misconduct in the primary and general election, Archie tried to convince the committee to save time by concentrating on the general election. "If I have not won the election fairly and squarely," Parr told the committee, "I shall step down and out." Hurling charges, Archie said "every affidavit secured by the contestant was gotten by a ranger at the point of a six-shooter."[37]

Recently recovered from an appendicitis operation, Glasscock rose to make his statement to the committee. He charged that Parr "was surrounded in his county by greasy Mexicans with long guns." He added that Judge Chambliss "had been driven from his county by his outraged people." Archie was furious and jumped to his feet to challenge Glasscock.

"Sit down," Glasscock exclaimed as Archie neared, "you can have your day in court."

"I don't want to speak to the committee," Archie replied. "I'm after you now—you can't insult me."

After the sergeant-at-arms restored order, Glasscock continued pleading for an impartial inquiry. In an executive session held that evening, the committee ruled it had the right to investigate both the primary and the general elections. More important, a motion would be made to have the entire senate sit as a committee to hear the evidence.[38]

While waiting for the motion to be heard, Glasscock's attorney filed affidavits gathered by Texas Rangers. Saying that he had heard Mexican voters calling Archie "El Presidente," one voter said he thought Parr was "president of the 16 states," referring to the district counties. One Hidalgo precinct cast all 157 votes for Archie. "The ballot was a long one, but these unlettered Mexicans knew who to support from the candidate for governor on down and strangely enough made no errors in marking their ballots." Comparing those districts to an Austin precinct, "where university professors vote" and ballots are thrown out because they are not properly made out, the petition said: "These Mexican voters are great for accuracy and never make a political bobble."[39]

By unanimous decision, the senate agreed to sit as a body to hear testimony. Glasscock's attorney asserted it was "folly" to issue subpoenas as most witnesses would "escape across the Rio Grande." He asked that Texas Rangers be enlisted to serve subpoenas, escort witnesses to Austin, and stay with them until they completed their testimony.[40] With the hundreds of witnesses Glasscock and Archie intended to call, the trial promised to be a lengthy one, costing Texas thousands of dollars.[41]

Hearings before the entire Texas Senate began in February and lasted over a month. In the circus-like atmosphere, Archie attended every session. A raised platform for witnesses was placed in front of the senate reading clerk's desk; an interpreter sat nearby and Archie sat alongside his attorney directly in front.[42] Not allowed to participate or vote, Archie quietly took his seat and listened to witnesses testifying about Duval politics and how he controlled it all.

Archie's attorney contended that only testimony concerning the general election should be heard. He reasoned that since records of the primary had been destroyed as required by law, and Glasscock had not filed to contest the primary, the senate should focus solely on the general election. The senate disagreed. Since the Privileges and Elections Committee had already voted to include the primary, the full senate would hear testimony relating to both contests.[43]

Outside the senate doors, a large crowd of Mexican witnesses brought to the capitol by Texas Rangers milled around waiting to be called to testify. Jesus Oliveira, an election judge at San Jose, was asked about the 270 votes cast in his precinct. He testified he was the only person in the polling place who could read English, so he "fixed all the ballots for Parr."

"How did you come to make out all the ballots for Parr?"

"They said they wanted to vote for Parr and all the men who Parr wanted," he replied.[44]

Testimony revealed that if an anti-Parr citizen in Duval County wanted to vote, it was difficult for him to receive a poll tax receipt. If a precinct didn't support his candidates, Archie solved the problem by not giving them a ballot box. If an insurgent independent tried to run for county commissioner, Archie altered the precinct boundaries, thereby eliminating the opposition. Election day practices such as helping illiterate voters mark their ballots by Parr-appointed precinct officials were commonplace.

Testimony continued but became a repetition of revelations already disclosed by previous witnesses. At one point Glasscock's attorney tried to clarify the aim of the Glasscock campaign. It was not a campaign against Mexicans, he said, but an "onward and upward movement" to purify the ballot and return decency to politics in the border counties. He added:

> This thing of these illiterate Mexicans voting down here is not the fault of the Mexicans, don't ever get that into your head. If you will let those Mexicans alone, they would be just as indifferent to the elections held in that country as the Negroes are in East Texas now. But it is the politician, the bosses, the white men who seek to control the offices and the policies of that country, and who pay the poll taxes for them, and drag them to the election and vote them as . . . they have been voted here.

Archie's attorney jumped at the opportunity to place the hearings in perspective by attacking Glasscock's motives. "It is a bitter political fight by the enemies of Senator Parr," he contended, "cloaked under the guise of an 'uplift movement.'"[45]

Archie's attorney began his case by calling twenty-three voters and three election clerks from La Salle County. Glasscock, who wasn't the untarnished angel depicted in the campaign, listened to testimony about abuses he had condoned. Witnesses testified that Texas Rangers warned Mexicans not to vote "if they could not read and write in English," effectively keeping many of Archie's supporters away. The U.S. Secret Service was questioned about its role in the primary when an agent testified that federal officers were in Duval—but "just to observe the situation." Archie's attorney announced he would end his case after calling one more witness.[46]

Judge James B. Wells of Brownsville, long considered the political boss in his area, was given due respect by the senate because of his reputation. Wells offered an explanation of bloc voting in the district. Most of the voters are Mexicans, he said, and "they are like Indians and they follow leadership based on trust and friendship." He denied being a political boss, saying he had the "confidence" of people in his district. He supported Parr because he considered him a "true Democrat," unlike Glasscock, who received Republican support. Wells proved a willing and articulate witness for Parr, but under cross-examination he became suddenly reticent. Glasscock's attorney managed to elicit that Wells "had scouts among the opposition" during the Corpus Christi convention and "knew all that was said and done in even the secret meetings."[47]

Even though the entire Texas Senate had been sitting as a whole, the Committee on Privileges and Elections took a vote on its recommendation to the senate. Two senators were absent and not paired when, by a vote of fourteen to twelve, Archie was recommended for the seat.[48] Heading into the final senate vote, Archie knew he had fifteen senators on his side, but this was exactly half the senate; he needed one more to avoid Lieutenant Governor Johnson casting the deciding vote.

The committee voted on two propositions: the first was to award Glasscock the seat, which was defeated twenty to six; the second was to award Archie the seat, but a third proposition was offered to declare the seat vacant and send it back to the district for another election. The third proposition was defeated fourteen to twelve, and the one to seat Archie was adopted by a vote of fourteen to twelve.[49]

After one thousand pages of testimony, the senate listened to one final round of debate from members on the floor. Most offered opinions or reasons for how they would vote, but not much was added to sway others. The roll call was taken and, one by one, senators cast their vote until the count reached fifteen for Archie and fourteen for Glasscock.

Senator Rienzi M. Johnson, who consulted with Governor Hobby before voting, rose to speak before casting the deciding vote. Because he spoke in a low voice, senators, stenographers, and clerks left their seats to move closer. When he said he agreed with Hobby's decision to send Texas Rangers to observe the election, Archie must have cringed. But Johnson wasn't finished. "Both sides to the contest sought votes by the old method," he said. "Did the evidence show Glasscock was legally elected? I believe Glasscock did not make out his case."[50] With Johnson casting the last vote, the final tally was sixteen to fourteen to seat Archie Parr.

It had been the most challenging test of the Parr machine, but Archie survived. He never made a major speech during his senate years; the state capitol seemed to be only a power base to further control back home.

Called "The Silent Senator" or "Dean of the Texas Senate," during his tenure he solidified his Duval power by delivering lopsided votes to candidates he supported.[51] Archie could always be counted on in the senate for his loyal support, but sometimes it got him in trouble, as happened in the case of James E. Ferguson.

Ferguson was governor until impeached and disqualified from ever again holding an elected office. Archie, a steadfast supporter, wouldn't let the matter rest. He introduced a resolution to expunge the impeachment record, but when it failed, Archie tried another tactic.[52]

Late afternoon on Friday, February 9, 1923, the state senate was without a quorum and repeated efforts to adjourn until Monday had failed. During a lull in the proceedings, Archie temporarily held the chair. He quickly recognized Senator Joe Burkett of Eastland, who after recalling the action of the senate when it impeached Ferguson introduced a resolution: "That said James E. Ferguson be and he is hereby declared to be henceforth pardoned, relieved and released from the terms and provisions thereof; and that he be hereafter qualified to hold any office under the State of Texas to which he may be elected by the people or to which he may be legally appointed."[53]

A quick voice vote was taken as senators shouted for recognition, but Archie kept pounding the gavel asking for votes, and the resolution passed. Still banging the gavel, Archie then recognized Senator I. D. Fairchild, who moved to reconsider the vote and table the motion to reconsider. This tactic effectively cut off other motions to reconsider—with the exception of one to rescind the action. But that required a two-thirds vote to carry and not enough senators were present. Fairchild then moved to adjourn the session, and the motion carried.[54]

The uproar in the chamber was immediate. Lieutenant Governor Davidson rushed to the platform and declared the senate was still in session. Absent senators were summoned, and Davidson quickly recognized Senator Bailey of Dewitt. "Mr. President," Bailey said, "I move that we expunge all proceedings that occurred from the time the Lieutenant Governor left the chair until he returned to it again." While Senator Fairchild shouted that the senate had already adjourned, Davidson pounded the gavel so hard that "shredded chips jumped up into the air." A voice vote was called and the motion passed. Ferguson had been exonerated by the Texas Senate, but only for thirty minutes.[55]

When the senate convened on Monday, every available senator was there as roll was called. Asking to be recognized, Archie rose to speak. He said he had "acted as he understood the rules, [and] the lieutenant governor did not know what was to occur when he gave the chair temporarily" to him. He apologized to those senators "who may feel hurt about the matter." After Archie sat down, Davidson said: "The chair appreciates those remarks." Several resolutions were proposed to condemn Archie's actions, but the matter was laid to rest.[56]

Archie's political power was firmly entrenched. Making the trip to San Diego to visit the Duke of Duval became a necessity for any office-seeker in a local or statewide election. Speaker of the House John Nance "Cactus Jack" Garner, who became vice president to Franklin Roosevelt; J. Frank Dobie, chronicler of Texas folklore; members of the Kleberg family, who owned the famed King Ranch; and a list of future governors, congressmen, and U.S. senators all came to see him, although some preferred to confer with him at the Nueces Hotel in Corpus Christi. As for Archie, his main concern was which of his three sons would take the reins upon his retirement.

CHAPTER 3
GEORGE PARR'S EARLY YEARS

George Berham Parr was born March 1, 1901, in San Diego, Texas, in a rented house his father kept in town. Named after his grandfather who fought in the Mexican War with Zachary Taylor, George was raised on his father's ranch, Los Horcones (the forked poles), south of Benavides. He was the second of three boys and the fifth of six children (his mother Elizabeth lost one child). His father insisted that George learn to speak Spanish before English and "think like a [Mexican]."[1]

The ranch house was a sprawling conglomeration that began with five rooms; as each child was born, Archie had ranch hands tie ropes to one of the tenant shacks and drag it to be attached to the house. By the time the youngest son, Atlee, was born, there was no place to attach the next unit, so a shack was dragged to the front yard and left on its own to be a bedroom. By then, the house had "a floor plan with the rough design of a fallen prickly pear cactus."[2]

Duval County, a semi-arid region with flat terrain undulating to eight hundred feet above sea level, was ranch and cattle country; oil would come later. Most of the arid climate and poor soil, typically a hard white caliche, would support minimal farming with less than 1 percent of Duval considered prime farmland. Surrounding hills were covered with *huajillo*, a thorny, dense brush offering protection to small wildlife and food for deer.

George was eleven when his father placed the family on a train to Corpus Christi after the Election Day massacre of three Mexicans. Violence was part of South Texas life, and George had an early initiation as to how it played a role in local politics. When Archie was elected to the Texas Senate, George, age thirteen, served as a legislative page. He loved exploring offices and archives at the state capitol. "I once knew where every bookcase and closet was," he recalled.[3] Archie began schooling his

27

son on the art of politics. "You'd better try to make some new friends every day," he told George, "just to take the place of the ones you're bound to lose when you're in politics."[4]

After his brief brush with the political scene, George attended West Texas Military Academy in San Antonio (the most notable graduate was Douglas MacArthur) for the next four years and spent the summer of 1917 in a cadet corps patrolling the Mexican border. His venture was cut short after he contracted a case of intestinal worms. Failing to graduate from the academy, he attended high school in Corpus Christi where he played football on the team that won the South Texas championship that year. He graduated at twenty.

George's college career was a series of starts and stops continuing until 1926 when he was twenty-five. In 1920 he began a two-year agricultural course at Texas A&M College before finishing high school, but he lasted only six days. His reason for leaving was the hazing he received.[5]

In February 1921, Archie Parr introduced a resolution in the state senate to investigate hazing at Texas A&M and was appointed to a three-member committee to conduct hearings. When the committee held hearings on the Texas A&M campus, students testified having been forced to "make love to kewpie dolls" and participate in "prune-eating races" to see who consumed the most.[6] The next witness heard by the committee was George Parr.

He testified that during his six days at A&M he had been subjected to three whippings from upperclassmen using long paddles. He had been required to attend "bull pens" every evening, a gathering where freshmen performed comic operas, farce comedies, and recitals to entertain upperclassmen. Following the sessions, freshmen ran a gauntlet while being paddled. George never reported his "ill treatment" to school officials because he had already made up his mind to leave. In a letter written to Corp Commandant Lieutenant Colonel Ike S. Ashburn Jr., George wrote that at other schools he was "treated like a gentleman, but at A&M like a dog."[7]

George next tried the University of Texas at Austin but left after one semester. His third attempt was Southwestern University in Georgetown, a Methodist school, thirty miles north of Austin, that his mother, brother Givens, and sisters (Lillian and Marie) had attended. His stay at the school was a complete disaster, ending in having to sneak out of town at night because of a football game. He loved football and fighting and managed to get a room in the dormitory section where the football team resided. Although he tried out for the team (at five foot seven inches, he weighed 155 pounds), he failed to make the cut, yet somehow managed to keep his room with the team.

Howard Payne College came to Southwestern for a game on November 6, 1920. Some players were former classmates of George, and Southwestern team members observed him conversing with them. The combination of a seventy-five-dollar bet he placed against Southwestern and their losing 21–0 made many players suspect him of divulging the team's play book. When George received word he was scheduled for a tar-and-feather session that evening, he asked the dean for an honorary withdrawal and took a late-night train back home.[8]

A college education seemed a distant possibility, so George tried getting work with a few of his friends at the Tampico oil fields in Mexico. He was ill-suited for the hard work, and one friend was told by a foreman, "Your friend doesn't want a job, he wants a position."[9] George came back to the family ranch long enough to rest up before going to a Kansas City trade school to study auto mechanics; his interest lasted only a few months before he returned to Texas in 1922. He enrolled as a special student at the University of Texas Law School, and the following fall married a girl he had met during his brief attendance at Corpus Christi High School. Pretty and head-strong, Thelma Duckworth was the daughter of a barber. Like George, she enjoyed playing high-stakes poker.[10] After studying law for three years, George quit school before graduating. He took the bar exam and, after passing, turned down a job offer in Laredo because he had decided to try selling Corpus Christi real estate.

George's oldest brother, Givens, had been tapped by Archie to succeed him as ruler of the dukedom, but Givens had other ideas. He entered Southern Methodist University at the age of fifteen and later studied mining engineering at the Yale University Sheffield Scientific School, graduating in 1913 with a PhB. Returning to South Texas, he worked as a surveyor before becoming a ranch manager. At his father's request, Givens was appointed county commissioner in January 1915, succeeding Archie, who had been elected to the state senate. In March that same year, Givens was appointed county judge.[11]

When war came, Givens went to Arkansas to train as an army aviator. After the war, Archie again called upon his son to hold down the county judge position, but Givens preferred to pursue a business career. He left the bench in 1926 when his father purchased a seat for him on the Dallas Cotton Exchange. His stay in Dallas lasted only a few years before he went back to Duval. Archie bought the Security State Bank in Alice and installed Givens as vice president after he renamed it the Texas State Bank.

Atlee, the youngest son, was never seriously considered a replacement for the Duke. All he ever talked about was becoming a cowboy, getting a ranch of his own, and raising cattle. His reluctance may have been the shyness he developed after a childhood accident. When he was a toddler his flannel nightgown caught fire, which badly scarred his face and body and disfigured an ear. Archie enrolled him in college, but higher education didn't sit well with the young man. When Archie heard his son wasn't at school but in "a whorehouse in San Francisco," someone asked if he was running it. Archie replied, "No—using it."[12] Atlee became a rancher and married in his forties. Archie's two daughters (Marie and Lillian) were not acceptable to take over his political domain because of the machismo mentality of his Mexican constituents, who would be reticent to accept orders from a woman. That left only George to inherit the dukedom.

In December 1926, George was summoned from his real estate venture to replace Givens as county judge. Although his life to this point had not shown promising indications of leadership, George soon displayed an aptitude for politics and administration of the political machine. Not only was he more fluent in Spanish than his father, he also knew common idiomatic phrases, including profanity and vulgarity, and many felt he thought like a Mexican. Archie, on the other hand, was becoming more distant from the electorate, partly because of his age and partly because of medical problems (he had diabetes and an eye disease).

George easily assumed the role of the younger patrón by calling on locals, learning their names, the names and ages of their children, and more important, listening to their needs and assisting them with their problems. After seeing he was capable of providing attention to their difficulties with Anglos, the Mexicans allowed him to be their benefactor and political voice. The nickname *El Tacuacha* (the Possum) given to George by Mexicans, was apt. "He may pretend he's asleep or dead, but don't be fooled. He's planning his next move."[13]

George and Thelma settled in Duval County and built a Spanish-style, red-tiled home just outside San Diego. He was a teetotaler, never having a drink of alcohol his entire life. At parties he and Thelma held at their new home, George imbibed only soda. "I can have fun at a party without drinking," he once said, "and I'll feel a lot better the next day."[14]

In the meantime, George's sister Marie who had married N. R. Weller, a worker for the Ford Motor Company, was heading for a divorce. Her son was born October 3, 1925, in Mexico City, and she brought him back to Duval County when he was two years old. Archie adopted him, renaming him Archer, which gave George a nephew who was also his half brother.[15]

In 1928 the Democratic National Convention was held for the first time in Texas—at Sam Houston Hall in Houston. George accompanied his father to see New York governor Al Smith nominated as candidate to run against Herbert Hoover. It was George's first taste of national politics, where he met Franklin D. Roosevelt (Smith's floor manager) and Texas congressmen John Garner and Sam Rayburn. He also met Sam Ealy Johnson Jr. a man Archie served with in the Texas legislature, who was there with his twenty-year-old son Lyndon. The elder Johnson was famous for saying, "When you're talking, you ain't learnin' nothin'!"[16] George later adapted the folksy saying as his guiding principle in politics.

George settled into a comfortable life as county judge, indulging himself in the pleasures of poker and polo. The way George and his polo team members played the game wouldn't fit on the playing fields of Palm Beach. In South Texas, where every man learned to ride at an early age, their style was considered too aggressive for the elitists of the sport. George convinced an international polo coach to train them, but the coach didn't last long after insisting players use proper polo saddles instead of Western-style.[17]

When the 1929 stock market crash plunged the nation into economic chaos, George's lifestyle remained unchanged because of the family's interests in oil and land, and the county treasury was always a source of funds. In addition to acting as county judge, George also maintained a law practice, sharing cases with attorney J. F. Clarkson. With control in local courts, George seemed untouchable by the law. What finally affected George came from the federal government in the form of an indictment for income tax evasion.

The only previous encounter for the Parr family with the federal government was the 1914 election inquiry, a distant memory. So when an investigator from the IRS appeared unannounced at his office, George told him he "didn't give a damn about the government's time and money." IRS agent Jim Cooner remembered, "I flatly accused Parr of failing to disclose $25,000 in income." Parr admitted taking the money and boasted, "There's nothing you can do about it because you can't prove it." He later recalled, "After that, they *really* got hos-tile." Unknown to George, he had been abrupt with an agent from the IRS intelligence unit, the same division that secured Al Capone's tax evasion conviction.[18]

The federal grand jury indictment came on March 12, 1932. Counts against George included receiving an unreported $25,000 "commission" and another for $17,140 "paid to him for 'protection,' by 910 proprietors of various gambling houses, 920 bootleggers, and 930 houses of prostitution!" The $25,000 was a kickback when the Houston construction firm W. L. Pearson and Company was awarded a 1928 road construction job for $85,000 by Duval County commissioners. George was chairman, and it was his signature on the contract. Accustomed to a Parr receiving a share of doing business in Duval, Pearson sent A. A. Sangster to handle a payoff in May 1928.[19] The government produced Pearson's checkbook showing the $85,000 deposit received from a warrant issued by Duval County and a cash withdrawal of $25,000. The prosecutor said George received the money in a "little black bag," and aside from the nontaxable $2,700 salary he received as county judge, George had failed to report $42,140 as additional income.[20]

George wanted to plead guilty to avoid embarrassment over the source of the $17,140, but Archie convinced him to wait until after the Democratic National Convention because Garner was certain to be nominated for president. An old family friend, Garner would be in a position to have the charges quietly fade away. Garner held on at the convention for three ballots against Franklin D. Roosevelt until Senator Thomas Terry "Tom" Connally of Texas persuaded Garner to support Roosevelt, who was nominated on the next ballot, eventually resulting in a Roosevelt-Garner ticket. One politician called it "a kangaroo ticket, being stronger in the hind quarters than the front."[21]

Archie still would not give up. After being sworn in as vice president, Garner pressured U.S. attorney general Homer Stille Cummings to call

William Robert Smith Jr., the U.S. Attorney for the Western District of Texas, to suggest that maybe the indictment was political in nature. "It's not a political indictment, General, it's a clear case of income tax evasion," Smith responded. A short time later, Smith learned that when Cummings had made the call, Garner was sitting next to him "pleading with him, practically with tears in his eyes" to dismiss the case.[22] With former Texas attorney general Claude Pollard (counsel for Glasscock in the contested senate seat case) handling his defense, George pleaded guilty on May 21, 1934.[23]

Several prominent Texans—including Governor James Allred and court of criminal appeals justices—sent a petition to the presiding judge, Robert J. McMillan, asking him not to give George a prison sentence. George was given two years, sentence suspended, and fined five thousand dollars. The judge admonished George, saying he was "no longer county judge of Duval County. You stay out of politics and behave yourself."[24]

Tax problems were also a concern for Archie as a defendant in an IRS civil suit. The government claimed he owed taxes on a hundred-thousand-dollar "fee" he collected from the same W. L. Pearson on another construction project. Paying the forty-thousand-dollar tax bill wasn't a problem because he could always raid a county fund; Archie's real concern was his upcoming state senate reelection. Not only was Archie being labeled a tax dodger, he was also opposed by a strong candidate, F. W. Seabury, who had proof the dean of the senate received kickbacks. He produced photostatic copies of bank deposit receipts in Archie's name, all coming from W. L. Pearson and Company.[25]

Although Archie contended that Pearson had promised to pay the taxes, Jim Neal, who would come in second in the primary against Seabury and Archie, forcing a runoff with Archie, plastered the district with banners reading, "Archie can't make it over the hill with that last $100,000."[26] To sidestep the issue, Archie focused on getting something for the electorate—a long-desired highway from the Rio Grande Valley to Corpus Christi. However, the expansive King Ranch (measuring one and a quarter million acres spread out over five counties) was in the way.

Founded by Captain Richard King, the ranch was the model Edna Ferber used in her Texas epic *Giant* and was now owned by the Kleberg family. Robert Justus Kleberg II, a Corpus Christi lawyer, married King's daughter Alice in 1886, a year after King died. Under Kleberg's direction, the ranch grew from five hundred thousand acres to over a million, and upon his death in 1932, his son Robert took over.[27] The Parrs had thrown their powerful machine behind Kleberg's son Richard for a vacant House of Representatives seat in 1931 and again in 1932. Always attentive to the Klebergs, both politically and neighborly (the two families traded pastureland in times of droughts), Archie and George took the long trip out to the King Ranch to ask for a favor.

Travelers to Corpus Christi had to circumvent the ranch with a sixty-mile detour, and for years Kleberg resisted having a road cut through the "Running W" cattle pastures. A concrete road ran from Raymondville to the property line of the King Ranch and stopped. Called the "Hug-the-Coast" highway, it had two alternative routes: along Padre Island or the more feasible cut through the King Ranch. When Archie announced he had secured right-of-way deeds for the highway from the King Ranch, it seemed he had accomplished the impossible. However, the many restrictions placed on the deeds made it difficult for him to deliver on his promise. "Senator Parr may someday secure the proper signatures to those rights-of-way deeds which have been entrusted to him," Seabury stated, "but by that time the state may not have the money which it at one time offered as a means of financing this road."[28]

If Archie could convince Kleberg to acquiesce, then one of his campaign problems would disappear. Giving the Duval political boss his due, Kleberg listened to Archie's impassioned plea to allow the concrete strip cut through his property (it was finally accomplished in 1940), but in the end Kleberg said, "I can't do it. I don't want a road through my pasture." Sensing the inglorious end of his father's political career, George shouted at Kleberg, "You're crucifying my father. I'll get you. I'll gut you if it's the last thing I do."[29]

Archie polled the most votes in the primary, but they were not enough to avoid a runoff. Seabury finished third, and the "dark horse" candidate Jim Neal came in second. Although the right-of-way deeds for the highway through the King Ranch were finally secured after the primary, Neal hadn't made it an issue during the campaign, so it came too late to help Archie.[30] Fighting for his political life, Archie waged a fierce campaign. Neal was not to be taken lightly since he had lost to Archie by only thirteen hundred votes in the 1930 election. Neal could narrow that gap, especially since the defeated Seabury was now asking supporters to vote for Neal. Archie's campaign efforts were bolstered by endorsements from four former Texas governors, including W. P. Hobby, who had championed Glasscock in 1919.[31]

Archie gave the campaign his full effort, but it wasn't enough to prevent Neal from closing the gap and winning by seven thousand votes. After congratulating his opponent, Archie thanked his friends, adding, "and as for my enemies, each and every one of them, they can go to hell." While conceding defeat, his "friends" in the Texas legislature were concocting a way to keep him in office. A bill was introduced to redistrict the Twenty-Seventh Senatorial District (Archie's domain), arranging for Archie to succeed himself.[32] The effort was dropped after considerable opposition.

Never to run again for office, Archie retired to Los Horcones and left the dukedom to his son. During his twenty years as state senator, he had managed two major accomplishments: the establishment of Texas A&M College at Kingsville and supporting lobbying efforts of Corpus Christi mayor Henry Pomeroy Miller and Representative Garner for congressional approval to construct a deep-water port at Corpus Christi. Although neither Archie or George held elective office, the political machine continued to flourish even when George's federal problems resurfaced.

George was also having problems on the local level. His federal conviction prevented him from handling firearms, but George had an extensive gun collection and loved to hunt. At the beginning of every deer season, George, his brother Givens, Duval County sheriff Walter Meek Jr., and several other friends set up camp on the Dobie Ranch where they had hunted since childhood. Unbeknownst to them, the ranch, located in part of Duval County and stretching into neighboring La Salle County, had just that morning become a game preserve.

George was the only one of the hunters approached by a game warden named Snow. After George was arrested, Snow, who was on horseback, ordered George to follow alongside him to the county seat at Cotulla. When George refused because he wasn't about to walk forty miles, the game warden rode away. The following day, Snow returned with an arrest warrant, telling George he had to be in court on Thursday. Sitting around a campfire with his friends, George shook his head. As George cleaned his rifle (Snow claimed it was pointed at him), several more dates were negotiated until one was finally accepted.

Under cross-examination by George's attorney, Edward G. Lloyd Jr., the game warden recanted the gun brandishing charge, but George was found guilty of the hunting charge, a misdemeanor in Texas that wouldn't affect his federal probation except that he had been using a firearm. Not taking any chances with his probation, George secured a pardon from Governor Miriam A. "Ma" Ferguson. George could thank his father because Archie helped Ferguson in two primary runoffs with typical lopsided Duval County votes.[33]

A federal conviction also barred him from owning a federally insured bank. But George needed access and control of a bank in order to filter county funds for personal use, payments to loyal lieutenants, and largesse to constituents. As a depository for county funds, whether for the school district, road projects, or county employee payroll, a Parr-owned bank could utilize the money as it pleased. Until Archie bought the bank, Duval County was paid 2 percent interest on deposits. From then on, the Parr-controlled county commissioners accepted 0.5 percent, giving the Parrs a virtual "interest free" loan. In 1943, they did away with the interest altogether.[34]

George also had personal problems. He divorced Thelma in 1933 after eleven years of marriage that had produced one child, a daughter born on November 27, 1932. She was named Georgia, and some said George named her after himself. At the end of 1934, the couple remarried in Houston, but a confidential FBI report released in 1978 revealed that George had married another woman in between. FBI agent George N. Denton discovered Parr had taken a young woman, Sandy "Fannie" Moss Williams of Beaumont, across state lines and lived with her in a hotel. It was alleged that Fannie had threatened George with the White Slave Traffic Act, so he married her. The marriage ended in divorce on October 2, 1934, in Duval County.[35]

On May 13, 1936, eight days before George's probation would end, the U.S. attorney filed a motion in San Antonio to revoke the probation and incarcerate him. George was charged with failing to report to his probation officer, assaulting an attorney, owning an interest in an illegal liquor business, receiving payoffs from gambling operators, and fraudulently altering oil leases. The assault charge stemmed from an old feud with Brownsville attorney Joseph T. Canales. In the 1934 election that Archie lost, Canales supported James Neal and publicly attacked Archie. On September 15, 1934, George was sitting in the Duval County courthouse when Canales entered, shook hands with the judge, the district attorney, the defending attorneys, then walked out of the courtroom. George felt slighted and was furious. Sitting next to George, Walter Meek heard him mutter, "Son . . . of . . . a . . . *bitch.*" George stormed out, catching up with Canales on the steps. Canales refused to engage in conversation so George slapped him across the face.[36] The following day, Canales filed a complaint of attempted murder against George.

The illegal liquor charge stemmed from George having a two-thirds interest (received the same day he received probation) in the Southwest Distributing Company, a local bootlegging concern. The gambling pay-offs were from A. H. "Big Boy" Compton who said he was granted permission to operate an illegal casino in the city of Freer, in return for a six-hundred-dollar monthly payment. He testified that the money "was delivered to Sheriff Dan Tobin and sometimes left in Parr's office."[37] Compton was not testifying out of civic responsibility. When he became delinquent on his payments, Judge Parr had his establishment raided and Compton indicted.

The oil lease charge stemmed from two incidents, which offer a glimpse into one of the ways George and his father obtained their oil wealth. George altered a lease dated June 11, 1934, with Texon Oil Company and J. P. Graham of Corpus Christi. Before signing and returning the one-year lease, George erased the words "oil and gas" in a clause providing for continuation of the lease if gas, oil, or sulfur was discovered. When a large deposit of oil was discovered a year later on the property, George sued in Duval County (where he was assured of winning) to have the lease terminated. He admitted making the alteration but said Texon Oil Company officers "simply hadn't read it" after he returned it.[38] The second charge claimed that George had altered a lease between Walter R. Tabor and George's wife, Thelma, by erasing a special warranty clause *after* it had been signed and filed with the Duval County clerk.

On June 3, 1936, standing before U.S. district judge Robert J. McMillan, George listened as his probation was revoked and he was sentenced to two years at the U.S. Southwestern Reformatory at El Reno, Oklahoma. His incarceration was delayed until an application for clemency he had filed could be acted upon. Several prominent political figures, including Democratic National Committeewoman Clara Driscoll Sevier and Texas governor Allred, petitioned for reconsideration, but to no avail.[39]

Despite his debilitating glaucoma and diabetes, Archie traveled by train in late June to attend the Democratic National Convention in Philadelphia. He was accompanied by his daughter Marie, who attended as a delegate from Corpus Christi. The convention was just a formality to recertify Roosevelt, who gave his "rendezvous with destiny" speech, but Archie was there to buttonhole old political friends into helping him get George out of jail. Garner, remaining on the ticket's second spot, halfheartedly said he would see what could be done.

When the convention ended, Archie insisted that Marie take him to Washington where he made the rounds of the government officials. He was met by more "I'll see what I can do" promises. One obstacle was Representative Richard Kleberg, who hadn't forgotten George's threat to his father during Archie's failed 1934 state senate campaign. Disillusioned and weary, Archie returned to Duval to keep the political home fires burning until his son's release from prison.

Records indicate that George was a model inmate during his incarceration at El Reno. He accepted his prison stay with the philosophy of a man who was not repentant but had been caught. "You've got to go by the law, whatever it may be," he said. "If it is for you, fine; if not, too bad." His homespun, pragmatic view of the system had him in a reflective mood. "You can do it some other way," he added, "but you don't last very long. Look at Bonnie and Clyde."[40] It was a remarkable analogy because he and the notorious couple had one thing in common—banks as a source of income. George worked in the prison library and taught reading and English to illiterate inmates who were mostly convicted moonshiners. After serving nine months, he was paroled on April 8, 1937, and discharged from parole on January 9, 1938.[41]

George showed no signs of allowing his power in Duval to diminish as he continued to rule on matters within his political domain. An indication that he would assume his father's throne came when a vacant seat for county commissioner in Freer had to be filled. The city of Freer, located in the northwest section of Duval, was populated mostly by Anglos, and although Archie consistently appointed Mexicans to official posts, this time George disagreed. Archie hesitated on the appointment, but George insisted that the man could be trusted. Archie acquiesced, and the Anglo proved to be just as loyal to the Old Party machine as the Mexicans.

CHAPTER 4

GEORGE BECOMES THE DUKE

From 1938 to 1948 George Parr was concerned in regaining his political hegemony in Duval County and the rest of the judicial district spreading into neighboring counties. The backbone of the political machine continued to be the Mexican American voter, and that population continued to hover around 90 percent, giving its patrón a power base that was virtually unbeatable at the voting booth. The vote was systematically gathered by various means of persuasion, and in some cases outright intimidation or force. George's description made it all seem like a grateful electorate being helped by an old friend: "We pass the word along who are our friends. Voting comes from long training. We teach them that it is their duty to vote in every election. It takes a long time, but if you teach them for a long time they will vote, and Latin-Americans are inclined to vote as a bloc because of race and religion. They stick together for self-preservation. They do what we ask only to the extent it is satisfactory to them. But we never ask them to do anything that is not calculated to be beneficial to them."[1] However, this was not the reason Parr-backed candidates consistently rolled up votes sometimes totaling 97 percent of total votes cast.

Using tactics learned from his father and systematically refined, George employed several methods to get out the vote and smoothly orchestrate elections. On Election Day several hundred "special deputies" were sworn in and given pistols or rifles. One squad, led by a veteran deputy, drove around the district "stopping and confiscating the ignition keys from cars with anti-Parr [candidate] stickers."[2]

One of George's trusted lieutenants told the county tax collector, "Give me three, four books poll taxes." With the thousand poll tax receipts, George would tell his deputy: "Go to every house and give them the poll tax [receipt] free." Using public funds, George would pay the poll taxes, telling his lieutenant, "Don't worry about the money; I don't pay for it out of my own pocket."[3] If Election Day turnout wasn't enough to deliver votes promised to the "upstate boys," George had his men stuff the ballot boxes by adding as many as were needed according to how many poll tax receipts remained.

Another advantage of the poll tax system was that voters over the age of sixty were exempt. By keeping track of who died past that age, the Parr forces had a handy list to draw from when the "machine votes the dead men" in a close election. "They even accuse me of snooping around in ballot boxes, trying to see how people voted," George responded when accused of controlling the vote. "Why, hell, I don't have to do that. I can tell how a man votes, whether he is for me or against me, just by talking to him."[4]

By 1930 thirty-eight states had provisions for poll taxes, either in their state constitution or enacted by statute. Although wide economic differences existed in society, the poll tax continued as a means of direct taxation. Because poll tax proceeds were used for highway maintenance and school support, it was felt that since everyone benefited everyone should pay an equal share. Many felt that citizens became more responsible to government's needs by paying the tax, and if not imposed, another source of revenue would be difficult to find.

Two-thirds of poll tax revenues in Texas went to support schools, and the remainder went into the general fund. Along with eight other southern states, Texas made poll tax payment a voting prerequisite, but most southern states enacted the provision after the Civil War to limit African Americans from exercising their voting rights. Texas passed a new poll tax law in 1870 requiring every male over twenty-one to pay. Indians, idiots, and persons non compos mentis were exempted. The following year males over the age of sixty were added to those exempted, and in 1882, "those who have lost one hand or one foot [were] exempted."[5] One can only imagine Archie and George combing the district looking for voters who had lost a limb.

On October 18, 1942, after suffering from glaucoma and diabetes, which left him blind during his last four years, George's father died in his sleep at the age of eighty-two. Banks and local businesses closed for the day to honor the patrón who had been a godfather to local people for a generation. Archie was laid to rest at the Benavides cemetery as three thousand people observed the solemn ceremony. The list of honorary pallbearers included four ex-governors, the incumbent one, Coke Stevenson, and a number of notable politicians throughout the state.[6]

During the war, Alice citizens voted for a twenty-five-thousand-dollar bond issue to be used for a tract of land for an airport, and George sought to use the project's federal funding to reward his friends and to garner votes. He had one of his men sort through the job applicants to find Parr supporters.[7] With more qualified workers than jobs, each was hired for only a few weeks.[8] One worker, Ascancio Trevino, owned a public-address sound truck, and he was asked to travel the county advertising Parr-backed candidates, collecting his paycheck for the airport construction job all the while.[9]

Getting county projects for a construction company in which he was a partner, was easy because Parr controlled the awarding process. A tax assessment was levied in 1943 against all independent oil companies in Duval County for the purpose of providing funds to construct new roads. During a meeting with county commissioners, oil company representatives asked where these roads were to be built. Present, but not a commissioner, George jumped up and declared, "It's none of your damned business where these roads are built, we'll build them wherever we most desire."[10]

In 1944 with funds provided by Duval County in the form of a "loan," Parr bought the 55,711 acre Dobie Ranch for $417,832. The sprawling ranch extended from Duval into two neighboring counties with the Nueces River flowing through the northern section. The loan came in two parts, the first $250,000, on April 24, 1945 in the form of a Road and Bridge Fund check from the county commissioners. On June 13, 1945, the commissioners wrote a second $250,000 check, this time to Wilder Construction Company, a dormant partnership with George the sole partner.[11] When his 1946 federal income tax bill for $172,000 became due, George (perhaps having flashbacks of El Reno Reformatory), paid it by "borrowing" from the county.

George formed the Duval Construction Company in 1946 with himself as silent owner and a trusted devotee, G. H. Dunn, as manager. Duval County commissioners awarded every road repair and improvement contract to the new company, contracts amounting to several million dollars during the following decade. Prior to 1946, every road project went to

W. L. Pearson and Company, the same outfit that was the source for Parr's 1932 tax evasion indictment.

George also controlled the San Diego Distributing Company, managed by friend Daniel Tobin Jr. (son of the Parr-anointed county judge). The beer distributor was the only one in Duval County (the county judge approved license applications). Reports circulated that beer retailers in the county were subject to a five cents per bottle "tax" being paid to "someone." When a visitor to the area inquired as to why beer cost twenty-five cents (anywhere else in Texas it was twenty), he was told the extra nickel was for "George."[12]

The money flowing in from construction and beer distribution was only a small part of Parr's income—the major source came from oil. With Earl Delaney as his partner in the Parr-Delaney Oil Company, George was a producer and developer of oil and gas leases and property, amassing 130 oil wells during the years following incorporation. Estimating the flow at 1,734 barrels of oil a day (the state allowed limit), the partnership grossed forty-five hundred dollars a day. The royalties from land leased to other oil companies through the partnership doubled that amount.[13]

Known to keep a roll of bills, "usually totaling $1,500, in his pocket at all times," Parr lined his pockets with money coming from all directions.[14] Mexicans in Duval County were not faring as well. Although they lived rent-free on the owner's land, ranch and farm laborers were expected to work (on days needed) for one dollar a day, averaging $150 a year in wages. Highway construction workers earned more, but not by much, since wage scales were determined by the Duval County commissioners. Unskilled workers received forty cents an hour; semi-skilled, seventy-five cents; and skilled, one dollar.

Since most uneducated Mexicans were unskilled pick-and-shovel workers, the best they could earn was sixteen dollars for a forty-hour week to support a customarily large family. They lived in squalor, usually shantytowns, frequently without plumbing or electricity. They received Parr handouts for extraordinary expenses, but they remained poor. "Well," said a member of Parr's inner circle, "you can't make everybody rich."[15]

Most of the time, Parr managed to acquire wealth at the expense of others. Kaye Northcott gave an apt description in an interview with a farmer who compared Parr's methods with dairy farming: "The dairies would separate the milk from the cream and the skim milk, *leche flaca* in Spanish, would be fed to the pigs. The farmer remembers, 'The Mexicans used to say that Duval County was George Parr's milk cow. They said that he was keeping the cream and giving the *leche flaca* to the people.'"[16] Separating the cream became a way of life for George, and he found many ways to spend the proceeds. In 1944 his income reported to the IRS was $406,000.

After amassing over seventy thousand acres of property, George built a mansion in San Diego. Only the local high school was larger than the two-story, Spanish-tiled-roof home featuring dark wood beams and stucco and styled with ornate exterior iron grillwork. Entrance to the three-acre property was a massive double side-by-side tiled archway leading to a tree-shaded courtyard with a swimming pool and an ornate fountain. Complete with live-in servants' quarters, the house had a fifty-foot den and a restaurant-quality kitchen with walk-in refrigerators and freezers.

Alongside manicured grounds in the back was a six-car garage, with the walls decorated with over a hundred deer heads George had collected as hunting trophies. Attached to the garage were a commercial laundry and a huge workshop. Next to the house was a forty-tree pecan orchard, watered with a regulation fire hose connected to a city hydrant.[17]

His ranch outside of town boasted a race track (*La Mota*) constructed by county workers, complete with a judges' stand and automatic starting chutes. His passion was quarter horses, and he maintained stables for twenty-five, often betting fifteen thousand dollars a race with neighboring ranchers. Former Duval County sheriff Santiago Barrera Jr. has fond memories of Parr and called him the "premier quarter horse breeder in the country" in his day. As a young man, Barrera worked as a trainer for Parr who gave him a horse as a gift. "I always dreamed of having my own horse," Barrera said. "Then George Parr gave me that mare. It was from that mare that I started my breeding program."[18]

Living the good life required paying attention to not only where to "borrow" money from but also how to bring in the votes. George consistently delivered the vote to candidates he supported, and his decision in choosing whom he backed depended on whatever political favors he expected from them. He had no ideology as to issues or platforms; supporting a candidate rested solely on what was good for the machine and its survival. Switching support from one political hopeful to another and back again was commonplace for the Duke of Duval.

In 1944 George sensed an opportunity to make good on his promise to "gut" Richard "Dick" Kleberg for Kleberg's father's refusing to allow a highway pass through the King Ranch. Although Parr supported Kleberg in his past congressional campaigns and was seeking Kleberg's help in obtaining a presidential pardon for his tax evasion conviction, outside pressure was being brought against Kleberg, which made it easier to unseat the congressman. Kleberg represented his district since 1931 and was well liked. A law graduate from the University of Texas, where he also received a master's degree, he was fluent in Spanish and an avid outdoorsman. An early supporter of Roosevelt and the New Deal, he began straying from the Democratic Party when FDR attempted to pack the Supreme Court. Two times an open supporter of the Republican nominee for president, "Mr. Dick," as his friends called him, had become a liability to the party.[19]

The smear campaign against Kleberg drew national attention when Drew Pearson in his radio talk show accused Kleberg of paying one of his page boys $129 a month and then forcing the boy to kick back $39. Pearson also asserted that when the boy reported the incident, Kleberg had him fired. Although Kleberg denied the charge, the seed of distrust had been planted. Pressure also came from the Congress of Industrial Organizations (CIO), which was contributing money to defeat any candidate "who would not line up with President Roosevelt."[20]

To oppose Kleberg, George chose John Emmett Lyle Jr., an army captain stationed with the 536th Anti-aircraft Battalion in Italy. Parr was well acquainted with Lyle, having helped him win a seat in the Texas House of Representatives in 1940. George had defied the incumbent Walter "Uncle Elmer" Pope, who held the seat for twenty years and had always carried Duval County.[21] When offered support for a U.S. representative bid, Lyle informed the Duke that army regulations forbade him to carry on an active campaign. George replied, "What for? . . . I told you that we were going to support you." Lyle won the primary against Kleberg by a substantial majority (over ten thousand votes) without "making a speech or shaking a hand," as James Rowe, in the *Corpus Christi Caller* put it, and went on to win the November election.[22]

In order to continue to enhance his political power George needed a presidential pardon. The felony conviction prevented him from holding public office. Even though he once remarked, "A political officeholder is nothing but an office boy," George came to realize he would be in a better position to favor the party faithful if he was holding an office.[23] Pulling the strings of a puppet official was not enough; he wanted visible demonstration of power. Also, in South Texas, Latino bravado—"ten-feet tall and bulletproof"—indicated stature in the community. By obtaining a presidential pardon, George would be in a position to demonstrate not only to the electorate but also to his network of fellow political bosses throughout South Texas that he had influence in Washington. Finally, a pardon would allow George to own a federally insured bank and maintain closer control of county funds.

He filed his application on August 7, 1943, to the U.S. Pardon Attorney for Executive Clemency.[24] Presidential pardons are entirely discretionary with a sitting president, and most often, the granting of them is usually influenced by an officeholding friend of the applicant. George had approached "Mr. Dick" Kleberg for the endorsement but was turned away. It would have been difficult for George to obtain the pardon anyway because the application would come across the desk of U.S. attorney general Francis Biddle, who would not have passed along his endorsement. Parr then enlisted the help of Congressman Lyndon Baines Johnson. In a letter to Johnson dated August 31, 1943, John Connally wrote: "I talked to Jim Rowe [White House administrative assistant] about George Parr. He tried to do what he could before he left. All the papers are in order—they are down with Dan Lyons of the Pardon Board now. On the face of things there is no reason why his civil liberties should not be restored. Jim left last night after talking with the President [Roosevelt] about an hour."[25]

In his letter to Rowe, written on House of Representatives stationery, Johnson was straightforward in supporting the Duke of Duval: "Here is George Parr's Application for Pardon to Restore Civil Rights which I would like to get filed. Would you mind taking it up with the proper people and seeing if you can get it in the mill for me?" In his closing remarks in the letter, Johnson displayed the folksy, down-home approach he often used to get whatever he wanted: "Why don't you and Elizabeth arrange to spend your vacation in Texas and let me show you what real living is in the best State with the finest people."[26]

Interviewed in San Diego on November 4, 1943, by FBI Special Agent George N. Denton, Parr seemed to take his application lightly. He admitted doling out money to Mexicans in Duval, but not for political purposes. George ended the interview by stating, "Frankly, I don't give a damn whether I get my rights restored or not."[27] The pardon was denied on January 22, 1944. Parr wrote a request to the Pardon Board on February 28, 1945, asking them to reactivate his application. In his letter to Pardon Attorney Daniel M. Lyons, Parr reflected on his statement to Agent Denton. Mentioning that the investigation had included interviews with "enemies" in the community, George wrote, "I merely meant to indicate that if the old wounds were going to be reopened, I had rather not go through with the ordeal."[28]

Newly reelected to a fourth term, Roosevelt also received a pile of letters dated January 15 or 16 from prominent Texas state Democrats, each containing glowing praises for "my good friend . . . humanitarian services . . . from one of the pioneer families of Texas . . . popular in South Texas . . . outstanding man in his community . . . invaluable to his community and state . . . highly respected." One letter, written by Brady Gentry, chairman of the Highway Commission, was particularly noteworthy in his understated praising that "Mr. Parr is always cooperative with the State Highway Department in our work in his section."[29]

Roosevelt died April 12, 1945, and the request sat dormant while Truman's administration came to power with a new U.S. attorney general—Tom Clark from Texas. No stranger to political maneuverings of South Texas, Clark was an astute, pragmatic practitioner of helping those who could help the Democratic Party. On February 20, 1946, Parr received a pardon to restore his civil rights. Some accounts credited Congressman Lyle with pushing the paperwork through the bureaucratic maze, but Parr always felt it was Lyndon Johnson who made it happen.

Two elections set the stage for the infamous "stealing" of the 1948 senatorial primary by Lyndon Johnson. Neither election led directly to the confrontation between Coke Stevenson and the always ambitious Johnson, but both races played an important role. The first was the 1941 special election for senator, and the second was the 1944 primary for governor. As lieutenant governor under "Pappy" O'Daniel, Stevenson found himself in a position of having to run the government because O'Daniel was about as incompetent as a governor could get. Robert Caro in *Means* of *Ascent*, described the problem: "He passed off most serious problems with a quip, appointed to key posts men with no experience, submitted legislation that he knew could not possibly pass so that he could blame the Legislature for not passing it, vetoed many of the significant programs passed by the legislature."[30] O'Daniel had to go. In the special senatorial election in 1941, Lyndon Johnson ran a close race against O'Daniel, and Parr supported Johnson with lopsided votes from Duval County, but in the end strong political powers in the state wanted "Pappy" out of Texas before he ran it into the ground. Sending him to Washington seemed to be the best solution. With Coke Stevenson as the new governor, everyone seemed more relaxed.

In his 1942 reelection Stevenson received the Duval vote. Parr hoped to work with the governor to "advise" him on selection of suitable political appointments in South Texas districts. In the 1944 gubernatorial election Parr outdid himself when Duval County went for Stevenson with a 99.5 percent vote. But Parr was only loyal to a politician if there was something in it for him. It was crucial to deliver patronage or lucrative state contracts to friends. This was the crux of his power in South Texas—providing for those who delivered votes to elect a candidate, who in turn provided jobs and government contracts for those who helped get him in office. George refined the triangular arrangement by establishing alliances with those who controlled other counties (Judge Manuel Box Bravo in Zapata, Judge Manuel J. Raymond in Webb, Sheriff Travis Hogue "Chub" Poole in La Salle, the Guerra brothers in Starr, and Parr's enforcer Luis Salas in Jim Wells County).

Through these alliances, Parr pooled resources to influence statewide elections. It was a fragile arrangement, enhanced by his presidential pardon, but steeled in South Texas politics. In the twenty counties of South Texas, Stevenson consistently received the backing of voters. He would have had the support of Parr and his fellow South Texas bosses in his bid for the U.S. Senate in 1948 except for a falling out after the 1944 gubernatorial election.

Following the election the Laredo district attorney resigned to join the U.S. Army, and Judge Manuel J. Raymond wanted Governor Stevenson to appoint his son-in-law and junior partner in Raymond's law firm, E. James "Jimmy" Kazen, to the position. Kazen had the backing of Parr, who lent his support to his political ally. However, Stevenson had been asked by the Laredo army air field commander not to appoint Kazen. The general argued that Laredo had become a "Sin City" under the present regime. "He said the prostitutes were running wild; half of his men were sick." According to Ernest Boyett, executive assistant to Stevenson, who was at the meeting, "Mr. Stevenson felt we were at war, and politics be damned."[31] Stevenson had already been called to task the previous year by the *Laredo Times*. An open letter to the governor, printed on the front page and ending with "We are going to expect something besides a whitewash," asked him to take action against a political machine permitting "a rotten, crooked, gambling red light district."[32]

At a Laredo hotel meeting, Parr pleaded, "Governor, why don't you just appoint this man that they want in there—they have the votes."[33] Stevenson ignored Parr and appointed S. Truman Phelps to the post. Like Godfather Vito Corleone, once denied, Parr never again asked a favor. Stevenson did not have aspirations for higher office at the time, but in 1948 he decided to run for the U.S. Senate. Knowing Parr might be carrying a grudge, he went to see him. James Callan Graham, who considered Stevenson his mentor (he had loaned him law books and encouraged Graham to pursue a legal career), described the conversation between Parr and Stevenson: "I've forgotten who all was in the room; but they were all very friendly. They said, 'Coke, we've liked you, and we supported you in the past many times, but we cannot tolerate a governor failing to go along with our patronage appointments. We're going to have to be all out against you. We're not against you personally. This is just what we have to do.'"[34] Ideology and loyalty to candidates did not hold much with Parr; if you couldn't help the Old Party machine, he was against you, plain and simple.

In an interview with a newspaper reporter after Lyndon Johnson won the 1948 Senate primary runoff, Parr stated: "We supported Jimmy Kazen for district attorney in Laredo because he was our friend. There was a vacancy. Coke could have appointed him, but he didn't." George never forgot the slight. "That's how come Lyndon Johnson got to be President of the United States," he later said.[35]

PART II
THE PEAK OF POWER

CHAPTER 5

THE 1948 SENATE ELECTION

The 1948 Texas U.S. senatorial campaign was the high point of Parr's political influence. It had all the earmarks of a classic Texas-style horse race, even without Parr's involvement; a popular vote-getter, Coke Stevenson was pitted against once-defeated, but now up-and-coming Lyndon Johnson. The outcome was crucial to President Truman, who faced Thomas Dewey and the Democratic bolting Dixiecrats led by South Carolina U.S. senator Strom Thurmond. Stevenson attacked Johnson for his New Deal liberalism, and Johnson called Stevenson a "calculating, do-nothing, fence-straddling opponent of mine."[1]

Parr supported LBJ in the 1941 election but balked at providing "extra" votes after polls closed. When his lead slipped Johnson's reaction was to call Parr for more South Texas votes. Parr refused. "Lyndon, I've been to the federal penitentiary, and I'm not going back for you." But in 1948 Parr either had a fading memory of prison or was determined to hand Stevenson a defeat. Callan Graham, quoted by Merle Miller, said, "The Parr machine had to demonstrate that *nobody* could stand up against them."[2]

The Parr machine geared up for the July primary months early. Parr's trusted lieutenant Luis "Indio" Salas was given responsibility to get out the Duval vote. An imposing six-foot-one-inch-tall over-two-hundred-pound native of Durango, Mexico, Salas was feared as a man who unhesitatingly resorted to brute force to get his way. When he was a teenager, the Mexican National Railroad hired him to train as a telegrapher. "When Pancho Villa came through Durango, I followed him for about 2½ years," Salas said. "I would send messages for Villa's army." He met Parr in 1940, when George helped him oust a local sheriff harassing Salas.[3]

Salas saw Parr as a patrón backing the Mexicans and who would legitimize his violence by making Salas deputy sheriff in three counties.

Always armed with a pistol, Salas enforced the rule of Parr in Duval with reckless abandon. Following orders, Salas intimidated anyone challenging the Old Party—"Indio, I want his place closed. Close his place, burn the shack or eliminate him." And Parr listened when Salas said he wanted someone removed from office—"I don't like that guy, he's against our people. Get him out."[4]

Salas also carried out Parr's patronage with the Mexican electorate. By seeing to their needs, Salas committed voters to Parr's candidates. Salas said, "a man's wife is sick. I would say to him: 'Go to the drugstore and get medicine.' I would tell the drugstore to give him the medicine and charge the bill to me. Parr would pay it. . . . I would tell the funeral home: 'Go ahead and bury them, and charge Parr.'" Salas received thousands from Parr to spread around. "Don't worry about the money," Parr would say. "I don't pay for it out of my own pocket."[5] Salas made the rounds of bars in the area throwing around money for drinks and grocery money, paying hospital bills, or helping someone out of work. Voters did what was expected of them, and candidates met their obligations by supplying money to the political bosses for the votes. "Ideology had nothing whatever to do with it. Liberals, conservatives, George Parr didn't care," recalled George E. Reedy, one of Johnson's press secretaries.[6]

Johnson wooed Parr for years, sometimes making the pilgrimage to George's San Diego office where a secretary ordered hamburgers from the Windmill Café—Johnson asked for "double the meat." Parr felt Johnson made the most boring speeches in the 1941 campaign, but he liked him for his perseverance and guts. "We all regret very much that you were beat out of the senate seat—when you really won it," he wrote to Johnson. "We will all be with you any time in the future that you decide to take another run at it." Johnson kept in touch with Parr by phone, although Lyndon "would talk on and on and on." Knowing Johnson was a religious man, Parr would say something irreligious just to get off the phone and it worked.[7]

As the July primary neared, neither candidate had approached Parr for support. Alvin Jacob Wirtz, an early supporter of Johnson, knew Parr and his father for years and was said to have made the deal for Johnson on the eve of the primary. After this, according to Wirtz, Parr told Luis Salas, "Concentrate on the senatorial race. Be sure we elect Johnson."[8]

Joe Phipps—writer and campaign worker who had been traveling with

Johnson by helicopter as he drummed up votes—gave another account. During a San Antonio stop on July 21, Johnson was approached by *San Antonio Express* reporter James McCrory who said his editor informed him that Parr hadn't yet committed to either candidate. Whether Stevenson was unsure if Parr would back him because he hadn't appointed Jimmy Kazen, or he felt he didn't need him, Parr hadn't been asked. "McCrory said he thought that if Johnson did no more than fly down to Parr's ranch at Duval's tiny county seat of San Diego and ask for 'the Duke's' support in person, he could probably get it. In fact, the editor of the *Express* had taken the liberty of chartering a small two-place puddle jumper to fly Johnson there." Johnson jumped at the opportunity and was off to Parr's ranch. The plane landed a few hundred yards from the ranch house, and Johnson knocked on the front door several times until it opened. Parr was standing in his house slippers. Flustered, Johnson took a formal, yet respectful approach while in the doorway.

"Mr. Parr, my name is Lyndon Johnson. I'm running for the U.S. Senate. And I have come to ask for your support."

"You have it," he replied as he held out his hand. Parr still hadn't invited Johnson in and the conversation seemed over.

"I am very thirsty after the flight down here," Johnson said. "I wonder if you could spare a drink of water."

If Johnson was hoping to prolong the meeting, he was quickly disappointed. Leaving him standing at the opened front door, Parr shuffled to the back of the house. Johnson heard a tap running and a few seconds later Parr reappeared holding a glass of lukewarm water. Johnson drank the water, shook hands again with Parr, and walked back to the plane.

"He didn't want anything?" Phipps asked Johnson upon his return.

"Nothing," Johnson said. "That was all there was."[9]

While Luis Salas was assuring a Johnson victory in Jim Wells County, Parr was helping the cause in Duval. Johnson garnered 4,622 votes to a mere 40 for Stevenson, a 99.1 percent margin. Lopsided returns in Parr-friendly Starr County (96.5 percent) and Zapata County (95.4 percent) assured Johnson the Duke had delivered. Judge Raymond in Webb County, probably still peeved over the fact that his son-in-law had not been appointed Laredo district attorney, turned in a 92.4 percent margin.[10]

When statewide returns came in, Johnson received 34 percent of the vote, Stevenson had slightly more than 40 percent, and their nearest rival,

George Peddy, 20 percent. Stevenson carried 168 counties to Johnson's 72, but more important, Johnson hadn't won big city votes. His power was in the Rio Grande Valley with the Parr machine. With neither candidate receiving 50 percent, an August 28 runoff election was scheduled. Johnson had a month to close the gap. "Stevenson has been slipping," Johnson declared, "and if that keeps up the next five weeks, I'll win."[11] Stevenson seemed headed for victory when advisers told him votes cast for Peddy would end up in his column.

Stevenson then made a costly error. He went to Washington, reportedly to find a place to live, instead of focusing on the runoff. John B. Connally offered another reason for Stevenson's trip. Johnson was "hammering" on foreign affairs, and Connally felt Stevenson went to Washington to be briefed by experts. "If he'd stayed in Texas and campaigned like he should have," a Johnson man later said, "he would have beaten Johnson."[12]

As the election neared, George paid Salas a visit. "Johnson made some agreement with Parr," Salas later said. "I know damn well he called George Parr about getting even with Coke Stevenson. That's why George came over here to see me." Salas said George told him, "Luis, do not hesitate. Spend all the money necessary, but we have to have Johnson elected."[13] Horace Busby, a Johnson campaign aide, offered another viewpoint. "Parr didn't deal—you've got to understand in a situation like that, those bosses in Texas, as everywhere in the United States, they couldn't care less about who's United States senator or president. They want to know who is going to be county commissioner. It's very difficult for people to get this through their head, that the Senate race was way—almost at the bottom of George Parr's priorities."[14]

Although there are accounts of Johnson playing a direct part in manipulating ballots with Parr's help, it is doubtful the accounts are true because Johnson was always concerned with public perception. This is illustrated by one example. During a San Antonio dinner held by local supporters, striptease dancers were brought out to entertain the guests. Johnson knew the local sheriff was a staunch Stevenson man, so he quietly slipped away to the men's room and climbed out a window.[15]

Politics had changed in the Rio Grande Valley since the war. When the military draft was enacted prior to the United States entering World

War II, George continued benevolent patronage by providing questionable classifications to the local draft board for friends—"no reason
a Mexican should get himself killed in an Anglo war," he said.[16] But
Mexican Americans who had gone off to war came back with a different outlook toward government. Emboldened by dangers faced in war,
coupled with an education that some had received during their service,
these war-hardened, young, and ambitious men returned with thoughts
of challenging Parr's machine. They formed the Freedom Party, encouraging Mexicans to take control of their destiny by backing reform candidates. Gordon Schendel reported in a 1951 *Collier's* article: "I found no
record of [Parr] ever having attempted to improve the living conditions of
the tens of thousands of Latin Americans forced to exist in squalid slums,
on near-starvation wages, throughout his domain."[17]

Anglo opposition was also brewing in the form of the Free and Independent Party headed by Jacob "Jake" Stokes Floyd Sr. Under new Texas
election reform laws, poll watchers were authorized to keep an eye on
balloting procedures. Floyd's party in Jim Wells County sent two young
men, H. L. Poole and James Holmgreen, to monitor Precinct 13, where
Luis Salas was election judge. Across from the polling place at the Nayer
Elementary School in Alice, Salas and his special Election Day "deputies" set up a tent where Mexicans were herded in, handed their poll tax
receipts, and given instructions on how to "properly" fill out the ballots.

Salas recalled: "Inside we had a table with plenty sample ballots to
teach some of our voters how to vote." When polls opened at 7:00 A.M.,
Poole and Holmgreen handed Salas a judge's order allowing them to see
each ballot as it was counted. "I just ordered them to go sit in a corner
and keep out of the way," Salas later said.[18] Holmgreen saw voters using
pre-marked sample ballots to refer to as they voted, a clear violation of
election rules, but when he objected he was told to sit down.

In the afternoon, Salas began counting ballots. "A ballot would be
pulled from the box marked for Stevenson," Holmgreen recalled, "but
would be called out for Johnson." Braving the wrath of Salas, who had
been threatening him all morning, the young poll watcher insisted on
seeing the ballots. "A police officer seemed to just grow out of the ground
and next thing I knew he took me to the city jail and locked me in a
cell, on the orders of Luis Salas."[19] Holmgreen was let out on a writ of
mandamus, but Salas repeated his warning to the two poll watchers to

keep out of the way. By ignoring the poll watchers and giving Johnson votes marked for Stevenson, Salas secured a Johnson victory in Jim Wells County—all from a single voting precinct.

On the day of the runoff, both Johnson and Stevenson poll watchers kept a close eye on the balloting. Each camp held back the count in districts favoring its candidate for fear the other would know how many votes were needed to close the gap. Johnson supporters especially remembered the 1941 fatal error and FDR's advice to "sit on the ballot boxes."[20]

As campaign manager in 1941, Connally blamed himself for Johnson's defeat. "I basically lost the election, I think, in 1941 by telling some of the election officials in South Texas to go ahead and report their returns to the Texas Election Bureau." Parr had told them not to. "Look, you're children; you don't know what you're doing," he said. "You're going to get all your votes in and then they're going to stop counting in their counties and after you've gotten all your votes out on the table they'll come in with however many votes it takes to beat you."[21]

Results reported after Duval County polls closed showed Johnson received 4,195 votes to 38 for Stevenson. Results in Starr County showed the Parr machine delivered a one-sided vote (Johnson—3,038, Stevenson—170). Salas reported the vote to the local newspaper after Jim Wells County polls closed at 7:00 P.M. Poll watchers observed Salas handing out 600 ballots that day, but returns gave Johnson 765 votes and Stevenson 60.[22] By midnight, Johnson was behind statewide less than 2,000—close enough that the election could be stolen.

The frantic scrambling for "extra" votes began. There are accounts that Parr received phone calls from the Johnson camp. "They were looking for George, they were anxious for George. They said it was Lyndon Johnson's office." One anecdote had the Johnson headquarters receiving a message from Duval County: "The moon is high. The river is low. How many votes do you need?" This not-so-skillfully veiled request referred to the Rio Grande River route taken by alien Mexican voters.[23] The race was closer than predicted, but Parr wasn't finished yet.

Late on Sunday, Duval County reported a precinct that had been "overlooked" having 425 more votes for Johnson (two for Stevenson), giving Johnson the statewide lead. When the final *official* Duval count was tallied, Johnson received two more votes. Since 4,679 poll tax receipts had been issued in Duval, the 4,662 votes for both sides (a 99.6 percent turnout) had to qualify for the *Guinness Book of Records* as a world record for civic duty of the electorate.

Thirty years later, Salas said in an interview that a meeting was held at Parr's office on Tuesday. Jim Wells Democratic Executive Committee member Ed Lloyd, Alice commissioner Bruce Ainsworth, Parr, and Johnson attended. Salas recalled Johnson saying, "If I can get 200 more votes, I've got it won." Speaking in Spanish, Parr told Salas, "We need to win this election. I want you to add those 200 votes." Salas balked, telling Parr in Spanish, "I don't give a damn if Johnson wins," but he said he would certify them if someone else handled the ballots. "I didn't want anybody to think I'm not backing up my party." Doing Parr's bidding was normal for Salas. "We had the law to ourselves . . . Parr was the Godfather. . . . We could tell any election judge: 'Give us 80 percent of the vote, the other guy 20 percent.' We had it made in every election."[24]

The later "confession" by Salas must be weighed against the fact that he was at the time promoting a book he was writing. LBJ biographer Doris Kearns Goodwin doubts that Johnson himself attended the meeting. "He was a very careful politician," she said. "He was subtle, not blatant. A bargainer. It's possible that the votes were added without his prior intervention." Salas stood by his statement, even though no record exists of Johnson making the trip to see Parr. "I don't think Lyndon Johnson was foolish enough to have something like that in his records," Salas countered.[25]

Salas's account of the meeting doesn't ring true with others. "He [Johnson] never left the house [in Austin]," recalled Mary Rather, Johnson's administrative assistant in 1948, "except to go out to the store." Campaign reporter William Bowling "Bo" Byers said he "practically lived" at the Johnson home during that week and would know if Johnson had left the area. "It's a long way to Alice, Texas," Mary Rather added. "It was even farther in 1948."[26]

No matter whether Johnson made the trip, Parr delivered the crucial votes. According to Salas, in the evening after the meeting with Johnson, he was in the Adams building in Alice watching as two men (deputy sheriffs Willie Mancha and Ignacio Escobar) proceeded to add another two hundred names to the Precinct 13 voting list. Salas noticed they were adding names in alphabetical order, but when he pointed it out to Parr, he was told, "That's all right."[27]

After completing the tally sheet both Salas as election judge and Democratic County Chairman Clarence Martens certified the "new" results. Johnson had his needed two hundred votes and Stevenson was given an additional two. Salas said it was Escobar's idea of a joke: "Let us give this poor man [Stevenson] a *pilón* [extra, small gift]." The tally sheets were put away until Parr was ready to spring the "amended results" on the Texas Election Bureau.[28]

Another version of that night in the Adams building had John Connally and Philip Kazen adding the 202 names. *Laredo Times* newspaper editor Lloyd Hackler said that during a car trip to Mexico with Kazen years later, he heard Kazen say that the details reported were mostly factual, except for his and Connally's parts. In a 1991 PBS television program, Connally swore, "I wasn't within 200 miles of him [Parr]. I was in Austin, Texas a battery of telephones, calling all over the State of Texas. I didn't know anything about it and that's the truth of the matter."[29]

According to John Cofer, an attorney close to Johnson, a meeting was held with Alvin Wirtz, Connally, and Johnson. The issue was whether to accept the Ballot Box 13 votes as they were certain to raise questions of legitimacy. Cofer said the decision was made to use them only after all other votes had been counted. When Salas made his 1977 revelation, archivists at the Lyndon Johnson Library found a draft of an undated and unsigned statement by Johnson: "I am without knowledge concerning the ballots in either Duval, Jim Wells or Zapata Counties. I have not been to any of those counties and have not conferred with the officials in those counties."[30]

Shortly before his death in 1975, in a tape-recorded interview Parr denied he had anything to do with the Jim Wells vote count: "the man that did it was Luis Salas. . . . And he is the one, the man who wrote in 200 names alphabetically on the damn poll list." But Parr's attorney, Anthony Nicholas of San Antonio, said George told him in 1973 that he had been in "direct telephone contact" with Johnson that week. Parr said Johnson had "told him how many votes to add to his total to pull the election out of the fire."[31]

With the gap whittled down to 351 on Thursday, the *Dallas Morning News*, a staunch Stevenson supporter, said the race was over. A prophetic editorial announced the election was "so close that the returns from a single box could alter the outcome," and "Duval County has come quite close to being represented in Congress by a Senator of its own."[32] By Friday morning Stevenson's lead dropped to 255, but he was still publicly confident. Privately, he was concerned, especially after hearing rumors that John Connally was in Duval County. Then corrected totals began trickling in from Parr territory. Although he had used every one of his Duval County poll tax receipts, Parr still had neighboring counties to tap: Cameron reported 38 more votes for Johnson, Dimmit added another 43, and Zapata "found" 45 more. By noon, Stevenson forces began worrying when his lead diminished to only 157 votes.

Parr played his hand by having the Jim Wells County corrected tally held back until the last minute. At 12:30 Friday afternoon, the election bureau, the informal group of media outlets that monitored Texas elections, received the phone call for the amended return. The Jim Wells Democratic Executive Committee had met that morning to certify final returns. When the Precinct 13 tally sheet was unfolded, the 765 for Johnson, which Salas announced on Election Night, had been changed.[33] The number seven had been altered to a nine, giving Johnson 200 more votes and the statewide lead. A few minor revisions trickled in, adjusting totals up and down by a few votes. Johnson was still ahead by 162 on Saturday, but when the final official count was tabulated, he had won by only 87 votes.

The controversy didn't end. The official statewide total had to be verified at the State Democratic Convention in Fort Worth by a subcommittee, and nominees had to be certified by the canvassing committee by September 17 to be on the November 2 ballot. Stevenson was growing angry over having the election stolen and in a statement after the Ballot Box 13 results from Jim Wells County had been added to give Johnson the lead, said: "On Thursday at noon, my opponent issued a 'victory' statement and urged his friends to 'do their duty.' Almost immediately, last-minute 'gains' for my opponent began to roll in from those counties of South Texas which are said to be dominated by a single man. I would like to know how my opponent knew so much in advance of the 'revisions' being made today."[34] Stevenson claimed that additional gains would be reported from other counties "dominated by this same individual"—an obvious reference to Parr. The *Dallas Morning News* continued its attack on Parr: "The boss of one of these counties passes down the word. The voting is according to order. 'El Patron' has his own ballot magnified a thousand-fold."[35]

Johnson claimed the *Dallas Morning News* published "fictitious" results showing his opponent leading. The newspaper suggested that the state senate conduct an investigation to "clear Texas' good name." Johnson countered that the FBI was the "proper agency" for an election probe. "Sure, Let the FBI Investigate," a *Dallas Morning News* editorial read "Let the chips fall where they may. . . . Let's investigate the vote in Duval and other bloc-voting counties."[36]

"They might as well save their time and effort," *Freer Enterprise* editor E. H. Shomette said. "If you open the ballot boxes you'll find a ballot for every vote cast. The ballots will be correctly marked and the count will be just as reported." Stevenson supporters said they would get affidavits from at least seventy people who would say they voted for Stevenson. "I told them I'd buy them a Stetson hat if they could find 40 people in Freer that had voted for Stevenson." Shomette added, "They couldn't find 40 people in the whole county that voted for Stevenson."[37]

Johnson charged in a radio speech that Stevenson complained about bloc votes in only one county but was "strangely silent" about bloc votes favoring him, including "behind the gates of King Ranch where not one single vote went to Johnson."[38] This was a direct reference to Richard Kleberg who supported Stevenson. "This is the first time anyone has cried votes for sale," Johnson added.[39] Answering charges of voting fraud, Parr replied: "Has Coke ever personally asked me to support him in his previous campaigns? Yes. He has personally asked me to do this, and I did. I never heard a complaint from him then about the bloc vote in Duval County. . . . The Duval County runoff was as clean an election as ever has been held. It will stand investigation by anybody and I invite investigation, for that matter."[40] Stevenson had already asked workers to check on voting in Duval. Pete Tijerina was in nearby Webb County checking votes for Lloyd Benson Jr., candidate for congress, and agreed to check out Duval for Stevenson. Although a Johnson supporter, the ten dollars a day plus expenses looked good to a struggling college student.[41]

When the Tijerina team began investigating those certified as having voted, "they told us their county commissioner had picked up their poll tax receipts and voted for them." It didn't take long for Parr's *pistoleros* to discover strangers in their midst. While looking for a notary public to get statements notarized, Tijerina recalled, "we were stopped by sheriff's deputies, one of whom had a sub-machine gun." It was a rude introduction to Duval as deputies "made us spread-eagle while they searched us." Satisfied they were unarmed, "they then told us we had 30 minutes to get out of Duval County."[42]

Stevenson then sent three young lawyers (T. Kellis Dibrell and James Gardner, both former FBI agents and now San Antonio law partners, and James Callan Graham, an attorney elected in 1948 to Coke Stevenson's old seat in the state legislature), down to Jim Wells County to check on the mysterious Ballot Box 13 and the additional two hundred votes for Johnson.[43] The three men received cold, blank-eyed stares from pistoleros carrying Winchester rifles when they went to B. F. (Tom) Donald Jr.'s office at the Parr-owned Texas State Bank. Donald was also Jim Wells Democratic Executive Committee secretary and would be in possession of the Precinct 13 tally sheet. When Graham asked for the lists, quoting Texas election laws that every citizen has a right to see them, Donald replied, "I know that. But you can't see them because they're locked up in that vault, and I'm not going to unlock the vault."[44]

Their suspicions aroused, they went to see B. M. Brownlee and Henry Lee Adams, both Jim Wells Democratic Executive Committee members. Adams, neither a Parr nor an anti-Parr man, had surprisingly won the chairmanship of the executive committee in the July primary. Unsure as to when he would officially take office, Adams was confused as to whether he should be in possession of the election paperwork. "Mr. Donald has the canvass of the official returns," he said. "I think I'm supposed to have it, but I don't know."[45]

As Callan Graham recalled in a later interview, Dibrell, Gardner, and Graham managed to talk Adams into going over to the bank and asking to see the voting records in the vault. After receiving the same response—"You can't get them because they're locked up in the vault, and I won't open it"—Adams returned to the trio to report. They came up with a strategy that Adams would return to the bank, tell Donald that, as the newly elected Democratic county chairman, Adams was worried that all sorts of inquiries were going to be made and he needed to be able to say the records were in the bank vault and he had personally seen them. It worked. He was allowed access to the vault for "about five minutes" to look at the Precinct 13 poll list.[46]

Prepped by the trio as to what to look for, Adams counted two hundred names up from the bottom, jotted down the name and the name above it and the last name on the list. They told him that in whatever time remaining, he was to write down as many names as he could. Before the list was quickly jerked away, Adams had jotted down 11 names. He also noticed the 200 names at the end of the list were all written in blue ink, while the previous 841 names were all in black. Additionally, the 200 names were in alphabetical order. Graham and Dibrell secured addresses of the eleven and found they were alive—no graveyard votes. However, none had voted. Ready to report back to Stevenson with their findings, they received a strange call that evening from Clarence Martens, secretary of the Jim Wells Democratic Executive Committee. He wanted to talk but would only meet them on a "graded dirt road" out in the county.[47]

Martens said he had signed the vote canvas certificate, which included the extra 202 votes, but was now concerned that his signature was affixed to a false document. Graham and Dibrell persuaded him to come to their hotel room and sign a new certificate—minus the 202 additional votes. As Graham recalled:

> Before I could finish typing it, the door—I won't say it was broken in, but it scared me when it was jammed in . . . I don't know whether it was locked or not. But some fellow came in and grabbed him [Martens] kind of by the scruff of the neck and marched him out of there. I don't know who the man was that did it. . . . But outside in the hall was Ed Lloyd, the lawyer for the Parr group there. . . . I knew who he was, for I'd seen him before. He was out in the hall when this guy came in and just literally lifted Martens out of the room.[48]

Not wanting to face pistoleros at the bank again, they reported back to Stevenson and prevailed upon him to come down to Alice. Stevenson was in Austin at the time and ran into former Texas Ranger Frank Hamer. He told him he was going to Alice to investigate the tally sheets. "Well, I'll just go down there with you," Hamer replied.[49]

Hamer was a Texas legend with the reputation of a tough, no-nonsense lawman who showed no fear facing adversity. His ranger career began in 1906, at the age of twenty-two, and lasted more than thirty years. Accounts of his bravery were part of Texas folklore. One story told of a Texas town besieged by a mob, resulting in the sheriff calling the rangers for help. When the train arrived, Hamer stepped onto the platform where the astonished sheriff asked, "Only one Ranger?" Hamer reportedly replied, "You've only got one mob, haven't you?"[50]

Facing a mob alone was a Hamer trademark. In 1930 he arrived in the small Texas town of Sherman to quell a lynching mob. A Negro in custody had been charged with assaulting a white woman and the angry mob was ready with a rope. On the courthouse steps, Hamer stared defiantly at the crowd. "Come on up if you feel lucky but if you try it there'll be a lot of funerals in Sherman tonight," he told them, sounding like *Dirty Harry*. The mob quietly dispersed.[51]

During his ranger career he was wounded seventeen times, and he killed fifty-three men. His most famous encounter occurred not in Texas but in Louisiana, where on May 23, 1934, he set a trap for Clyde Barrow and Bonnie Parker. Hamer discovered the notorious pair were using a hollowed-out tree stump on a desolate Louisiana road to receive messages. Staking out the location, he waited until Bonnie and Clyde appeared and stepped out of their car to approach the tree stump. "Stick 'em up!" he ordered. When the bank-robbing duo reached for their guns, the other officers opened fire. Seeing Bonnie's bullet-ridden body sickened him before remembering how many men she had shot in cold blood, but he paid his respects by attending their funerals. Always dressed in black, Hamer personified a Hollywood film Western lawman. J. Edgar Hoover once called him "one of the greatest law officers in American history."[52]

As soon as Stevenson and Hamer arrived in Alice, word quickly spread that the famed lawman was in town. After meeting Dibrell and Gardner at their hotel, Hamer instructed them to remove their jackets so everyone would see they were unarmed. Hamer also removed his, but to show that he *was* armed. "He had tremendous confidence," Dibrell recalled. Leaving the hotel, they walked down the street toward the bank. Reminiscent of a Western movie high-noon showdown, spectators lined the way as they neared the bank, which now had more armed men guarding the entrance. "Git!" Hamer told the pistoleros blocking his way in the street, and like the Red Sea for Moses, they parted. At the bank door, he told the guards to "fall back," and after facing him for a few tense moments, they also gave way to the imposing peace officer.[53]

Corpus Christi Caller-Times reporter James M. Rowe, who covered Duval County for years, offered a different version of the showdown. "I followed the party into the bank and was the only reporter there," he said. "I never heard Frank Hamer say a word, nor did I see the *pistoleros* at or near the bank entrance"[54] Callan Graham recalled, "Frank Hamer didn't do anything except sit there. His presence was all we wanted. He sat there to insure that there wouldn't be any problem."[55]

Inside the bank, Stevenson met with Donald and demanded to see the tally sheet and the poll list. The tally sheet summarized total votes cast and the poll list recorded names of individuals in the order they voted. Intimidated by the presence of an ex-governor and the legendary Hamer, Donald agreed to allow them a few moments to look at the sheets.

In his earlier peek at the lists, Adams noticed the color of ink changed around the 842nd voter. "It did look to me like there had been a change in ink," Homer E. Dean Jr. recalled, "and it looked like 200 or 202 or 203 names had been added to the poll list in a different ink by a different hand."[56] Dibrell and Gardner looked for the ink change and jotted down the name of voter number 841—apparently the last legitimate voter. One factor Adams had missed, but they now noticed, was that the "additional" names all appeared to be in the same handwriting and in alphabetical order. "It stuck out like a sore thumb," Dibrell later remarked.[57]

When Donald saw them copying names from the list, he quickly snatched it away. "We didn't have a court order or anything," Dibrell said, "and legally there was nothing we could do about it." While jotting down names, they also memorized as many names of "false" voters as they could. Dibrell and Gardner now set off on the difficult task of securing affidavits from voters on the list to ascertain whether they really had voted.[58]

Asking questions and, even more important, securing affidavits in Luis Salas's county was dangerous business. Ever alert to being followed by special deputy sheriffs in the county, Dibrell, Gardner, and Graham began looking for as many people on the list as possible. People in the county, especially Mexicans, learned you stood a better chance at a long life if you kept your mouth shut. E. L. Wall of the *Houston Chronicle* reported a local newspaper editor as saying, "I'll give you a good hat if you'll find a man who is willing to make an affidavit or produce any legal evidence on anything political [in South Texas]." But the attorneys managed to get people to talk and (more important) sign notarized affidavits. Gardner found the 841st voter on the list, Eugenio Soliz, and while sitting in his car in front of the Alice Hotel with a portable typewriter on his lap, Gardner listened to Soliz's statement in the presence of a notary.[59]

Soliz said he voted shortly before the polls closed at 7:00 P.M. When he exited the polling place, he noticed no one else entering. Number 842 on the list, Mrs. Enriqueta Acero, later testified she was the only person of that name in the precinct and she hadn't voted. Juan A. Martinez (number 891) and Louis Salinas (number 911) both swore they did not vote. Texas College of Arts and Industries at Kingsville student Hector B. Cerda (number 920) testified he wasn't even in Alice on the day of the primary, but was in Pharr, a town two hundred miles away. Dibrell and Gardner also came up with three names of deceased persons on the list who had miraculously voted.[60]

CHAPTER 6

INVESTIGATIONS AND COURT BATTLES

In later years Lyndon B. Johnson, who loved anecdotes and homespun Texas stories, enjoyed telling (complete with Mexican accent) about a young boy sitting on the curb in a small Texas town crying his eyes out. A friend passing asked why he was upset.

"My father was in town last Saturday, and he did not come to see me," he replied.

"But, Manuel, your father has been dead for ten years."

"Sí, he has been dead for ten years," Manuel said. "But he came to town last Saturday to vote for Lyndon Johnson, and he did not come to see me."[1]

With evidence gathered of voting irregularities, Kellis Dibrell filed an affidavit with the county clerk of Jim Wells County. It called for the Jim Wells Democratic Executive Committee to recertify a correct tally of the county's votes, and any from Precinct 13 "should be entirely discarded."[2] Time was a factor because the state convention in Fort Worth opened on Monday. If the entire Precinct 13 vote was discarded, Stevenson would be declared the nominee.

Not to be outdone, Johnson's legal team hurriedly filed an affidavit in Austin before 126th District judge Roy C. Archer, charging that Stevenson, Dibrell, and Hamer "by threats and intimidation have attempted to have the votes of one or more of the voting boxes of [Jim Wells] eliminated." In wording that was astonishing to veteran political observers, Johnson's lawyers asked for and received a temporary restraining order to prevent the Jim Wells Democratic Executive Committee "from eliminating or attempting to eliminate any votes on the ground of illegality, irregularity, or fraud, or from hearing or considering any contest concerning the votes cast in said election."[3] Claiming "I want only the votes I got," Johnson attacked Stevenson, accusing him of showing up "with a pistol-packing pal" to meddle "with tally sheets in counties that he lost." Stevenson countered by saying he had only been trying to determine where "additional votes" for Johnson came from in "bloc counties."[4]

The unprecedented order of a judge blocking a committee meeting in another judicial district had Stevenson's legal advisers in an uproar. They countered by requesting a hearing to have the restraining order lifted. Johnson's team, aware of the time frame, needed to split their legal efforts on two fronts. The court proceedings had to be delayed to prevent losing crucial Jim Wells County votes. At the same time, the canvassing subcommittee in Fort Worth would be considering certifying the original county tally. Without a revised tabulation, Johnson would keep his additional two hundred votes from Ballot Box 13 and receive the party's nod by eighty-seven votes.

Wilbur L. Matthews of San Antonio, heading the Stevenson team, argued that under Texas law, intraparty primary elections were matters "far beyond the power of the court to enjoin." Aware the clock was running, Matthews said "time was a vital factor," taking only one hour for his argument. Attorney Benjamin Dudley Tarlton Jr. argued for Johnson, attempting to delay the injunction hearing. When Tarlton rose to present his case, his delivery was longer and purposely drawn out. He took his time by citing verbatim every election statute that might apply, ever watchful of the clock on the courtroom wall.[5] While Tarlton was speaking, Parr, neatly dressed in a brown suit with red pinstripes, walked in the courtroom, passed through the low gate dividing spectators from the attorneys, and sat with Johnson's lawyers. This was home turf, and he made his physical presence a demonstration of his potent political power.

Stevenson's attorneys may have felt intimidated by the Duke in their midst, but out-of-town newspapermen felt differently. Commenting that he had turned on Stevenson, Parr replied to reporters, "Yes, it was about 3,800 to 40, I believe. And we certainly gave him every vote cast for him, too." Asked about bloc voting Parr said, "No one could tell them how to vote. . . . If we vote the same way, it is because we see eye to eye and have the same interests."[6] Reporters then asked about his influence in the election. "You don't control votes," he replied coolly. Pressed further, he became perturbed, and as one reporter wrote, Parr "stopped short. His eyes seem to pierce his glasses and his smile and hearty laughter quickly molded into a resolute expression."[7]

Meanwhile, a battle was being waged in Fort Worth, where Johnson would have to seek certification of the Jim Wells County returns before the full executive committee.[8] Every available seat in the Blackstone Hotel Venetian Ballroom in Fort Worth that evening was taken to watch the Johnson-Stevenson showdown. Heated debates brought out every bit of nastiness concerning voting practices, not only in Jim Wells and other Parr-controlled counties but also in those dominated by Stevenson. After close to three hours of debate, a vote was called. It was going to be close—so close that when executive committee member and Johnson supporter Jerome Sneed, collapsed earlier with an apparent heart attack in the hotel lobby (later diagnosed as ptomaine poisoning), he was asked to sign a handwritten proxy as he lay on the floor.[9]

In seesaw voting changing lead several times, the final vote (29–28) went to Johnson. His supporters went wild, backslapping and congratulating their candidate. In the confusion Chairman Robert Calvert, presiding over the meeting, pounded his gavel to resume order and officially announce the results. After everyone had settled down, a hand suddenly popped up in the crowd—it was Mrs. Seth Dorbandt, a committee member who had voted for Johnson. Now she wanted to change her vote to "present, but not voting."[10] Scrambling for pro-Johnson members quickly began, with John Connally finding committee member Charles C. Gibson of Amarillo, in the men's room. Pushing Gibson through the crowded ballroom, Connally managed to get him close enough so his vote for Johnson could be heard. With his one vote lead restored, Johnson shouted to Calvert: "Announce the result now, Bob, before someone else changes his mind."[11]

At the full convention held at the Will Rogers Memorial Auditorium the following day, the executive committee's report was read giving Johnson the 29–28 vote. Chairman Tom Tyson called for a convention voice vote, and aside from a scattering of "no" votes, Johnson was accepted as the Democratic candidate for the November ballot. Johnson, waiting in the wings, was called to the platform.

As the convention roared its approval, Parr was brought out to join them. With Johnson's and Sam Rayburn's arms around Parr, Rayburn called him "the hero of the Democratic Party in Texas, the Savior of our cause." Johnson jokingly praised Parr as "the man that casts more Democratic votes than anybody else in the state." A *Houston Post* front page editorial called the election a "hairbreadth, photo-finish climax," and "the closest major political race in all Texas history." But it wasn't over. Sensing this was his last hurrah, Stevenson refused to quit.[12]

There were three venues in which to appeal the nomination. Stevenson could take his case to the state legislature, called for in the election code, but that was time consuming. The deadline for a candidate's name to be placed on the ballot was October 2, less than three weeks away. Ballots had to be printed and distributed to 254 county election boards, taking at least a week. Stevenson's window of opportunity was effectively cut to two weeks with the clock running. His second recourse was to challenge the fraudulent votes in state court, but that would also take time. Adding to the problem, the case would have to be heard in a Jim Wells County courtroom and Stevenson wanted to be as far away from Parr territory as possible. The third alternative, arguing the case before a federal district judge, seemed more promising. Attorney Gerald Weatherly suggested bringing suit in equity based on a U.S. law allowing civil action for deprivation of rights guaranteed by the U.S. Constitution.[13]

The next decision would be to select a sympathetic judge who would be open-minded to their plea. All three Northern District of Texas federal judges were Democrats, but one stood out as a possibility—Judge T. Whitfield Davidson (the former lieutenant governor who had blocked Archie Parr's attempt to reinstate the ousted governor Ferguson). Appointed by Roosevelt, Davidson had "soured" on the New Deal, making him the ideal choice for the civil suit.[14]

Dallas attorney Connie C. Renfro, along with T. Kellis Dibrell, drove through the night looking for Davidson until they found him on his farm in Jefferson, Texas, near the Louisiana border. Arriving just after dawn, they found the judge already awake, still in his pajamas, making coffee. A strict jurist, Davidson insisted on proper courtroom procedures. He set up a makeshift table as a bench and instructed the two lawyers to stand before it. "Then I read it to him word for word," Renfro said. "He asked a couple of questions and then signed it."[15] Davidson scheduled a full hearing for September 21 in Fort Worth to decide if a permanent injunction was merited.

Renfro and Dibrell went to Fort Worth to file the petition and temporary restraining order with the federal district court clerk. They had an unexpected surprise when they walked into the clerk's office. "When I saw John Connally, it convinced me again that someone in the Johnson camp had the ability to listen in on our telephone conversations," Dibrell recalled. "It had taken us hours to drive up to that farmhouse . . . , and hours to drive back. But we did call in and left word that the judge had signed it, and that we were en route to Fort Worth to file."[16]

Johnson's attorneys quickly filed for a writ of mandamus with the Texas Supreme Court. They asked the court to order Texas secretary of state Paul H. Brown to certify Johnson as the nominee and print his name on the ballot. Hoping to disengage himself from legal action, Brown petitioned the court, saying, "That's what I intend to do anyway [certify Johnson] unless I am served with some court order stopping me." Since Brown intended to do what the writ called for, the court refused Johnson's petition. Judge Davidson then expanded his restraining order to preclude Brown from printing Johnson's name on the ballot until he heard legal arguments.[17]

Both candidates were at the Fort Worth federal courtroom for the hearing. Davidson quickly established authority by banning smoking in the courtroom. Stevenson was a pipe smoker while Johnson preferred chain-smoking cigarettes, immediately making him edgy. The morning was spent hearing opening statements and accusations of election wrongdoing. "About this time the hour of noon recess was approaching," Davidson recalled in his memoirs, and "I made a proposal to the attorneys."[18] According to the *Corpus Christi Caller* Davidson said, "I suggest and it is only a suggestion . . . that the names of both candidates be placed on the general election ballot in November. . . . Let the people of Texas decide the winner. . . . If this case goes to the U.S. Senate, which it may, then you will have the feeling among some in Texas that the winner has won on a technicality."[19] Stevenson was quick to tell reporters during the noontime break he was willing to accept Davidson's suggestion. Johnson, however, wanted to consult with his legal staff.

Behind closed doors his lawyers advised him to accept, but Johnson was adamant. In 1941 he had lost by 1,311 votes and had accepted the outcome; he expected Stevenson to do the same. The primary and runoff had exhausted him; another fierce campaign would be too much. He berated his legal team saying he would fight for the decision in court. "This is a free country!" he shouted. "I won it fair and square, and you want me to trade it away!" Back in court, Stevenson accepted the compromise, but Johnson preferred to "fight to the political death."[20]

The legal battle came down to one man's control of the vote in three South Texas counties where a total of 8,160 votes were cast in an election of just under a million votes. Thirteen witnesses called by Stevenson's lawyers testified about voting fraud that gave Johnson the three counties and tipped the balance in his favor statewide. Johnson's lawyers squirmed listening to voters (or in point of fact, alleged voters) testify that they hadn't participated in the election but that their names appeared on tally sheets as having voted. James Gardner, one of the lawyers sent to South Texas, testified he saw poll lists at Parr's bank. For the first time, bloc voting practices in Parr-controlled counties were being aired in court, and although Parr wasn't there, he must have felt the heat coming from that packed Fort Worth courtroom.

After Davidson heard motions (Stevenson wanting a permanent injunction—Johnson looking for a final ruling on jurisdiction), the judge made his ruling. On September 22, 1948, Davidson issued a temporary injunction "for the reason that there was evidence of fraud in the official returns from certain election officials in Jim Wells, Zapata, and possibly other counties"[21] If Parr felt uneasy over a court hearing about his control over the electorate, Davidson was about to turn up the heat. "We would like to know further about Box 13 Jim Wells, Zapata, and Duval," the judge said. "In cases of fraud, the rule is to throw open the door and let the light in."[22]

He appointed Masters in Chancery (officers appointed to assist a court of equity) to investigate and hold hearings in the three counties with authority to subpoena witnesses and submit reports of findings to him by October 2. In effect, Davidson prevented Johnson's name from appearing on the ballot. The injunction could still be lifted in time, but Johnson's people were worried that, when the Masters submitted their reports, Davidson would have confirmation of the election fraud and would rule that Stevenson's name should be the one on the ballots.

Parr did his duty in supporting Johnson by supplying the votes and having a Parr-controlled judge prevent new certification of the tally, but the matter was now out of his hands. Making matters worse, the Master appointed by Davidson to investigate Jim Wells County was former U.S. attorney for the Western District of Texas William Robert Smith Jr., who had previously prosecuted Parr on tax evasion.[23] Smith had boarded at the same rooming house as George while attending law school in Austin and had also served in the Texas State Legislature with Archie.[24] Attending to matters in both Duval and Zapata Counties was San Antonio attorney James McCollum "Mac" Burnett.

Power granted to Masters included gathering physical evidence—the ballot boxes could be impounded and opened in their presence. Parr and Johnson had a lot to lose if that happened. George had "voted the dead," and inquiries of voting fraud might generate enough publicity for state officials to consider their own investigation. His control of votes hadn't been seriously questioned, but with a U.S. Senate seat up for grabs, the door was beginning to open.

Johnson had been overly cautious in avoiding direct dealings with Parr, but newspapers might not make that distinction—his name would be alongside Parr's in the headlines. With his reputation at stake, Johnson couldn't afford this—his political life would come to an inglorious end. He knew that once the veil of secrecy was penetrated he would lose, but his main concern was what Parr would do to protect his dukedom. George was sitting in his office talking to Duval County Democratic chairman J. C. King when Johnson phoned.

"George," Johnson pleaded, "Don't burn those ballots. It'll be a reflection on me."

Parr, more concerned with not wanting any physical proof to surface, responded, "To hell with you. I'm going to protect my friends."[25]

Johnson needed Davidson's injunction overturned before the Masters reported their findings. If that failed, the investigation had to be staunched to prevent probing into Parr territory wrongdoing. State courts offered no relief; Johnson's only recourse was to continue at the federal level, so he called an old friend—Abe Fortas. As luck would have it, Fortas was already in Texas. After listening to various strategies, Fortas quickly cut to the heart of the matter. The case had to be heard by the U.S. Supreme Court, but to get there a brief had to be first filed in federal district court. "I felt very strongly that if we tried to go directly to the Supreme Court from the District Court we would be rebuffed," Fortas recalled, "and that would mean the loss of some precious days."[26]

The plan was risky; everything would ride on one roll of the dice, but to his astute legal mind the constraint of time made this the only possible approach. First, a weak case based on jurisdictional grounds would be presented to a federal circuit court judge with the hope of being turned down. With an unfavorable decision, they could appeal directly to a single supreme court justice and present their strongest arguments. The Fifth Circuit Court of Appeals in New Orleans quickly obliged, and Johnson's legal team called on Supreme Court Justice Hugo Black, who agreed to hear their petition.

The South Texas investigations were scheduled for September 27, 1948, with a meeting of lawyers from both sides in Corpus Christi. The day before, President Truman's whistle-stop campaign train, the *Ferdinand Magellan*, pulled into San Antonio. Johnson was there to greet the president and join him for a few days of conferences and campaigning during part of Truman's visit to the Lone Star State. There are several accounts that Parr also met with Truman at the time. One report had Parr meeting with the president in a hotel room for a half hour while others had him visiting Truman on the train.[27]

Seeking publication of his "Ballot Box 13" manuscript, Luis Salas gave an interview in 1977 to James W. Mangan of the Associated Press claiming that Parr boarded the train on September 29 in Corsicana, Texas. Salas said Truman made a call to Justice Black ("That's the way it works in party politics") to apply pressure. However, the story does not jibe with the facts. The train was in Oklahoma that day, and according to the Truman Library, which has a complete record of who boarded the train, Johnson did board in San Antonio, but Parr was never on it at any time. Truman did publicly support Johnson as the party's candidate, drawing a comment from Stevenson that, "It's not to be wondered at that a candidate of the Kansas City machine endorses a candidate of the Parr machine."[28]

At the conclusion of a meeting with Johnson's and Stevenson's lawyers and the Masters, subpoenas were issued for witnesses and physical evidence—ballot boxes, poll tax lists, and tally sheets. While the Masters were anxious to begin hearings, Johnson's legal team wanted to slow them down, hoping the team's Washington colleagues would have a Supreme Court resolution before ballot boxes were opened. Johnson tried remaining confident while on the train, but his thoughts were on courtrooms several thousand miles apart. If the Supreme Court maneuver failed and the Alice and San Diego inquiries revealed what he knew they would, his name would not be on the ballot in November.

Parr did what he could to stall the inquiries. Federal marshals began serving subpoenas, but they discovered that witnesses had suddenly taken Mexican vacations. More than fifty subpoenas were issued, but only eight appeared in court. Tom Donald, who had denied Stevenson a look at election records at the bank, mysteriously left town for a vacation in Mexico. Precinct 13 election judge Luis Salas and former Democratic County Executive Committee Chairman Clarence Martens could not be found. Another surprise came when the Master for the Zapata and Duval investigations was informed that Zapata County had no poll tax lists. Demanding to know why the law wasn't complied with, Johnson's attorney replied, "The election judges knew everyone in the county."[29]

Master W. R. Smith began hearings in the Alice courtroom with Stevenson sitting in the spectators' section. Every seat was taken, "dozens blocking the doorway to listen," as the drama began. After hearing a U.S. marshal testify on non-delivery of subpoenas, Smith issued a hand-written subpoena for deputy county clerk Juanita Hulsey to bring all the county's ballot boxes into court. Hulsey brought only one—the infamous number 13. Under Texas election laws, three copies of the tally sheet and poll tax lists were required to be kept: one for the secretary of the county Democratic committee (the Mexican-vacationing Donald), one for the precinct election judge (Luis Salas for Precinct 13), and the last for the ballot box itself. Sitting on the table before them appeared to be the only available source of election lists in Precinct 13—lists that would verify Stevenson's charge of two hundred extra fraudulent votes for Johnson. For the rest of the session that day, lawyers from both sides argued as to whether the court had the right to open the ballot box—a secretive container Stevenson must have looked upon as the salvation for his political career. When court adjourned, the ballot box still hadn't been opened.[30]

Both the Supreme Court and Alice hearings were scheduled for the following day. With time a crucial factor, Johnson had the advantage of a one-hour time zone difference with both proceedings beginning at 9:30 A.M. Knowing that instant communication was vital, Parr posted a deputy sheriff next to a phone in the county judge's office with orders to the long-distance operator to keep the lines from Washington clear. James V. Allred, former Texas governor and member of the Washington legal team, had been given the phone number to call the instant that Black's decision was known.[31] If it was favorable (lifting Davidson's injunction),

Parr wanted the Alice inquiry immediately stopped to prevent further inquiry into ballot box stuffing.

Parr was becoming a national figure with media coverage of his political maneuvering. *Time* magazine, in an article titled "The Duke Delivers," dubbed him a "powerful king-maker," and the "man most responsible" for Johnson's win.[32] Holding on to that power was Parr's foremost concern; Johnson's court battle was secondary, so Parr continued to engineer whatever control he could over the court process. Ever the astute manipulator, Parr next ordered Luis Salas to be available for service of the subpoena he had been avoiding. Confident and swaggering into the Alice courtroom, Salas took the stand. Before Smith could open the ballot box, he needed first to establish its identity and the chain of events surrounding its possession. As Precinct 13 election judge, Salas was the official responsible for sanctity of the contested ballot box.

Salas appeared unafraid of testifying. Years later he would say he had talked to Ed Lloyd, Parr's attorney, about testifying. Salas said Lloyd told him, "We talked to Truman on the train. Don't worry about the investigation."[33]

Salas said he complied with election laws by making three copies of each tally sheet and poll tax list and giving one set to Clarence Martens, who turned them over to Tom Donald at the bank. Salas said he placed one set in the ballot box and kept the third. Under further questioning, he said he borrowed Donald's copy to make a "comparison," but both copies were stolen from the glove compartment of his car. Frustrated, Smith announced the ballot boxes were going to be opened to find the only copies still in existence. Johnson's lawyers immediately protested that the ballot boxes had not been properly identified, they may have been tampered with, and opening them violated the Texas Constitution.[34]

J. M. Burnett, Master for the Duval County investigation, wasn't faring too well in the San Diego courtroom either. Ernesto Benavides, Precinct 6 election judge, testified he had also lost his list and the other two were locked inside the ballot box. When pressed as to how he was able to call in the results if the only copies were locked in the box, he said, "I do not know." Burnett questioned Duval County tax collector E. B. Garcia, who was responsible for the poll tax lists. Under Texas law, poll taxes were allowed to be paid by persons other than the voter, but an authorization certificate was required. Pressing the witness as to who paid for the several hundred poll taxes, Garcia had a loss of memory when Parr, sitting in the courtroom, shook his head. Asked where the certificates were now, Garcia said he couldn't find them.[35]

Six Johnson lawyers in Washington presented their case to Justice Black as Dan Moody, the lone Stevenson attorney, argued that fraud was the major issue. Fortas kept hammering away that it was jurisdiction and federal courts had no business interfering with a state primary election. Justice Black retired to consider his decision before announcing his verdict: "It would be a drastic break with the past to permit a federal judge and the federal courts to go into the business of conducting a contest over elections in a state. I think it's impossible to interpret present statutes that federal courts may go into a state and suspend its process of electing a senator or governor."[36] With that said, Black's decision was to "grant a stay until the full Supreme Court has an opportunity to consider the matter."[37]

While Black was instructing Johnson's lawyers to draft the stay order, Allred placed calls to the Alice and San Diego courthouses to let Parr's waiting deputies know the decision. Parr, in the San Diego courtroom, passed a note to the attorneys informing them, and Burnett called a recess, saying the inquiry would continue pending word from Judge Davidson.[38] Black scheduled a full Supreme Court hearing for October 4, in effect, assuring that no matter what happened, Johnson would be the only Democratic nominee on the ballot.

In hindsight, many political observers felt that if Stevenson had originally filed suit in state courts, the ballot boxes would have immediately been impounded, and Fortas would not have had his jurisdictional argument. However, as one writer noted, if Stevenson stayed on the state level, the issues would not have been narrowed to just three South Texas counties. He also had "additional" votes to hide, and an inquiry might have resulted in Johnson winning by an even wider margin. One Texan politician later wrote, "The really vital change [in the vote] took place in the larger counties where there was no one man who could control the vote."[39]

Special Master Smith was still adamant about opening the ballot boxes, even though word had reached him of Black's decision. The following day, Smith began by saying he would proceed with opening the remaining ballot boxes until Black's order came. When it came, Smith announced, "Judge Davidson has instructed me to close this hearing."[40] Following the cessation of the investigation by the two Masters, Tom Donald, the bank cashier "vacationing" in Mexico (U.S. marshal B. S. Ainsworth located him in a Monterrey, Mexico, hotel but couldn't serve the subpoena), strolled into the Alice bank and remarked, "I understand someone is looking for me. Well, here I am."[41]

Even though the Supreme Court refused to hear his petition, Stevenson wouldn't quit. Bolting the Democratic Party, he had, he said, "no hesitation in announcing my support of Jack Porter [the Republican candidate] for United States Senator." Johnson quickly commented, "Mr. Stevenson is like a spoiled child . . . when the party rejects him, he picks up his marbles and tries to break up the game." Parr's sister, Marie Thompson, also bolted, telling voters in a radio address that if her father "knew what the so-called Democratic Party . . . has degenerated into, he would turn over in his grave."[42]

In an effort to settle the matter once and for all, grand juries were convened in Duval and Jim Wells Counties (carefully orchestrated by Parr). The Duval grand jury found "no evidence of improper conduct" in the primary and congratulated election officials "on the orderly manner in which the election was handled." The Jim Wells grand jury lasted longer, due to several delays. Eventually, its report concluded, "We were unable to definitely fix responsibility for irregularities to such an extent that we felt criminal proceedings should be instituted."[43]

On a request from Stevenson to look into the primary, the U.S. Senate Committee on Rules and Administration sent an investigator to check on allegations of election fraud in Duval and Jim Wells Counties. Horace Busby recalled seeing LBJ at the Federal Building in Austin and showing him a newspaper article about an investigator going into Parr territory. "My blood runs cold," Johnson told him. "You've got a stranger down there. He's got a badge. He may have a gun. He may be dead by sunrise, and there's not a goddamn thing I can do about it."[44]

Another senate investigator began checking nearby Zapata and Starr Counties. Using federal subpoenas, both investigators impounded ballots and records surviving from seven counties, including Jim Wells, Zapata, and Duval. To their dismay, they discovered contents of thirty-nine ballot boxes in Duval had been destroyed. A request had come from Judge C. Woodrow Laughlin to supply empty ballot boxes for the upcoming

November election. The Duval County Democratic chairman obliged by ordering courthouse janitor Epifiano Betacourt to get thirty-nine ballot boxes from the basement. The janitor dumped the contents of the boxes in a trash container across from the courthouse and set a match to them. During an interview with *Dallas Morning News* reporter Wick Fowler, Parr was told that someone suggested the "Duval political machine should erect a monument" to the janitor. Relaxing in his San Diego office, George leaned back and "laughed heartily."[45]

It was over. Parr's machine delivered Johnson the vote, saving his political future. Manipulation of the ballot box in Texas was not uncommon, but the focus had centered on one precinct in Parr's backyard. In the process, he received national attention, unwittingly placing himself in the limelight. Never again would he be able to run his dukedom in secrecy.

LBJ's political life had been saved, and he never forgot how close it came to ending. As president, he gave an interview to Ronnie Dugger, who asked about the 1948 election:

> One night, up in his bedroom, he started laughing and he seemed to wonder if he could find something and he said he was going back into Bird's bedroom, which was next door. And he rummaged around in a closet. . . . And he came in with this photograph of these five guys in front of this old car with Box 13 balanced on the hood of it. I looked at him and grinned and he grinned back, but he wouldn't explain it to me. I asked him, "well, who were these guys and why did they have Box 13 on the hood of this car? What did it mean?" And he just—nothing. He wouldn't say. As we'd say in Texas, "he wouldn't say nothin.'" So there it is—history turning on a mystery.[46]

In the years to come, George Parr would look back on the 1948 U.S. Senate race and view it as the zenith of his power. Parr continued to dominate the region with boss rule and to plunder public funds, but at a price sometimes measured in human life.

CHAPTER 7

BILL MASON

If the year 1948 was a shining moment for George Parr, then 1949 was the beginning of a slow downward spiral. Initial opposition came from returning Mexican war veterans, now wanting to be known as Mexican Americans, taking pride in their culture but also reminding everyone they were free Americans just like any Anglo. "We were Americans, not 'spics' or 'greasers,' because when you fight for your country in a World War, against an alien philosophy, fascism, you are an American and proud to be in America," said Dr. Héctor Perez García. Horrified to see fellow Mexican-descent veterans segregated in military hospitals, García, a former army medical major, formed the American GI Forum, a nonpartisan group encouraging returning servicemen to participate actively in the political process. By the end of 1948 the GI Forum had established chapters throughout South Texas, and García actively supported Lyndon Johnson in his 1948 senatorial campaign. The Civil Rights movement for African Americans hadn't shown much progress in Texas, but Mexican Americans were starting to find a common voice. There was no American GI Forum chapter organized in Duval County.[1]

Parr shared their language and customs and even appointed them to county positions, but he was apprehensive about an educated Mexican. An illiterate and uneducated electorate was easily assimilated into bloc voting as instructed by their patrón, and although candidates may have been of Mexican descent, the new emerging Mexican Americans wanted a say. Many serving in World War II and the Korean conflict completed high school and then earned college degrees under the GI Bill of Rights. This core of intelligent and educated men, coming from poverty-stricken backgrounds, was becoming a potential danger to Parr.

Even Anglos began to see a seam opening in the political fabric. They became active supporters of the new movement along with Mexican

Americans and backed reform candidates. This new breed of candidates didn't win at the polls, but they made their presence known, forcing Parr to keep on his toes. George was starting to become hostile to the electorate that had been his power base for years.

Ignoring Parr's admonition that an officeholder is nothing but "an office boy," when Judge Dan Tobin Sr. died in office, Parr appointed himself to the unexpired term. It may have been pressure he was feeling from opposing groups motivating him to be closer to the seat of county power, but as usual, he was quiet as to his reasons. In his personal life, he went through a second divorce from Thelma in 1949. In addition to a community property settlement of a one-half interest in the land and oil leaseholds, Thelma received $425,000 in cash. She moved to Corpus Christi with their daughter, Georgia, who attended the University of Texas and received an allowance of $1,000 a month until she turned twenty-five. Thelma built a $125,000 home overlooking Corpus Christi Bay and formed an oil and gas partnership with John J. Pichinson. Within a few years, she was a millionaire.[2]

On July 29, 1949, an event occurred in South Texas which again focused national attention on Parr. Although no evidence ever surfaced linking him to the incident, the fact it had taken place in his political backyard was sufficient to arouse his enemies to mount a formidable attack on the Duval political fortress. William Haywood "Bill" Mason was a newspaperman for thirty years after serving in World War I. He began with the *Minneapolis Journal* as a police reporter, then became city editor, before working in California as a journalist with San Francisco-Oakland area newspapers. He lost his position with the *San Francisco Examiner* after running afoul of Earl Warren's campaign for district attorney by publishing information he had agreed not to use (according to Warren in his memoir). After a stint as state editor of the *San Antonio Light*, in 1947 Mason arrived in Alice to become managing editor of the *Alice Echo*.[3]

Shortly thereafter, Frank B. Lloyd and George Parr, co-owners of the radio station KBKI in Alice (Parr would own 75 percent of the stock by 1953), hired Mason as a program director. A relentless crusader, Mason purchased fifteen minutes of daily airtime to report news and opinions on local matters. On January 1, 1949, he began broadcasting "Bill Mason Speaks," a program covering a variety of topics: traffic safety, proper garbage disposal, and meat-packing plant sanitation.[4] Although much of the daily commentary attacked local politics, Parr felt secure enough to have Mason at his radio station where he could keep a close eye on him.

Mason began a blistering attack on Jim Wells County sheriff Hubert T. Sain. In one broadcast, he accused Sain of charging exorbitant rent on property leased to the county. Undeterred by threats, Mason continued his attacks until one evening he was called out of the local bowling center by Deputy Sheriff Charles Brand. Sain, and another deputy sheriff, Charlie Brown, stood by as the incident unfolded.[5] As they walked down the street, Brand grabbed Mason by the belt and began smacking him on the back of his head. The belt broke and Mason's trousers came off, leaving him half-naked. In defiance, Mason hung the pants on a street lamppost with a sign stating they belonged to him and "if anyone else wanted to meet him he would meet them there."[6]

His attacks continued, this time against Deputy Sheriff Sam Smithwick, whom he accused of secretly owning Rancho Alegre (The Ranch of Joy), a beer joint on the outskirts of Alice. He criticized Smithwick's owning a place "where loose women ply their trade" and spread venereal disease. Smithwick owned the property, but the beer license was registered to Bitero Flores. "I paid Mr. Smith [Smithwick] $100 a month for the place," Flores said. Smithwick, a half-Mexican infuriated at hearing his name on Mason's program, decided to take action after hearing that Mason was going to mention one of Smithwick's children in his next broadcast.[7]

"I've known Sam Smithwick all my life," a friend said. "You could push him around, maybe you could talk mean to him. He would just smile and go on his way. But if you rubbed his fur the wrong way, Look out!" Father of seven children, Smithwick was a portly, 263-pound, 60-year-old lawman who always removed his hat before speaking to anyone. Born to an Irish father and a Spanish mother, he had been deputy sheriff for twenty-four years. Fluent in English, he chose to speak Spanish but could read or write very little in either. His friend recalled hearing Mason's broadcast. "Just as soon as I heard it, I knew there was going to be trouble."[8]

On July 29, 1949, Mason's wife received a phone call from a woman who wouldn't identify herself. "I just overheard a conversation," she said. "Your husband is in danger." The warning was ignored. "The family didn't pay any attention . . . since Daddy was being threatened almost daily," Mason's son, Burt, recalled. Mason always wrote out the text of every broadcast, and his next scheduled program would accelerate the attack on Smithwick. "I am going to take the gloves off today in the prostitution situation and start swinging," the text read. "The word has been passed to me I better shut up or else."[9]

Avelino Saenz was the only eyewitness to the gruesome encounter that occurred. Saenz, a city employee, accompanied Mason as they surveyed local streets looking at the deplorable conditions, even though a considerable amount of funds had been allocated for their repair. Mason drove as Saenz pointed out deteriorating roads when Smithwick, in a red pickup truck, approached from the opposite direction. Smithwick made a signal for Mason to stop by sticking his hand out the window and both vehicles pulled to the side approximately ten feet apart. He got out of his pickup truck and approached Mason's vehicle.

Leaning into the driver's side window, he asked, "Are you Mr. Mason?" When Mason replied he was, Smithwick pulled out his service revolver and ordered Saenz out of the car. Mason began waving his hands in front of his face, saying, "Wait a minute. What's the matter with you?" As Saenz was getting out, Smithwick shot Mason in the chest. Saenz walked to the front of Mason's car as the wounded man was getting out and staggering to keep on his feet. "I saw Mason crawl under Smithwick's pickup," Saenz later testified. "Smithwick was standing between the two cars working with his gun."[10]

Apparently the gun jammed. After repeated attempts to get his gun working, he got into his truck and drove off. Mortally wounded, Mason began walking away "looking backward all the time as if he were afraid he was going to be shot again." He "staggered southward, crossed a vacant lot," and "managed to climb a fence. After traveling two hundred feet, he reached the porch of the Alice Pipe and Supply Co."[11] Sprawled out on the porch, Mason said, "I can't make it any further." An ambulance rushed him to the hospital where he died. While Mason was fighting for his life, Smithwick drove directly to the county jail. "He had a key and went in and locked himself up," Sheriff Sain said.[12]

News of the crusading reporter's death spread quickly. Texas Ranger Ben C. Krueger, stationed in Alice, immediately telephoned Ranger Captain Alfred Young Allee, who dispatched two rangers to patrol the Alice streets. After Smithwick was arraigned before a justice of the peace,

Sheriff Sain spirited him off to Corpus Christi "for safekeeping and to avoid trouble breaking out here."[13]

He was right—trouble was on the way. At 11:30 that night, two cars with five men drove to the Rancho Alegre and blasted the building with shotguns. Fortunately, it was unoccupied and only a few windows and a light meter on the outside were shattered with one shot blowing a hole in the outside wall.[14] Two weeks later, an attempt was made to burn down the roadhouse. Rags soaked with gasoline were stuffed under flooring in the rear of the building and set afire. A night watchman living nearby saw the flames and extinguished them before they spread. After the attacks, Flores gave up and opened a small grocery store at another location. "I don't want to operate any more beer joints," he said. "You make too many enemies."[15]

After the death of his father, twenty-two-year-old Burton Mason, who had his own radio program on KBKI—"Duval Doings"—asked Ed Lloyd for permission to broadcast his father's final script. Lloyd deemed it "inadvisable at this time," so the son quit his job at the station. Burt wanted to continue his father's crusade and managed to secure broadcast time on Station KWBU in Corpus Christi. Two weeks after inauguration of the program, he was in a Houston hospital with a fractured leg and bruises over his entire body.[16]

Burt had been with his girlfriend visiting her parents in Victoria and said he wanted to visit Houston. Around one in the morning he stopped at a traffic light. "While I was waiting for the light to change a car with three men came alongside," he recalled. They began swearing at him—he didn't know why—so he pulled to the curb, got out of his car, and confronted them. They beat Mason relentlessly until bystanders separated them. When he noticed his leg was broken, Burt was helped back into the car. His girlfriend took the wheel, but after three blocks the three men caught up to them. They forced the car to the side and started beating Mason again.[17]

Burt did not know the men, nor did anyone know of his last-minute plan to visit Houston. "I don't think it had anything to do with the radio programs which led to my father's death," he said. "But then, I don't know." The men were eventually arrested, but when one confessed, a different story was given. He said Mason's car narrowly missed hitting them, but his version of the beating and second encounter verified Mason's story.[18]

Although Mason continued broadcasting his show after his hospital release, a few days later he quit. "The advertising income is not enough to support the show," he said.[19] He moved to Galveston, where a local radio station owner, who had known Burt's father for years, gave him a job. After a short time, he was let go. Unfortunately, Mason's troubles weren't over after losing the job. In February 1950 he was caught robbing a bar in Galveston and sentenced to a five-year suspended sentence.[20]

After tension following Mason's death subsided, Smithwick was brought back to face an examining trial. Unlike a grand jury hearing, an examining trial hears sworn testimony and serves to preserve evidence and allow defendants to present testimony to determine the amount of bail to be set. If a witness dies before a later trial, his testimony at the examining trial may be entered as evidence. Smithwick sat quietly at the defense table hearing a step-by-step report of his encounter with Mason. Dressed in khakis and cowboy boots, he "wore a brightly-colored tie that had a figure painted on it resembling a large hourglass. All of the sand appeared to be in the bottom of the glass."[21] Bail denied, Smithwick was held over until a grand jury could convene.

Judge Lorenz Broeter, a Parr-backed Seventy-Ninth District magistrate, called a special grand jury to investigate the Mason murder. Broeter could limit the scope and testimony heard by the grand jury, but he announced, "The grand jury will be charged to investigate all angles of the case." He implied the scope of the inquiry would not be limited, even if they chose to investigate organized gambling and prostitution in the county. The fact that he was facing prostate surgery for cancer may have motivated Broeter to see justice prevail. Against Parr's suggestion, Broeter appointed Corpus Christi judge Paul A. Martineau to handle the grand jury in his absence.[22]

With no allegiance to Parr, Martineau told the grand jury not to limit their investigation to the Mason murder but to expand their authority to include any corruption in the county. "If any public official is not doing his duty—if he is guilty of malfeasance of office—investigate that, too," Martineau charged them. "All public officials are subject to your scrutiny." Encouraged in their civic responsibility by Martineau the almost all Anglo grand jury, three days after being impaneled, returned an indictment of "murder with malice" against Smithwick, and they disclosed to District Attorney Sam G. Reams that they were broadening their scope to include the election fraud surrounding Ballot Box 13.[23]

Knowing reluctant witnesses might take sudden "Mexican vacations," the grand jury issued subpoenas for Ballot Box 13 election judge Luis Salas and for Tom Donald, the bank cashier who had been in possession of the election records.[24] At least one witness called was anxious to testify—Kellis Dibrell, former investigator for Coke Stevenson during the 1948 primary. Salas was questioned for forty minutes by the grand jury. Before entering the grand jury room, Dibrell announced he had "new evidence" never disclosed.[25] After leaving the courtroom, Dibrell would not disclose what he had told the grand jury.

During the lengthy grand jury investigation, several witnesses were called. These included Jim Wells County Democratic Executive Committee chairman Clarence Martens; voters who previously testified during the election probe; and Salas, who was called a second time and spent close to two hours on the stand. Although ballots from the 1948 primary still existed, impounded by order of Judge Broeter—another bone of contention between Parr and the errant judge—the grand jury could not examine them. Under Texas law they could only be examined under supervision of a district judge.[26]

After hearing more than fifty witnesses over ten days, the grand jury presented its final report to Judge Martineau. One of the last to testify was *Corpus Christi Caller* reporter James Rowe, who had covered the 1948 primary and the resulting controversial aftermath. Unfortunately, having sworn to keep secret any testimony given, Rowe couldn't even write his own story. In the end, the grand jury returned two indictments: one against Smithwick and a perjury charge against a man involving mortgaging of an automobile. Not one indictment was returned against anyone involved in the 1948 primary.[27] Parr could rest easy, for the moment at least, but Smithwick still had to face trial for murder.

Transferring the trial to Bell County, Martineau felt confident an impartial jury would hear the murder case. Worried what Smithwick might say in his defense and concerned about resurrecting the investigation of voting procedures in his dukedom, Parr quickly raised eight thousand dollars for Smithwick's defense. Years later, Luis Salas recalled a conversation he had with Parr: "I asked George B. what he was going to do to help Sam. He told me he could do nothing since Sam had killed an Anglo. I asked him if the victim had been a Mexican could he do something? Parr said he thought he could because an Anglo and a Mexican were two different things. That was enough for me. I was through with Parr from then on."[28] Smithwick was defended by four attorneys (reportedly paid by Parr), while James K. Evetts and Homer E. Dean Jr. prosecuted. After a postponement, and a week to select a jury, the trial began in January 1950.

On the night of January 23, 1950, Evetts arrived at his home at 8:00 P.M. after a long day in the courtroom. Pulling into the two-car garage, he began getting out of his car. Suddenly, from a corner of the garage, he caught a glimpse of a figure stepping from the shadows. A World War II veteran, Evetts reacted quickly and jumped backward. Two shots rang out; the first creased the car trunk and was buried in the garage wall; the second slammed into the wall where his head had been only a moment before. Hearing the shots from inside the house, Evetts's wife turned on the garage light. Surprised by the light, the would-be assassin fled down an alley on foot.[29]

Numerous footprints found near the garage indicated the gunman had been lying in wait. Bloodhounds brought to the scene failed to pick up a scent. Unable to determine if the shooting had anything to do with the Smithwick trial, Evetts decided the sequestered jurors would not hear about it. They will "not see a newspaper," he told reporters. Two days after the ambush, the local sheriff took four men in custody but after questioning set them free. The would-be-killer—suspected by Texas Ranger Captain Alfred Y. Allee to be Juan Barrera Canate—reportedly fled across the border into Mexico and was never found.[30]

Having shed thirty pounds before the trial, Smithwick testified in his own behalf and pleaded self-defense. He claimed he flagged down Mason's car just to talk to him. "I want you to take my name off the radio," he told Mason. He said Mason cursed him, calling him a Mexican. "When he said that I pulled my gun. He made a move and grabbed my gun. Then I shook loose, stepped back and fired my gun."[31] Later in his testimony, he tried to justify his actions by saying he feared his life was in danger. Considering that Mason was unarmed, it was a tough sell to the jury, and in closing arguments the state asked for the death penalty.

"A trust had been placed in him as a peace officer," District Attorney Homer E. Dean Jr. told the jury. "He has long forgotten the gun was given to him to protect the people and not to murder a defenseless, helpless

52-year-old, fat, be-spectacled man sitting trapped under the steering wheel of his own car." Defense attorney Byron George Skelton attacked the victim, calling Mason "a viper, a serpent, a smear artist, slanderer and character-destroyer."[32] At the age of sixty-two, Smithwick was sentenced to ninety-nine years and sent to the state prison at Huntsville.[33]

There never was any evidence linking Parr to the Mason killing, but rumors made the connection, and in the 1950 primaries for offices in Duval and Jim Wells Counties, every Parr-supported candidate won, except for Jim Wells County sheriff Sain, who was defeated by a Freedom Party–backed Anglo candidate. That small victory, paid for with the life of Bill Mason, was the beginning of a foothold that members of the reform movement would use to their advantage. Parr never regained control of Jim Wells County. Even in prison, Smithwick would continue to add press coverage by mentioning Parr's name.

On March 23, 1952, Smithwick wrote to Coke Stevenson from his prison cell that he knew the location of the infamous Ballot Box 13. Five days before he shot Mason he arrested two men who had the ballot box in their possession; apparently it had been given to them by a third person who told them to destroy it. He said he took the box and, after "getting it put safely away," was on his way to contact Stevenson when he encountered Mason. "I am quite sure that I can produce it if you are interested," he wrote.[34] Three weeks after writing the letter, and before Stevenson had an opportunity to meet with him, Smithwick was found dead in his cell. No autopsy was performed and the death was ruled a suicide.

Segregated from the prison population because he was a former peace officer, Smithwick had been placed in a cell by himself. Prison officials said he was found hanged by a towel tied to the lower edge of his bunk, but it was later discovered the bunk came away from the wall when very little pressure was applied. A hefty 245 pounds, Smithwick would have fallen to the cell floor with the bunk on top of him. Even though ruled a suicide, rumors surfaced that Parr had engineered the death. "Oh, sure," Parr responded. "I had him hanged inside one of those prison walls. It's a physical impossibility."[35]

Stevenson, contemplating running against Lyndon Johnson for his Senate seat in 1954, released the Smithwick letter to the press. Johnson replied that he didn't know what "a convicted murderer might have done prior to committing suicide in an attempt to get released from prison," adding that "a group of disgruntled, disappointed people" were looking to resurrect the 1948 campaign. The controversy wouldn't die for Johnson, who in 1956, was accused by Texas governor Allan Shivers of having Smithwick killed. According to one of LBJ's biographers, the only source of the accusation came from Johnson himself.[36]

A polished headstone in the local Alice cemetery marks the final resting place of Bill Mason. Along with dates of his birth and death, it has an inscription quoting a statement given by prosecutor Jim Evetts in closing remarks to the jury during the Smithwick trial:

> HE DIED BECAUSE HE HAD THE
> NERVE TO TELL THE TRUTH
> FOR A LOT OF LITTLE PEOPLE[37]

Bill Mason attempted to chip away a small segment of the Parr political foundation, and he made the ultimate sacrifice so as to have his voice heard. Others would follow to carry on the fight, and some also paid with their lives. Backed with armed men wearing badges, having county tax funds and political candidates to draw from, and an electorate who supported his choices at the polls, George Parr continued to rule his fiefdom in South Texas. But cracks in the foundation were beginning to erode the strength of his political machine.

CHAPTER 8

GATHERING FORCES

Parr might have weathered the storm surrounding the Mason–Smithwick incident if it hadn't been for the untimely death of Governor Beauford Halbert Jester on July 10, 1949. Parr had supported Jester in the 1948 election by delivering a massive plurality vote in the Parr-controlled districts, and Jester promised George a judgeship appointment for a friend. Succeeding Jester was Lieutenant Governor Robert "Allan" Shivers of McAllen, who also benefited from Parr's bloc votes in the past. When they held a meeting with Shivers in McAllen, the new governor told Parr and Ed Lloyd, "Boys, if you want anything from Corpus, from anywhere in our district, whatever you say goes."[1] That was all Parr had to hear. Lyndon Johnson would provide patronage from the U.S. Senate in Washington while Shivers would see to Parr's needs from the state capitol in Austin.

On October 21, 1949, Chief Justice Edward W. Smith of the Fourth Court of Civil Appeals in San Antonio announced his retirement. Shivers honored his pledge to Parr by appointing Corpus Christi district judge Harry M. Carroll to the vacated post. Parr expected Carroll's old spot to be filled with his friend Luther E. Jones Jr., but when informed by Shivers that Jones's appointment was receiving opposition from an influential group of Corpus Christi businessmen, Parr arranged a meeting with Shivers in a hotel room. Parr insisted on Jones, while Shivers sought another candidate who would satisfy everyone. The meeting ended without a satisfactory resolution. The new governor was not showing the "friendship" that George expected from those he supported. If Shivers wouldn't abide by his choice, Parr was ready to "gut him" as he did Dick Kleberg. When Judge Carroll heard about the contested replacement, he went to George and asked what he should do. "I told him he should write the governor and withdraw his name from consideration," Parr recalled. "We didn't want just anybody as a district court judge in Corpus Christi."[2]

Carroll did as instructed. In an effort to placate Parr, Shivers appointed Judge Broeter to the vacated post, not knowing Parr held Broeter in disfavor because of his actions in the Smithwick case.[3] Shivers then appointed District Attorney Sam G. Reams to Broeter's old spot and elevated Homer E. Dean Jr. to district attorney, despite the fact that Parr preferred his friend and attorney Raeburn Norris for the judgeship. Attempting to honor his promise of "whatever you say goes," Shivers had further infuriated the South Texas boss.

Parr blatantly showed disapproval of Shivers in the 1950 primary by turning his back on the incumbent governor. His choice was railroad commissioner Olin Wellborn Nichols Culberson, but when he dropped out of the race due to a heart attack, someone else was needed. "I'm in a quandary," Parr told a Houston reporter in a telephone interview. "It's true that I was supporting Judge Culberson, but now I don't know what I'll do."[4] Out of seven remaining candidates, George decided on Caso March of Waco as his anointed choice.

To ensure that March received as many votes as possible in Duval County, Parr made it easier for his mostly illiterate electorate to mark ballots. He had long known that ballots with his candidate's name at the top simplified the process. Accordingly, March appeared at the top of the ballot listing seven candidates and Shivers was at the bottom. Shivers—a popular governor, who would remain in office a record seven and a half years—carried every county in the state except Duval, where he received 108 votes to his opponent's 4,239.[5]

Before the primary, the *Corpus Christi Caller* carried an article by James Rowe detailing how Parr's choice always received top billing on the ballot, providing a "clue to the personal preference of George B. Parr, political overlord of the county." Outraged at the reporter's snooping and at being referred to as an "overlord," Parr rounded up the eleven Duval County Democratic Executive Committee members and had them file a $550,000 libel suit against the newspaper (each member suing for $50,000). They claimed their "honesty and integrity" had been impeached by the article, which "suggested to the minds of readers" that they were guilty of "official misconduct sufficient to warrant their removal from office."[6]

According to James Rowe (in an article in the *Corpus Christi Caller* written twenty-five years later), before the suit went to trial, Parr was sitting in Judge Sam Reams's chambers, both being paid a visit by Webb County political boss Manuel J. Raymond.

"George," the Webb County boss said, "what do you want to fight the *Caller-Times* for? It won't get you anything but bad publicity. Why don't you make friends with them?"

It was good advice and George knew it. "Maybe you're right," he told Raymond. "Do you think it would do any good to dismiss the libel suit?" Parr asked Reams.

"It sure wouldn't do any harm," Reams answered.[7]

Although not a party to the lawsuit, Parr had the suit dropped. He had enough enemies without adding a newspaper to the list. With a district judge and district attorney owing no political allegiance to him, and a governor he had denied a unanimous victory, Parr was heading into turbulent times.

Local opposition came in the form of the Free and Independent Party led by Alice attorney Jacob S. Floyd, an outspoken Parr critic for twenty years. Dubbed *El Vibora Seca* (The Dry Snake) by Mexican Americans, Floyd sponsored a slate of reform candidates against Parr's Old Party nominees. Jim Wells County clerk C. H. (Hap) Holmgreen, who joined Floyd in opposing Parr, called upon Governor Shivers to oversee elections by having Texas Rangers monitor polls because "the opposition controls all the law-enforcement agencies in the city and the county." It was ranger policy to send men only if both sides in an election submitted requests, so Old Party approval was needed. "We are not going to ask for them," Sheriff Sain announced.[8]

The July 1950 primary became a hotly contested election. After the polls closed, one precinct held back its totals—once again, a repeat of the infamous Ballot Box 13 incident. Holmgreen won reelection, but three posts were forced into a runoff. These were county judge C. Woodrow Laughlin, Sheriff Sain, and county commissioner Dan J. Scruggs—all Parr-supported incumbents.[9] While Laughlin won by a narrow margin and Sain was soundly beaten, Scruggs lost by only a few votes, so Parr decided to challenge the results.

In a role reversal a Parr legal team of Raeburn Norris, Luther Jones, Hector Lopez, and Nago Alaniz challenged the results based on voting fraud. They accused the reform party of keeping absentee polls open until midnight, marking ballots for illiterate voters, providing transportation for voters, and "double voting" absentee ballots who also voted at the polls. Although no counter charges were filed, the Parr machine had fought the reform party with terror tactics. Business owners supporting the reform party had their parking lots blocked by deputy sheriff cars, welfare recipients were told not to patronize those places if they wanted to retain their benefits, and even children of reform party members were ostracized at school activities.[10]

Judge Reams ordered ballot boxes impounded "to preserve the records."[11] A loyal follower of Parr since he was elected district attorney in 1948, and subsequently appointed district judge when Broeter was elevated to the Court of Appeals, Reams suddenly turned the tables on Parr. Ordering ballot boxes opened, he declared ninety-seven votes illegal and Perkins remained the winner. With a renegade Judge Reams on his hands, Parr began planning to unseat him. Playing possum Parr, who allowed Reams to run unopposed in the primary, summoned his faithful lieutenants.

Secretive about his plans, Parr made no overt actions against Reams until the November election. The reform party, enthusiastic to support anyone bold enough to oppose Parr, wasn't expecting opposition from the Republican candidate and Parr would never back a Republican, but they hadn't counted on a last-minute surprise. Rumors began spreading that a massive write-in campaign was being conducted against Reams, but nothing definite could be substantiated.[12]

Prevailing upon Starr County attorney Arnold J. Vale, who had been renominated to his state representative seat, Parr coerced him into running against Reams in a write-in campaign. When results came in from three of the four district counties, Reams had a substantial lead, but Duval hadn't sent in its results. Thinking he had lost, Vale said he "would not take the job even if the vote in Duval County" gave it to him.[13] Six days later, Parr released the Duval totals.

Newspapers around the state sent reporters to cover Parr's announcement, anticipating a surprise like the Stevenson-Johnson results. They were not disappointed. Relishing the attention, Parr took his time going down the list of votes received for each office, saving the best for last. "I know this is the one you are interested in," Parr said. "Our totals show 43 votes for Reams and 4739 for Vale." Added to totals from the three other counties, Vale had won by 250 votes. "Kept my little secret, didn't

I?" George told the press. "That's just good strategy."[14] Once again, Parr outfoxed his opposition, but Governor Shivers wouldn't let the matter rest.

Reams hadn't planned to contest the election, but Shivers urged him to file a complaint. Vale was also a problem for Parr because he had no desire to be a judge, preferring to serve in the state legislature. Vale's reluctance meant if he was certified the winner and refused the post, Shivers was authorized to appoint whomever he wanted to the vacant bench. When the Election Canvassing Board met to certify the votes, Texas Secretary of State John Ben Shepperd, in a precedent-setting action, refused to allow Duval votes added to the total. "Under the circumstances, I can not consciously count the Duval County votes in this race," he told reporters. Realizing he had failed to seat Vale, Parr told him to refuse the judgeship. Asked why he wasn't pressing the issue, Parr replied, "What for? We voted and won. Our man simply didn't want the job."[15] An astute political game player, he knew when to retreat. But gathering forces—emboldened by victory—would continue the attempt to unseat the Duke from his long-held throne.

After a meeting to test the extent of political unrest in Duval, a Mexican American group headed by San Diego grocer Manuel P. Sanchez announced the formation of the Freedom Party. Their platform was "to oppose the political rule of County Judge George B. Parr." Matias D. Garcia, a veteran who was an instructor at the Veterans' Vocational School in San Diego and secretary of the new party, charged that "control of the county has been used for the purpose of personal advancement," and he could not live in a county "where even our heritage of voting does not count without doing something about it."[16]

The political tide was changing, not only in Texas for Parr but nationally, in a Republican Party controlled federal government. Under Eisenhower, the Justice Department came under Republican control, and Parr faced a formidable outside foe. If matters weren't bad enough, Governor Shivers had supported Ike with crossover Democrat voters. This gave new impetus to the perennial stepchild Texas Republicans. The Freedom Party was also beginning to gather voters. They taught illiterates to read and write (and thus, how to mark ballots on their own), and their efforts showed their political destiny could be wrested from the sly possum.

When Sheriff Sain was defeated there was no longer a Parr-controlled sheriff in Jim Wells County. Even the grand jury was fomenting reform.

Under a new Texas election code, grand juries were empowered to open ballot boxes and investigate election irregularities. The Jim Wells grand jury informed Judge Reams that because "our county has been notorious for alleged misconduct at prior elections," they would ensure that future elections would be a "true expression of the will of the voters."[17]

Internal opposition in Duval County came from the defection of Sheriff Dan U. Garcia Jr. Passed over for a judgeship when Judge Tobin died in 1949 (George appointed himself to the vacancy), Garcia began aligning with the reform movement. Getting rid of the recalcitrant sheriff wasn't easy because Garcia demanded twenty thousand dollars in "severance pay." A practical man, as well as an astute political practitioner, Parr instructed the county treasurer to stuff an envelope with twenty thousand dollars and deliver it to W. C. Johnson, Garcia's business partner. "The office was for sale and I bought it," Parr would later say.[18]

To tighten control in his county, Parr gave up his judgeship and appointed himself Duval County sheriff. He filled the vacant judgeship by appointing Dan Tobin Jr. In a county as small as Duval there were two hundred armed deputies, now under Parr's control. He was also in a position to keep a close eye on the grand jury nosing around in financial records of the Benavides Independent School District (BISD), a favorite source of funds for Parr.[19]

Parr controlled the county, but Governor Shivers had the state with Texas Rangers at his command. When a delegation of Duval citizens registered complaints, he ordered rangers into Duval to protect citizens "beaten, molested and threatened because of their political beliefs."[20] Unleashing them on Duval, Shivers had the rangers begin an investigation of prostitution and gambling in the San Diego area.

The previous year, Texas Ranger Clinton Thomas "Clint" Peoples had set up surveillance of El Ranchito, a local bar reported to have backroom gambling and a row of ten one-room cottages on the back property for prostitution. After a raid in which twenty-two people were arrested, Judge Reams issued a temporary restraining order to padlock the place.[21] In the hearing that followed, border patrolman Edwin H. Wheeler testified to having frequented the place at least once a month during the past five years looking for illegal aliens and observing what he described as obvious evidence of prostitution in the back cottages. One interesting fact arising during the hearing was that Mrs. Thelma Duckworth Parr was listed as property owner. In truth, George had taken over the property under the divorce agreement. At the conclusion of the four-day hearing, Reams ordered El Ranchito closed for one year, and Parr could only grin and bear this latest assault on his dukedom.[22]

The Freedom Party tested their power by offering a full slate of candidates in the 1952 primary. It was a concerted effort to "eliminate George B. Parr as the dominant factor in Duval County politics," said Freedom Party president Manuel Sanchez.[23] Parr fought back the only way he knew: his deputies harassed Freedom Party rallies, pressured local merchants and their customers with their presence, and detained Freedom Party members for hours to be searched before releasing them. Duval County became a war zone with the casualty of a border patrolman, an outspoken critic who had crossed swords with Duval County officials.

"We noticed this car coming towards us with his bright lights on," a passenger in a car driven by Milton Mareth said. Mareth flicked his lights on and off to get the approaching car to dim his lights, but "he just kept right on coming." The two cars collided, and the other slowed until it stopped as a result of a flat tire. Slumped over in the car was the lifeless body of Edwin H. Wheeler, head of the local Texas Border Patrol, the same officer who had exposed the El Ranchito bordello. What seemed an accident became a murder investigation when the mortician preparing the body discovered a bullet hole in Wheeler's head. Because Wheeler was a federal officer, the Immigration Service asked the FBI to investigate.[24] After an exhaustive inquiry, no arrests were made, and no connection was ever established between Parr and the murdered U.S. border patrolman. The case is still open to this day.

George Parr had other matters to tend to—his empire was indirectly being threatened by Judge Reams, who was using the grand jury as a weapon. "They planned to indict my friends and then remove them from office," Parr said. "Pending a hearing, Freedom Party men would be named to the offices." He wasn't a dictator and didn't control the vote, he contended. "I couldn't even control my wife's vote when I was married."[25]

Reams was hostile toward the Parr machine, and George put defeating him at the top of his political agenda. Parr controlled all local officeholders, including the school board, the county commissioners, and the sheriff's office, but the Seventy-Ninth Judicial District Court was still in enemy hands. In his words, "Politics is a game we play 365 days in the year. I've been boss around here for quite a while—and I don't intend to retire for a long time yet."[26]

Playing the game also meant hurting an opponent where it mattered most—his means of livelihood. Donato Serna, Freedom Party candidate for Duval County judge, owned a drugstore in San Diego and was becoming an outspoken Parr critic: "For nearly half a century we have been living under the political influence of the Parr regime, a regime controlled by one man. . . . There exists here one dictator, a man in absolute control of all county affairs, all school affairs, and all city affairs. . . . Mr. Parr not only controls the political life in this county, but also a great share of the economic life. . . . The present one-man dictatorial regime has driven the rich people away and kept the poor man poor."[27] Serna had to be silenced, and Parr knew how to deliver the message. A bus stop that brought steady business to Serna's drug store was suddenly relocated, and a restaurant owned by Serna's brother was harrassed by Parr's deputies who blocked the driveway of the eatery.[28]

"Parr would do anything to punish a man who opposed him, no matter how mean or little," Texas attorney general John Ben Shepperd said. "A Freedom Party man couldn't even get his cotton ginned. At the 4-H Club shows, children of Freedom Party members couldn't sell their fat lambs and calves."[29] Undeterred, Serna refused to remove his name as a candidate.

Parr's anointed candidate for district judge was Jim Wells County judge C. Woodrow Laughlin, who would put an end to the anti-Parr crusading if elected. Getting him elected required manpower provided by the Old Party machine, and Parr spared no expense. An added impetus to his concern was that Alice attorney Jacob S. Floyd offered his services to the Freedom Party as general counsel; he would provide legal expertise in getting judges to issue writs of mandamus or any other actions to limit voting fraud.

It became a bitter, name-calling campaign with both sides accusing each of immoral conduct. "If the people of Duval County want bigger and better houses of prostitution, let them vote for George B. Parr," Serna proclaimed. Covering the election for the *Corpus Christi Caller-Times*, James Rowe editorialized on the Parr machine: "There is no lack of money to carry their campaign to every end of the county." Rowe quoted Parr as saying that Judge Reams is "anti–Latin American" and wants to "send them to the penitentiary."[30]

The day before the primary Texas Rangers were assigned to watching posts in three of the four counties. Eleven rangers would be patrolling polling places in Brooks, Starr, and Duval Counties; only Jim Wells County would be without ranger presence on primary day. Newspaper reporter Jim Greenwood noted: "Just outside Duval County, was a group of black, official-looking cars, a bus equipped with a powerful mobile radio station and a group of booted men upon whose chest shone the badges of Texas Rangers. You remembered the old saying, 'one riot, one Ranger' and begin to wonder what type of situation demands a group of nine Rangers." To assure a democratic voting process, Judge Klein allowed Freedom Party supervisors to be at polls where they could challenge prospective voters to assure they were not carrying pre-marked ballots. When the polls closed, Klein ordered all ballot boxes impounded.[31]

Parr spent the day at his election headquarters, set up at the county garage next to the courthouse, where he refused to comment to reporters. Polling places took on an aura of a banana republic election with Texas Rangers armed with Winchester rifles standing alongside Parr's deputized pistoleros. The show of force was effective because there were no reports of violence that day.[32] Whatever tactics Parr used to frighten voters prior to Election Day, his hands were tied while ballots were cast. He could not even "vote the dead" as in the past.

When the final results came in, Parr's candidates had made a clean sweep of every office. The Duval tally was 3,084 for Laughlin, 1,151 for Reams, and Parr (running for reelection as sheriff), received 2,149 to his opponent's 752 votes. One newspaper reporting on the disparity of votes between Parr and Laughlin surmised "he [Parr] must have instructed the voters to vote only for district attorney and district judge," so as not to tax them as they read the ballot.[33]

The Duke delivered, but notice had been served that he would no longer be able to engineer lopsided 99 percent margins. Prior to the 1952 primary, 1,151 votes for an opponent in Duval County was unheard of, and as Freedom Party president Manuel Sanchez stated, "We have just begun to fight."[34] No longer fearful of Parr's rule, reformers began planning their next assault on the dukedom.

CHAPTER 9

BUDDY FLOYD

"Jake, I'm glad to hear your voice," the caller said. "I want to talk to you."[1] It was the night of September 8, 1952, when Jake Floyd received the call from Nago Alaniz, partner in a law firm with Raeburn Norris and close friend of George Parr. Floyd and Alaniz were not friends, but both practiced law in Duval and Jim Wells Counties, and although on opposite sides of the political fence they kept a professional acquaintance. Floyd invited him to his home, but Alaniz insisted they meet at Jewel's Drive-In restaurant on the outskirts of town.

"Nago, I have always told you when you called me, I would come," Floyd responded.

"Come out right away, Jake: Do me that favor," Alaniz pressed. "Come in a taxi; I don't want anybody to see you. Don't come in your own car they know it. Take a taxicab."

"All right, I will be right out," Floyd told him.

During the phone conversation, Floyd's twenty-two-year-old son, Buddy, a law student at Baylor, was listening from the stairway to the upstairs bedrooms. After hanging up, Floyd called a taxi, and although he had difficulty in finding one, he finally succeeded.

"I'm going to meet a Parr man," Jake told his son. Floyd's wife, Edith, had left the house earlier to attend a Baptist Church social and wasn't expected back until later. Buddy's fiancée, Elynor Lewis, was visiting and saw the father leave. Buddy and his father had a lot of similarities: he resembled his father physically, weighed almost the same, had the same distinctive walk, and both carried their arms in the same peculiar way. Concerned his father was having a late-night rendezvous in an out-of-the-way place with a Parr associate, Buddy told his fiancée he would be back shortly, having decided to follow his father.

When Jake Floyd arrived at the drive-in restaurant, Alaniz appeared nervous and edgy. Alaniz was sitting in his car, and Floyd opened the passenger side door, waiting for a moment to allow the headlights of the taxi to shine inside before getting in.

"Jake, I called you out here to tell you that they are going to have you killed," Alaniz said. "I cannot tell you who they are, Jake, they would kill me."

"Why should anyone want to kill me?"

"They are afraid you are going to put Judge Reams back in office in November in the general election."

"Has George Parr got anything to do with this?" Floyd asked.

"I don't know, but somebody is putting up the money."[2]

Floyd listened attentively as Alaniz told him two professional killers had been brought in from Mexico; one of them was now waiting in Floyd's garage to ambush him. Apprehensive about meeting with a Parr associate in the dark of night, Floyd was curious and pressed for details. Alaniz told him a man named Sapet was leading the killing team and driving a green Packard. Floyd recalled that Sapet was a Duval County deputy sheriff.

"I have agreed to say that the killer was with me when he kills you," Alaniz said. "He had to have an alibi."[3]

"I can't tell you who the killer is," Alaniz added. "If I did they would kill me; they would kill me if they knew I was talking to you now."

Still skeptical, Floyd told Alaniz the election was over and he knew nothing about a planned write-in campaign. Alaniz was frantic; he was certain the attempt on Floyd's life had been planned and wanted to convince him he was serious.

"You won't believe me, Jake, but let me tell you something. You know how close I am to George Parr? Do you remember two years ago when the county clerk's office was broken into. I did that—George made me."[4]

"You didn't get in the vault," Floyd replied, "you just got in the office."

"No, Jake, I got in the vault. We bribed one of the deputies."

The raid on the county clerk's office Alaniz described referred to a contested election in Jim Wells County. Although the late-night entry into the courthouse had been successful, the final goal was not achieved. County Clerk C. H. Holmgreen, being wise to the ways of Parr, had hidden the official ballot boxes and left worthless ones in their place.[5]

Floyd asked if he could tell Sheriff Halsey Wright everything Alaniz was telling him. "If you do, they'll kill me." When Floyd offered to tell the sheriff "somebody from Rio Grande City told me," Alaniz agreed, but added, "Don't go see Halsey—telephone Halsey." While waiting for another taxi, Floyd discussed Duval politics with Alaniz. The nervous lawyer was disgusted with what was happening. He said, "when they start killing people I'm leaving."[6]

Floyd still didn't believe the story, but he decided it would be prudent to go directly to the sheriff's office. When he arrived, the office was empty, so he headed home. As the taxi pulled up to the house, Floyd saw flashing lights of emergency vehicles and a crowd gathered near the sheriff department's cars. Rushing to see what had happened, Floyd arrived just in time to see his son being placed on a stretcher.

Investigators pieced together the following scenario. Floyd's home was equipped with a loud-ringing attachment to the telephone, which was easily heard from the garage. The killer, later identified as Mexican national Alfredo Cervantes Martinez, apparently heard the phone ring when Alaniz called Floyd. Expecting Floyd to use his car, Cervantes waited in the dark and fired five shots when Buddy Floyd entered the garage. One shot hit him in the wrist, another in the head; he died nineteen hours later in the hospital only two hundred yards from his home. Fleeing the scene, Cervantes dropped the murder weapon, a Mexican version of a .38 caliber Colt Detective Special, in a nearby garbage can. It was later determined to be similar to one owned by Mario Sapet. A "very clear" set of fingerprints was found on the gun.[7]

Buddy's mother returned from her church meeting a little after 10:00 P.M. When she turned into the garage driveway behind the house, the "lights flashed into the driveway," she said, "and I saw my son lying there. I got out of the car, ran over to him, kneeled down and felt of his pulse." Buddy was still breathing. Mrs. Floyd ran to the nearby home of Dr. G. G. Wyche Sr., who went back to the garage with her and rendered first aid until the ambulance arrived.[8]

Buddy's fiancée was in her bedroom when she heard "several rapid explosions" and then a car speeding away. Looking out the bedroom window toward the garage, she didn't see anything. Mrs. Floyd's screams alerted Elynor that something had happened.[9] At the hospital, Dr. Wyche and his son G. G. Wyche Jr., worked with Corpus Christi orthopedic surgeon Dr. Rayfus, who operated on Buddy. "Part of the bullet that entered his head was outside near the right temple," Dr. Wyche later testified, "and the rest of it lodged in the rear of his skull in the brain and destroyed the brain tissue." Buddy died at 3:45 P.M. the following day.[10]

Jake Floyd later testified that Alaniz told him Judge Reams was also targeted for assassination that same night. Reams recalled he was awakened by his barking dog. "I started to get up and look around, but turned over and went to sleep." A while later his phone began ringing. The caller was Deputy Sheriff Jack Butler, who told Reams that Buddy Floyd had been shot. "He told me to stay in the house, not to turn on any lights, and that he would be out in a minute." After a search of the neighborhood, and finding nothing suspicious, the officer advised Reams not to leave his house until the following morning.[11]

Gathering evidence and interviewing witnesses in the days following, the sheriff's department was able to reconstruct events leading up to the killing. On the morning of the murder, Cervantes stopped in a San Antonio bar called The Golden Horn (Inez's Place) and told the owner's wife (Inez Mendez) he was going to see "The Turk," for a job to be done. "If he did it," she said Cervantes told her, "I would never see him again. If he didn't, he would be back in a week." Forty-five-year-old Mario Sapet Arteaga, a San Antonio tavern owner Cervantes referred to as "The Turk," had been issued a Duval County deputy sheriff's card dated August 12, 1952, and signed by "George B. Parr, Duval County Sheriff."[12]

Sapet, who used several aliases, was a dangerous man with a criminal record going back twenty years.[13] Known among his associates as *El Turko* (The Turk), Sapet waited for Cervantes at his place of business on the day of the murder. Together, they drove in Sapet's 1952 green Packard coach to Corpus Christi where Cervantes dropped Sapet off at the bus station to buy a return ticket to San Antonio. While Cervantes headed toward Alice in the car, Sapet boarded a bus and arrived back in San Antonio around 10:00 P.M. He went directly to the county sheriff's office on the pretext of seeing a friend, but in reality to establish an alibi.

Several of Floyd's neighbors saw a car cruising the area earlier that evening fitting the description of Sapet's car. Shortly before 9:00 P.M., Cervantes parked a block away from the Floyd home and approached the garage via an alleyway. After mistakenly shooting the wrong man, he crossed the Rio Grande bridge at Laredo into Mexico and abandoned the vehicle in Nuevo Laredo. He stopped in Ricky Callione's International Gardens for two shots of tequila, paid three pesos (twenty-five cents) for them, and vanished.[14] The following morning, Sapet strolled into a San Antonio police station and said, "I hear you are looking for me."[15] He was arrested by Texas Rangers and brought back to Alice.

Testimony by a Corpus Christi bar owner linked Sapet to the gun, or one closely resembling it. Duval County resident Justo Tijerina testified seeing Sapet in his Packard around 4:00 P.M. on the day of the murder. Riding with Sapet was Duval County chief deputy sheriff Jose "Pete" Saenz, and following behind "was a black Cadillac driven by Sheriff George B. Parr." Alaniz was linked to Sapet by Freer resident Henry Norris, who reported seeing Alaniz in a car with Sapet and J. C. King, chairman of the Duval Democratic Party Executive Committee.[16]

Circumstantial evidence kept linking Parr with the murder. In a rare public statement, he sent a typewritten letter to a Corpus Christi newspaper in an effort to quash rumors of his involvement. He dictated the letter at his home in San Diego to his brother-in-law Nueces County judge B. Green Moffett, who delivered it to the newspaper. Parr's statement read in part:

> It was with shock and deepest regret that I heard of Jake (Buddy) Floyd, Jr., and my sympathy goes out to the parents of this young man and I sincerely hope that the perpetrators of this atrocity will be brought to speedy justice.
>
> It is true that Jake Floyd, Sr., and I have been on opposite sides politically for over twenty years, but contrary to rumors that have been circulated, I have always played the political game open and above board and have taken my chances on the open field of political activity. I have never taken an undue advantage either legal or illegal of my opposition. I have always fought an open battle, true to my own convictions, and I offer no apology to any man or set of men for my activities.
>
> Many rumors have been circulated and spread against me in this section of Texas. However, I have never done anything in my public life for which I offer anyone an apology. And despite rumors current at the present time my conscience is absolutely clear and I can only say to Jake and Mrs. Jake Floyd, Sr., that in this their hour of sorrow and trial they have my heartfelt sympathy and compassion.[17]

Despite his passionate plea, George couldn't shake the belief among many that he was somehow connected to the murder. "Parr controls everything except the way the wind blows," was a popular sentiment among South Texas residents.[18]

Alaniz was arrested on a murder charge and conspiracy to commit murder; both he and Sapet were denied bail. Cervantes was indicted for murder, but the charge was dropped. Knowing he had fled to Mexico, prosecutors felt it would be wiser to deal with him at a later date. Alaniz was represented by Percy Foreman, a flamboyant (and expensive) Houston attorney who was reportedly paid his twenty-five-thousand-dollar fee by Parr, although no evidence ever supported the rumor. Sapet's attorney was Fred Semaan from San Antonio, who once claimed to have tried more death penalty cases than any other attorney. None of his clients ever received the death penalty, including one claiming self-defense who sat in the backseat of an automobile and fired five shots into the driver's back.[19]

Before the grand jury met to return indictments, Parr, in a surprise move, resigned as sheriff on October 1. His nephew Archer Parr, discharged from the Marines after serving in the Korean War, was appointed as his replacement. Two other Duval County officials, Joe Hancock and J. A. Tobin, both precinct commissioners for more than twenty years, also resigned.[20]

Concerned over the possibility of a whitewashing trial, Governor Shivers appointed Houston attorney Spurgeon E. Bell as special prosecutor to handle the case. Judge Reams was to preside over the grand jury, but when Foreman and Semaan argued that Reams would not be impartial, Shivers replaced Reams with district court judge Arthur A. Klein from Brownsville. Shivers also appointed two Texas Rangers as court bailiffs while the grand jury sat. Parr, among the witnesses called, testified for a little over an hour and left. Passing by Alaniz in the hallway, Parr quipped in Spanish, "You're getting fat."[21] On October 14 indictments were returned against Alaniz and Sapet, and the trial was moved to Brownwood—far away from any possibility of Parr's influence.

After two attempts to be granted bail, Alaniz was released on December 19, 1952, after D.C. Chapa and Lorenzo Garcia posted the twenty-one-thousand-dollar surety bond.[22] Sapet was refused bail and remained in jail. His trial began March 16, 1953 (Alaniz had won a motion for separation), and after two days to select a jury, the state presented its first witness—Jake Floyd.

Floyd's testimony lasted for four hours, during which he repeated the conversation he had with Alaniz the night of Buddy's death. Interwoven throughout his testimony were vivid details of the political history of Duval County. When defense attorney Semaan began his cross-examination he wasted no time getting to the heart of the matter:

"You would like to see the Parr party destroyed and wiped out wouldn't you?" Semaan challenged the witness.

"I certainly would," Floyd fired back.[23]

After Ranger Captain Alfred Allee testified on recovering Sapet's car in Nuevo Laredo, a lunch recess was called. In the courtroom corridor one of Sapet's attorneys, Werner A. Gohmert, jokingly asked the ranger if he had "maliciously lied" in his testimony. Reacting to the remark, Allee slapped the lawyer across the face with an opened hand. Gohmert staggered and dropped his briefcase. When he started to say something, Allee told him to "shut up." Another defense attorney stepped in and led Gohmert away. After the lunch break, Semaan brought the two combatants together and suggested they forget the incident.[24]

Contending that registration papers for Sapet's Packard were "illegally acquired" by police before Sapet was arrested, Semaan asked the court to hear testimony on the matter. The judge agreed but removed the jury during testimony. When Semaan called Sapet, the prosecutor objected to the defendant's limited testimony, requesting Sapet should be heard for "all purposes." He was overruled, and Sapet recalled the events leading up to his arrest. He said he didn't know about Buddy Floyd's murder until after being taken into custody and reading it in a local newspaper. "They stopped sending me papers after I read about the killing," Sapet said.[25]

The state concluded its case at 9:54 on a Friday night, after which Semaan berated the prosecutor's tactics. "They are trying to paint a picture of Parr as a crooked and dirty politician and indicated that the defendant was working hand and hand with him," the attorney raged. "George Parr is not being tried here, Mario Sapet is the defendant."[26]

When court convened the next morning, the jury was instructed to disregard Floyd's testimony concerning his Duval County political activity. The judge then told the defense, "Call your first witness." The packed courtroom waited in silent anticipation, hoping rumors were true that Parr would testify. He didn't. Seven minutes into the session, defense attorney Gib Calloway stood up and announced, "The defense rests." Courtroom spectators, many of whom had packed lunches in order to retain their seat during the noon break, were stunned. Sapet's fate would go to the jury without their having heard him testify.[27]

After five hours of closing arguments, during which the state asked for the death penalty, the jury was given instructions before beginning their deliberation at 11:13 Saturday night. On Sunday, after deliberating for close to twenty hours, they returned with a verdict at 6:55 P.M. Sapet was found guilty, and the jury set his sentence at ninety-nine years in prison. Commenting on the trial, Parr said, "That's a big Baptist town and there used to be a lot of Ku Kluxes there. Mario Sapet was a dark Mexican, and a Catholic. You can see he didn't have a chance."[28]

Before Alaniz was brought to trial, a strange development occurred that added further mystery to an already confusing case. Betty Bushey, a redheaded, twenty-nine-year-old woman being held in Pensacola, Florida on a charge of passing bad checks, told Florida officers she had evidence pertaining to the Floyd murder. Claiming "her life had been threatened twice and that she had been kidnapped once" while attempting to contact Texas authorities, she refused to tell her story to anyone except Jake Floyd or a Texas Ranger. Texas attorney general John Ben Shepperd, hoping new evidence might point to Parr's involvement in the murder, was interested in hearing Betty, but "wouldn't vouch for her credibility." He had good reason not to.[29]

Born in Hamburg, Germany, but a U.S. resident since the age of two, Betty had a dozen aliases and a string of arrests for passing worthless checks. She told police she had a two-year-old son, but she was uncertain about her marital status. "I don't know whether I am divorced or not," she said. Whether she was lying to get out of jail or really had concrete information, Jake Floyd wanted to know. Arriving in Florida with a Texas Ranger, Floyd listened to her story. "She has confirmed my belief that other parties were involved in the murder of my son," Floyd said after the jailhouse interview. Florida authorities agreed to allow Betty to be taken to Texas and testify before a grand jury, if Texas wanted her.[30]

Duval County attorney Sam Burris refused to grant immunity, but he expressed interest in questioning her. He wanted to know how Betty had managed to retain one of the best criminal lawyers in Pensacola. "It seems strange that a woman picked up on hot check charges would have money to hire an expensive lawyer," he said. "I believe someone else is footing the bill." Shepperd was betting that Parr put up the lawyer's fee. Hoping for any evidence linking Parr to the murder, he arranged for her to appear before a Duval County grand jury.[31]

"I don't know who she is working for and I have been trying to figure it out," Parr said during an interview on his radio station in Alice. "I don't know this woman personally," he said. "But she must be a stoolie for the Texas Rangers or has privately been hired by Jake Floyd." Parr wasn't the only one curious to know what she had to say.[32] Escorted by two rangers wherever she went, Betty drew a lot of attention while having coffee in an Alice cafe. Ignoring stares and whispers like "good actress," Betty waited for the grand jury call.[33]

During her grand jury appearance, Betty doled out bits and pieces of her upcoming testimony. She said she had served as a messenger between people in Duval and San Antonio. She claimed papers were stashed in a San Antonio safe deposit box, among which were a map of the Floyd residence and notes she had retrieved from a wastebasket. Unfortunately, the box was in another person's name, and while she was certain the man would give permission to open it, he was too ill at this time. She also said, "I have met George Parr and he is a friend but I am not his girl friend." Her story was beginning to sound far-fetched and evidently the grand jury felt the same. The prosecutor handling the Alaniz case decided not to call her as a witness, and Betty Bushey's story remained untold.[34]

Although Betty was dismissed as a potential witness in the Floyd murder case, she still managed to create news of her own. After her testimony, she was arrested in Waco on a charge of theft by bailee involving a car. Her attorney, former Waco assistant district attorney James R. Morris, visited her in jail to discuss the case. A romance soon blossomed. After her release, Betty and James Morris were married on January 2, 1955, in Durant, Oklahoma.

Betty's past came back to haunt her. A month after the wedding, she was arrested after failing to appear in court on a year-old charge of passing a bad check for $87.66 to purchase dresses and lingerie at a Waco store. Pregnant at the time, Betty felt other Waco lawyers resented her marriage to one of their own. "They're awful clannish down there in that small town," she complained. "They don't like me." Morris stuck by his paperhanger wife. "We're going to fight that check case," he declared. "If I can't get a good lawyer to defend her I'll do it myself." Pleading guilty to check forgery, Betty received a two-year probated prison term.[35]

Having rescued his errant wife for the second time and with a child on the way, it would seem Morris could hope life would return to normal for the strangely paired couple, but the tabloid saga of Betty Bushey had a bizarre chapter added the following month. On the evening of April 3, 1955, the couple were returning to Waco from Houston. Betty was driving and they began to argue. "I told him I'd leave when I got to Waco. When he told me he'd jump out of the car, I told him he didn't have the guts enough to." Morris told her to step on the gas. With the car speeding down the highway, he opened the passenger door and jumped. Betty stopped the car and ran back to where her husband lay on the side of the road. He was dead after suffering a massive cerebral hemorrhage from the fall.[36]

An inquest returned a verdict that Morris died of a "voluntary fall" from the car, but others were suspicious. Local newspaper publisher Pat Midkiff and Waller County attorney C. W. Kirisch filed a murder on complaint charge against Betty. She was arrested while preparing for her husband's funeral but was allowed to attend under escort. After an examining trial held by Justice of the Peace A. M. Wallingford, who had rendered the original suicide verdict, all charges against her were dropped.[37] Having had enough of the limelight, Betty dropped out of sight and was never heard from again.

Getting Alaniz to trial was a long, tedious process. After a change of venue, the case was scheduled to begin in Waco in July 1954, but it was delayed when Alaniz had to have an appendectomy operation. Postponed until October, the trial was again delayed, this time by Alaniz's attorney Percy Foreman, who submitted two motions to quash the indictment.[38] After the motions were denied, jury selection began, but Foreman delayed the process by questioning each prospective juror at length. Alaniz sat stoically at the defense table listening attentively. His wife sat in the spectators' section with their two daughters, both preoccupied with coloring books.

While the prosecutor questioned jurymen on their feelings concerning the death penalty, Foreman asked about "beer drinking, suspended sentences," and how they felt about the "Parr Regime." After a marathon session lasting eleven hours with no supper break, Judge B. W. Bartlett called a halt a little after midnight. Only six jurors had been chosen.[39]

Jury selection continued the next morning. During questioning of jurymen, the prosecutor mentioned that the case originated "from those counties in South Texas with some widely publicized political troubles." After being quizzed about his opinions, one prospective juror asked, "Has this got anything to do with George Parr? If it has, then I got an opinion." He was not selected. By 7:15 the second night, only eleven jurors had been picked, and the panel of 115 had been depleted. The judge ordered the sheriff to round up fifty additional men and have them ready by morning. The jury was completed the following day after the twelfth man from the additional list was selected just before eleven o'clock.[40]

The first witness called was Jake Floyd. After testifying about meeting with Alaniz he told the jury how he arrived home to see his son being placed in an ambulance. During Floyd's testimony, Foreman kept objecting to the father's continual reference to "my murdered son," saying such statements served to arouse sympathy among the jurors. The prosecutor had no more questions and turned Floyd over for cross-examination by Foreman.[41]

"Isn't it a fact Nago Alaniz warned you of a plot against your life because you had been his friend, counselor and guide?" Foreman asked.

Floyd snapped back quickly with an angry "no." Foreman attempted to establish that a close relationship existed between the two men, but Floyd wouldn't agree. Several times he said, "I don't remember," when asked about ties with Alaniz.[42] After several heated exchanges, Floyd lost his composure. "You ought to be fair to me and this jury and this court," he snapped. "If he [Alaniz] had gone to the law as he should, he would have saved my son from being murdered."[43] But the flamboyant defense attorney kept bearing down.

"Isn't it a fact that Alaniz risked his life to tell you of the murder plot?"

"No," Floyd answered. "He said he would be killed if 'they' knew he told me what he told me. He tried to keep me from going to see [Sheriff] Halsey Wright."[44]

Foreman began the defense by calling witnesses to attack the credibility of state witnesses, but under cross-examination the prosecutor kept bringing in Parr's name, hammering away at the idea that the death of Buddy Floyd was directly linked to Duval politics. After calling former

Benavides justice of the peace H. Q. Heras, who had been at Alaniz's home the evening of the murder, Foreman called Alaniz's wife, Elvira. Leaving the two daughters with their father at the defense table, Elvira began her testimony. Having difficulty keeping her composure, she often broke down in tears recalling events of that fateful night.

Prior to her husband arriving home she received a cryptic phone call from a Spanish-speaking man who wouldn't identify himself. "I am the man that talked to [Alaniz] Saturday," he told her, "and this matter in Alice is true and it will be tonight." When her husband came home she repeated the message, but before she could ask what it meant he abruptly cut her off. "I've got to go," he told her and the visiting Heras. "It might mean saving a man's life."[45]

The trial continued through the weekend and closing arguments began at 8:00 Saturday night. The prosecutor labeled Alaniz a "miserable tool of George Parr," while Foreman claimed his client risked his own life to save another, but the "fickle wheel of fortune" claimed Buddy Floyd. As Foreman was making an impassioned plea to the jury, Alaniz's three-year-old daughter began crying and had to be taken from the courtroom by her mother. After a charge to the jury lasting fifteen minutes, shortly after midnight the judge placed the fate of Nago Alaniz in the hands of the twelve jurymen.[46]

The jury immediately began deliberating the case, taking four ballots until retiring at 3:45 Sunday morning. At one point they asked that Jake Floyd's testimony be read to them concerning the meeting with Alaniz at the drive-in. The next morning at 9:40 they announced a verdict had been reached. Veteran courthouse observers could not recall a verdict having been returned on a Sunday in Waco. After taking nearly an hour to round up the judge and lawyers, the judge was handed the verdict at 10:27. Although the courtroom had been crowded every day during the weeklong trial, there were only twenty-five people present when the verdict was read—Jake Floyd not among them. "Not guilty," Judge Bartlett announced. As his wife clung to his arm, Alaniz raised his hand to his eyes and wept for a few minutes.[47]

Alfredo Cervantes was hiding in Mexico fearful of his life and complaining he was never paid for the killing.[48] Testimony during Alaniz's trial positively identified him as the trigger man. Fingerprints on the murder weapon, combined with prints taken from Sapet's Packard, were checked against a set of Cervantes's prints taken in 1943 in Mexico City. Jake Floyd worked tirelessly to have him extradited back to the United States, but the Mexican government refused. Floyd claimed someone was paying Cervantes to remain in Mexico and worried some day he would be killed. "I don't want him killed. I want him here alive to tell the whole story. I know in my heart who tried to have me killed, and killed my boy instead."[49]

In 1954 Texas governor Allan Shivers made a formal request to the U.S. Department of Justice to issue a fugitive warrant for Cervantes and have him returned to Texas. Not until September 25, 1955, three years after Buddy Floyd's death, was Cervantes indicted. Four years later, Governor Price Daniel pressed the issue, but to no avail. "The State Department said the Mexican government has found no trace of him," Daniel reported. President Eisenhower signed an extradition request for Cervantes on June 6, 1957. He also appointed attorney Sidney P. Chandler and Sheriff Halsey Wright to press the Mexican government to search for the wanted killer. "With the ties of friendship this country now has with Mexico," Chandler said, "I am hopeful that Mexican authorities will respect our efforts to see that justice is done."[50]

In June 1960 Cervantes was arrested in Tepatitlan, a small town fifty miles east of Guadalajara. He had been living there for a number of years training fighting cocks for a living. "I had almost given up hope," Jake Floyd said. Although Cervantes was a U.S. citizen, he was born in Mexico and entitled to the rights of a Mexican national. Extraditing him was difficult because Mexico would not turn him over unless it was guaranteed that he would not receive the death penalty if found guilty.[51] One month after his capture, Cervantes was deemed to be a Mexican citizen by the First Federal Court of Mexico and would not be extradited.[52]

An appeal to the Mexican Foreign Ministry to overrule the Mexican court's decision was denied in 1961. After John F. Kennedy took office, William Bradford Huie wrote a letter to the president asking for his help in the case. A popular novelist who wrote the best seller *The Revolt of Mamie Stover*, Huie pressed JFK to use his influence to extradite the man "hired to kill by Texans to whom Vice President Lyndon B. Johnson is indebted." Huie chronicled in his letter the rise of Parr and the help Johnson received in the 1948 election, but whether Kennedy did anything about the case is not known.[53]

In 1963 the Mexican Supreme Court refused to overturn the denial for extradition. There seemed no hope Cervantes would ever stand trial for murder in Texas. The battle to have his son's killer brought to justice took its toll on Jake Floyd. In February 1964, after suffering for a year with a lung ailment, he died at Houston's Methodist Hospital. His body was brought back to Alice and buried alongside that of his son.[54]

Later that year, Cervantes was finally brought to justice for killing Buddy Floyd. The Mexican courts still refused to extradite him, preferring to try him there. After a trial before a Mexican judge without a jury, Cervantes received a thirty-year sentence at hard labor.[55] Mario Sapet was paroled on July 17, 1972, but neither he nor Cervantes ever implicated anyone else in the murder. For Parr, who was never tied directly to the Floyd murder, life in the political arena continued; this time, however, his foes were becoming increasingly more difficult to overcome.

CHAPTER 10
EMPIRE UNDER ATTACK

If the aim of killing Jake Floyd was to prevent a write-in campaign for Judge Reams it failed. Not only did the Freedom Party fight to keep Reams on the bench, they also organized a write-in campaign to unseat the newly appointed sheriff Archer Parr. To vindicate his son's death, Floyd worked tirelessly arousing voters to defeat the Parr machine. An ad hoc group of mothers from Alice rallied to the cause "so our children can grow up without fear of political assassination."[1] With sympathies aroused because of the brutal and senseless murder, Parr found himself in a passionate battle against a swelling opposition of reform.

With armed deputy pistoleros at his command, Parr initiated a reign of terror so as to remind constituents who it was had the power. Stores owned by Freedom Party officials were searched for narcotics, their business disrupted as deputies tore the places apart. Freedom Party member Andy Griffin lost income at his auto and truck repair shop when patrons were threatened that their taxes would rise if they did business there. "Men who supported the Freedom Party in the July primaries are being practically put out of business," said Alice grocer E. W. Carpenter. Parr let it be known that if anyone shopped at Manuel Sanchez's grocery store they would lose their welfare benefits. To combat the American Legion literacy campaign (an illiterate voter being to his advantage), Parr abolished the program.[2]

Undaunted, the Freedom Party continued gathering members to its growing list. "We must be prepared to die in order to win this fight," Freedom Party organizer Richard Beasley told his friends. "We must also be prepared to kill to keep from being killed."[3] Peace-loving individuals began arming themselves. Even with opposition coming from Austin (Governor Shivers requested supervisors stationed at the polls) and a grand jury impaneled by Judge Reams to investigate improprieties in the county (which was quashed by Judge Klein in a motion submitted by Parr), all Old Party candidates were victorious on Election Day. Having Judge Laughlin presiding over the Seventy-Ninth Judicial District and Duval County sheriff Archer Parr reelected, with his band of armed deputies keeping order, Parr fended off insurgents—for the time being.

Laughlin came under attack when he was indicted by a Jim Wells grand jury for selling his personal law library to the county for $2,185 and a second count of "swindling" for receiving the county check. He had "forgotten" to secure competitive bids for the law library, but to get out from under the indictment he had to return the money the county had paid him. Controversy continued to surround Laughlin. He impounded Duval County ballots and turned them over to Sheriff Archer Parr. Many voters were concerned that with Archer Parr in possession of the ballots, the sacred secrecy of the electorate would be compromised. Their fears were well-founded because George had boasted, "There's no secret between heaven and earth that I can't find out."[4]

Laughlin then dismissed the grand jury that indicted him. When demands for Laughlin's impeachment gained support from the state capitol, he responded by rescinding his dismissal order. Before the grand jury adjourned, the jurors met with Governor Shivers in Austin to appeal for help, charging that Laughlin put "stumbling blocks and delays" in the way of their investigation. Shivers responded with legislation calling for Duval County to be split from Jim Wells County in the Seventy-Ninth District and placed under the jurisdiction of the 111th Laredo District, "a set-up where the vote of the people would elect a district judge instead of George Parr's doing it."[5]

Not only did the state legislature consider the governor's proposal, they also decided to investigate Laughlin's possible removal from office. If removed, Laughlin could still run for the same seat he held. During hearings to consider both motions, Jake Floyd testified: "I've fought those political dictators, and you've read in the papers that it's cost me." Senator Abraham "Chick" Kazen Jr. of Laredo—a neighboring-county Parr supporter—attempted to suspend the hearings, but they continued with testimony from Freedom Party members who were concerned that with Duval under jurisdiction of the 111th Judicial District they would still be facing the same problems because that district was controlled by Parr's political ally Judge Manuel J. Raymond.[6]

The State Bar Association added pressure by accusing Laughlin of "reprehensible conduct in office," basing their allegations not only on the sale of library books and the ballot-impounding issues, but on the fact that he allowed his brother, a Jim Wells County commissioner, to sell property to the county and that he also appointed the judge (Ezequiel David Salinas) who heard his law library case. The battle in the legislature continued when the senate called for an immediate investigation by a committee. Gerald Weatherly (one of George Parr's attorneys) appeared before them to defend Laughlin. He said Laughlin's appointing Judge Salinas from the 111th Judicial District to sit on the law library case was not unethical, nor was the sale of the books improper because the county had been using the judge's library for free for fourteen years.[7] Parr called on Senator Kazen to stop the hearings by bringing the matter to the floor of the Texas Senate, where it failed to garner the necessary two-thirds vote.

With the urging of Texas attorney general Shepperd, Jake Floyd and ten other lawyers practicing in the Seventy-Ninth Judicial District filed a motion with the Texas Supreme Court calling for removal of Laughlin. Their plea was based on an obscure, and never before used, section of the Texas constitution allowing the Texas Supreme Court to have jurisdiction to hold hearings to remove a sitting judge for cause when reasons are "presented in writing upon the oaths taken before some judge of a court of record of not less than ten lawyers, practicing in the courts held by such judge, and licensed to practice in the Supreme Court; said presentment to be founded either upon the knowledge of the persons making it or upon the written oaths as to the facts of creditable witnesses."[8] Including charges presented to the legislature, this new petition listed twelve allegations of misuse of judicial power by Laughlin. He was now facing a more formidable inquest—Parr's influence did not extend to the body of jurists who would determine the facts in their inquiry.

Hearings began before the Texas Supreme Court with witnesses who rehashed previous charges against Laughlin. Representing the beleaguered judge was Clint Small, who claimed the charges were motivated by sore losers at the polls who now wanted to unseat the judge. At the conclusion of the hearings, the Supreme Court appointed Twenty-Sixth Judicial District judge J. B. Wood as Master in Chancery to conduct a thorough investigation. Laughlin was the first witness called, and during four days of testimony he denied all allegations, adding that the *Corpus Christi Caller-Times* had been waging a campaign against him. "If Parr's opponents don't like a man, they call him 'a Parr man'" he said. "That's the same as calling him a bad name."[9]

Among the new charges being levied against Laughlin, one involved the case of David Carrillo "D.C." Chapa, a political leader in the Parr machine. Laughlin gave Chapa a five-year suspended sentence, justified on the ground that all previous convictions against the defendant had been overturned on appeal. Another Old Party faithful, José S. Hinojosa, had sixty indictments of voting irregularities dismissed by Laughlin—a record for a South Texas court. In another case, Laughlin awarded a Parr man—Jessie Grimes Jr. of Brooks County (whose father was sheriff)—custody of his son without giving notice of the hearing to the child's mother. In a March 1953 murder case against former Benavides city commissioner Luis Garza, Laughlin allowed attorney O. P. Carrillo to prosecute the case, even though Carrillo's law partner had previously represented Garza. In a plea agreement, Garza waived a jury trial and pleaded guilty to murdering Duval County deputy sheriff Oscar Briones, upon which Laughlin gave him a suspended five-year sentence. The charges against Laughlin kept piling up, and George Parr could do nothing to prevent them from being aired in public.[10]

On the issue of impounding ballots and turning them over to Sheriff Archer Parr, one witness observed "ballots being studied by deputies" in the sheriff's department. Texas Ranger Captain Allee testified "we thought it peculiar they [the ballots] were rolled up like that [tied with string and separated into groups] instead of being folded." Allee managed to get on record that it was common knowledge "Parr says he knows how everybody votes." Raeburn Norris, who prepared the court order to have ballots impounded, testified that he saw no reason for "singling out" Duval County for irregularities since it had been a fair election. Robert Leo, who lost his teaching position because of his Freedom Party affiliation, testified that people were afraid to speak out because of economic pressures. When asked by Judge Wood who they were afraid of, Leo said, "They were afraid of George Parr."[11]

The Laughlin investigation became a secondary issue as Judge Wood expanded the inquiry to include political tyranny in Duval, with special attention focused on George Parr. Donato Serna testified about the bus stop removed from in front of his drug store. He said his brother José left the county after treatment he received from pistoleros at his drive-in across the street from Parr's office. When Serna tried taking photographs of official cars blocking the driveway, Parr hit him on the head with a five-cell flashlight. "I was taken to his office," Serna said. "There one of his deputies smashed my camera." Parr then told him, "Get out."[12]

After hearing the last witness—Manuel Raymond, Laredo political boss and ally of Parr—who said, "I think the main fight is against George Parr," Judge Wood closed the hearings. Spoiling Laughlin's Christmas holiday, Wood filed his sixty-five-page recommendation with the Texas Supreme Court on December 23, 1953. Out of twelve charges, Wood found merit in five: Laughlin's impeding the Buddy Floyd grand jury; giving impounded ballots to the Duval County sheriff, which "was motivated solely by a desire to favor George B. Parr and his political party"; hand-picking the judge who heard the law library case; dismissing the Jim Wells County grand jury and appointing commissioners who would select grand jury members favorable to the Parr machine; and handling of the Garza murder case.[13]

Before the Texas Supreme Court reached a decision on the Laughlin matter, Parr began creating his own controversy. Sensing blood in the water, the Freedom Party began preparations to offer another slate of candidates in the 1954 primaries. Membership in the reform movement was gaining steadily, and meetings were now in the open and seeing increased attendance—giving Parr an unsettling feeling. It was evident something had to be done. Assigning deputies and loyal associates to monitor Freedom Party meetings was a customary practice, but on the night of January 16, 1954, Parr took action on his own.

The Freedom Party held a meeting outside San Diego at the Hacienda Drive-In. Parr, along with Juan Barrera, Mauro Garcia, and D.C. Chapa, sat in an automobile in the parking lot observing those attending the meeting. Tortilla maker Manuel Marroquin, the Hacienda owner, and vocal member of the Freedom Party, along with Manuel Corrales, approached the parked car. Marroquin claimed he wanted to learn the identity of the car's occupants, but when he neared the vehicle, the driver's side door swung open and Parr stepped out, threatening him with a pistol. He said Parr was angry "cussed me out and told me he would kill me and the rest of the guys inside if we didn't quit holding meetings."[14]

A few months earlier, Parr had been involved in another gun-toting incident. Cristobal Ybanez was a quiet religious man who minded his own business. On August 17, 1953, he was sitting on a sidewalk talking and laughing with a friend. Parr drove past, suddenly made a U-turn and parked on the wrong side of the street. Jumping out with a Winchester rifle in hand, Parr accused Ybanez of laughing at him. Without warning, he swung the rifle to hit Ybanez in the head, but fortunately the blow landed on the arm raised to ward off the attack. Ybanez defiantly tore his shirt open and boldly dared Parr to shoot, but George backed down. Ybanez tried three times to file a complaint of assault with Duval County attorney Reynaldo F. Luna, but each time the paperwork was either lost or pigeonholed. He tried to get the grand jury to hear his complaint, but they refused.[15]

Marroquin found a sympathetic ear in Sheriff Halsey Wright of Jim Wells County where the threat had taken place. He swore out complaints against Parr and Barrera, and after obtaining arrest warrants Wright set out to serve them. He found Barrera at a local restaurant, but the elusive Parr proved more difficult. When he contacted Sheriff Archer Parr, Wright was told that George was out of town at a horse race but Archer said he would find and arrest him for Wright.

Wright was led to believe that Parr would appear Monday morning to give himself up. Barrera showed up, but George didn't. He sent his lawyer Ed Lloyd instead, but county attorney Sam H. Burris insisted Parr appear in person. Ranger Captain Alfred Allee dispatched Rangers Walter Russell and Joe H. Bridge to pick him up. As a courtesy, Bridge contacted Sheriff Archer Parr, who told the rangers to come to his office. When they arrived he told them to wait there while he went to pick up George. "Archer gave me the run-around," Bridge said. "I called him and told him we were coming over. He promised to bring George to his office. He didn't. He came straight to Alice, leaving us sitting over there."[16]

After waiting several hours, Bridge realized he had been duped and set out to find George on his own. He went to the Jim Wells courthouse where he found him in the hallway with his nephew talking to Captain Allee. George had already been fingerprinted and photographed. Seething over being the butt of a joke, Bridge approached Archer Parr. "Well, I don't appreciate the run-around I got," he told him. "Well, I know of some things you've done unbecoming . . . ," Archer began replying.

Before he could finish his sentence, Bridge slapped him across the face, knocking Archer's glasses to the floor.[17]

Alice Daily Echo reporter Caro Brown, who was in the hallway, turned to a man she was talking to and said, "Something's fixing to happen." It wasn't long before she knew she was right. George, reacting to his nephew being slapped, lunged at Bridge. Allee grabbed George and, at the same time, reached to disarm Archer, who had drawn his gun. In the fracas Allee twisted George's ear, causing it to bleed, and punched him before sticking his gun in Parr's ribs. While blood ran down Parr's face, Allee held him by the shirt collar and shoved him backward.[18]

"I've had all I'm going to take off you and the way you've been handling things," Allee threatened. Sensing Allee was angry enough to pull the trigger, Caro Brown stepped between the two men, begging the Ranger, "Cap, please don't, please don't."

Manhandling George by his shirt collar, Allee pushed his frightened captive into the empty courtroom, motioning Joe Bridge and Archer Parr to join them. "We're going to get this thing settled right here," Allee told them.[19]

According to the *San Antonio Light*, Parr pleaded with the angered ranger captain. "Alfred," he asked, "what have I done to you?"

"I'm fed up with you," Allee replied, still holding Parr by his shirt collar. "If you want to get rough we'll get rough."

"Nobody wants to get rough," Parr said nervously.

"If I ever make up my mind to kill you," Allee threatened, "there's nothing to keep me from doing it."[20]

Archer retrieved his eyeglasses, which miraculously hadn't broken, and nervously polished them while Allee was face-to-face with George, who kept nodding in agreement.

"I'm not going to put up with any whipping with pistols or Winchesters in Duval County," Allee warned. "Those people have a right to have political meetings without being molested." During the twenty-minute dressing down, no more punches were thrown, but George was visibly shaken after Allee released him.[21]

The Marroquin gun-brandishing and the courthouse scuffle had meaningful significance for Parr because for the first time he was shown to be vulnerable. In the eyes of many Mexican Americans, their patrón lost some of his machismo aura. "I knew they were doing everything in their power to embarrass me, so I made up my mind to grin and bear it," George said.[22] After posting a fifteen-hundred-dollar personal appearance bond, Parr was released.

According to the *San Antonio Express*, Parr later gave his version of the gun-toting incident at the Hacienda. "I wasn't carrying a pistol," Parr told reporters, "and I didn't threaten anyone. I was sitting in a [San Diego] cafe when someone said, 'Say did you know there was a meeting of the Freedom party?' No, I said. Let's go see who's at it."

Parr said when he and Barrera arrived at the Hacienda there were from twenty to thirty cars in the parking lot. He parked about a hundred feet from the meeting place, "but you couldn't see anything," because it was cloudy. While sitting in his car, another car passed by with three men in it. The car made a U-turn and came back.

"It stopped about 40 feet away and this fellow got out," Parr said. "I got out too, because I knew he had recognized the car."

Claiming he had a pair of binoculars in his hand, not a pistol, Parr said he asked the man [Marroquin], "What the hell do you want?" Parr then said, "Get on away." He said the man got back in his car and drove away.[23]

Two Parr associates, D.C. Chapa and Mauro Garcia, testified before the grand jury that they were in the backseat of the car and Parr was holding only a pair of binoculars. A week later, the grand jury handed down indictments of assault with attempt to murder against both rangers. George expressed "surprise" at the grand jury's action. "I didn't have anything against [the two rangers] and I still don't."[24]

The binocular incident not only provided a South Texas newspaper with material to run a series of political cartoons, it became part of the local lore. A typical yarn had Parr walking into a local drugstore where he spotted a youngster wearing a cowboy outfit and sporting a pair of toy six-shooters. According to the *San Antonio Express*, George walked over to the boy and patted him on the head.

"Sure a nice pair of pistols you got there young fellow," Parr remarked.

Apparently not realizing who he was, the boy blurted out, "Them's not pistols, mister, them's binoculars."[25]

Allee was not a man easily intimidated. Duval residents may have feared Parr, but the ranger captain held only disdain for him. Through a reliable informant, Allee heard he had been targeted for assassination by two Parr supporters, Jose Rodrigues and Raul Barrera. Allee went with three other rangers to the Windmill Café in San Diego. "I just wanted some of my men to see what these men look like," he said. "I wasn't going to arrest him."[26] They didn't find them, but when they got to the cafe, county attorney Raeburn Norris was just walking out. According to Allee, Norris made a sarcastic remark to him as he passed by. "Norris' attitude ever since I've been indicted had been a sneering one," Allee felt.[27]

Norris gave a different version. "As I was leaving, Allee and three or four other rangers walked up. Allee jumped on me and cussed me out." Norris claimed he didn't lift a hand to defend himself. "I knew all he was waiting for was for me to do it and then he'd pull a gun." Allee slapped Norris around and kicked him several times. "I've got four or five big bruises on my shin where he kicked me with his boot," Norris said. "He [Allee] said he was damn tired of the way I had been acting and not to ever look his way again."[28]

A half block away, Parr was outside his office watching the confrontation. Allee and the rangers got back in their cars and drove to where Parr was standing. "George, come here," Allee called from the car. Parr walked over and Allee said, "If anything happens to my men or myself, I'm going to get you." Allee then accused him of sending his nephew Archer to Mexico to hire men to kill the rangers. "I told him my nephew had gone to New York City to see a girl friend," Parr said. Dismissing Parr's explanation, Allee said, "If you want to shoot it out, we'll be ready." Allee then jumped out of the car and stood toe-to-toe with Parr. He accused Parr of bringing in the men to kill Jake Floyd. "Allee's face was white, his eyes bloodshot and his face flushed with rage," Parr recalled. "I was quiet and calm because I knew Allee's terrible temper." After saying his piece Allee got back in the car and drove away.[29]

Whether frightened or wanting to add more ammunition to the case against the rangers, Parr's next move was to seek court protection preventing the rangers from harassing him. In a petition before federal judge James V. Allred (former Texas governor) in Corpus Christi, Parr accused Allee and Bridge of having "given convincing evidence of a desire" to kill him. Parr claimed they threatened "he must forfeit his life . . . if any person or persons whether under his control or not, cause injury to be inflicted on any ranger stationed in or near Duval County." This threat "is one to take plaintiff's life, without any investigation or trial, with defendants acting as judge, jury and executioner." Seeking an injunction under the Fourteenth Amendment, Parr asked the court to enjoin the lawmen to "refrain from unlawfully interfering with, molesting, abusing, attacking and assaulting, beating or killing plaintiff."[30] Allred scheduled a hearing in Houston and ordered the two rangers to appear before a panel of three federal judges to show cause why an injunction should not be granted.

To beef up his claim, Parr made an unprecedented move by bringing in outside counsel to present oral arguments. For a reported fifty-thousand-dollar fee, he engaged the services of a prestigious New York lawyer, Arthur Garfield Hays, a longtime crusader of civil rights. The seventy-two-year-old attorney began law practice in 1905, but his international fame came as counsel for the ACLU soon after it was formed in 1920. He joined Clarence Darrow in Dayton, Tennessee, as a member of the Scopes legal team in the famous "Monkey Trial," defending the right to teach evolution in public schools. He defended Sacco and Vanzetti at their murder trial; and after the Reichstag fire in Berlin, Hays sat on a London examining commission condemning Hitler for his actions. After the war, he headed a delegation making recommendations to guarantee civil liberties to Germans under the occupation.[31]

News of Hays coming to Texas prompted the state attorney general Shepperd to fire off a telegram to the ACLU: "Since when is it your policy to represent a political dictator against an oppressed and outraged people?" Accustomed to controversy in handling emotional, politically unpopular cases, Hays was beginning to get a taste of Texas–style justice. "I am here as a private attorney," he explained, "the Civil Liberties Union knows nothing about George Parr and I doubt if it even knows I'm down here."[32] When asked if he would withdraw from the case if it became "explosive," Hays replied that it "would be contrary to my experience to leave the case."[33]

Taking their cue from Parr, five Freedom Party members submitted a motion to Judge Allred. They filed a plea of intervention, saying "Parr has violated our civil rights with threat and violence," adding, "We are prepared to tell the court of Parr's iron-handed rule in Duval County." Among the petitioners, Cristobal Ybanez hoped to finally get his day in court for the beating Parr gave him; Donato Serna wanted to tell of his plight when the bus stop in front of his drug store was moved;

and Manuel Marroquin would rehash the still pending "binocular" case. Judge Allred agreed and signed the order for intervention.[34]

A three-judge panel convened the federal district court in Houston on February 22, 1954. Outside the packed courtroom, U.S. Marshals held back spectators arriving late for a seat. People besieged a newsboy to buy copies of the local paper. "I can't get in," was a common complaint. "Let me read about it . . . at last, now we'll know what's going on." The newsboy sold every copy before being told it was against the rules to sell newspapers in the building. U.S. senator Strom Thurmond from South Carolina was among the fortunate ones to make it inside. "I'm not too familiar with the Parr case," he said, "but I thought I'd take a look."[35]

Markel Heath represented the five Freedom Party members; Jake Floyd represented the two rangers as did Houston attorney Frank J. Knapp; Gerald Weatherly and John J. Pichinson argued for Parr. The real drama expected would come from the battle between Hays and Texas attorney general Shepperd, who was there for the state. The hoped-for clash never occurred as Shepperd kept an observer's position, but the performance by Hays was well worth the wait.

Supporting his frail body with a mahogany cane, Hays wore horn-rimmed glasses, but behind them were razor-sharp eyes and a keenly honed legal mind. His immediate task was to separate Freedom Party members from the suit. He argued they were in court to "create a legal Donnybrook," with charges going back twenty years.[36] "I brought my case here to protect [Parr's] civil rights," he argued. "What possible connection has their contention he has violated their civil rights?"[37] Hays went straight to the heart of the matter during his twenty-two-minute argument. "If what they say is true," he said, "they could have brought a suit of their own at any time in the past, and not waited to intervene in a suit brought by this plaintiff [Parr]."[38] Without leaving the courtroom, the three judges conferred briefly before rendering a decision. "It is the consensus the petition [to intervene] should be dismissed," Judge Thomas Martin Kennerly announced.[39]

Filing answers to Parr's chargers, Rangers Allee and Bridge said that Parr "does not come into court with clean hands," adding "Nor does he show himself free from guile, but seeks to take advantage of equity to relieve himself of the consequence of his own wrong doings."[40] In defending the rangers, Jake Floyd began by recalling the night of September 8,

1952. "A tragedy took place on that date which as this court knows has meant so much to me," he said in a voice trembling with emotion. Parr, sitting three chairs from Hays, displayed no emotion. He kept his eyes turned to the ceiling during most of the session with hands folded in his lap, but when Floyd spoke, he focused his look on the back of Floyd's head.[41]

Hays called nine witnesses, but spectators wanted to hear only one—George Parr. A buzz of excitement stirred the courtroom as he walked to the stand. Early in his testimony, Judge Kennerly rapped his gavel when laughter broke out among spectators, warning that he would clear the courtroom if there were any further outbursts. Hays led Parr through his testimony as he recalled events leading up to the Duval courthouse scuffle, including the pending gun-toting charge against him and the altercation between Norris and Allee.

During cross-examination, Jake Floyd repeatedly brought up his son's murder but mostly aimed his questions to reveal the past history of the witness and the hold Parr had over Duval County. According to the *Corpus Christi Caller* in February 1954, Floyd began by asking why Parr had resigned as county judge in 1936.

"My parole was revoked and I was sent to the federal reformatory at El Reno, Okla.," Parr answered matter-of-factly.

When Floyd asked about Parr's connection to the resignation of several Benavides school board members, Judge Kennerly asked the relevance to the present case.

"The situation was tense," Floyd replied. "This helps show why the Rangers were sent down there." Kennerly allowed the questioning, but Parr was evasive as to his role in the school board members' actions. Floyd did manage to get Parr to admit he had been signing checks on behalf of the school district.[42]

According to the *Houston Chronicle*, Floyd asked, "Is it true that you carry a submachine gun in your black Cadillac?"

"No, sir," Parr replied.

"When you were sheriff," Floyd pressed the witness, "you appointed one Mario Sapet as your deputy, did you not?"

"I gave him a card that was for the purpose of carrying a pistol and it read that he was a full-time deputy," Parr said. "But he was never paid and he never did act as a deputy sheriff."[43]

Floyd had waited eighteen months for the opportunity to question Parr under oath in connection with his son's murder, but George proved reluctant and evasive. Frustrated at being denied, Floyd ended his questioning and Parr returned to sit next to his attorneys. Attempting to maintain a modicum of his distinguished demeanor, Hays asked Parr for a list of character witnesses to support his claim of being an upstanding community member. On cross-examination, one witness admitted running a whorehouse in San Antonio. Another was described as the "sloppiest, poorest looking specimen you ever saw in your life—shabby clothes and soup stains."[44] Hays was now left with cross-examining Ranger Captain Allee as the only remaining hope of having the injunction granted.

Both son and grandson of Texas Rangers, Allee was five feet, nine inches tall and a bit on the chunky side, but as tough as any ranger who ever lived. After a short career as a rodeo bronc rider he became a ranger. Considered one of the quickest men on the draw, Allee also had a temper, "but it takes a long time to work him up to the point where he loses it. When he does, the flare-up can be spectacular." Stubborn, but highly respected, "when he is mad, Allee drops his deep black eyebrows, works his face into a fierce scowl."[45]

According to the *Fort Worth Star-Telegram* in February 1954, defense attorney Frank Knapp opened direct examination by going straight to the heart of the case. "Did you attempt to kill him [Parr]?" Knapp asked.[46]

"I believe not," Allee answered calmly. "If I had attempted to kill him I believe I would have done it." Knapp then questioned Allee on circumstances leading to his being assigned to Duval County and how he handled the situation upon arrival.

"There were plans under way for organizing the Freedom Party in opposition to the Parr Party," Allee testified. "They were being molested by Parr and his deputies. George and his deputies were trying to break up their meetings."

Knapp asked why Allee went directly to see Parr upon arriving there.

"Because I know the conditions in Duval County," he said. "I knew that George Parr was head of the political party and that a majority of the people looked to and listened to him until the Freedom Party was organized."

Knapp then asked about Allee's assignment to investigate the Buddy Floyd murder. Allee testified he first saw Mario Sapet at a Freedom Party rally two months before the killing. Juan Barrera accompanied Sapet, whom Allee described as "the man known as the bodyguard to George Parr." Hays objected to Sapet's name being brought into the case. "They are trying to show guilt by association," he contended. The objection was overruled.[47]

According to the *Corpus Christi Caller* in February 1954, under cross-examination Hays led Allee through a history of his assaults, including slapping Sapet's attorney, Werner Gohmert, and the scuffle with Raeburn Norris.

"You hit him to assuage your feelings?" Hays asked about the Norris assault.

"Well, I did it that time," Allee replied bluntly. "Had I not been a Ranger I still would have done it."

"You now admit you made a mistake?"

"I might have but, by golly, I'm not sorry I did it."

Hays did manage to get Allee to admit his feelings about Parr. "I just personally don't like nothing about him." Hays was satisfied he had demonstrated Allee's penchant to assault anyone he felt insulted him and even shook Allee's hand as he was leaving the stand. "I want to pay tribute to this witness," Hays told the court. "I think he is an honest man."[48]

Ranger Joe Bridge testified about the courthouse brawl, but nothing was added to clarify the incident. Four Freedom Party members who had been denied to be part of the case were allowed to testify. Each described the violent confrontation they received from Parr, but a "steady barrage" of objections from Parr's attorneys who contended the incidents were not relevant to the present proceedings, disrupted their testimony to the point of distraction.[49]

In his closing argument, Hays stressed that his client's "life is in danger." His depicting Parr as a mild-mannered citizen who turned the other cheek when confronted with violence seemed a bit far-fetched. "I am amazed at the meekness of the people on my side," Hays said. "They have been assaulted and kicked with heavy boots and they have done nothing."[50] Not granting the injunction "could result in bloodshed," Hays predicted.[51]

Jake Floyd again reminded the court he lost his son because of Parr. "My feelings in this matter go down to my toes," he said. Pointing directly at Parr, he added, "All this matter has come about because of the conduct of this man." Defense attorney Frank Knapp warned of the danger in handcuffing the rangers' efforts to bring law to Duval. "Lurking in the background and shadows of this case are thousands of Duval County citizens who have been oppressed by ruthless and unconscionable actions. . . . To grant this plaintiff the relief he asks would be a monstrous thing."[52]

After closing arguments, the three judges rendered their decision: "The issuance of such an injunction would be a step in the direction of destroying the long preserved relations between a Federal court of equity and a state's administration of its own criminal law." They "gravely doubted" jurisdiction lay in their court. Recognizing Allee may have used tactics that should not be condoned, nevertheless, they refused to grant an injunction.[53] The *Houston Post* agreed: "A contrary ruling would have been a revolutionary interference in a state's right to enforce its laws and police a county where it believes there is wholesale lawlessness and corruption and fear of violence." Allee felt justified. "He's a dangerous man who would do anything under the sun," he later said, "and I don't treat a tiger like I do a rabbit. I'm not sorry I hit Mr. Parr."[54]

Before leaving, Hays had a parting comment. In a tongue-in-cheek remark, he suggested an ACLU branch be established in Duval with Parr and Allee as charter members. "It will have an educational value, if not to the public, at least to all those involved," he said. Taking up the offer, Parr quipped he "will be glad to do all I can to help in this connection."[55]

Although he lost the case, Hays was asked by the five Freedom Party members to represent them in a civil liberties action against Parr. Hays had said he would represent "even the Texas Rangers" if their rights were violated and now the five were asking him to "keep your promise made in the federal courtroom in Houston."[56] Citing conflicts of interest, Hays declined.

Archie Parr as Texas state senator. Thirty-Fourth Senate Composite, 1915, detail, accession ID CHA no. 1989.598, preservationist Jesse Herrera. Courtesy State Preservation Board, Austin, Texas.

Stokes Micenheimer, Jim Wells County deputy sheriff; Hubert T. Sain, Jim Wells County sheriff; Givens A. Parr, brother of George Parr; Ed Lloyd, Jim Wells County Democratic Executive Committee chairman; and Barney O. Goldthorn, president, First State Bank of San Diego, grouped around Ballot Box 13. Courtesy LBJ Library.

Hearing in Alice, Texas, concerning the outcome of 1948 U.S. Senate primary election. Governor Coke Stevenson is seated behind the table, third from left, with cigar. September 28, 1948. Courtesy LBJ Library.

William "Bill" Haywood
Mason, March 17, 1943.
RGD0005F6164–R01, Houston
Public Library, HMRC.

Sam Smithwick (*right*) escorted by Dick Knowles Sr., jailer, at Bell County
Jail, Belton, Texas, January 8, 1950. Courtesy *Fort Worth Star-Telegram*
Collection, Special Collections, University of Texas at Arlington Libraries.

Left to right: Texas Ranger Captain Alfred Young Allee, Texas Ranger Joe H. Bridge, and Jim Wells County deputy sheriff Jack Corby Butler. RGD0005F6709–R01, Houston Public Library, HMRC.

Duval County Commissioners Court meets to canvass votes after the November 7 election, November 14, 1950. A write-in vote gave J. Vale a victory over incumbent Seventy-Ninth District Court judge Sam Reams Jr. In the center is county judge George Parr, clockwise from Parr are chief deputy county clerk Garcia, Precinct 3 commissioner John Turnham, Precinct 4 commissioner Felipe Valerio Jr., and Precinct 2 commissioner Joe Hancock. Red Moores, *Corpus Christi Caller-Times.*

Jacob "Jake" Stokes Floyd Sr.
RGD0005F6676-002, Houston
Public Library, HMRC.

George B. Parr and Arthur
Garfield Hays in hallway at
federal courthouse, Houston,
Texas, February 18, 1954.
RGD0005F6676-002 EWM,
Houston Public Library, HMRC.

George Parr, February 22, 1954. *Corpus Christi Caller-Times.*

Archer Parr and wife Anne
Blair Furman Parr. Date
unknown. Archie and Anne
were married on August 12,
1954, and divorced in 1963.
RGD0005F0262-001
EWM, Houston Public
Library, HMRC.

Thelma Duckworth Parr after appearing
before Houston federal grand jury.
investigating tax evasion charges against
her former husband, George Parr, on
October 5, 1954. RGD0005F6676-001
EWM, Houston Public Library, HMRC.

Caro Brown, 1955 Pulitzer Prize–winning *Alice Daily Echo* reporter.
RGD0005F6676-003 EWM, Houston Public Library, HMRC.

George Parr and eight other defendants after the federal mail fraud trial in Houston
ended with a hung jury, on December 18, 1956. *Left to right*: Oscar Carrillo Sr.,
Jesus Oliveira, Jesus G. Garza, D.C. Chapa, Attorney Percy Foreman, George Parr,
B. F. (Tom) Donald Jr. (*in rear*), O. P. Carrillo, Santiago Garcia, and Octavio Saenz.
RGD0006N-0946N001, Houston Public Library, HMRC.

George Parr with attorney Luther E. Jones during New Braunfels trial for theft of Benavides school district funds, on January 25, 1957. *Corpus Christi Caller-Times.*

George Parr's mother, Elizabeth Allen Parr (age ninety), at the federal courthouse in Houston after testifying at Parr's mail fraud trial, on July 2, 1957. RGD0006N-1262N001, Houston Public Library, HMRC.

George Parr with attorney Percy Foreman outside the federal courthouse, Houston, Texas, on July 30, 1957. Courtesy *Fort Worth Star-Telegram* Collection, Special Collections, University of Texas at Arlington Libraries.

George Parr (*center*) with San Diego attorney Nago Alaniz (*hand on Parr's shoulder*) leaving federal court in Corpus Christi after sentencing for income tax evasion, on May 3, 1974. In the foreground is Clinton Manges. *Corpus Christi Caller-Times.*

Jody Martin Parr with her lawyers Jack Pope Jr. and William Bonilla in San Diego before being sentenced for contempt of court, on June 7, 1974. *Corpus Christi Caller-Times.*

Archer Parr, April 2, 1975. *Corpus Christi Caller-Times*.

An estimated 150 cars stretched one mile for George Parr's funeral procession on the way to the Benavides Cemetery, on April 3, 1975. *Corpus Christi Caller-Times.*

Archer Parr (*center*) escorted by Texas Rangers Ray Martinez (*left*) and Rudy Rodriguez (*right*) at Duval County Courthouse to be arraigned on charges of official misconduct, on September 24, 1976. *Corpus Christi Caller-Times.*

PART III
TREADING WATER

CHAPTER 11
UNCOVERING THE HIDDEN

Parr's gun-toting trial began March 22, 1954. According to Caro Brown in the *Alice Daily Echo*, Marroquin gave his "pistol-brandishing" version and Parr countered with his "binocular-brandishing" story. County attorney Sam Burris entertained the crowded courtroom recalling the fable of Br'er Fox and Br'er Rabbit. Caught by the fox, the rabbit begged, "Don't throw me in the briar patch, please. Just throw me in the cool, cool well."

Burris explained to the jury "the rabbit lived in the briar patch, and that was just where he wanted to be thrown." Pointing to Parr, he said, "Don't throw this rabbit in the cabbage patch, for he's got plenty of cabbage. Throw him in the cool, cool jug."

The jury took less than an hour to return a guilty verdict. Illegally carrying a gun in Texas was a misdemeanor, and although facing a year in jail, Parr was fined $150 plus $10 in court costs. After taking eight $20 bills from his wallet to pay the fine, Parr walked over to Burris and shook his hand. "Sam, you put up a darned good fight," he said.

"Well," Burris said, "we didn't put you in the cool, cool jug, but we got into that long green cabbage."[1]

According to Harold Martin in the *Saturday Evening Post*, upon leaving the courtroom Marroquin met a friend, Conception Peña, the owner of a local barbershop. "Manuel, do me the great favor," Peña pleaded. "Do not patronize my shop any more. The red light is upon you. You and all who know you will be made to suffer."

"Have no fear, amigo," said the smiling Marroquin. "*El Tacuacha* [The Possum] has no power to hurt us any more. He may not know it yet, but he is dead."

"That cut the Duke down to size," one observer noted. "If he can't beat a common pistol-toting rap he can't play *papacito* any more."[2] The

Corpus Christi English Spanish weekly *La Verdad* labeled Parr "the Binoculars Man" and considered him dangerous. The editor said a man dropped by the newspaper and told him, "Sure, Parr was carrying a pair of binoculars the night he went to see who was attending the Freedom Party meeting."

"Are you positive of that?" he was asked.

"Yes," the man asserted, "but he never told the Rangers that the binoculars were attached to a 73 Winchester!"[3]

At the Dallas Press Club's annual gridiron show that year, political notables such as President Eisenhower and Senator Joe McCarthy—and Parr—were lampooned in musical skits. The actor portraying Parr sang:

> I'm a ding-dong daddy from Duval
>   You oughta see me do my stuff.
> I'm a ballot stuffer from San Diego
>   I can be plenty rough.
> My binoculars are loaded (pats large, obvious holster
>   on hip) for the opposition.
> They say I'm totin' pistols, but that's superstition—
> I'm a ding-dong daddy from Duval
>   You oughta see me do my stuff.[4]

The floodgates opened to inundate Parr in the attempt to sweep him out of South Texas politics. Texas attorney general John Ben Shepperd gave notice that the year "1954 will bring an end to George Parr's power." Governor Shivers called Duval County "a cancerous growth on the good name of Texas," announcing, "that all state and federal resources are being used to 'stamp out' political tumult in Duval County." The *New York Times* printed three consecutive days of articles outlining battle plans being implemented to defeat the Duke, even if it meant imposing "martial law." Shivers disclosed that state officials—along with the IRS and the Post Office Department—had been investigating Duval County's use of public funds for more than a year, "a county in which the light of freedom has been almost snuffed out."[5]

Parr tried to head off investigations by launching one of his own. Chances were good that Judge Laughlin would be removed and replaced by a Shivers hand-picked judge, but before that happened Parr wanted to get as much mileage out of Laughlin as possible. Convening the Duval grand jury, Laughlin charged them to make an extensive probe into county affairs. "I further charge you to extend to the attorney general of Texas . . . an invitation to appear before you and present any evidence," he added.[6] It was strictly a fishing expedition; Parr wanted to know what evidence Shepperd had against him in order to combat it.

Parr had nothing to fear from the probe because the grand jury was stacked with friends.[7] The grand jury called the *Houston Press* assistant city editor Jack Donahue, who had written a series of articles on Duval, including a probe of the Benavides school system funds. After his session with the grand jury, he said, "As near as I can tell, half of them were confused and the other half didn't give a damn."[8] Donahue's testimony helped the grand jury decide where to probe next. They didn't have to wait long because the Texas attorney general's office released affidavits from several Duval citizens outlining dispersal of sixty-seven thousand dollars in school funds, paid in vouchers to fictitious persons. Most of the vouchers had been countersigned by Parr, even though he had no official connection with the school district.

Gathering affidavits hadn't been easy. "We took the affidavit of one man in the dead of night, out in the brush," Assistant Attorney General Willis E. Gresham recalled. "He was so scared that sweat was literally pouring off his face."[9] The most incriminating affidavit came from Diego Heras, acting secretary of the board of trustees of the Benavides Independent School District (BISD) from 1940 to July 1951.

His affidavit was taken by IRS agents investigating Parr's tax liability. Heras detailed methods that Parr used to receive funds from school district accounts. He said the BISD books were kept at Parr's office and audited by William M. Benson, who had been appointed by the school board. Benson also served as Parr's office manager and bookkeeper, which made access to school funds convenient. Heras said Parr would walk into the office, make lists of names on scratch pads with amounts to be paid and notes of "services allegedly performed," and "instruct me to write checks from his list." Heras endorsed the checks and took them to the Texas State Bank in Alice. Cashier B. F. (Tom) Donald Jr. totaled the checks and filled an envelope with fifty- and hundred-dollar bills. "I would drive back to San Diego and deliver same to Mr. Parr," Heras added.[10]

The Duval grand jury couldn't wait to hear Heras. Not only had he given the IRS an affidavit, he also gave one to the Texas state attorney's office. In that affidavit Heras expanded his testimony on how BISD vouchers were handed out. Parr's brother-in-law B. Green Moffett received five hundred dollars monthly for "legal services," but Heras couldn't recall any services Moffett performed. Heras also provided a list of vouchers made out to 101 persons "who do not exist," and another list of 24 persons who did exist, but "never received the money."[11]

Acting on Judge Laughlin's suggestion, the grand jury asked Texas attorney general Shepperd to appear before them. It was more of a challenge than an invitation. Citing Shepperd's promise to "prosecute law violators" in Duval, the grand jury wrote in a telegram: "We will be at your service." Shepperd wouldn't take the bait. "I don't want to be a party to a whitewash or a fishing expedition," he wired back to the grand jury.[12] "Enough material has been printed in Texas newspapers to give you ample leads to start on." The battle of telegrams continued with the grand jury replying: "We do not want to base indictments on newspaper articles as you suggest." Both sides released copies of their messages to the press, with Shepperd including additional comments. In an obvious remark aimed at Parr's departed father, he said, "we need more people down there before the courthouse burns down."[13]

Events in Duval were being played out daily in newspapers as reporters from around the country descended on Alice and San Diego. Newsmen stayed at the Hotel Alice, where, as Don Politico put it, "the desk clerk is harried by barrages of incoming and outgoing long-distance telephone calls." Western Union was hard-pressed by the wire traffic volume as reporters fought to meet deadlines. Caro Brown, writing for the *Alice Daily Echo*, acted as unofficial host to fellow reporters. Gladwin Hill, Los Angeles bureau representative for the *New York Times*, was already writing a series on Duval. "The office phoned me back that they liked the stuff fine," he told Brown. "But it's really hard to capsule this business down here in short enough form for a small series of articles."[14] Reporters wanted the inside story on Duval politics, interviewing anyone for local color.

Most reporters gathered at the Windmill Café to swap stories over a cup of coffee. A nondescript, commonplace diner, the Windmill had four tables with four chairs each and a counter with six stools. Beer ads with cowboy themes decorated the walls.[15] The place took on the aura of Rick's Café Americana in *Casablanca*, including a cast of characters seemingly out of place in the small dusty town of San Diego. But the man everyone wanted to see was Parr, who sat at a table at the Windmill Cafe every day talking to associates or listening to constituents who needed financial help. Getting a seat in the Windmill was easy; interviewing "Boss Parr" was not.

"Our bosses don't understand the situation down here," a newsman said, "and they think nothing of telling us to get Parr's reaction to certain things that are going on. I've phoned and tried to make appointments, I've sent telegrams, and I've sat around coffee shops hoping he'd drop in—but no luck yet." In 1951 Parr told *Collier's* magazine writer Gordon Schendel, "I don't care what you write about me. My people don't read Collier's." The magazine sent another writer to Laredo to interview political boss Manuel J. Raymond. The writer was given VIP treatment during his stay, including a complimentary Mexican vacation. Upon returning, the writer told *Collier's* there was "no story" in Laredo, but Schendel's article on Parr in the June 9, 1951, issue was titled, "Something Is Rotten in the State of Texas."[16]

In contrast, a *Saturday Evening Post* writer met Parr at the Windmill and had no difficulty getting an interview. "The big conservative newspapers are the ones who are after my hide," he told the writer. "They know I've always been a liberal, looking out for the interests of the little man."[17] The *New York Times* may have been one of those "conservative newspapers" because when a *Times* reporter asked for an interview, he was told to send his request in the form of a telegram, which received no reply. Even away from his office and the Windmill, Parr was elusive. Elvira Alaniz, a neighbor, recalled how Parr wore old clothes while mowing his lawn, and anyone asking to see Mr. Parr would get a reply in Spanish from the poorly dressed George, saying that Mr. Parr wasn't home.[18]

Corpus Christi Caller reporter James Rowe covered Duval politics for years and was on somewhat friendly terms with Parr. That was before Texas state officials, U.S. federal officers, and the IRS began homing in, making Parr edgy. In early 1954, W. W. "Bill" Johnson, Texas bureau chief for *Life* and *Time* magazines, asked Rowe to introduce him. The two newsmen entered the Windmill and saw Parr sitting at his usual spot talking to a white-haired old woman.

"I guess you want to see these men," the lady said to Parr when she saw Rowe and Johnson approach the table.

"That's all right," Parr told her. "I don't have anything to do with them." Apprehensive on overstaying her welcome, the woman rose and slowly walked away. Rowe stepped closer.

"How do you do, Mr. Parr?" Rowe asked.

"Move on," Parr replied in a gruff tone, giving both newsmen a cold, glaring stare from his blue eyes behind gold-rimmed spectacles.

"I'm Bill Johnson of *Life* and *Time* . . . ," the newsman said before being cut off.

"Move on," Parr repeated in a raised and more demonstrative tone. "Move on, get away."

"Johnson wants to talk to you to get your side of the story," Rowe added. A reporter who persists may get a story, but with armed men on guard, Rowe knew he was taking a chance.

"Get away from here," Parr snarled. "Move on." Parr placed his hands on the table as if he were about to stand up. Knowing he was confronting a man capable of sudden violence, Rowe backed off and walked away.

"There is a scared and angry man," Johnson told Rowe after they left.[19]

Uncovering Parr's hidden empire had begun in 1952, when Mrs. R. H. Wilkins at the Texas Education Agency in Austin discovered in the state school payroll records that large amounts from the Benavides school district were being paid to individuals she didn't recognize.[20] A separate investigation was undertaken by Freedom Party member James L. McDonald, who visited Austin to search records that all banks handling school funds were required to report. He met Wilkins, who disclosed her discovery of suspicious payments.

McDonald became a bitter foe of Parr when Judge Reams appointed McDonald to the commission assigned to pick a grand jury. Parr visited McDonald at his Benavides home on April 28, 1952, with an offer: "Mac, I'm going to put you on my payroll for $500." When asked why, McDonald was handed a piece of paper with three lists of names Parr wanted to be named to the grand jury and two petit juries.

"I understand you have an interest in the ———— lease on my property on which there is an R.F.C. [Reconstruction Finance Corporation] loan," Parr said. "If you will take care of this for me, I will see that you get that lease. I'll send you in to Lyndon Johnson in Washington and have him clear it through R.F.C."

Parr left without giving McDonald a chance to accept or turn down the offer. While he was on the jury commission, not one name on Parr's list was placed on the grand or petit juries. McDonald then received a phone call one night from a stranger.

"McDonald," the caller said, "you have double-crossed Mr. Parr. No one in Duval County ever double-crossed Mr. Parr and lived. This is your first and last warning, McDonald. You leave Duval County. If you don't you will be killed."

Similar threats followed and in July 1952, McDonald was stopped by four Parr deputies with a warrant to search his car for weapons. When they didn't find any, one deputy said, "We are taking you to San Diego to see George."

After sitting in the sheriff's office for a long time, McDonald got up to leave when Parr walked in. Parr was irate, accusing McDonald of double-crossing him. When McDonald said he never agreed to anything, an argument broke out. He recalled Parr said "he would run me out of the county, and that he had had better men than me killed."[21] McDonald wasn't easily scared and, after meeting with Mrs. Wilkins, gladly joined the investigation.

Tall, rugged, and a veteran of both U.S. and Canadian Armies, McDonald searched through agency records finding fictitious payments—a possible postal law violation because they had been transmitted by mail. Enlisting the aid of Diego Heras, who agreed to help locate canceled checks and records, McDonald showed the evidence to Governor Shivers. Using Heras's affidavit, McDonald convinced the IRS to send agents to Austin. Two agents arrived, but they reported back asking for more agents to complete a thorough inquiry. Their request was denied. When U.S. attorney general Herbert Brownell attended the Tarlton Law Library dedication ceremony at the University of Texas on December 5, 1953, he stayed the night at the governor's mansion. Shivers mentioned the stalled investigation, and the following week four more IRS agents were assigned to the inquiry.[22]

Texas attorney general John Ben Shepperd also continued investigating Duval affairs. He added pressure by inviting the U.S. Post Office to search for potential criminal mail fraud activity. He also instructed state auditor C. H. Cavness to investigate Duval County funds and those of the local independent schools.

Standing in the doorway of his San Diego office facing reporters, Parr first declined to comment but then broke his silence. On the Judge Laughlin ouster attempt, he said: "If they're wanting to throw him out for dismissing a grand jury in Jim Wells county, why are they asking him to dismiss the grand jury in this county [Duval]?" On state officials: "Just like a hockey game, Shepperd and Shivers passing the buck back and forth."[23] He accused them of "trying to try the case in the newspapers." Reporters pressed for his views on the IRS investigating his tax returns, and "that is an annual procedure," he said. "They do it all the time. The investigators began work on my income tax in May, 1953. They worked until December and found everything in order." He knew Shivers asked U.S. attorney general Brownell for a thorough inquiry. "They are on a fishing trip. They are looking for anything that can be used against me politically."[24]

Parr's empire received another blow; this time from a visiting judge. While Laughlin was in Austin fighting charges levied against him, Judge Arthur A. Klein of Brownsville was brought in to fill the empty bench. Klein had no sooner convened court when he was presented with a motion to tie up the Benavides school district records. IRS investigator William H. Ninedorf testified that since the probe had begun "about 800 canceled checks" had suddenly disappeared from the Duval county auditor's office. Klein immediately issued a temporary restraining order to county and school board officials not to destroy any records.[25]

Klein then issued a court order to impound all records of the Benavides and San Diego school districts, Duval County's road and bridge accounts, and various other county records. He granted immunity from criminal prosecution to three key state witnesses, including Diego Heras. Parr began to take it personal. "These boys seem to want to play for keeps," he said, referring to Shepperd and his cadre of attorneys. "We will play for keeps if they want to."[26]

While the state auditor C. H. Cavness was in San Diego preparing to go through the three-foot-high stack of impounded records, Judge Laughlin hurried back from his ouster hearing. "As I understand the law," he said, "if I'm in the district, I'm the judge." He was prepared to take back his court and preside over the hearing set by Klein to determine if the order to impound county records would be made permanent. Laughlin also informed Attorney General Shepperd that he would hear oral arguments on the motion to dismiss the Duval grand jury.[27]

Parr had his handpicked judge to control court battles, but he was losing his grip on the Benavides school district. Constituting a majority, four new board members were appointed, and they vowed they were independent of both Parr and the Freedom Party. Two members—Joe D. Vaello and his uncle Frank Vaello Jr.—were prominent members of a family respected in the area since 1876, while the other new members were local businessmen with no ties to Parr or anti-Parr forces. "Mr. Parr gave us all kinds of assurances," the new members said, "that no one would try to tell us what to do as far as he is concerned." When asked if Parr would be signing any more checks, Frank Vaello said, "I don't think he'll ask, but if he does, I'll resign just like that," snapping his fingers.[28]

Parr then tried using a characteristic ploy to mollify his foes—that is, bribery. Remarkably, he chose the one man who previously had denied him. James McDonald was approached by an intermediary—Dr. J. C. Gonzales, a Benavides surgeon and Parr supporter—and offered Archer Parr's job of Duval County sheriff. When word of the offer leaked, George claimed he had been approached by McDonald for the position, adding that Shepperd had agreed to "soft-pedal" his investigation if McDonald received the posting.[29]

"I'm not making any deals," George vehemently asserted when rumors of the offer spread. "I know nothing about this." Shepperd acknowledged that McDonald had told him about the offer, adding that he too had been approached by a Parr man. He denied sanctioning the deal. "It looks to me like an attempt to break up the Freedom Party," Shepperd told reporters. "That is an obvious tactic of George Parr for many years." In truth, McDonald had been selected as a candidate for sheriff by the Freedom Party, but he declared that it was up to the voters to decide if he was fit for the job, not Parr. "George Parr has his back to the wall," McDonald said. "He is fighting with his last weapon—a propaganda of lies, a whispering campaign."[30]

Shepperd vowed to "end boss rule" in Duval, calling upon citizens to actively participate in local government by supporting independent parties.[31] Heading into showdown week, Parr began counterattacking by going public in a tape-recorded radio broadcast on KTRH in Houston. In a plea to the community concerning the charges (mixed with rumors spread about him), he tried countering with an apology: "I am very sorry my friends of Duval County, where I was born and grew up, are being subjected to the unfavorable publicity because of the inordinate truth-sacrificing ambition of John Ben Shepperd to be Governor of Texas."[32] There was some truth to the claim that the attorney general was wanting to seek higher office, but Parr's accusation wouldn't provide reprieve from the multiple probes that were aimed at him.

Shepperd, a self-proclaimed "do gooder," had brought a strict work ethic to the Texas attorney general's office. Shepperd did have political ambition, and he hoped the Parr inquiry would generate enough publicity for him to seek higher office—that of governor or maybe even Lyndon Johnson's Senate seat, which would be up in 1954. In a letter to Johnson, Everett L. Looney warned that the investigation "could very well affect you quite adversely. This Parr business has been resurrected to the point where it is now the hottest it has ever been," George Reedy, another Texas friend, wrote Johnson. "Your name has certainly been used in a bad way as regards the present investigation."[33] Johnson denied ever helping Parr "except once Parr asked him for some Kentucky Derby tickets."[34]

The news coming out of Duval prompted *Time* magazine to run an article titled "The Land of Parr." In a summary recalling the birth of the Duval duchy under Archie and the rise of George, leading to his "arrogant zenith" in the 1948 senatorial election, the article chronicled Parr's "Coming of Trouble." Mentioning the Bill Mason and Buddy Floyd murders, and the "openly declared war" Governor Shivers was waging, the article said that under pressure, "Parr's affability has turned to moroseness" and may be crumbling. "Don't bet on it though," one observer noted. "This is mesquite country. You know how hard it is to kill a mesquite tree; you can chop it, you can burn it, but the roots go way down deep and it'll keep coming up again."[35]

On February 17, 1954, State Auditor Cavness submitted his report on Duval County public funds. The ten-page summary made no mention of Parr, but Shepperd was positive he had a hand in improprieties alleged by Cavness on how money had vanished. Shepperd boasted, "I think I'm the first state official to oppose George Parr openly." The Republican administration was only too glad to join in the effort to dethrone Parr. U.S. attorney general Herbert Brownell was quoted as saying that the investigation initiated by the Justice Department "would bear fruit."[36]

Cavness examined records between 1946 and 1953 and found disturbing discrepancies and practices. Several Duval County checks and invoices were missing for the Road and Bridge Special Fund—a favorite coffer for Parr. Cavness uncovered a practice of paying "one individual" for services that in turn were supposedly used to pay for services of others. The major payee was the Parr-owned Duval Construction Company, which received over one hundred thousand dollars between 1951 and 1952 for "Partial estimate" and "Rentals on machinery." Advances on county employee salaries (an illegal practice) showed "some deductions" made, but no record of employees ever paying any money back. In the Jury Fund checkbook he found eighty blank checks pre-signed by the county treasurer, and in the county auditor's canceled checks he discovered ninety-six checks that had not been endorsed but that had been paid by the Parr-owned depository bank. When Cavness questioned the county auditor, he received an "I don't know" answer.[37]

Independent of the Cavness audit, Texas state banking examiners appeared at the Texas State Bank at Alice on February 18 to inspect their records. The bank's vice president—George's brother Givens Parr— agreed to give them access to the records, but George, who was the bank president, arrived to say he wouldn't allow them in without a court order. Two days earlier, IRS examiners had appeared at Parr's other bank, the San Diego State Bank, to examine microfilmed checks paid through the bank. "All the recorded films are missing," bank vice president C. G. Palacios told them. The same response was received when agents asked to see records at the Texas State Bank. The Texas banking commission recommended records be kept "not less than 10 years," but state law had no specified time period requirement.[38]

Parr knew that to raid school and county funds, the best place to start was at the bank. The Texas State Bank opened for business in 1941 at a newly constructed building in downtown Alice, with Atlee Parr as president, and Givens Parr and Lillian Parr (George's sister) as vice presidents.[39] For several years, the bank was the sole depository for city and school funds, while the Alice Bank & Trust (not controlled by Parr) held county funds. Both banks submitted bids for accounts they held until 1949, when George, president of the Texas State Bank, decided to go after the county account.

Parr offered to pay the county 1.5 percent on all funds the county had on deposit for more than six months. Previously, the Alice Bank & Trust had not paid interest. A spirited bidding war ensued as each bank offered slightly higher interest rates than the other until Parr's bank sent in a bid to pay one-tenth of 1 percent more interest than "any offer submitted by the Alice Bank & Trust Company." Jake Floyd, representing the Alice Bank & Trust, immediately filed suit in Judge Laughlin's court. Instead of ruling in favor of Parr, Laughlin decided to avoid legal squabbles by throwing the controversial matter before the county commissioners, who in turn chose to reopen the bidding. After receiving new bids, the commissioners voted to accept the Texas State Bank as the new county depository.[40] With his two banks holding county and school deposits, Parr had been sitting in the catbird's seat until IRS probers began sniffing around.

CHAPTER 12

COURT TIME

Having been stonewalled in examining records at the two banks, the IRS petitioned federal courts to prevent the banks from "destroying, hiding or secreting" county and school district banking records. On February 19, 1954, federal judge Ben Clarkson Connally of Houston issued a temporary restraining order against both banks. Although it was a federal order, Texas Rangers were immediately assigned to guard both banks until U.S. marshals arrived with the court order. After a night-long vigil, rangers turned over guard duties the following morning.[1]

The next day, Judge Laughlin heard arguments on the motion to dismiss the Duval County grand jury. Parr sat quietly in the courtroom as Manuel Raymond and District Attorney Raeburn Norris argued that Texas attorney general Shepperd had no legal right to ask for the dismissal. Both argued the only time a grand jury may be challenged is before impaneling. "The attorney general is too late," Raymond said. Shepperd said the grand jury was "stacked with Parr henchmen and not qualified to perform its duty." After listening to both sides, Laughlin made his ruling—the present grand jury would remain in place. He added: "The grand jury should study the report of the state auditor on his findings in an examination of the records of Duval County and its school districts." When announced, "a trace of a smile crossed the sphinx-like features" of George Parr.[2]

The score was even in the courts—Parr won the grand jury ouster case but lost the restraining order against the rangers. The next round would take place in the federal court at Corpus Christi before Judge James Burr V. Allred, who would hear arguments on the temporary restraining order issued to Parr's two banks to preserve records. George didn't attend the hearing, which lasted only five minutes. Allred ruled the restraining order kept and set a May court date for another hearing to decide if the order should be permanent.[3]

While Norris continued leading the grand jury, supposedly investigating finances in the county and school district, Judge Laughlin, still having the ouster case hanging over his head, called for the opening of a new court term on March 6, 1954. The first order of business was hearing a motion to dismiss the assault-to-murder indictment against two Texas Rangers involved in the courtroom scuffle with Parr. The defense contended three commissioners who appointed the grand jury should have been disqualified because one hadn't resided in the county the required six months and two were already serving on a grand jury when appointed. After hearing witnesses in a three-hour hearing, Laughlin denied the motion. The rangers would have to stand trial, although the venue was moved to Brownsville.[4] While interested observers awaited the showdown between Parr and the rangers, another event took place in Duval County that overshadowed everything else.

On March 17, 1954, Judge Laughlin was scheduled to preside over a regular court session at 10 A.M. He failed to show because news had been received that the Texas Supreme Court had rendered its decision in his ouster case. Basing their finding on only one of the eight charges, the court ordered Laughlin off the bench effective noon that day. The unanimous ruling was based on the charge that Laughlin dismissed the Jim Wells grand jury immediately upon assuming office while the grand jury had already returned two indictments against Laughlin and was investigating charges against his brother. Laughlin was also ordered to pay $3,079 in court costs. Although the court declared "that no motion for rehearing will be entertained," Laughlin could file an appeal with the U.S. Supreme Court. For the first time, a Texas district judge was removed from the bench based on a civil suit brought by attorneys practicing in his court.[5]

With an empty bench in his district, state senator Abraham Kazen Jr. said he would meet with Governor Shivers to discuss appointing a successor. Kazen added he would not recommend any of the eleven lawyers who filed the civil suit and his selection would be someone "who has not been connected with the Duval County political feud."[6] Kazen was speaking from a position of power. Texas Senate tradition held that if the legislature was still in session no appointee made by the governor would be confirmed unless approved by the senator from that judicial district, which effectively gave Kazen veto power.

If matters weren't complicated enough, in their eleven-page decision, the Texas Supreme Court said that there was no "statute making removal of a district judge a ground for disqualification for the remainder of the current term of office or otherwise." In effect, Laughlin could run again for the bench. Although not speaking to the press, Laughlin let his presence be known. As one of his last official acts before the noon deadline, he appointed a new Duval County auditor, W. M. Benson, who was also Parr's tax consultant and bookkeeper.[7]

Whomever Shivers picked for the vacant bench seat, the appointee would only be serving the remainder of Laughlin's term. In eight months the voters would select their choice, and in January, if the interim judge wasn't the anointed one, his term would expire. But that was in the future; what mattered to Shivers was selecting a replacement judge who satisfied all factions—a seemingly impossible task. Surprisingly, Attorney General Shepperd stayed out of the fray, concerned only that when a new judge was seated a new jury commission would be appointed. Only when an "impartial and honest grand jury" was selected would Shepperd proceed to act against corrupt officials in the two counties.[8]

Complicating matters, the replacement judge Shivers picked had to be at least a one-year resident of the Seventy-Ninth Judicial District. Advisors to the governor sought a way to solve the dilemma and one possibility arose. Under the Texas Judicial Retirement Act, the chief justice of the Texas Supreme Court could call a judge out of retirement to fill the vacant post. It was a viable option, although never used in the case of an ousted judge, but it would get Shivers off the hook. An added feature was the appointment did not require senate approval, thereby nullifying Kazen's veto power.[9]

Chief Justice John Edward Hickman, without consulting Shivers, took matters into his own hands by appointing retired judge Albert Sidney Broadfoot of Bonham to sit ad interim in Laughlin's vacant seat. "Judge Broadfoot is from the other side of the state and is not involved in the situation in any way," Hickman said. "He has no axes to grind and I think he will make those people a fine judge." Calling him a "judges' judge," the *Dallas Morning News* applauded the move, noting Shivers had been saved from "embarrassment" by not having to battle Kazen.[10]

Broadfoot was from the old school, having served twelve years as district judge before retiring to his farm. A country-style judge, he often listened to testimony while whittling away on a wooden kitchen match after lighting his curved-stem pipe. During twelve years on the bench, he had only five criminal cases reversed by higher courts and was known to go to great lengths to reach out-of-court settlements in civil cases. Reserved and soft-spoken, normally wearing modest clothes and high-top shoes in court, he "was happy at home [on his farm], not looking for a job," but would carry out his duties and "try not to disappoint Justice Hickman."[11]

On his first day on the bench, Broadfoot encountered an experience he had never before faced in a courtroom. Jim Wells County petit jury panel members were being questioned by attorneys when a court interpreter was called to assist Spanish-speaking members. "This is something in all my experience as a judge I have never ran up against," he remarked, "a court interpreter."[12] As he soon discovered, a language barrier would be the least of his problems.

Broadfoot wasted no time delving into lawsuits left over from Laughlin. The first was a motion to prevent the Texas State Bank of Alice from paying out Duval funds improperly. He listened to four witnesses, including State Auditor Cavness, who testified about checks made out to fictitious persons. Broadfoot issued a temporary injunction preventing the bank from cashing any checks of a dubious nature. Hearings on remaining lawsuits were postponed to the following week. Broadfoot had other matters to attend to first, one of which was to order all ballots impounded in the upcoming Benavides school district election.[13]

Then Broadfoot dropped a bomb. Demonstrating that he was independent and would not have his authority questioned, he dismissed the new Duval County grand jury, the petit jury panels, and the three jury commissioners who had selected them. He said "because of personal and business relationships . . . the grand jury, so selected by the commissioners is not now a fair and impartial grand jury."[14] As for replacing the jury commission, he needed time to ensure an impartial grand jury would be selected.

This left the present Duval grand jury to deal with, and they were scheduled to submit their final report at the end of the week. As expected, the report stated that the grand jury heard no evidence to "support any indictment against any public official of Duval County." However, the report did have something to say about the Texas attorney general.

Misspelling his name, they attacked Shepperd, saying his staff "refused to assist us" and charging them with putting "stumbling blocks" in their way.[15] Shepperd dismissed the accusations, saying he felt sorry for them "because they are so tied in with . . . George Parr they couldn't do anything else." He labeled their report a "whitewash." According to the *Fort Worth Star-Telegram*, he added, "there was enough evidence available to return indictments and institute removal proceedings against at least 75 per cent of the officials in Duval County."[16]

While Broadfoot was establishing control in his court, Parr faced a crucial test of his power at the ballot box with three of his hand-picked candidates running for reelection for the Benavides school board. The other four board seats—previously held by Parr men, all of whom had resigned—had been filled by independent trustees and were not up for reelection. After the four resigned, school district operating costs dropped thirty thousand dollars in the first month, an indication as to how much had previously been siphoned away.[17]

With more than half of Duval County voters living in the Benavides school district, the election turnout was higher than expected, and although all three Parr men won, their winning margins were not as great as in the past. "The only question in my mind had been how much strength my opponents had gained," Parr said. Despite lack of large pluralities, he declared any candidate he backed for office would win "in spite of anything they do." The Old Party had prevailed, but their invincibility was developing a chink in its armor. "We can now vote without gunslingers molesting us," a Freedom Party spokesman said, adding that the number of votes they received was "encouraging."[18]

With the elections over, attention turned again to Broadfoot's courtroom. There were still several lawsuits pending, but this was "Parr Country" where the unexpected was expected. In a surprise move, W. M. Benson, appointed Duval County auditor by Laughlin in his last official act as judge, resigned because of pressing "private business." The county commissioners acted quickly and abolished the position, turning duties over to the county clerk. Ignoring the order Broadfoot appointed John Arthur Thomason of Brownwood, secretary of the State Public Accountants Association, as the new Duval County auditor.[19]

Appointing a new auditor was one matter, but getting him installed was another. Broadfoot swore in the new auditor, but Thomason had to post a required five-thousand-dollar bond before the commissioners' court. When he went looking for the commissioners they were nowhere to be found. Under state law Broadfoot had authority to appoint an auditor and the commissioners were required to accept the appointment and pay his salary. Word came from the commissioners, wherever they were, that "technical difficulties," including Thomason's salary, had to be worked out. One meeting after another was scheduled by the commissioners, but each meeting failed to materialize. The excuse was that two of the commissioners lived out of the city and neither had a telephone. When they finally met, three of the four commissioners voted to ask the district and county attorneys for their opinion, further delaying the appointment.[20]

After waiting a week, Thomason asked Broadfoot to withdraw his application for the auditor's position. Two weeks later, Broadfoot named another candidate. In a move calculated to demonstrate a new order of law was being established in Duval, he appointed Donato Serna, founding member and leader of the Freedom Party. Broadfoot also wrote a letter to each member of the commissioners' court asking them to hold a special session to approve Serna's bond. Signing a temporary restraining order, he declared county officials could not issue any vouchers, and the Texas State Bank of Alice could not accept any for payment, unless signed by the new county auditor.[21]

Meanwhile, Serna appeared before the county clerk to post the required bond. The commissioners held a special session prior to the regular one but only "to approve bills," saying they didn't have time to consider the auditor question.[22] Two months after being appointed, Serna was informed by the commissioners that they could not approve his bond. The reason given was that, since Broadfoot had vacated the office of auditor, the post no longer existed. "If there is no office," one commissioner said, "we can't pass on the bond." Walter W. Meek, a friend of Parr since childhood, had been appointed to the commissioners' court a few days before Broadfoot named Thomason as auditor. Speaking for the commissioners, Meek revealed their true feelings. They objected to being "bullied" by the visiting judge. "It is a slap in our face when the leader of the Freedom Party is appointed," he said.[23]

Undaunted, Serna filed for a mandamus suit to force the commissioners to accept his bond. He got his day in court, but in front of Judge Maxwell Welch of New Boston, Texas, who was called in to help the crowded court calendar. After Serna testified that he had tried repeatedly to have the commissioners approve his bond, Duval county clerk Alberto Garcia Jr. was called to the stand. When Welch asked Garcia why he never gave Serna's bond to the commissioners, he said he "just forgot," adding he knew the commissioners wouldn't consider it anyway. Welch had heard enough; citing statutes providing for an auditor for counties in the fifteen-million-dollar bracket, as Duval was, he issued an injunction against the commissioners, restraining them from interfering with Serna assuming the post.[24]

At the same time that Serna was trying to get his posting made official, Ranger Captain Alfred Allee and Ranger Joe Bridge were filing motions to have their assault with intent to murder George Parr indictments quashed. With Judge Laughlin no longer hearing motions on the case, the charges against Bridge were dropped at the request of the state. District court judge Arthur A. Klein granted the motion but set the trial of Allee for April 19, 1954. In a surprise move, Allee requested all efforts to quash his indictment be dropped; he was ready to face trial.[25]

Attention now turned to the Brownsville courtroom where spectators crowded together to hear the trial. While Allee sat with five fellow rangers, Parr sat with his nephew, Sheriff Archer Parr, as questioning of the thirty-two-member jury panel began. Cameron County district attorney F. T. Graham frequently referred to newspaper accounts of events in Duval during his examination of potential jurors, asking if they had a preconceived idea "George Parr is a scoundrel or had this coming to him." When Allee's attorney, Claude Carter, questioned the panel, he put on a showmanship display of his remarkable memory. Without referring to a list, he addressed each man by name, having memorized each while being questioned by the district attorney.[26]

After the jury was selected and sworn in, Judge Klein called a thirty-minute recess. When the session resumed, Parr asked to make a statement to the court. Catching everyone by surprise, he announced, "The complaining witness [Parr] has no desire to further prosecute the case," adding that he held "no ill will or any resentment or any kind of ill feelings" toward Allee. Disappointed newspaper and radio reporters, expecting a week-long trial, sat in silence as Klein dismissed the case. Parr, standing a few feet from Allee, extended his hand, which the ranger captain briefly accepted before they were separated by newsmen hoping to get statements. Parr's response to reporters was he had "nothing against Alfred," adding, "politically we differ, but there are no personal feelings."[27] The attention of the news media turned back to Judge Broadfoot's courtroom.

Broadfoot was correct in his assessment that he needed help in the troubled Seventy-Ninth Judicial District "to clear up a crowded docket," and although his plea was granted, he faced a morass of lawsuits.[28] In addition to pending lawsuits, Broadfoot had another issue to confront. The grand jury he had dismissed wouldn't go away quietly. Two attorneys hired by the dismissed jurors and jury commissioners presented Broadfoot with a reconsideration motion. Attorney General Shepperd labeled it "a scurrilous petition." He was outraged and knew who was behind the action: "It is inconceivable to me that another hand-picked instrument of George Parr should be crammed down the throats of the people of Texas."[29]

When Broadfoot told them his court had a busy schedule and would get to their motion in time, the attorneys decided not to wait. They filed suit in the Texas court of criminal appeals asking Broadfoot's order to dissolve the grand jury be set aside. They charged that Broadfoot heard only seven witnesses, not one of them from the grand jury, before issuing his dismissal order. They also charged that Broadfoot "appropriated" records from the district clerk's office and refused to allow attorneys to make copies, and the judge barred the court reporter from making available any transcripts of the proceedings.[30]

The appeals court accepted the suit and set a hearing date. Broadfoot was also ordered not to seat a new grand jury until disposition of the suit. Not to be outdone, Broadfoot retained Fort Worth attorney Atwood McDonald to challenge the suit. In his brief, McDonald contended the appeals court had "no jurisdiction to supervise, direct, or control a trial court in the exercise of its discretionary powers," and that the court did not have jurisdiction in a civil case.[31]

In a two-to-one decision, the appeals court dismissed the commissioners' suit on the ground that it was not within their jurisdiction. In his dissenting opinion Judge W. A. Morrison strongly denounced Broadfoot's action. "In my opinion," he wrote, "such an act smacks of the police state and is not in keeping with the policy of the law." Morrison made reference to the fact that Laughlin had been removed from the bench for discharging a grand jury. "I cannot see how we may consistently uphold Judge Broadfoot when he does the same thing."[32] Although Broadfoot had no comment on the favorable decision, Attorney General Shepperd predicted it would "send shudders of fear through the ranks of certain Duval County politicians."[33]

Back in his Alice courtroom, Broadfoot took immediate action by appointing a new Duval County jury commission. He said grand jurors appointed by the new commissioners would be directed to investigate everything from "handling of public money in the county," to school district funds and reports of nepotism in hiring public workers and appointing officials. When asked if he felt the new commissioners would act fairly, Parr said, "It all depends on what they do. I don't recognize any of the names." Acting swiftly, the new jury commission drew up a list of prospective grand jurors.[34]

Attempting to block the impaneling of a hostile grand jury, Parr mustered his Old Party members. A motion was filed on behalf of the dismissed grand jury to delay seating the new grand jury until the dispute was settled in federal court. Although federal judge Thomas Martin Kennerly refused to issue the injunction, he did allow the suit to continue. Always seizing the opportunity to publicly denounce Parr with barbed comments, Shepperd called this latest lawsuit "a desperate attempt by the Parr forces to save their bucket of whitewash." He said he would be making an appearance before the new grand jury to offer his input.[35]

Sitting in the back of the courtroom, Parr silently watched as the new grand jury was impaneled. He had no doubt that this group of Duval citizens he labeled "100 per cent anti-Parr" were going to stir up trouble, and he was right.[36] The next day the new grand jury made its first report to Broadfoot. Stating that they intended to fully investigate handling of county and school funds, and that their inquiry would likely include the offices of District Attorney Raeburn Norris and Duval County attorney Reynaldo F. Luna, they said they "did not desire the services or the presence in the grand jury room of either." If the grand jury members needed assistance "from time to time" on matters of law, Norris and Luna would be called.[37] This was a serious blow to Parr. Not only were his hand-picked officials being investigated, but neither attorney would be present when witnesses testified before the grand jury, making it virtually impossible for Parr to know what to expect.

Dubbed the "Praying Grand Jury" because the jurors opened each session with a prayer, they subpoenaed Freedom Party candidate for sheriff J. L. McDonald. Following his testimony, they called Sheriff Archer Parr. Then Cristobal Ybanez (who had tried unsuccessfully to get previous grand juries to hear his year-old complaint on George Parr hitting him with the barrel of a rifle) was finally asked to tell his story.[38]

"Judge Colt is no longer the law in Duval County," the grand jury wrote in a report to Broadfoot, "and the days of pistol packing are over." Referring to ID cards issued to special and honorary deputies, they recommended abolishing the use of "extra" pistoleros and allowing them to carry weapons. It was only a recommendation, but if carried out, Parr would lose one of his most powerful means of establishing order in his fiefdom—physical fear. Going on the offensive, Parr gave a radio interview and described the new grand jury as "composed entirely of Freedom Party members and appeared to be stacked." Charging opponents of hand-picking grand jurors as he had in the past, he said "it's all a case of the pot calling the kettle black."[39]

Nevertheless, before retiring to a closed-door session, the grand jury ordered fifty blank indictment forms from the district clerk. Courthouse observers anxiously waited to hear how many would be used and whose names would appear on them. Eighteen indictments were returned, but only two names appeared on them. Former Duval County auditor C. T. Stansell Jr., was charged with seventeen counts of forgery, and George Parr was indicted on a charge of assault to murder, stemming from the rifle-beating incident of Cristobal Ybanez.[40]

The identity of those indicted wouldn't be revealed until arrest warrants were served, but Parr knew one was for him. While waiting for the district clerk to prepare the warrants, he relaxed in the sheriff's office, smiling and quipping with friends. "This is a hell of a note," he jested. "Man gets indicted and can't get arrested." Continuing his banter, he added: "Arthur Garfield Hays told me man's greatest right under the Constitution is the right to be arrested. And here I am—waiting and can't get arrested." As reporters gathered, Parr entertained them with bravado humor. "I'm going to hire John VanCronkhite," he said, referring to an Austin public relations man and former political aide to Governor Shivers. "I need influence."[41]

After being arrested, Parr posted a twenty-five-hundred-dollar bond,

signed by Earl Delaney, his oil company partner. Stansell's bond was set at
five hundred dollars for each charge, totaling eighty-five hundred dollars,
which was posted by Parr and Delaney. Retaining Corpus Christi attorney Luther E. Jones to defend him, Parr filed a motion before Broadfoot
to quash the indictment. He claimed double jeopardy, based on the fact
he had pleaded guilty to a charge of aggravated assault on Ybanez for the
rifle-beating and was fined $150 and costs. "It shows they are so anxious
to prosecute someone they failed to check the county records," Jones said.
A second motion charged "prejudice and bad faith" on Broadfoot's part
for dismissing the previous grand jury and approving one hostile to Parr.
While his attorney filed the motions, Parr was in the corridor, buying
soft drinks for county employees, keeping a close eye on any subpoenaed
witness climbing the nearby stairs leading to the grand jury room.[42]

One witness Parr noticed was local schoolteacher Robert Leo. Loaded
with an armful of photostatic copies, Leo spent two hours before the
grand jury, leaving with the records still in his possession. The next day,
V. L. Fewell, tax assessor-collector and secretary of the Benavides school
board, was summoned. Waiting in the hallway was R. W. Milligan,
superintendent of the Benavides school system for the past sixteen years.
Two more witnesses, both employees of the school district, also awaited
their turn before the grand jury.[43]

The Duval County school system was already under attack by a five-
man group filing removal proceedings against Superintendent Reynaldo
L. Adame. The request for removal followed a lawsuit asking for a temporary injunction preventing Adame from signing any more vouchers
drawn against school funds. Pressed to pursue Adame's removal, Duval
County attorney Reynaldo F. Luna at first agreed to take action, but then
he backed away, saying he wanted to await the outcome of the injunction
suit. Broadfoot granted the temporary injunction against Adame, but
Luna failed to follow up on his promise. Taking matters into their own
hands, the Duval grand jury indicted Adame on eight counts of theft of
more than fifty dollars from various school fund accounts. In another
indictment, they charged D.C. Chapa, former Benavides school district
tax assessor-collector, with one count of illegally converting public
money. These were the only indictments returned against school officials,
but the grand jury had more testimony to hear, and it was almost certain
that more charges would follow.[44]

While the Duval grand jury continued probing, Broadfoot faced a serious challenge of his authority. A suit initiated by District Attorney Raeburn Norris, District Clerk Julian Perez, and Duval County attorney Reynaldo F. Luna named Broadfoot, Attorney General Shepperd, and the Duval grand jury as defendants. The plaintiffs sought to prevent Shepperd from working with the Duval grand jury, to prevent Broadfoot from issuing impounding orders and names of Duval County jurors, and to have their rights reinstated to be with the grand jury during its sessions.[45]

Because Broadfoot was a defendant in the case, Governor Shivers named Judge H. D. Barrow of Jourdanton as special judge to hear the motion. After listening to both sides present arguments, Barrow tossed out two of the complaints. He ruled that the grand jury had a right to bar Norris and Luna from hearing testimony and that Broadfoot's actions were perfectly legal. On the matter of Shepperd having the right to help the grand jury, Barrow said he would take the matter "under advisement" and render a decision later that month. Calling the decision a victory for justice, Shepperd warned there would be more Parr tactics on the way, "all of them of the delaying type, attempting to preserve George Parr's bucket of whitewash." The following week, Barrow completed his temporary duty in Duval by dismissing the suit seeking to prevent Shepperd from acting with the grand jury.[46]

CHAPTER 13

FIGHTING TO KEEP CONTROL

Judge Maxwell Welch, presiding over Parr's assault-with-intent-to-murder case, arrived in the San Diego courtroom only to discover the air-conditioning unit was being replaced and there were no fans in the room.[1] The new air-conditioning unit was finally installed, which eased the discomfort resulting from the heat wave sweeping through the area, but a motion presented before Welch by Assistant Attorney General Eugene Brady again heated up the courtroom. Acting as amicus curiae, Brady asked that District Attorney Norris be disqualified as prosecutor in all cases stemming from indictments passed down by the new grand jury because Norris was, according to a report in the *San Antonio Express*, "socially, economically and politically connected with the defendant, George B. Parr."[2]

Jumping out of his chair, Parr's attorney, Luther Jones, vehemently protested. "We all know John Ben Shepperd is trying to take over this court and operate it," he said in a voice loud enough to be heard in the corridor. He added that if anyone felt Norris, a duly elected official, wasn't performing his duties, then the proper recourse would be to initiate a removal action. "Is there some halo that nestles over the heads of the attorney general's men?"

"What difference does it make to you in representing your client who represents the state," Judge Welch asked Jones, "as long as it is fairly and legally done?"

"We are entitled to a fair trial under the law," Jones replied. "Not according to the caprices of your honor or the caprices of this gentleman," he added, pointing to Brady. "If the court is not going to follow the law, I might as well sit down. I say you are bound to follow the law; I say you are violating your oath, if you don't follow the law. That is my answer to you."

Attacking the assistant attorney general was one matter, pointing a finger at the presiding judge was an entirely different and dangerous approach, but Jones was irate. Now that he had elevated his argument to the level of soapbox oratory, Jones continued in the same vein.

"It is high time somebody talked," he added as his voice grew louder. "There is one public official who had the guts to speak out: Judge W. A. Morrison of the court of criminal appeals, who said that this 'smacks of a police state.' The law has not been followed in prior hearings before Judge Broadfoot."

Having patiently listened to the tirade, Judge Welch raised his hand to interrupt Jones, who, he felt, had stepped over the line.

"The court does not appreciate remarks made about a former judge," he said in a stern tone. Welch added that his court would be run according to the law, and if Jones did not feel the judge was being fair, he would have to show proof. Reproved by Welch's remarks, Jones brought the tone of his rhetoric down a notch.

"I think apologies are definitely in order," he offered, "but the rights of my client have been kicked around the last six or seven months."

Welch, sensing order was being restored, offered a way to sort out the issues. The question, he said, was whether the motion should be heard, not whether Norris was disqualified. "Let's get the laws and avoid political speeches." But Jones wouldn't let the matter rest.

"We can prove that Judge A. S. Broadfoot flagrantly disregarded the law in former hearings," he told Welch.

The newly installed air-conditioning unit couldn't cool Welch's temperature. He had heard enough. Struggling to maintain his demeanor and modulating his voice to the sternest tone he had used up to this point, he warned both attorneys: "I say to you, gentlemen, this is not going to degenerate into a rat race." Jones again apologized and Welch set a hearing date the following week to hear arguments on the motion.[3]

During the vocal fireworks, the courtroom was packed with spectators. Every seat was occupied, while some listeners lined the staircase leading to the balcony, which held only one row of seats. Parr sat near the side of the room behind the railing, quietly watching his attorney heat up the room with his words; Attorney General Shepperd sat with spectators in the back, also listening without participating.[4]

Represented by two lawyers, Parr listened as motions were presented to Welch that were designed to limit the scope of the hearing. Manuel Raymond asked the court to consider only if Norris was qualified to prosecute Parr, not to broaden the argument to include everyone indicted by the grand jury. Luther Jones contended that Judge Welch had no jurisdiction to disqualify Norris, asking that he appoint a member of the state bar to settle the matter. Welch overruled both motions, then called for arguments on whether Norris should be disqualified.

Jones and Brady presented their arguments for and against Norris. Announcing his decision with "a sense of regret," Welch barred Norris from prosecuting Parr and others indicted by the current grand jury because Norris had been "adversely interested in the case file in this court, attacking the very proceedings which will be before the court."[5]

The question then was who would replace Norris to prosecute the cases. Welch chose Karnes City lawyer John F. May, and at May's request, Welch allowed San Antonio attorney John Peace to assist.[6] With a temporary prosecutor arriving in Duval to take over, everything was placed on hold. That didn't mean politics came to a standstill, however; Parr loved playing the game and always seemed to have another surprise up his sleeve.

Judge Laughlin was out and Judge Broadfoot filled the vacated bench, but the July 1954 primary would determine who would be the new judge. The first to announce his candidacy was Falfurrias attorney James Breckenridge South, a Spanish American War veteran, who said he would be "a fair and impartial judge." Markel Heath, one of the eleven Laughlin ouster attorneys, announced he was running with the "unanimous endorsement" of the ten other ouster suit lawyers. Two other notable filings for Duval County offices were also made. County attorney Sam Burris announced he was running against District Attorney Raeburn Norris, and decorated World War II veteran Bob Mullen tossed his hat in the ring for state representative. "If elected," Mullen said, "I'll be the first anti-Parr representative in the history of this district."[7]

On the last day for filing an application to run in the July primary, ousted Judge Laughlin announced he was running for his old spot on the bench. "I will be a candidate for MY unexpired term," was the only statement he made.[8] His announcement was anti-climactic, however, because the real story in the turbulent politics of the area had occurred the day before.

Attorney General Shepperd had long complained of Parr's control over the district judge because with that control, "You cannot be arrested, indicted, prosecuted, tried, convicted or sentenced." On May 2, Parr announced his candidacy for Seventy-Ninth Judicial District judge. "My opponents said I control the district judge," he said in a phone interview. "Why not let me be the district judge? Then no one will control the district judge but me." Tongue in cheek, he added he would rule "as honestly, fairly, and impartially," as did the Supreme Court in ousting Laughlin, as Attorney General Shepperd had acted toward Duval County, and as the *Corpus Christi Caller-Times* did in reporting the facts about him.[9]

"George Parr wouldn't get ten votes that cannot be controlled," Jake Floyd commented on Parr's announcement. Floyd called it a "smoke screen" because Parr will eventually choose another candidate to run and then direct voters to switch over at the last minute. "This is the same old Parr political trick."[10]

Eliminating the middle man sounded easy for Parr, but there was a problem. He passed the bar examination in 1926, but the Texas State Constitution required a candidate to be a practicing attorney or a presiding judge for four years preceding the election. Parr was a county judge in 1950, too far back to qualify, and he had never practiced law. "That's a question of interpretation—a matter for the courts," he told a reporter. "You didn't think my opposition would take it lying down, did you?" When told his opponents said he didn't know enough law to qualify being a judge, Parr laughed. "The attorney general came down here with nine assistants," he joked. "Maybe I could hire one or two to tell me the law."[11]

Parr running for district judge wasn't the only surprise. At the last minute Sheriff Archer Parr announced he was running against Bob Mullen for state representative. The current representative, A. J. Vale, wasn't seeking reelection, but Archer would also be up against Bob Grimes, an Alice radio station manager who filed just before the deadline.[12]

The race for the district judgeship in Duval grew tighter when James South withdrew. When Parr failed to file the necessary fee for his candidacy, the primary ended up a two-man race. The Parr experts were correct in their prediction about his tactics. At the last minute he withdrew and announced he was backing Laughlin.[13]

While candidates began seeking votes, politics took a backseat to what was happening with the Duval County grand jury. After hearing testimony on misuse of Benavides school district funds, the grand jury returned nine indictments, bringing the total issued since their being seated to thirty-seven. The newest charges were brought against Parr confederate D.C. Chapa and his sons, Oscar Carrillo Sr. and O. P. Carrillo. Spread over nine indictments, the trio were charged with misappropriation of more than twenty-two thousand dollars of school funds.[14]

There was more bad news for Parr. The Federal Deposit Insurance Corporation (FDIC) gave an ultimatum—either he surrendered his interests in the two banks he owned or they would cancel deposit insurance in both banks. Without FDIC backing, the banks would have to close. Realizing he had no choice, Parr sold his stake in both banks to a group of investors headed by Alice attorney Frank B. Lloyd. Terms of the sale stipulated that neither Parr nor any family member would be associated with the banks. Under a reorganization plan, the Texas State Bank of Alice was renamed the First State Bank of Alice, and the San Diego State Bank became the First State Bank of San Diego. Parr still faced an ongoing IRS investigation of concealing and destroying bank records.[15]

The bad news kept coming. The IRS announced it had referred, "at least one" income tax evasion case against Parr to the Department of Justice. Texas attorney general Shepperd called the IRS action "another link in the chain of justice," predicting that 1954 "will mark the end in Texas of . . . the George Parr reign of terror."[16]

Watching court proceedings became a way of life in Duval. Daily life came to a standstill as each session was packed with citizens who had never before been inside a courtroom. "If these court battles and investigations aren't over pretty soon most of us are going to be broke," admitted one man. Housewives left chores undone to sit and watch lawyers in action; even courthouse employees, accustomed to the legal scene, took breaks by catching a few minutes of court time.[17] The grand jury didn't have time to observe the legal battles; they always had a full day of work.

The "Praying Grand Jury" proved to be a dedicated, close-knit band of citizens who sacrificed their personal time so as to fulfill their duty. Though some members drove forty miles each day, none was ever absent or tardy. Gathering at 9:00 each morning for coffee at the cafe across from the courthouse, they began each session promptly at 9:30. They seldom took any breaks, preferring to send the bailiff for refreshments while they continued working. Carl Hofstetter, the youngest, typified the dedication of each member. Married only two days before receiving notice to serve, Hofstetter didn't shirk the call to duty. After he was sworn in, his brother, who helped him operate a seventy-three-cow dairy farm, was hospitalized for an illness. So Hofstetter was getting up at 3:00 A.M. to milk cows, then driving forty miles to San Diego to attend grand jury sessions, and returning to his farm to work late into the night cutting feed for his herd.[18]

Judging from those subpoenaed, the grand jury seemed to be focusing on school funds and the two banks formerly owned by Parr. Several employees of the Texas State Bank of Alice were brought in for questioning on county and school funds. When one witness refused to testify about a $750 check he received from the Benavides school fund, they asked Judge Welch to persuade the reluctant man, Willus Wright, to reconsider. Welch questioned Wright, but he still refused, so Welch ordered him jailed to think it over. After spending the night in jail, Wright agreed to tell what he knew about the check.[19]

After a week of testimony, the grand jury handed down a fistful of indictments against thirteen persons. R. W. Milligan—superintendent of the Benavides school district for the past sixteen years, whose contract wasn't being renewed—was charged with felony theft, but he was only a small fish. The bigger fish being reined in included Givens Parr, former vice president of the Texas State Bank, B. F. (Tom) Donald, former cashier at the bank, and the biggest fish of all—George Parr, former president of the bank. All three were charged with conspiracy to convert Benavides school funds to their own use.[20]

Unperturbed over the day's courtroom events, Parr spent the evening doing what he did best—courting voters. With primary elections less than two weeks away, he was out in the field gathering votes. While the Freedom Party held their rally, attended by two thousand supporters, all being fed barbecue from two cows and two yearlings, the Old Party held their get-together seven miles away. Almost four thousand attended to hear speakers blast their opponents, with Parr adding jibes in Spanish from the sidelines. He donated ten large steers for the barbecue "and there was not any meat left over." Sheriff Archer Parr provided deputies to watch the crowd, while Texas Rangers offered their protection at the Freedom Party gathering.[21]

Politics aside, Parr focused on the courtroom in San Diego where his freedom was at stake. Judge Welch allowed Parr and five other defendants to have their motion heard to quash the indictments against them on the ground the grand jury was impaneled illegally after Judge Broadfoot had dismissed the previous panel. To argue this, Parr's attorney, Manuel Raymond, made a bold move by calling Broadfoot to testify.

Seemingly unperturbed, the seventy-year-old jurist whittled on wooden kitchen matches while answering questions "slowly and deliberately." Twice during his testimony, Raymond declared him a hostile witness as he pressed for details. Broadfoot revealed that "Texas Rangers and a member of Shepperd's staff helped select the new jury commissioners and jurors." But, he said, he was not influenced by Parr's nemesis, Jake Floyd.[22]

While hearsay testimony is not usually allowed into evidence, to elaborate on what had influenced his decisions, Broadfoot was given the opportunity to discuss rumors he heard upon arriving in Duval. In one incident, he overheard a conversation between two traveling salesmen in the lobby of the Alice Hotel. Both remarked that local merchants were "close mouthed" about local politics and seemingly "intimidated" when discussing county and school affairs. After dismissing the grand jury and before naming a new one, Broadfoot said he overheard two IRS officials say that more than two hundred thousand dollars a year were being misappropriated from Duval County funds. Hearing these two conversations, Broadfoot said, he resolved to appoint jury commissioners who would name a "fair and impartial" grand jury panel not intimidated by powerful men in the community.[23]

After Broadfoot completed his testimony, Judge Welch postponed the hearing until July 27. He explained the delay was necessary because the court of civil appeals was scheduled to review Assistant District Attorney Gonzalez's claim that Gonzalez should prosecute the cases under discussion.[24] The recess didn't mean political activity would take a vacation. The primary would be held on July 24, and both sides intended to use the time to prepare.

According to Caro Brown in the *Alice Daily Echo*, at a Freedom Party rally held within a stone's throw of the Windmill Café where Parr sat with his friends, former Benavides school district trustee Richard Barton rose to speak. "I was with Parr in stealing money from the school kids," he told the two thousand people gathered. "I am ashamed to be here before this crowd because I am trash, a killer and a rat, as George Parr called me last night." His remarks stunned and quieted the crowd. "My sisters got together tonight and begged me not to come to this rally because they were afraid Parr would kill me," he said. "But I am here, George. If you want to kill me, do it yourself," he challenged, pointing a finger toward the Windmill. "But don't hire somebody else to do it for you."

Elaborating on his confession, he referred to the murder of Luis Reyna seventeen years before. Barton said when he and his brother were tried for the murder, Parr said he would take care of everything. "The trial went just as George had ordered it," he said. When Barton's brother, Jimmie, balked at going to prison as part of the agreement, another deal was struck. "To get out of trouble and go free, my brother Jimmie had to promise George Parr to resign as constable and get out of the county," Barton confessed. "George made him resign in front of me and then he made him promise to leave before he would let him go free. Jimmie left the county and has been gone 16 years."[25] Parr never denied these charges nor offered any comment.

On primary day, Old Party faithful sat under a large shed erected earlier in the week across from the San Diego polling place. Cold drinks and a huge fan greeted visitors seeking comfort in the blistering one-hundred-degree heat. Dressed in a white sport shirt and brown slacks, Parr dropped by throughout the day to check with poll observers. "*Ya no tienen animo*," he said, referring to the Freedom Party—"They don't have any life." Just before polls closed at 7:00 P.M., he strolled across the street to vote. Nine minutes later he walked out. "George must have had a hard time making up his mind," a Freedom Party member joked. "It took him longer than it did some who have a hard time reading the names."[26] Parr hoped others would vote the straight Old Party line because his candidates faced stiff opposition.

Even Governor Shivers, seeking an unprecedented third term, faced difficulties when his closest opponent, Ralph Yarborough, garnered enough votes to force a runoff. In Parr country, when the final results were tabulated they showed that voters had split their choices. Archer Parr lost by a handful of votes to Robert Mullen for the Texas house seat. More ominous for George, incumbent district attorney Raeburn Norris lost to Burris. The only saving grace was that Laughlin won back the judgeship he had been ousted from earlier that year. Parr now had a friendly judge again but an anti-Parr prosecutor who would try indictments handed down by the grand jury.[27] All primary winners were certain of being elected in November, but Laughlin wouldn't be taking office until January. This left several months for the present grand jury to continue working and to hand down more indictments against the Parr machine.

Handing down more indictments was exactly what the grand jury did. After the primary, they announced more defendants would be standing trial, and some previously indicted officials faced even more charges. Former sheriff Jesus Oliveira, who won the Duval County tax assessor-collector post, was indicted on four counts of theft and conspiracy related to his former job. County school superintendent R. L. Adame had seven more counts of theft tacked on, and D.C. Chapa, former tax assessor-collector of the Benavides school district, had one more count for conversion of public money added to his previous charges.[28]

Having postponed hearings until after the primary, Judge Welch reopened court and the battle continued. Back on the stand, Judge Broadfoot was grilled on how much influence the attorney general had on the decision to discharge the grand jury. "It did have weight," he said, but he denied Shepperd had guided his decision. Attempting to prove a conspiracy against Parr, the defense called Shepperd. Under heavy attack, Shepperd made no revelations bolstering the charge, and after thorough questioning by both sides he was dismissed.[29] After several more witnesses testified, Welch turned to Parr's motion to quash his indictment.

Luther Jones, one of Parr's attorneys, argued that when Parr pleaded guilty to aggravated assault and paid the fine, the case had ended. Any further charges stemming from the incident would constitute double jeopardy. Parr's conviction was "a mere puppet show," attorney for the state John Peace said, "with every string pulled by George Parr." County attorney R. F. Luna was asked why six months had passed after the alleged attack and before the hearing was held, and why the victim, Ybanez, hadn't been notified of the hearing. Luna said he had been "unable to get witnesses together," and when notified that Parr would plead guilty, he "didn't want to let the opportunity go by." Everyone, including Welch, knew they were listening to a "whitewash," but no one painted themselves into a corner. With all testimony heard, Welch rendered his decision. The assault-to-murder-charge against Parr was dismissed, but Welch delayed ruling on the other thirty-nine indictments against Parr and four others until he had time to review the cases.[30]

The following day Welch denied motions to quash the remaining indictments and ordered change of venues on the cases. So Parr had dodged one bullet but still faced two charges for conspiracy to convert school funds for private use. Former county auditor C. T. Stansell Jr., with twenty-two counts pending, had his trial transferred to Fort Worth; county school superintendent R. L. Adame, with eight felony theft charges, had his case transferred to Bryan in Brazos County; and D.C. Chapa and Oscar Carrillo Sr. with six and three counts respectively, would both be tried in Tyler in Smith County.[31] Parr's case remained in Duval County for the time being because he had filed an appeal on his motion to quash the remaining two indictments.

A lull seemed to settle over Duval as the summer months dragged on under sweltering heat. Two items of interest made otherwise lackluster news in the area. The first was the resignation of Sheriff Archer Parr. Having lost his bid to become state representative, he said he was entering law school at the University of Texas. He also married Ann Blair Furman of Corpus Christi. Debutante of the 1952 Christmas season, Ann was a Texas University graduate and a Girl's Cotillion Club member. After Archer resigned, the county commissioners court immediately appointed Julian P. Stockwell, who had won the primary, as the new sheriff. The second news item was a U.S. Department of Justice announcement that Parr's income tax case was being forwarded to U.S. Attorney Malcolm R. Wilkey in Houston to be placed before a federal grand jury.[32]

Near the end of August Judge Broadfoot resigned his post due to illness. Two weeks later, Judge Welch announced he was leaving Duval because of a loaded docket in his own district. With the Duval court calendar packed with scheduled hearings and no judge to hear them, criminal district judge A. C. Winborn of Houston was shifted to the strife-torn judicial district to handle the workload. While judges were being shuffled around, the Duval grand jury kept busy. Duval County tax collector E. B. Garcia was indicted for "misapplication" of county funds. Duval County attorney R. F. Luna found himself on the other side of the law when indicted on the same charge. In early October, the grand jury added another Parr crony to the list. This time it was county judge Daniel Tobin Jr., who was charged with five counts of theft.[33]

When Judge Winborn took over the Duval County bench, he wasted no time in clearing the overloaded docket. After a forty-five-minute hearing of oral arguments on motions to quash numerous indictments, he denied every one and transferred fifty-one of them, covering twenty-eight defendants, to six courts in other parts of the state. Among defendants in the courtroom, Parr listened as his case of conspiracy to convert school funds was assigned to the court in La Grange.[34] But Parr had more important matters on his mind. Having engineered a primary victory for ousted Judge Laughlin, who would certainly defeat his Republican opponent in November, there was still another obstacle to overcome.

On September 22 the Texas State Bar Association had filed suit to have Laughlin disbarred. In the seventeen-page petition, ten out of eleven charges were repeats of those originally in his ouster case. The newest charge claimed that Laughlin held an informal hearing for Nago Alaniz so his attorney, Percy Foreman, could file for a habeas corpus motion. Neither the state's special prosecutor assigned to the case nor the county attorney had been notified of the hearing for Alaniz, scheduled to be tried for conspiracy in the Buddy Floyd "mistake murder." Under the Texas State Constitution, if Laughlin was disbarred he could not serve as judge because only a practicing attorney could be seated on the bench. Even if elected, he could not be sworn in until disbarment proceedings were settled.[35]

Once again Laughlin had a target pinned to his chest, but Parr couldn't deal with that either just now. His hand-picked candidate for district attorney, Raeburn Norris, lost the primary to Burris, an avowed anti-Parr nominee, and Parr didn't want a foe prosecuting cases in his district. To combat Burris, who would assuredly win the general election, Parr began gathering the required five hundred signatures to have another friend, Gerald Weatherly of Rio Grande City, placed on the ballot as an independent candidate.

Being backed by Parr had its drawbacks, one of which was to be thoroughly scrutinized. Weatherly was challenged by Texas secretary of state Cecil Everett Fulgham, who rejected the application after discovering that more than one hundred names on the petition were forgeries. "To accept this petition would make a farce out of the purity of our Texas ballot," he asserted. Weatherly protested, and Burris was even harsher in condemning his potential rival. Weatherly's outrage, Burris said, was "a typical George Parr cry of anguish"; when they are caught "they hol-ler like little kids." Burris also maintained: "If Weatherly would like to investigate how he got his signatures from Duval county, I could give him some leads to follow, such as the deputy sheriff of Duval going to see old people, with their guns on their hips, and telling them they had to sign."[36]

With the general election less than a month away, Weatherly filed suit in the Texas Supreme Court asking that his name be placed on the ballot. After oral arguments, the court ruled that the secretary of state had no discretion in the matter and ordered Weatherly's name placed on the ballot. Burris had no choice but to fight another election battle, this time against an opponent he termed "an out-and-out, second-string candidate of George Parr."[37]

The election was approaching, but Governor Shivers needed to find someone to take the Seventy-Ninth Judicial District bench on an interim basis. In a surprise move, the governor called Laughlin to the state capitol to discuss the matter. "I had talked to just about everybody else down there about the judgeship except the man who got elected," Shivers said, "and I thought I ought to talk to him about it." Attorney General Shepperd couldn't believe the governor was toying with the idea of seating Laughlin and he severely criticized Shivers for even considering the possibility. "It would throw fear and consternation into the ranks of the people who have had the courage to oppose George Parr," he said. Shepperd praised the Duval grand jury for the job they were doing "and I don't think Judge Laughlin ought to be allowed to touch their work."[38]

The Dallas Bar Association was even more adamant on Laughlin being appointed. In a telegram, members blasted Shivers with a blistering statement: "The organized bar will never accept the degradation of the judiciary by appointment of a man removed from this very office for misconduct, and who is now the subject of disbarment proceedings by the State Bar of Texas." Whether Shivers was showing impartiality or was seriously considering Laughlin, the matter became moot when the presiding administrative judge of the district made the decision for the governor. In an unprecedented move, two judges from other districts were assigned to sit side by side on the district bench in Duval.[39]

Ironically, the first case heard by the duo-jurists would be the Laugh-lin disbarment suit brought by the State Bar Association because state law required such cases tried in the home county of the defendant. Although a civil suit, it was titled *The State of Texas* vs. *C. Woodrow Laughlin*, and at the last possible minute Laughlin asked for a jury trial. The presiding judges set November 22, 1954, for a hearing to consider the merits of the allegations.[40] Since the hearing would take place after the election, Parr had to make a decision, and make it quickly.

If the State Bar Association's suit to disbar Laughlin was successful, Governor Shivers would appoint a judge to replace Laughlin, who seemed assured of winning. Fearful of having another unfriendly judge like Broadfoot or Welch presiding over the indictments that were showering down like confetti, Parr decided on a last-minute write-in campaign as had proven successful against Judge Reams in 1950. Parr even convinced A. J. Vale, the same write-in candidate against Reams, to run against Laughlin. Having lost Parr's backing, Laughlin chose to make a clean break. "Woodrow Laughlin will not be dominated by anyone," he told reporters. "When my troubles are over, my head may be bloody but it will not be bowed down to any political boss."[41]

To help his write-in candidate, Parr distributed a circular in Anglo American sections of Alice urging voters to write in the name of Jake Floyd's law partner, Clarence Perkins, for the same judgeship. Using his radio station KBKI, Parr had broadcasts repeatedly aired to report the intended write-in by Perkins. The ploy was designed to pull enough votes away from Laughlin to assure a Vale win, but Perkins adamantly denied being a candidate, saying he would have nothing to do with "another typical Parr trick." An avid poker player, Parr was going "all in" with his political chips. If his two write-in candidates (Weatherly and Vale) lost, Parr would have fierce opponents in two key district positions. "There was no other alternative," Parr said about the write-in campaign against Laughlin. "I hope we are still friends."[42]

Despite the Vale and Weatherly write-in campaigns being successful in Duval, Laughlin and Burris carried enough votes in the three other judicial district counties to win the election. Laughlin still faced disbarment and if he was ousted a second time, Governor Shivers would certainly appoint an anti-Parr judge to take his place. To demonstrate his avowed break with Parr, after being sworn in, Laughlin began working with newly elected district attorney Sam Burris on cleaning up corruption. When Laughlin circulated a petition among lawyers practicing in his district to oppose continuation of the disbarment proceedings, Burris added his name.[43]

The State Bar Association ignored the petition and pressed for a trial. After several delays, the jury trial was held in the Alice courtroom, presided over by visiting judge Louis T. Holland. After listening to oral arguments for more than six hours, Holland surprised everyone by announcing he was instructing the jury to return a verdict of not guilty. Citing that the law in this case was vague, and when there is a question "the law should be resolved in favor of the person injured by it," Holland said he had no other choice. Acting on his instructions, the jury did as it was told. Laughlin was acquitted and went back to work.[44]

Losing control of the prosecutor and judge in the judicial district was a serious blow to Parr's political power. No longer could he conduct "business as usual" with the understanding that he had key players in his pocket. But now he had even weightier problems to face—the tax case being prepared against him by the U.S. government.

CHAPTER 14

INDICTMENTS, TRIALS, AND A PULITZER

The Justice Department assigned Parr's tax case to U.S. Attorney Malcolm Richard Wilkey in Houston. Convening a federal grand jury in late September 1954, Wilkey issued thirty-five subpoenas for persons from the Duval area to testify about Parr's finances. Among them was Parr's ex-wife, Thelma. Witnesses were told to bring any records pertaining to the investigation, including bank statements, copies of oil leases, canceled checks, and microfilms of ledger accounts and checks paid through Parr's banks from 1949 through 1953. Three witnesses were scheduled to testify at the Nago Alaniz trial in Waco on the same day they were wanted in Houston—a distance of two hundred miles apart. They were allowed to appear in Houston first.[1]

The first witness was IRS special agent William H. Ninedorf, who had investigated Parr's finances. The three men scheduled to appear in the Alaniz trial were heard and dismissed. Next was Thelma Parr who, although divorced, was still a partner in her ex-husband's Parr-Delaney Oil Company. Wearing a dark gray wool dress, "like she'd just come [from] Dior's in Paris," she was besieged by newsmen before entering the grand jury room. When one reporter asked if the rumors were true that George had been making several visits to see her in Corpus Christi for the purpose of reconciliation, she "tossed her head" and kept walking without a reply. After one and a half hours before the grand jury, she was again surrounded by reporters. She refused to comment but sarcastically told them their job was "a sordid way to make a living."[2]

More witnesses testified, with emphasis on Parr's oil leasing business and illegal use of Duval County funds. Parr's oil company partner Earl Delaney was grilled on profits that Parr made from oil leases, which the government contended were never reported as income. San Diego auto

dealer J. C. King testified to having a seventy-five-thousand-dollar canceled check for oil leases he sold to Parr "at a profit," but he declined to
say how much profit. Bank employees and Parr's personal accountant, W.
M. Benson, were asked to explain discrepancies in records from Parr's
defunct Texas State Bank. County employees were asked about transactions from county and school funds.[3]

Before the Parr tax probe, grand jury witnesses usually waited their
turn in the corridor outside the jury room. Due to the excessive heat,
the lack of air-conditioning in the corridor, and the number of witnesses
called, the waiting area was relocated to an unoccupied jury room on
the fourth floor. The air-conditioned room, furnished with a television
set, may have eased their discomfort and boredom, but waiting to be
summoned left some uncomfortable.[4] Except for a short break to allow
Wilkey to attend the annual conference of U.S. attorneys in Washington,
the Parr investigation continued until the end of October 1954.

On November 15, 1954, the federal grand jury handed down a three-
count indictment against Parr on income tax evasion. According to tax
returns he earned an income of $164,372 between 1949 and 1951, and he
paid $83,555 in taxes. The government said his actual income for the three-
year period was $278,284 and the tax should have been $169, 209. Federal
judge Allen Burroughs Hannay issued a bench warrant for Parr's arrest and
set bond at $10,000. After receiving notice of the indictment and before
the arrest warrant was served, Parr surrendered to a deputy U.S. marshal in
Corpus Christi and was fingerprinted before posting his bond.[5]

Two weeks after being indicted, Parr received more bad news from
the IRS. Federal tax liens were filed against him and his ex-wife, charging
that the pair owed more than a million dollars in additional taxes for the
years 1945 and 1947. The liens were a civil not a criminal matter and were
not related to the tax evasion indictment. The IRS filed in every county
where either George or Thelma held property or bank accounts, thus
preventing either of them from disposing of any assets until the government's claims had been satisfied.[6]

At his December arraignment in Corpus Christi, Parr strolled into
court wearing a tailored brown flannel suit with matching light brown
shoes, and a dark brown tie. He was in good spirits and smiling as he
entered the courthouse but had a solemn, serious look on his face when
he stood before the judge. In a session lasting fifteen minutes, federal

judge James V. Allred set dates in January to hear motions from both sides, announcing that the trial would be held "sometime in March."[7]

Before the year ended, superintendent of Duval County schools Reynaldo L. Adame went on trial for fifteen counts of theft. Transferred to Bryan, the trial was held in a former furniture store while the new courthouse was being built. Missing ledgers, vouchers with the payee line left blank, reluctant witnesses, and Adame's taking the stand as the only defense witness were the highlights of the short trial. After four hours of deliberation, he was found guilty and quickly sentenced to a two-year prison term. After he submitted his resignation "effective immediately" to the Duval County commissioners court, the commissioners appointed Adame's wife, Consuelo, to succeed him as school superintendent.[8]

Adame appealed on the ground that the grand jury indicting him had been illegally formed. It was the same contention that the court of criminal appeals heard when Judge Broadfoot had dismissed the previous jury in favor of an anti–Parr one. In a split decision the court reversed its previous ruling and threw out Adame's conviction. They also wiped out 104 indictments from the same grand jury, including one against Parr for conspiracy to commit felony theft. Calling the decision "tragic," Texas attorney general Shepperd vowed "someday George Parr's political debts will be paid, and we can start with a clean slate."[9] Reacting to Shepperd's vow, Parr said, "He is desperate; he needs something to peg his so-called crusading campaign either for attorney general or governor."[10]

Shepperd filed for a rehearing before the appeals court, hoping they would reverse their reversal. Having prepared a lengthy motion, he spoke as fast as he could during oral arguments, racing to finish before his allotted fifteen minutes were up. He didn't make it, so he pleaded for additional time but was denied. District Attorney Sam Burris used only five minutes. Burris contended that the original 1954 appeals court decision had given Broadfoot a "green light" to impanel a new grand jury. "We're not magicians and we're not mind readers," he said, leaving him uncertain of "what to do" in seeking indictments. Under the court rules, Adame's attorneys were not allowed to present oral arguments but were permitted to file a written brief. Without issuing a written opinion, the appeals court denied the motion to rehear its decision.[11]

Three weeks before the appeals court decision, Parr was indicted by the Duval grand jury on four counts of removing records from his San

Diego State Bank "for the purpose of suppressing evidence." Adame was charged on seven counts of theft and embezzlement of public money. He was also indicted in December 1955 by a federal grand jury for evading $3,064 in taxes on three returns. After the appeals court threw out Parr's indictment, the following day the Duval grand jury reindicted him on the same charge of theft.[12]

Adame went on trial for the felony theft charges in March 1956. Witnesses testified that Adame had been given signed blank vouchers to purchase supplies for the school at a local lumberyard. A lumberyard employee testified that whenever a voucher was presented it was for an amount greater than the purchase price and Adame took the difference in cash. Found guilty, Adame received a five-year prison sentence—three more years than he had been given after his first trial. One month before his appeal was to be heard and before his tax case went to trial, Adame died. He was fifty-one.[13] He had been the first of the Parr regime to be convicted, but he never served a day in prison.

Attorney General Shepperd predicted that 1954 would see the end of Parr's control in Duval. It hadn't happened, but it was beginning. Shepperd estimated that the Parr political machine had been "siphoning off public funds into private pockets at the rate of from $1,000,000 to $2,000,000 a year." Shepperd now predicted that with "the rake-off system broken down," and with "Parr and his gang standing before the bar of justice," Duval could "look forward to a new era of freedom and prosperity."[14]

The "praying" grand jury returned 103 indictments during its five-month tenure, and the new grand jury sworn in on November 1, 1954, seemed destined to continue dismantling the Parr empire. Parr's attorneys objected that members appointed to the new panel were Freedom Party supporters, many of whom had publicly stated that Parr's Old Party was a group of "crooks who should be in the penitentiary." With an anti-Parr grand jury and a newly elected district attorney not beholden to Parr, Shepperd pulled his staff out of the county after being there almost a year. "I am firmly convinced we are going to prevail," he said, "because we are right."[15]

As Shepperd would learn, however, being "right" did not necessarily translate to prevailing, and Parr was not going away. Tenacious in keeping control, Parr could be compared to the mesquite covering the Texas landscape. A tough, resilient tree, it refuses to be eradicated. As one

Texan politician noted, "you can chop it, you can burn it, but the roots go way down deep, and it'll keep coming up again." The mesquite tree sucks moisture with its root system so efficiently that even grass won't grow under it. Ranchers who use mesquite posts for their fences often see it sprouting to life and taking root to grow again.[16]

Anything Parr did was news. Whether in the courtroom or holding court at the Windmill Cafe, George always managed to make the daily editions of newspapers throughout Texas. Caro Brown, reporting for the *Alice Daily Echo*, with byline articles and a daily column, kept locals informed on the doings of the Duke of Duval, and she was about to receive national attention for her efforts.

Born in Baber, Texas, the daughter of sawmill worker, she found her early school years difficult. Bullied in school for her humble beginnings until the family moved to Beaumont, she attended junior college for a year and then enrolled at the College of Industrial Arts in Denton, which later became Texas Woman's University. She took a journalism class before she left, but didn't continue with it.[17] When the Great Depression came, she returned to Beaumont and enrolled in a local secretarial school.

It was while working as a secretary at a local law firm that she met Jack Brown, a civil engineer working as a surveyor. Marriage and three children later, she followed her husband to Alice, where he worked as an engineer for Texaco. Bored as a housewife, she answered an *Alice Daily Echo* job ad for a proofreader, to be paid fifteen dollars a week. Converted from a weekly to a daily newspaper, the *Echo* was short on reporters, so editor Curtis Vinson shifted Caro to the reporting staff. "He started by training me on little automobile accidents and reporting from the courthouse," she recalled. Then Vinson turned a daily column he was writing—the "Street Scene"—over to Caro, which she continued to write until the day she left the newspaper.[18]

When Buddy Floyd was murdered, she was assigned to cover the story, and she realized that the murder, the local elections, and the Parr political machine all formed part of the same story. Doggedly determined to tell the story by placing events in proper perspective, she worked long hours attending court sessions, and visiting and interviewing people reluctant to reveal anything, before returning to the newsroom after a long day to write her articles.[19]

Covering South Texas resulted in her being directly involved in articles she was writing. "The whole series of stories started with that murder because . . . you have to get down to the human element before the public will understand," she said. Her incisive reporting described the unfolding story so well that the Associated Press relied on her to keep newspapers across the country informed on the rapidly changing story of the Parr empire. Being close to events resulted in her being at the courthouse when tempers flared between Ranger Captain Allee and Parr. "I thought sure there was going to be a killing," she said at the time. She later remarked she had looked "into his [Allee] eyes and saw death."[20]

As 1954 drew to a close, the managing editors of Associated Press newspapers picked Duval and Parr as the top news stories in Texas for the year. Chances were that Parr would make the top-ten list the following year. "The Associated Press, at its annual convention in Florida recently, voted the Daily Echo as the Number One newspaper in Texas in its annual recognition of member newspapers' 'participation' in AP news coverage."[21] The newspaper also received national recognition when the advisory board of the Pulitzer Prizes announced that local reporter Caro Crawford Brown had been nominated for the award.[22]

When the Pulitzer Prizes were announced in May 1955, Caro won for local reporting to meet edition deadlines. Three women had won the award before, but she was the first to win for local reporting. National recognition didn't change the circumstances for the housewife-turned-reporter, however. "So help me, my salary for that paper never was over fifty dollars a week," she said. "Even after I was nominated for the Pulitzer, I was still only making fifty dollars a week." The sports reporter for the *Echo* received fifteen dollars a week more. A week after winning the Pulitzer, she quit her job and never again worked as a journalist.[23]

By 1955 the economy was expanding under the Eisenhower administration. Business was booming, but not in South Texas where there was little industry to provide jobs. The coming national recession was already developing in Duval County. It continued as an agrarian culture mixed with oil and gas income, but most employment came from county and city jobs controlled by Parr. As long as he was the primary source of employment, Parr felt he would always be in power. Three elements were needed to maintain control—he and his henchmen had to stay out of jail, access to public purse strings had to remain open, and his candidates had to win elections.

Delaying the trials was the best tactic for Parr and his men to stay out of jail, and he found a unique way to accomplish this. Eligio "Kika" de la Garza II, a young attorney who was a member of the state legislature, was engaged as a member of the defense team. Under state law, a member of the state legislature could not be compelled to make court appearances within thirty days prior to the beginning of the legislative session, during the session, or thirty days after the session ended. Although he denied being employed for the purpose of delay, Garza filed notice of immunity to several of the counties where the cases had been transferred.[24]

The first trial scheduled was for D.C. Chapa and his son Oscar Carrillo Sr., with a total of thirteen charges against them. Garza filed the motion for immunity and Judge Otis T. Dunagan of Tyler postponed the trial until April. Former Duval County auditor C. T. Stansell Jr., facing charges of theft and forgery, fared even better. His case was transferred to Tarrant County, but the district judge complained that witnesses lived far from his court and his docket was so crowded that the case wouldn't be heard until next year.[25]

Trials could be delayed, but no one could stop the Duval grand jury. While awaiting his day in court, Carrillo had three more charges for theft tacked on to his lengthy list of pending indictments. Trial dates for others were being set, but more motions resulted in delays. Chapa and Carrillo were granted postponements until September, but when neither showed up on the scheduled date, the trial judge ordered their arrest. After a night in jail, both were brought into court to explain why they had failed to appear. Their attorney, Percy Foreman, argued he was engaged in another trial in Corpus Christi and told Chapa and Carrillo they wouldn't have to appear. New bonds were posted and a trial date set for November. With his delaying tactic accomplished, Garza withdrew, leaving Foreman as the attorney of record.[26]

When the case came to trial, prosecutors decided to try only D.C. Chapa. Percy Foreman immediately filed five motions, which had to be heard before jury selection began. One motion asked for dismissal because two indictments were for the same crime, putting the defendant in double jeopardy. Another motion challenged the change of venue, which placed the trial 450 miles from the defendant's home. Another argued that because Chapa was of Latin American descent, and Duval had an 80 percent Latin American population, while the county he was being tried in had less than 0.5 percent, the defendant would not receive a fair trial. The last motion asked that Sam Burris be disqualified as prosecutor because Smith County had a qualified district attorney who was ready for trial.[27]

Setting the tone of the trial, Foreman called Burris to the stand and began grilling him on his involvement in the case. Attacked for being "anti-Parr," which Foreman said is what the case was really about, Burris said, "I'm not anti-anybody. I'm just for justice." After several more witnesses, Judge Dunagan overruled all but the double jeopardy motion. Foreman then asked for a continuance, which the judge denied.[28]

Jury selection was a slow drawn-out process with Foreman grilling prospective jurors at length. To speed up the process, Dunagan ordered a night session that lasted until 9:00 P.M., but ended with Foreman qualifying only fifteen men. Thirty-two veniremen were required from which the twelve-man jury would be selected, so Dunagan ordered fifty more brought in. The delays had a rippling effect felt all the way back to Duval. Witnesses and attorneys scheduled to appear were also wanted for hearings for over one hundred indictments in San Diego. Dunagan added another delay by recessing court for one week because of the Thanksgiving holidays.[29]

The trial finally got under way with a jury of eight men and four women. Because Chapa was being tried for theft of school district funds, the state began by establishing that he had never been duly appointed as school district tax assessor-collector. Paul J. Green testified being a Benavides school board member for nineteen years, but he couldn't recall how Chapa received the job. School district auditor William E. Ponder said records showed Chapa received a monthly salary of $300, one of Chapa's sons received $300 a month, and another son received $217.70 a month. Ponder said he discovered a $21,000 shortage in funds and couldn't find records to support more than $3,000 in disbursements. The money "should have been in the bank but just never got there."[30]

The state attempted to establish that Chapa had received tax checks and converted them for his own use. A rubber stamp bearing Chapa's signature that had been used to cash checks was introduced into evidence, but Foreman produced a second rubber stamp, contending that someone else may have had the "ability and design" to "purloin" the school funds. A handwriting expert testified Chapa had signed several tax receipts in his own hand. Foreman countered by bringing in a cashier at the San Diego State Bank who testified that the signatures were not Chapa's.[31]

Texans are very serious, almost religious, about high school football. Public meetings and social gatherings are never scheduled during game time. Business comes to a halt and stadiums are packed for every game. Even criminal trials are affected. With Roy Miller High School of Corpus Christi in a playoff game against John Tyler High School, Dunagan called a Saturday afternoon recess so those in court could attend the game. Keeping his word that the trial would move along without delays, he scheduled a Saturday evening session after the football game.[32]

The defense opened with evidence that Chapa received money from a source other than school funds. A Mexican attorney, whose testimony was translated by an interpreter, said he represented a client who purchased a horse named "Indian Charlie" from Chapa for six thousand dollars in cash. After Foreman introduced the bill of sale, he said Chapa had come by the money through legitimate means, not from school funds. In totaling up the amount, Foreman was one cent short. In a display of courtroom dramatics, he reached into his pocket, pulled out a single penny, and tossed it onto the state counsel's table. It remained there the rest of the session without being touched by the prosecutor.[33]

According to the *Corpus Christi Caller*, former Benavides school board president Octavio Saenz testified that Chapa had a contract with the school board to collect taxes for a 4 percent commission. Under cross-examination by Burris, which became heated at times, Saenz said he never checked to see if Chapa was taking his fee. "You mean you let a man who didn't get past the third grade collect half a million dollars of your money and never file a report on it?" Burris asked. "That is correct," Saenz answered calmly. "That is what was going on."[34]

Foreman called Mrs. Velia O. Bridges, a former employee of the school district tax office, who intimated that someone else was responsible for the missing money—Diego Heras, whose affidavit said Parr and his men had been robbing the county blind. She said Heras often flashed large amounts of cash in the office. She recalled an incident occurring one evening while she was with her father and brother. Passing by the tax office, they noticed a light burning and went to investigate. Upon entering, they saw Heras jumping out of a window. She noticed that school district record books were missing.[35]

After closing arguments, during which Foreman said that the only thing the state had managed to do was hold "up to ridicule the utter lack of bookkeeping in the school district," the judge charged the jury and they retired to consider a verdict. The trial had lasted eighteen days, but after two hours the jury returned their verdict at 9:21 that evening. Chapa was found not guilty of all charges. He was free, but he still had other charges pending, and Burris had every intention of getting a conviction. "There'll definitely be no let up in our efforts," he vowed. "In fact, we plan to work even harder in the prosecution of these cases."[36] Prosecuting—especially Parr—wasn't an easy matter, but the federal government showed no hesitation.

Having secured liens against Parr and his ex-wife, the IRS dug deeper. Two agents arrived in San Diego on February 23, 1955, posting themselves in front of the county treasurer's office waiting for it to open. One hour past the regular opening time, the county treasurer made his appearance. Locking themselves in the office, the agents pored through county records. At the end of the day they emerged carrying two large boxes.[37]

The following month Parr received notice from the IRS that he owed an additional one-half million dollars in back taxes, penalties, and interest from 1945 and 1947, bringing the total amount Parr and his ex-wife owed to one and a half million dollars. Three months later, the IRS tacked on one hundred thousand dollars in taxes and penalties owed from the 1951 tax year.[38]

With his tax evasion case scheduled for trial, Parr filed a change of venue motion. A common motion in criminal cases, it is seldom granted unless substantial doubt is raised that a fair trial cannot be had in the district where the defendant is being tried. Parr contended there was an ongoing campaign of "vilification, defamation and abuse" being waged by the *Corpus Christi Caller* and *La Verdad*, a Corpus Christi weekly. He charged that federal agencies (the FBI, the IRS, the U.S. Post Office, and the Department of Justice) had "blanketed" the area in an attempt to convict him before the public. Contending that "virtually the same situation prevails" in the Houston, Galveston, Brownsville, and Victoria judicial divisions, he said the only site remaining where he could receive a fair trial would be Laredo.[39]

Supporting his motion, Parr filed a truckload of attachments, including sixty-five affidavits from Nueces County residents and thirty-five folders containing newspaper clippings going as far back as 1945. "Corpus Christi papers have done an extremely effective job of creating mass hatred against Parr," read one affidavit. Another, from a close friend of Parr's, said he introduced people to Parr who were "surprised that he was such a nice person," and "not at all like they would have supposed" after reading about him in the local newspapers.[40]

Calling it a "unique" motion, U.S. Attorney Malcolm Wilkey entered ninety-seven affidavits to show why the trial should not be held in Laredo. Circulation figures from Corpus Christi newspapers showed that 2.55 percent of the Laredo population received or read Corpus Christi newspapers, as compared with 0.05 percent in Houston and 0.127 percent in Galveston. He admitted there was a "division of opinion" as to whether Parr could receive a fair trial in Corpus Christi, but this wasn't true for Houston, Galveston, or Victoria. He added that the government would be under a "severe handicap" to prosecute the case in Laredo.[41]

Judge Thomas Martin Kennerly ruled there was "so great a prejudice against Defendant" that a fair trial could not be had in Corpus Christi. Citing news clippings attached to the motion, he felt there was "much publicity, generally very unfavorable and sometimes most unfavorable." He noted the government never claimed it wouldn't receive a fair trial in Laredo, and Parr had consented to the case being transferred there. Outraged that the trial would be held in Laredo, state representative Bob Mullen of Alice said the government "may as well dismiss the case and save the taxpayers money." Having promised to keep Senator Lyndon Johnson informed, Parr's attorney, Everett L. Looney, sent a copy of the ruling to Johnson's office in Washington.[42]

Wilkey refused to concede defeat. Presenting the case before a federal grand jury in San Antonio, he obtained a three-count indictment against Parr for tax evasion based on the same evidence. Returning to Kennerly's courtroom, Wilkey submitted a motion asking for dismissal of the original tax evasion indictment so that Parr could be tried on "similar" charges in San Antonio. A Corpus Christi Caller editorial on May 6 cited Wilkey's "resourcefulness" for the maneuver, adding that although Parr would "much rather be tried in Laredo," it would be difficult for him to argue he wouldn't receive a fair trial in San Antonio.[43]

During a hearing on the motion, Wilkey argued that if the case was held in Laredo there would be an "adverse effect in getting the truth from witnesses who are reluctant and in some instances hostile." Looney contended the government "was trying to do indirectly what it could not accomplish directly." Kennerly sided with Wilkey by dismissing the original indictments and ordered the new trial to be shifted from San Antonio to Austin. According to the *Alice Daily Echo*, Parr showed up, smiling for photographers, and posted a five-thousand-dollar appearance bond on the new charges. "I could have posted the bond a week ago," he joked, "but if the government can wait, I'm sure not in any hurry."[44]

Filing a motion in the Fifth Court of Civil Appeals in New Orleans, Parr asked to be tried in Laredo on the original indictments. Wilkey labeled the appeal "frivolous" and "obviously taken for purposes of delay." Parr also filed a motion before federal district judge Ben H. Rice Jr. in San Antonio to "stay arraignment and all subsequent proceedings," and another to dismiss the indictment. After both motions were denied, Parr asked for a change of venue from Austin to Laredo on the new indictment. Arguing that if held in Austin, where juries are drawn from a substantial number of state employees, who "are in one way or another dependent upon the government's favor," he would not receive a fair trial.[45]

After denying a change of venue, Judge Rice set July 18, 1955, as the date for Parr's tax evasion trial in Austin. Getting Parr to trial had been a long drawn-out process, but another delay was added. The Fifth Court of Civil Appeals in New Orleans, by a two-to-one vote, rejected Parr's appeal to have his case tried in Laredo. That should have ended the appeals, but the court left the door open for a U.S. Supreme Court review. Keeping Lyndon Johnson informed, Everett Looney wrote to advise him of the next step. "I have been in touch with [Thurman] Arnold and [Abe] Fortas," he wrote, "and they are preparing the necessary papers for the Supreme Court." Looney added they had a "fifty-fifty chance" of winning. Fortas followed up by sending Johnson copies of briefs filed by his law firm and those by the government.[46]

With the possibility of the high court taking up the matter, Judge Rice, concurring with the Justice Department, decided to postpone Parr's tax trial indefinitely. In his petition Fortas argued that Judge Kennerly had transferred the case to Laredo, after which the government had Parr indicted again in San Antonio, making "a unique and unprecedented attempt to circumvent a valid and effective order of transfer."[47] The prosecution felt there was "nothing to indicate that [Parr] will be unfairly prejudiced" by a trial in Austin, supporting their claim by quoting Judge Kennerly, who "found that it would be more fair to both parties that the case be tried elsewhere" than Corpus Christi or Laredo. Opening their October 1955 term, the U.S. Supreme Court agreed to hold a hearing on the matter, effectively delaying Parr's trial until the following year.[48]

The U.S. Supreme Court ruling was handed down June 11, 1956. The court recognized the government attempted "to avoid a trial in Laredo, which it regarded as *the defendant's seat of political power*," but in a five-to-four decision (with Chief Justice Earl Warren, Hugo Black, William Douglas, and Tom Clark dissenting), the motion was denied. The majority opinion, written by Justice Harlan, contained a very strange proviso: "True, Parr will have to hazard a trial under the Austin indictment before he can get a review of whether he should have been tried in Laredo under the Corpus Christi indictment, but bearing the discomfiture and cost of a prosecution for crime even by an innocent person, is one of the painful obligations of citizenship." In other words, if found guilty in Austin, Parr could appeal based on where the trial should have been held in the first place! The dissenting opinion noted that "for the last 20 years preceding, the Government had filed all tax-evasion cases arising in that district in Austin," and the new indictment to get the case from Laredo to Austin attempted to "circumvent the court's order." A *Corpus Christi Caller* editorial said, "The possibility of a useless trial, expensive both to Parr and the United States, has been sanctioned by the Supreme Court."[49]

"Parr was guaranteed a speedy trial," Wilkey remarked. "He was indicted over a year and a half ago, and we want to try the case on its merits as soon as possible." Judge Rice, however, wouldn't set a trial date because Parr had already filed a motion for a rehearing before the high court. At the opening of the October 1956 term, the U.S. Supreme Court refused to reconsider their decision, opening the way for Parr to be tried for tax evasion in an Austin federal court.[50]

CHAPTER 15

AWAITING TRIAL

There were always newsworthy events in Duval—most centering on George Parr. During the period when the federal government was trying to pin down a trial date for Parr's charge of income tax evasion, he provided more than enough controversy to keep reporters busy. Duval had been the featured story in Texas newspapers in the year 1954, and when 1955 began, newspaper coverage of Duval picked up where the previous year had left off.

The Duval grand jury kept digging into local matters, and no one was immune. Six former Duval commissioners, including Judge Dan Tobin Jr., were indicted in June 1955 on charges of misappropriation of public funds. The following month, George Parr and his partner in the Oil Belt Chevrolet Company, J. C. King, were indicted on charges of receiving misapplied public funds. Twelve others, including present and former Duval County officials, were also named in indictments, all for misappropriation of public funds. The grand jury indicted eight more, including Raeburn Norris, the former Seventy-Ninth Judicial District attorney who had been defeated by Sam Burris. Norris was being charged with conspiracy to misapply five thousand dollars in county funds, unlawfully paid to Parr's San Diego State Bank.[1]

The turmoil stirred up by the grand jury prompted some to hide. Three Duval County commissioners under indictment resigned their posts and were quickly replaced by their wives.[2] Others chose to fight it out tooth and nail within the court system. As each new indictment was issued, George's attorney, Percy Foreman, filed motions to have them quashed. Representing twenty-two defendants with a total of seventy indictments against them, Foreman began by attacking the methods employed in returning the indictments.

Judge Frank E. Fulgham, sitting in for Judge Laughlin, who had recused himself, allowed Foreman wide latitude in arguing the motions, which he took full advantage of by calling Sam Burris and Carl Gromatzky, an IRS agent who had been present during grand jury deliberations, to the stand. "The indictments were the act of the district attorney and not of the grand jury," Foreman contended. "The grand jury was simply the outer ego of the prosecuting attorney." To prove his point, he spent hours grilling Burris on who was present during grand jury sessions and what was said. Burris remained cool under relentless questioning, refusing to ascribe to Foreman's accusation that indictments had been politically motivated.[3]

At the conclusion of the hearing, Fulgham denied all defense quash motions and ordered changes of venue, scattering the cases to nine courtrooms throughout the state. J. C. King and Parr would be tried in Midland on September 1, 1955, but with more motions from Foreman, it was doubtful the date would stick. There was also more grand jury action that would further delay trial dates. Examining affidavits used in the defense quash motions, the grand jury indicted Parr and eighteen others for swearing to false affidavits. Parr received three more indictments, charging him with making an unauthorized fifteen-thousand-dollar loan to himself and falsifying bank records while president of the San Diego State Bank.[4]

Parr was given hope when the Texas court of criminal appeals threw out the conviction of school superintendent R. L. Adame, along with 104 indictments handed down by the Duval grand jury. Parr filed suit in federal court charging that the present Duval grand jury had deprived him of his civil liberties. Named in the suit were the entire grand jury, District Attorney Sam Burris, and Texas attorney general Ben Shepperd. "The present grand jury has one more month to run," Burris commented on Parr's ploy. "If they can tie it up for that month in federal court, possibility that no re-indictments will be returned and the defendants will go scott free."[5]

In an attempt to prevent the Duval grand jury from re-indicting them, Parr and the other defendants challenged that the statute of limitations had run out on some of the charges. These stemmed from 1951, and with a three-year limit, they claimed time had expired. Burris disagreed: "The period an indictment is pending does not count as part of the limitation time," but he admitted there may be "controversy" on that point.[6] Burris and Shepperd filed for a criminal appeals court rehearing on the ouster ruling of the original 104 indictments. They also asked one of the judges in the majority opinion, Judge Lloyd Witten Davidson, be disqualified.

District Attorney Sam Burris claimed not only that Davidson had expressed an opinion on the case "before it was considered," but that Davidson was "the choice of Parr on the marked ballots distributed by his organization before the election." If Shepperd and Burris thought their statements would force Davidson to recuse himself, they were grossly mistaken. Public defense of the judge was immediate and came from very powerful and influential voices.

Shepperd's timing couldn't have come at a more inopportune moment because the judiciary section of the Texas State Bar was opening its convention in Corpus Christi. Speaking before the conclave of judges, district judge Penn J. Jackson said that any improvement of the courts "must begin with the Legislature, and can not be accomplished by unwarranted criticism or assaults upon a great court." Heavy applause followed Jackson's speech.[7]

Feeling pressure from lawyers and judges throughout the state, Shepperd backpedaled. "I have been distressed," he began in a telegram to the convention of judges, "to learn that certain remarks of mine intended to apply to a general situation have been misinterpreted by some as reflecting upon integrity of our courts." Leaving Burris alone out on a limb, Shepperd said he would not seek Davidson's disqualification. "The final decision will be up to Sam Burris."[8] Without Shepperd's support, Burris had no choice but to drop the matter.

The public apology by Shepperd should have ended the matter, but the Texas State Bar Association felt otherwise. Directors of the state bar announced they had referred Shepperd's criticism of the courts to the local grievance committee to investigate "the ethical propriety of such public criticism." Although Shepperd said he welcomed the inquiry, he was displeased when he learned the committee would be holding closed door sessions. He demanded the hearings be public because he wanted to bring his own witnesses, including two Texas Rangers, who would testify on political conditions in Duval County. His request was denied.[9]

As an advisory group, the grievance committee could only make recommendations to the state bar, but their decision carried considerable weight. They could recommend an official reprimand or even ask for Shepperd's disbarment, which was highly unlikely. Refusing to hear witnesses Shepperd had brought to the hearing, the committee grilled him and two assistants during a four-hour session. When it ended, the committee voted to take no action.[10] Although the outcome wouldn't affect the cases pending against him, Parr may have delighted in having his adversary on the hot seat, if only for a short time.

Even before the Shepperd disciplinary action ended, the Duval County grand jury began probing deeper into district corruption. Subpoenas were issued to potential witnesses, including Parr. Ten witnesses, including Parr, refused to testify, evoking the Fifth Amendment. "We all but wore the constitution out today," remarked Assistant Attorney General Sidney P. Chandler, who was sitting in for the absent Shepperd. Two dozen other witnesses called were described by Chandler as being "very fine, very cooperative."[11]

Any potential witnesses needed were being called, no matter how far away they lived. Shepperd even reached out to a sixty-two-year-old man living in Sacramento, California, but there was a slight hitch: the man was a convicted felon. James L. McDonald—the man who opposed Parr by refusing to accept a bribe, the man who held a special Texas Ranger badge, the man who ran unsuccessfully for Duval County sheriff in 1954—had a criminal past. Sheppard petitioned California governor Goodwin Knight for a pardon so that McDonald's testimony could not be impeached on account of his past.[12]

By mid-October, the grand jury was ready to hand out indictments. These were the first batch issued since the appeals court had thrown out the previous 104. Parr was charged with removing bank records "for the purpose of suppressing evidence." Former Duval County auditor C. T. Stansell Jr. was hit with seventeen indictments ranging from forgery to theft.[13]

With these indictments, cracks in Parr's political machine began to appear in the form of desertions of the party faithful. The first to jump ship was county judge Dan Tobin Jr. who announced he was "putting principle above politics," opting to go it alone as an independent. Soon after, county commissioner Maria C. Leal, who had replaced her husband, Juan, after he had resigned, joined Tobin. County treasurer Victor Leal became the third to break ranks. Even with their departures, Parr still had three county commissioners who could easily nullify Mrs. Leal's vote.[14] But Parr was soon to lose one of his three "pocket" commissioners.

In a civil suit filed by F. A. Vaello—joined by the State of Texas—Duval County commissioner Estella G. Garcia was charged with "nepotism, official misconduct, and of being incompetent." The nepotism charge stemmed from her act of placing her son Lorenzo on the county payroll. Mrs. Garcia also approved payment of salary to Mrs. Maria Estella Haught, her daughter, who was on leave from the state welfare office. When the civil suit was filed, Judge Laughlin, who had already demonstrated he was no longer a Parr man, suspended Mrs. Garcia from her post. In her place Laughlin appointed Tomas H. Molina, a longtime vocal opponent of Parr. With the crossover of Mrs. Leal combined with Molina's being added to the commissioners' court, the anti-Parr forces now controlled a three-to-two vote on board decisions.[15]

Filing a brief on behalf of his client, attorney Gordon Gibson of Laredo claimed the ouster of Mrs. Garcia was invalid because Duval County attorney R. F. Luna, whose name hadn't appeared on the order, was the only qualified official who could initiate the case. In their answer, the state said that Luna, although sympathetic to the ouster, hadn't joined in "due to fear of personal violence toward [himself] and his family." Luna denied ever saying he was "afraid" of getting involved, and filed to join the suit "regardless of any danger to my personal safety."[16]

While the ouster case was pending before the Texas Supreme Court, Luna changed his mind. He filed a motion to be removed from the suit, saying "evidence available would not support the charges." Did Luna have a change of heart, or was he concerned in going against Parr? No one knew for certain, but by the end of the week, Luna appeared to be jumping the fence again to be back in Parr's good graces. To counter the move against Mrs. Garcia, Luna filed a petition before Judge Laughlin to have county judge Dan Tobin removed from office. The surprise action, charging Tobin with "misconduct and incompetency in office," was designed to nullify Tobin's vote on the commissioners' court, even though Tobin was only empowered to vote in case of a tie. Although Luna had requested Laughlin to immediately suspend Tobin, as had happened to Mrs. Garcia, Laughlin refused and set a trial date for after the first of the year.[17]

During December 1955, events in and out of the courtroom began to set the tone of what was happening to Parr's control of his empire.

The Texas Supreme Court gave its decision on the Garcia ouster—Judge Laughlin's action was deemed valid. The unanimous ruling held that Attorney General Shepperd didn't have authority to initiate the removal proceedings, but that District Attorney Sam Burris did. The second event took everyone by surprise. Victor Leal, who had broken ranks from Parr, suddenly submitted his resignation as Duval County treasurer. He said he had friends on both sides of the political fence and didn't want to hurt any of them. Leal preferred to sit on the sidelines while the battle raged. The third event, pivotal in the South Texas judicial district, was a ruling by the court of civil appeals. When Laughlin won his disbarment case, the State Bar Association appealed. Upholding the directed verdict of not guilty, the appeals court effectively assured that Laughlin would remain on the bench.[18]

Parr now had two unfriendly judges on the bench, district judge Laughlin and county judge Tobin, and there was more bad news coming. On December 14, 1955, Tobin met with Freedom Party members in an "informal" session to explore the possibility of joining forces in a united front against Parr. If differences separating the two groups could be resolved, Parr would be facing a coalition at the polls that would be seriously challenging Old Party candidates. As meetings were held over the next two months, District Attorney Sam Burris acted as middle-man between the two groups, hoping they could find common ground.[19]

When the Tobin forces and the Freedom Party were on the verge of a united front, the merger talks broke down. They had agreed on every issue except one—which faction would put up candidates for elections that summer. "They will have their full slate and we will have ours," Freedom Party official Donato Serna announced after the failed merger. Tobin would not be opposed for his seat by the Freedom Party and Tobin would not officially form a third party. However, that wouldn't eliminate the possibility that a member of his faction would run against a Freedom Party candidate for another position.[20] Parr must have breathed a sigh of relief because without a unified coalition the splintered groups would be easier to defeat at the polls.

While facing prosecutions coming at him from every direction, and political opposition challenging him at elections, Parr still found time for his personal life. In 1954 he had been living with a thirty-nine-year-old woman, Maria Luz Garcia, but the romance didn't last long because

George began turning his attention to fifteen-year-old Evangelina (Eva) Perez. Shortly before Christmas 1954, Eva, who for the past eight months had been working part-time at George's home, shot herself with a shotgun. No motive was given for the apparent suicide attempt, but it may have been due to Eva's father, Gregorio, having filed charges against Parr for contributing to the delinquency of a minor. In any event, on December 10, 1955, Parr married the teenager in Nuevo Laredo, Mexico.[21]

During a revealing interview with probation officer Calvin H. Bowden in 1974, George admitted his only vice was "chasing women." Bowden noted in his report that Parr was very jealous and possessive of his teen bride—to the point of being obsessive. The report detailed an incident when Parr took a shot at a roofer working on a house near his home because he thought the man was looking at Eva. "Threatening to shoot others who have looked at his wife is not a new thing with Mr. Parr," Bowden noted. "There have been quite a few incidents where threats were made with a weapon against people he accused of looking at his wife."[22] George's temper wasn't limited only to protecting the virtue of his wife.

San Diego real estate agent Juan Carrillo Jr. encountered Parr on Sunday morning, November 20, 1955, in front of the post office building. A discussion of Carrillo's political activities soon led to an argument, during which Parr pulled a pistol. Fortunately, Chon Pena, a former court interpreter, was standing nearby and grabbed George's arm before anything could happen. Shaken by the confrontation, Carrillo swore out a complaint of assault with intent to murder against Parr, who was arrested. After posting a one-thousand-dollar bond, Parr was released. Since no shots were fired and Carrillo had not been struck by Parr, the grand jury chose not to indict.[23]

On July 11, 1956, Mrs. Soila Olvera, a worker in the Duval County treasurer's office and member of the Old Party, ran into Parr's office. "She was crying and in a semi-hysterical condition," Parr recalled. After calming her, he asked what had upset her. She told him Tomas Molina had insulted her. "Molina said that the Old Party men are nothing but a bunch of thieves and the women nothing but a bunch of prostitutes," she told Parr as tears ran down her face. George was furious: "I made up my mind to go over and talk to Tomas Molina."[24]

Storming out of his office, Parr headed toward the courthouse, but he stopped on the way to get a .30 caliber semi-automatic rifle from his car. "I always carry this little carbine between the seats in my car," Parr said. "I went over with the rifle because I knew there would be a row." Bursting into the courthouse, Parr screamed, "Why doesn't that s.o.b. Tomas Molina jump on men instead of women." Witnesses said Parr raged through the courthouse, shouting at the top of his voice, "Where is that old Tomas Molina, I want to kill him, he ain't going to make *no* fun out of me." Not finding Molina on the main floor, Parr headed into the courthouse basement, carrying the rifle and still shouting. Molina, who was upstairs in Judge Tobin's office, was unaware of the commotion until someone told him to stay out of sight because Parr was armed and looking for him with blood in his eye.[25]

Texas Ranger Walter A. Russell was in the courthouse sitting in the sheriff's office when someone burst in and said Parr was ranting and raving, carrying a rifle, and hunting for Molina. Accompanied by a sheriff's deputy, Russell headed for the basement where he found Parr still gripping the rifle in his hand. "I reached over and took it away from him and said 'let's go.'" Parr went quietly with Russell back to the sheriff's office. Charged with "seriously threatening life," a misdemeanor, Parr was released after posting a one-thousand-dollar bond.[26]

Concerned there might be further disturbances, District Attorney Sam Burris asked Texas Rangers to assign extra men to "patrol Duval County so there won't be any gunslinging." Three days after the gun-toting incident, Parr was placed under a seventy-five-hundred-dollar peace bond. On September 17, 1956, the case came to trial. Defense attorney Percy Foreman argued that Parr had never threatened Molina directly and had only been venting his anger over the mistreatment of an innocent woman. After a two-day trial the jury apparently ignored George's chivalrous attempt at defending the virtue of a woman. They found him guilty and assessed a fine of $1,500 and $460 in court costs. On appeal, the judgment was affirmed and Parr paid the fine.[27]

Despite being under compliance of a peace bond, Parr's fiery temper continued to erupt whenever he felt insulted. On the night of March 3, 1957, he entered Angelina's Cafe in San Diego and began shaking hands with several men. When Eloy Ramirez refused to shake his hand, Parr cursed him, left the cafe to get a pistol from his car, and returned to curse Ramirez again while waving the pistol in the air. Ramirez still refused to shake hands. After Ramirez swore out a complaint, Parr was arrested at his home by Texas Ranger Walter Russell on a charge of "unlawfully carrying a gun." Parr was released after posting a five-hundred-dollar bond, but before a trial date could be set, he got into another gun-toting fracas.[28]

Parr was driving through San Diego on a Friday night two months later, when he spotted a group of high school students. After flashing a light on the boys, Parr parked his car, walked back to the group, and struck one of the boys with his fist while pointing a pistol at him. Eighteen-year-old high school honor student Ramon H. Tanguma, who had recently received a congressional appointment to the Air Force Academy, had never been in trouble with the law and could give no reason for the attack. Once again, Parr was arrested by Ranger Russell and posted another five-hundred-dollar bond on a charge of aggravated assault.[29]

District Attorney Sam Burris had had enough. On June 14, 1957, he filed suit in district court to have Parr's seventy-five-hundred-dollar peace bond revoked and court costs tacked on. The peace bond required Parr to "keep the peace toward Molina and all other persons for a period of one year," which Burris contended Parr had failed to do. The suit listed the threat on Ramirez, the attack on Tanguma, and a third charge that Parr was carrying a rifle and a pistol on the night he was arrested on the second charge. The two assault cases and the revocation suit were never heard in court. No record exists that any of these cases ever reached a conclusion.[30]

That still didn't stop Parr from reaching for a weapon whenever he was angered. According to the *Alice Daily Echo*, on the night of July 12, 1958, Agapito Luera stopped his pickup truck at a San Diego intersection, got out, and approached two boys in a parked car to ask for a cigarette. Parr, driving a green Chrysler, pulled up behind the car, which was blocking the street. When the youths saw Parr take out a rifle from under the front seat, they "scattered like quail." Luera jumped into his pickup truck and was pulling away when Parr thrust the rifle barrel through the pickup truck window, smacking Luera on his neck. After Luera signed a complaint, Texas Ranger Walter Russell, who seemed to have a steady job arresting Parr, found him at a drive-in theater that night. Parr posted a three-hundred-dollar bond and was released.[31]

Pleading not guilty to assault, Parr waived a jury trial and went to court the following Monday before Justice of the Peace Cato Perez.

"Don't you think you could have politely asked the boys to move their cars, instead of getting out of your car and brandishing a rifle?" county attorney Walter Purcell asked Parr.

"There are a lot of rumors going around this town and I don't know what's going to happen when I see the street blocked," Parr answered. "It's my skin—not yours."

Parr claimed he never hit the boy. While Luera was on the stand giving testimony, Parr interrupted. "I didn't hit you boy," he said. "If I had, you wouldn't be here today."

Found guilty, Parr was ordered to pay a $25 fine, the maximum penalty for assault and battery, plus $15.50 in court costs.[32]

There were times when Parr found other ways to show his displeasure, even if it meant taking it out on someone's children. Duval is farm and ranch country and had a 4-H club that held annual shows for young members to enter their livestock in a competition. The grand champion calf is auctioned off at the end of the show. Local businessmen bid on the calf, usually running the price to as much as two dollars a pound—a price that in the 1950s reflected accomplishment of the youth, not the value.

The son of a Parr opponent won the top prize one year, but when the calf was auctioned, Parr and his friends refused to offer bids. As a result, the calf went for seventy-five cents a pound. The runner-up calf, owned by the son of a Parr supporter, sold for twice that amount. The following year, the daughter of an anti-Parr man won the top prize for her calf, but not a single bid was offered. After that year, the annual auction was discontinued.[33]

Targeting children at livestock shows wasn't the only way Parr punished his opposition. He also used county welfare programs to let them know who was still in charge. "The county welfare department has been a disgraceful example of favoritism, discrimination and misuse of funds for political purposes and vote getting," a Duval grand jury report said. When doling out county funds, "no investigation has been made to determine actual need, but instead, only as to how the applicant voted." The grand jury investigated the school district's free meals program and "found that the parents of all children receiving free meals were so-called 'Old Party' members."[34] No one escaped Parr's attention when it came to loyalty—he demanded it, or else.

As a powerful and dominant figure in South Texas politics, Parr could easily target for retribution any individual who displeased him. But for all his power, he could not prevent the government agencies that were trying to bring him to justice. Legal proceedings against him were coming from all directions—both civil and criminal. The best he could do was to hire a battery of lawyers and oppose each proceeding tooth and nail in the courts. The civil suits alone would keep his attorneys busy for several years.

PART IV

DERAILED BY CIVIL AND CRIMINAL CASES

CHAPTER 16

CIVIL SUITS

Two back-to-back civil suits were filed against Parr in July 1955. The first was for money received in a circuitous route to pay his 1947 income tax bill. Records revealed that on January 13, 1947, a total of $60,000 had been withdrawn from the Duval County Interest and Sinking Fund, along with $45,000 from the Duval County Road Bond Series 1941 Sinking Fund, another $30,000 from the Duval County Special Road District No. 1 Fund, and also $45,000 from the Duval County Road Bond Series 1944 Sinking Fund. Each transaction took place at the Parr-owned Texas State Bank of Alice and on the same day the total amount ($180,000) had been deposited in the Duval County Road and Bridge Special Fund. The following day, two withdrawals were made on that fund ($162,000 and $10,500) and both were deposited to Parr's personal account. Records showed that George paid the IRS $181,319.81 on July 28, 1947, with a check drawn on his account.[1]

The civil suit filed by District Attorney Sam Burris also listed Thelma Parr as a defendant, because the money paid was for taxes levied on the community estate held by both of them. The former Texas State Bank of Alice was charged with "acting either fraudulently or with gross negligence when it allowed the public moneys of Duval county to be paid out illegally." The suit sought return of the $172,500 plus 6 percent interest per annum.[2]

In the second suit George and Thelma were sued for money "loaned" for purchase of the 55,711-acre Dobie Ranch in 1945. Attorney General Shepperd joined Burris in the suit to recover the money or confiscate the ranch. The county commissioners' court was asked to join in, but after three commissioners resigned and were replaced by their wives, Shepperd and Burris chose to pursue it on their own. Papers filed showed that George and Thelma received $500,000 in 1945 to purchase the Dobie

Ranch, spanning La Salle and Webb Counties, of which $416,138.52 was used to purchase the ranch and the remaining sum of $83,861.48 was placed in George and Thelma's bank account.[3] Complicating matters, Shepperd and Burris found it necessary to file suits in both counties because the sprawling ranch extended into two jurisdictions.

Owned by J. M. "Jim" Dobie, uncle of legendary Texas writer J. Frank Dobie, the ranch on the Nueces River ran from eastern La Salle County into Webb County. After Dobie went broke, the ranch was purchased through bankruptcy proceedings by an Illinois man named Griffin Watkins. After he died, the estate sold the ranch to Parr. Taking possession, Parr began spending money on improvements to provide a second home where he could hunt and raise cattle.

Turning his enclave into a fortress, Parr brought in truckloads of fence posts and barbed wire to close in miles of the property, including a public dirt road that cut through the property. Blockhouses were built at each road entrance with armed guards stationed to prevent anyone using the road without permission. The ranch house had burned down years before, so Parr built a new one. Selecting a new site, Parr sank a well that provided bitter water and erected a bunk house with a refrigerated room capable of holding whole deer carcasses.[4]

The Dobie Ranch suit was amended by the plaintiffs to include an additional five hundred thousand dollars for property rental fees and an unspecified amount for mineral rights. To eliminate any confusion as to who was suing, the amended brief listed Burris as the petitioner with Shepperd as the attorney of record. Parr's attorney filed a plea of privilege asking the La Salle County suit be transferred to Duval County. Attorney for Thelma Parr, Dean B. Kirkham of Corpus Christi, asked to have the suit against her moved to Nueces County, the county seat where she resided.[5]

Left out of the recovery suits, the Duval County commissioners' court hired attorney Arthur A. Klein to investigate and make recommendations on their position. Sensing trouble, Burris attended a commissioners' meeting to request they join in the suits, stating that any money recovered "will go back into the Duval County treasury." The commissioners said they needed time to read the Klein report.[6]

The report suggested that the commissioners file a motion to seek dismissal of the two suits and initiate their own. Agreeing, the commissioners hired Klein as their attorney with a five-thousand-dollar retainer and an agreement to pay him 15 percent of any funds recovered. The reaction from Burris was immediate. He labeled their actions as "an attempt to defeat efforts of the Internal Revenue bureau to collect income taxes allegedly owed by Parr." In his report, Klein said money given to Parr was merely a "loan" from the county, which had to be repaid. Burris said if the courts agreed, then "there would be no tax, no penalty or interest required."[7]

Complicating matters, when Klein filed suit on behalf of the commissioners, he did it in Laredo, located in Webb County. Assistant Attorney General Sidney Chandler, co-counsel with Burris on the recovery suits, wasn't surprised. "It is well known that some of Parr's strongest political allies are residents of Webb County," he said. Freedom Party leaders labeled the suit an "unnecessary waste of taxpayers money and a ruse to aid George Parr." They asked Attorney General Shepperd to seek ways to nullify Klein's contract with the commissioners.[8]

The Duval commissioners sat behind closed doors with attorneys on both sides in an effort to reach an agreement. Parr wasn't a participant during the three-hour conclave but made his presence known by sitting outside the room. As commissioners and attorneys came and went, Parr held whispered conversations with cronies and county officials passing in the hallway. No resolution was reached. Klein withdrew from the case the next day saying that "controversy" over the legality of his fee and the inevitability of protracted court action, combined with a recurrence of ulcers, forced his resignation.[9]

While the commissioners met to discuss hiring another lawyer, both Maria Leal and Judge Dan Tobin Jr. chose not to participate. Tobin admitted a "falling out" with the three remaining commissioners, resulting from a disagreement with Parr and having conferred with Burris and Shepperd on the recovery suits. "I've been called a turncoat," Tobin said, "but the meetings don't mean I'm going in politically with Sam or Shepperd." That didn't rule out the possibility of his joining the Shepperd-Burris suits as a plaintiff. "At this stage of the game," he said, "I believe I would." When asked by a reporter if the suit filed by Klein on behalf of the commissioners' court had been Parr's idea, Tobin nodded without elaborating.[10]

Acting without two absent members, the three commissioners agreed to hire Klein's assistant, Gordon Gibson of Laredo, in their recovery action. As soon as Gibson took over, Burris filed a plea of abatement in Laredo, contending that the commissioners' suit should be halted on the ground that prior action in his two suits took precedence.[11] Sorting out motions filed in courts spread over four counties was a task that would have been confusing for any judge, but not Judge Frank Fulgham, sitting in for Judge Laughlin in San Diego. Fulgham threw out Parr's motion of jurisdiction, nullifying the state's plea of abatement. The judge was only interested in hearing arguments on the plea of privilege.

"I'm confused, really I am," Parr's attorney Luther Jones pleaded. "I want it made clear to the court, judge, what is going on. There have been so many motions and pleas filed."

"It is clear to the court," Fulgham said firmly. "Proceed."[12]

During testimony, Givens Parr, vice president of the bank, cashier B. F. Donald Jr., assistant cashier Jewel Mayfield, and Mildred Daniel, who worked the microfilm machine used to record canceled checks, were called. No one knew where the records were or how they mysteriously had disappeared.[13] Fulgham declared a recess, telling the lawyers to file briefs, after which he would hand down his ruling.

Before Fulgham had a chance to render his decision, Judge Laughlin was back on the bench. Having pledged he was no longer a Parr man, he now had an opportunity to live up to his promise. Acting on a motion filed by Burris, Laughlin issued a restraining order against the county commissioners preventing them from taking any further action in their recovery suit. The order also barred any payments made to their attorney, Gordon Gibson. Laughlin then scheduled a hearing to decide if the restraining order should be dropped or replaced with an injunction. A few days later, Parr received bad news. His change of venue motion to have the suit initiated by Burris moved from La Salle County to Duval County had been denied and a trial date set for October 31, 1955.[14]

During the six-hour hearing on the restraining order in Laughlin's court, arguments often lead to heated debates. Gibson contended that the commissioners' suit was the only one allowing a lien to be placed on Parr's property prior to a federal one—a valid point. "I think you boys are throwing Duval county's rights out the window," he said, referring to the Burris-Shepperd suits. At the end of the hearing, Laughlin ruled in favor of the original suits brought by the state, granting the injunction and effectively giving Burris and Shepperd the green light. Three days later, the Duval County commissioners held their regular monthly meeting, during which they hired former district attorney Raeburn Norris to represent them in further actions.[15]

Barred from being paid by the commissioners, Gibson filed an appeal with the court of civil appeals in San Antonio. Meanwhile, Everett Looney, acting on behalf of George and Thelma Parr, filed a motion in Laredo to seek an injunction against Burris and Shepperd from proceeding with their suits. Judge R. D. Wright in Laredo granted a temporary injunction, which along with Laughlin's injunction brought all civil actions to a standstill. Shepperd filed a petition in the Texas Supreme Court asking them to clarify who had authority to go after the Parrs in the various recovery suits.[16]

While the Shepperd petition was being considered, Burris asked Judge Laughlin for a trial date on one of the suits. "Aren't you enjoined?" he asked Burris, referring to the Laredo ruling. Burris said he didn't feel the order was valid, adding that he might have to get clarification. Despite the uncertainty, Laughlin set a trial date for December 1955. Further complicating matters, Parr's attorneys approached yet another judge to block the Laredo suit. After studying the plea of abatement, district judge H. D. Barrow of Jourdanton, denied the motion and set a trial date on the La Salle County recovery suit for the end of October.[17]

Motions began flooding courts in three counties, all with one purpose in mind—either to stop or delay the suits. To counter, Burris and Shepperd papered the courts with their own motions. In a speech delivered before an association of dairymen, Shepperd said he would file more suits to recover more than three million dollars that had been "misappropriated or stolen" in Duval. Hoping to break the deadlock, Judge Wright in Laredo agreed to rehear arguments on the temporary injunction. After briefs were submitted, Wright rendered his ruling. Nothing changed when he reinstated the temporary injunction to prevent the state from prosecuting their suits.[18] Everything was back to square one, but two new twists were added to liven up the cases.

The Duval grand jury indicted Parr and his attorney, Luther Jones, for the suborning of perjury in connection with the recovery suits. The charge—eliciting perjury of another person—involved the affidavit given by Duval County treasurer Victor Leal. In his signed statement, Leal said he hadn't authorized filing of the suits against the Parrs. The indictment charged Parr and Jones with "designedly" inducing Leal to commit perjury in swearing to the affidavit.[19]

Then the Duval County commissioners dropped a bombshell. They had been divided, with two members voting the Parr line and two voting against, but county judge Dan Tobin Jr. decided to break the tie by casting a vote favoring the anti-Parr duo. Three actions were involved in the voting: First, they decided to negate their contract with Gordon Gibson; second, they voted to give Burris and Shepperd authority to dismiss the suit they had filed to counter the state's cases; and third, they gave the state full authority to prosecute any recovery suits on behalf of Duval.[20]

The commissioners' rulings may have been intended to clear up the jurisdictional matter and get the recovery suits moving again, but Parr was not a man to be taken lightly. Burris filed motions to have Gibson's contract canceled and for a restraining order on the commissioners' Laredo case, but his briefs were quickly followed by motions filed by Parr. Gibson filed a cross-action in Judge Laughlin's court, claiming that the commissioners had acted "in haste and without proper information" when they canceled his contract. He also petitioned the Texas Supreme Court to set aside the suspension of county commissioner Estella Garcia, whose replacement, Tomas Molina, had voted to have his contract nullified. Gibson also wanted Burris and Shepperd prevented from picking the county where the recovery suits would be held.[21] While the Texas Supreme Court was considering the petitions, Judge Laughlin issued a restraining order against Parr, his ex-wife, and their attorneys. The order enjoined them from taking further action until the matter was settled in the higher courts. When finally rendered, the Texas Supreme Court ruled that the suspension was legal; therefore, any actions taken by the present commissioners were valid. They had every right, according to the decision, to drop out of their recovery suit and transfer power to Burris and Shepperd.[22] Heading into the New Year, recovery suits against Parr and his ex-wife were still alive in Webb, La Salle, and Duval Counties.

Maneuvering, jousting, and fighting for a legal foothold to thwart Parr's efforts to delay any recovery trial, or at least have it taken from Webb County, the state filed for relief in the court of civil appeals. Adding another attorney, R. D. Moorhead of Austin, to the roster of his legal team, Parr fought the appeal. Two petitions were to be heard. One was the refusal of Judge Wright in Laredo to dismiss the Duval commissioners' suit; the second was the injunction issued by Judge Wright preventing the state from prosecuting its two recovery suits.[23]

Agreeing with the state, the appeals court reversed Wright and dissolved the injunctions blocking Burris and Shepperd. The panel of three judges also declared that La Salle and Jim Wells Counties had jurisdiction in the suits. With the high court ruling, on a motion filed by the state, Judge Laughlin released Parr and his ex-wife from the injunction he had imposed. This allowed the state to begin taking pretrial depositions on the long-delayed recovery suits.[24]

The first deposition was from former Texas State Bank cashier Wallace Roach. His testimony focused on identifying copies of checks, deposit slips, bank statements, and drafts cleared through the bank as depository for Duval County funds.[25] According to the *Alice Daily Echo*, next on the stand was Parr, who was in a jovial mood during the two hours he was questioned by Burris. Establishing background information before getting into transactions involving the Dobie Ranch, Burris questioned Parr on his marriage and his political hold on Duval County.

"How many times were you married?" Burris asked. The question was innocent enough, but Parr was hesitant in being forthcoming.

"I don't recall," Parr answered.

"Are you saying you didn't marry her a second time?" Burris asked, referring to Thelma. Unfortunately, Burris had no knowledge of Parr having married another woman in between his two marriages to Thelma.

"I wouldn't say that," Parr slyly replied.

Burris then began lengthy questioning concerning the political situation in Duval and Parr's role in dominating elections.

"You pretty well dominated political affairs of Duval county in 1944, 1945 and 1946," Burris challenged the witness.

"That's a pretty broad statement," Parr replied. "Do you mean as the honorable Jake Floyd in Alice? I didn't dominate in the sense of telling everybody what to do."

"Was there ever any candidate elected not backed by you?" Burris asked.

"That's all dependent on public opinion," Parr answered. "I had to put up people attractive to the voters to win."

"You mean they were free and independent?" Burris fired back.

"Well, if you don't know that now, Sammy, you will find it out."

"Yeah, I found it out in 1952," Burris retorted before continuing. "These men on the commissioners court were all men who had been supported by the machine, isn't that true?"

"Didn't know of any machine," Parr answered coolly.

"Don't argue, just answer the question," Burris shot back. That remark brought Luther Jones to his feet, who objected that his client was being lectured.

Having failed to succeed in getting the political boss to admit to anything substantial, Burris then turned his questioning to matters directly concerned with Parr's purchase of the Dobie Ranch and where he acquired the necessary funds to pay for it. According to Parr, he had paid "around $450,000" for the ranch, partly with his own money and part borrowed from the county. This was the crux of the matter, because if it was established he had only "borrowed" the county funds, then the only action against him would be for recovery of the loans, not income tax evasion.

In Parr's version of the loan's history he said it began in a conversation with then county judge Dan Tobin Jr., who later told Parr that the commissioners' court had approved the loan. Parr said the transaction was a five-year loan, divided between five notes of $100,000 each, all bearing a 1 percent interest rate. He added that only one $28,000 interest payment had been paid. He said that his lawyer, Ed Lloyd, had prepared the notes and assured Parr they were legal.

Burris questioned Parr as to how the county funds were transferred to him, and how the money went from him to the seller of the ranch. Parr said he "wasn't sure" how the money had gotten to the St. Louis Union Trust Co., which handled the sale. Copies of two $250,000 checks were introduced, both made out to the Wilder Construction Company. One was endorsed "Wilder Construction Company by G. B. Parr," but Parr wouldn't swear it was his signature. He said that Wilder Construction was a partnership with Harry Wilder, Atlee Parr, D.C. Chapa, and himself. After Burris finished, Luther Jones excused Parr without asking a single question.[26]

Following the depositions, events began escalating at a quicker pace. Parr's attorneys filed for a rehearing in the court of civil appeals but were denied. Receiving notice from the high court, Judge Laughlin set a trial date for the $172,500 suit against Parr, his ex-wife, and the Texas State Bank. Having cornered Parr in the legal battle, Burris and Shepperd were anxious to bag their prey before he could wiggle out. They filed for a summary judgment in the civil suit before Laughlin. In effect, they contended that since there were no questions of fact in the case because Parr had admitted in his deposition he owed the money to the county, then a judgment for that amount should be granted.[27]

Laughlin set a hearing date on the motion, but before that Burris and Shepperd were in Cotulla, Webb County, filing the same motion to end the recovery suit there. Down to their last legal maneuver, Parr's attorneys filed an appeal in the Texas Supreme Court for a review of the decision by the court of civil appeals.[28] Parr was getting desperate; there was little hope the high court would grant him relief. To survive he had to try a different tactic, and as usual, he always had another card up his sleeve.

Before any motions could be heard, Parr pulled off an end-run catching everyone off balance. As he was about to have the door slammed shut on him, Parr announced he had reached a settlement with the Duval County commissioners. The agreement called for Parr and Thelma to give the county a warranty deed to the Dobie Ranch in exchange for dropping all claims against them. The commissioners also agreed to drop claims against the Texas State Bank and to grant Parr a one-year lease on the ranch to give him time to settle accounts and dispose of the cattle. The lease stipulated it could be canceled if the ranch was sold during the year.[29]

The news was unsettling to Burris because he just lost a co-plaintiff in the suits. The commissioners instructed the county attorney to "dismiss and non-suit" all litigation against the Parrs, and they also revoked all "prior authority given the district attorney, the attorney general, or any assistant attorney general." Despite the agreement, the attorney general's office said it would continue the suits. "The deal placed legal title to the Dobie ranch in the County of Duval," Assistant Attorney General Sidney Chandler said, "and the deal did no more than that." Since Burris was plaintiff in the recovery suits, Chandler claimed, "no one but . . . Burris can dismiss the suit," adding that if county officials failed to cooperate, they could be sued.[30]

The state's position improved when the court of civil appeals ruled that the state had the right to bring suits in Jim Wells and La Salle Counties. Five days later, the Texas Supreme Court upheld a lower court decision dissolving the injunction that had halted the two suits in a jurisdictional dispute. Burris and Shepperd could now go after Parr's money in both counties. Burris gloated, "Maybe this decision will teach Luther E. Jones, Everett Looney, and George B. Parr some law so that next time we tell them what the law is they will listen to us."[31]

Judge Laughlin reacted to the decisions by rescheduling the summary judgment motion. But this was Parr country, and nothing ever went as planned. Duval County attorney Luna filed a motion on the eve of the hearing to dismiss the suit as instructed by the county commissioners. Countering, Burris filed an amended petition asking that eighteen more defendants be added to the recovery suit. He wanted to include anyone remotely connected to the case so as to assure that no one else filed their own motions.[32]

As if all this wasn't enough, another suit was filed before Laughlin. Acting on behalf of the First State Bank of San Diego, attorney Ed G. Lloyd sought collection of twenty-four thousand dollars in principal, interest, and attorney fees on a series of notes Parr had signed in 1954. Parr had put up a 3,728 acre parcel of Duval County land as collateral and now the bank wanted to foreclose. Although this latest action had nothing to do with the recovery suits already in progress, it did affect the federal government's tax case against Parr. The suit contended that the government's lien on Parr's property was secondary to the bank's lien. Laughlin caught a break when a motion by federal attorneys to move the case into federal court was granted.[33]

If Laughlin had any thoughts of holding the hearing, his hopes were dashed when Parr's lawyers filed for a rehearing on the decision passed down by the court of civil appeals. The request was eventually denied, but it delayed the recovery suits. Undaunted, minutes before the summary judgment hearing, Parr's attorneys filed two more motions. One contended that the recovery suit was "being prosecuted without proper authority," and the second was another plea in abatement. Both Burris's and Parr's attorneys asked for another delay in order to sort out the files that were getting thicker each passing day. After listening to both sides for less than ninety seconds, Laughlin granted the postponement.[34]

The second recovery suit in Cotulla wasn't faring much better. To cover all legal bases, Burris and Shepperd filed an amended suit to add more defendants to the already bulging roster. The Duval County commissioners' court, the county treasurer, and the U.S. government were all now involved because of the new filing. The federal government was added as a precaution to clear the title on the Dobie Ranch due to the IRS liens.[35]

Back in Duval County, more complications arose when a county commissioner submitted a resolution to have the order rescinded releasing Parr from other claims after signing over the Dobie Ranch deed. Having enough anti-Parr votes, in a split decision, the commissioners voted to kill the liability release on Parr, but nothing was said about returning the Dobie Ranch deed back to Parr. More paperwork followed because the commissioners were defendants in the recovery suit; now they wanted to be plaintiffs.[36]

By the middle of summer 1956, all pleadings and motions had run their course. The first decision came from Judge H. D. Barrow, presiding over the $1.4-million suit in Jourdanton. After a full-day hearing, Barrow rendered a summary judgment giving Duval County title to the Dobie Ranch. "Parr said he borrowed the money from the county to buy the land," the judge said. "Well, you can't borrow money from the county. Just like you can't borrow money from a bank from the janitor."[37] As for "a whole bushel of other things," such as rental and oil lease fees, Barrow set a trial date to settle the rest of the case.[38]

A year after filing of the $172,000 recovery case in Alice, Judge Laughlin was finally ready to hear arguments on a summary judgment against Parr. After dismissing every one of Parr's motions, Laughlin denied the state its summary judgment and set a trial date to settle the recovery suit before a jury. Laughlin noted in his ruling that he rarely granted a summary judgment.[39]

Just when everything appeared to be headed for a solution, another roadblock was thrown up by Parr. When the Duval commissioners made their agreement with Parr on the Dobie Ranch, which was later rescinded, Parr brought suit in Laredo against Duval County to uphold the one-year lease agreement. Judge R. D. Wright in Laredo entered a judgment for Parr, and ten days later, during which the state hadn't appealed, declared his ruling final. Both Burris and Dan Tobin Jr. objected since neither had received notice of the original judgment claiming they learned of the judgment only after reading about it in the newspaper.[40]

Acting quickly, Attorney General Shepperd filed a motion in the court of civil appeals, asking that Judge Wright, Parr, and others be cited

for contempt of court. The brief stated that Wright did not have jurisdiction—but more importantly, "a false certificate of service was made"
indicating that county judge Dan Tobin Jr. had received notice of the
judgment. Moving against the judgment itself, the state filed a writ of
error with the court of civil appeals, asking the judgment be set aside.[41]
Once again, Parr's attorneys were back in the higher courts.

Although Judge Barrow in Cotulla awarded the Dobie Ranch to
Duval County, this still left the question as to rental fees and other revenue that George and Thelma had to pay. Before this was heard, Thelma
settled with the Duval commissioners. Including her share of oil royalties,
rent, interest, and back taxes on the Dobie property, she agreed to pay
$338,307. After a day-long hearing, Barrow agreed to the settlement and
entered a judgment against George, ordering him to pay Duval County
$300,000 as his share. He also ruled that since Duval had always held
title, federal tax liens placed on the Dobie Ranch were not binding. As
expected, Parr filed an appeal.[42] On October 13, 1956, Duval County
took physical possession of the Dobie Ranch. The county installed new
gate locks and posted five men to guard the property. Burris said that
once the federal liens on the ranch were cleared, Duval would sell the
property, which could bring one and a half million dollars.[43]

The Duval commissioners invited the local Boy Scout troop and a
Future Farmers of America chapter to use the property for overnight
camping trips. Other organizations were permitted to use the land if
they requested. But Parr wouldn't give up without a fight. He filed for a
rehearing before Judge Barrow but was denied. Still not content to let the
matter rest, Parr filed an appeal with the Fourth Court of Civil Appeals
in San Antonio.[44]

Heading into 1957, Parr lost another piece of property in a court
action. The 3,728-acre parcel formerly known as the William Hoffman
Ranch was located a short distance from Parr's San Diego home. The
First State Bank of San Diego received a judgment to recover notes owed
by Parr, and the ranch was put up for auction. With the auction held
on the steps of the Duval County courthouse, the bank opened with
a bid for the thirty-one thousand dollars Parr owed. Armondo Canales, a local rancher, won with a bid of ninety-six thousand dollars. The
bank received its money for the notes, and the balance was applied to the
six-hundred-thousand-dollar federal government tax lien.[45]

On February 14, 1957, the Duval County commissioners announced that the Dobie Ranch would be sold at public auction on May 7. The federal tax lien hadn't been settled yet, but the commissioners were hopeful it would be settled before the auction. Their hopes were premature, however, because Parr still had an appeal pending on the Cotulla ruling that awarded the ranch to Duval County. On July 19, 1957, the court of civil appeals reversed the lower court ruling and ordered a new trial for the recovery suit against the Dobie Ranch. The sticking point with the appeals court was that not all the money used to purchase the ranch had come from county funds. Records showed that the Parrs had used $135,000 of their own money for the purchase. After receiving title, they obtained money from the county for the amount they had laid out. In effect, the court ruled, the Parrs had received county funds after purchasing the ranch, making it a debt owed to the county not connected with the property.[46] The recovery suit was once again back to square one.

Despite the ruling, Duval County was going ahead with the Dobie Ranch auction. The IRS agreed to allow the property to be sold to help satisfy their tax lien. Once the property was sold, the agreement called for the proceeds to be placed in escrow until all litigation had been settled. But another hitch developed when the Texas Supreme Court held that it had found no reversible error in the court of civil appeals opinion. Without offering a written opinion or giving its reasons, the higher court upheld Parr's right to another trial.[47]

While George kept up the fight to prevent the sale of the Dobie Ranch, Thelma distanced herself from the recovery suits. Already a wealthy woman, drawing close to seven thousand dollars a month as her share in the Parr-Delaney Oil Company, she began paying Duval County the debt she owed on the agreed settlement. Owing $388,000 as her share, she made a $40,000 payment, followed by a second payment of $60,000 in March 1957. Later that year, she paid $200,000 on the debt and agreed to pay an additional $6,000 a month until her obligation was met.[48]

Parr had fought the recovery suits tooth and nail, keeping the case alive for several years, but these were civil matters. The criminal cases being readied against him were entirely different because he stood a fairly good chance of losing his freedom. The income tax evasion case had stalled, but the federal government still had the mail fraud charges against him, which they decided to prosecute first.

CHAPTER 17
MAIL FRAUD

With the tax evasion case on the back burner, the federal government's mail fraud case seemed to be the best way to convict Parr. Federal prosecutors saw merit in J. L. McDonald's suggestion of going after Parr for using the U.S. mail as an integral part of the scheme to drain funds from local school board accounts. The core of the government's argument was that in order to steal money the defendants had to mail out tax statements to collect funds. Texas was also going after Parr for stealing more than one thousand dollars from the Benavides Independent School System funds—a case similar to the federal one. Parr was cornered, feeling his troubles, including federal ones, were the result of a personal attack by Governor Shivers. "He's used everything in his power to gut me," he told reporters. "In a certain sense, I guess he has."[1]

Already two years old, in January 1956 the mail fraud case was finally brought before a Houston federal grand jury. Subpoenas were issued, but names were withheld. "We are dealing with some evasive witnesses," U.S. district attorney Malcolm Wilkey said, "and we don't want to warn the opposition." Witnesses included Parr's brother-in-law B. Green Moffett, employees at the former Texas State Bank, U.S. postal inspector William E. Main, who spent ten months on the investigation, and Diego Heras, who received immunity from prosecution.[2]

The grand jury sessions lasted over a month. Oil firms paying taxes to the Benavides school district were subpoenaed, along with school officials and employees. Anyone remotely connected to tax notices sent out, remittances collected, and funds deposited was called. Even Freedom Party members, who had no connection to the tax chain, were called for background on the political situation.[3] Wilkey was taking no chances as he led the grand jury in the direction that would result in indictments. Notably, Parr was never called to testify.

After hearing sixty-eight witnesses, on March 6, 1956, the federal grand jury handed down twenty indictments for mail fraud and conspiracy. Parr headed the list—followed by eight others, along with the Texas State Bank of Alice and the San Diego State Bank. The indictments charged the defendants with formulating a scheme to defraud taxpayers by using the U.S. mail to send out tax statements and receive payments. They claimed vouchers and checks were issued on school funds for equipment, supplies, and services, none of which ever benefited the school district. Forging endorsements on checks, issuing false reports, which were also sent by mail, and using the two banks to accomplish the thefts, were given as methods used to illegally convert school district funds for their private use.[4] All nine defendants, represented by Percy Foreman, pleaded not guilty. The trial date was set for November 5, 1956, in the court of federal judge Allen Burroughs Hannay in Houston.[5]

To prepare for the trial, Wilkey assigned two assistants to interview potential witnesses. Although Wilkey described his action as "routine pretrial preparation," many who followed the political situation in Duval felt the federal prosecutor wasn't taking any chances that witnesses might suddenly disappear. Meanwhile, Parr's attorneys had their own pretrial work. By order of Judge Hannay, government records concerning the case were ordered delivered to the defense. They filled two mail carts, giving Parr's legal team a formidable task in preparing for trial.[6]

A month before trial, Hannay moved it up two days. Unfazed by the short delay, Wilkey issued subpoenas for thirty witnesses to appear in Houston for the trial. The government witness list would jump to 103, with the defense calling an additional fifty. The reason for the delay was because several defendants were running for public office or serving as election judges in the November election. Among those running for office was George Parr, Democratic candidate for Duval County sheriff.[7]

Leading the defense, heavy-hitting Houston attorney Percy Forman brought his no-fear-of-the-opposition attitude into the courtroom. In his remarkable career, he handled close to one thousand capital crime cases with only fifty-five sentenced to prison and, even more remarkably, only one getting the death penalty. A millionaire from his law practice, he represented such front-page cases as James Earl Ray, Jack Ruby, and Nago Alaniz, who was acquitted in the Buddy Floyd murder. Foreman's tactic was to ignore the facts of the case and attack others instead. "You should never allow the defendant to be tried. Try someone else—the husband, the lover, the police or, if the case has social implications, society generally," he said, "but never the defendant."[8] The "others" in this case were Attorney General Shepperd and Jake Floyd, both of whom Foreman would accuse of staging a "political persecution" against his client, who he claimed was innocent. Wilkey, who was later appointed by Nixon to the court of appeals and would rule against publication of the Pentagon Papers, told the jury he would call witnesses to tell "who George Parr and these other people are . . . how a kingdom was built, and how it was used by one man to perpetuate himself."[9]

Foreman set the tone of the defense when the first government witness testified. T. J. O'Connor, business manager of the Texas Education Agency in Austin, was asked by Wilkey to identify annual reports of expenditures submitted by the Benavides school district. Foreman objected on the ground that the prosecution had not shown any official authority existed requiring filing of such reports. His objection was overruled. Wilkey then called Texas Ranger Joe Bridge to testify about a sixteen-page list of 268 names attached to one of the reports identifying persons receiving payments from school funds. Wilkey began by bringing in a large map of Duval and Jim Wells Counties, but Foreman objected to the map having large red lettering for Duval and smaller red lettering for Jim Wells. After Wilkey tacked on pieces of paper to cover the letters, Foreman objected that the map had not been identified by experts as a true map of the area. His objection was upheld and the map was scrapped.[10]

Wilkey may have felt intimidated by the ever-watchful Foreman as he questioned Ranger Bridge, but not one objection was made. Bridge said he searched Duval County for two weeks trying to find persons on the list. The search was thorough because he talked to "county officers, sheriffs, filling station people, merchants and tax collectors" in every Duval community. "No one on the list did I find living in Duval County," he said. Postmasters from the Duval area were paraded to the stand to testify they had never heard of anyone on the payment lists.[11]

Having established payments had been made to fictitious persons, Wilkey proceeded to show how checks were cashed. Carl Williams, chief teller at the Texas State Bank, said former Benavides school secretary Diego Heras "once or twice a month" would bring him "bunches" of checks totaling as much as twelve thousand dollars. "I asked him to endorse the checks and he refused," Williams said. "I told Mr. Donald [bank cashier and codefendant] and he told me to go ahead and cash the checks without the endorsement." Other bank employees testified that some of the school account checks were countersigned by George Parr.[12]

Federal offices were closed on Veterans Day, but Hannay's court remained open. Joe D. Vaello, a Benavides construction company owner, testified about work his firm did for the school district. Having testified in three other trials against Duval leaders, Vaello spent two months in courtrooms that year. "I'm getting a little tired of it," he said. "I hope I don't have to stay here too long." He said that between 1949 and 1950, his construction firm built a school cafeteria and band building for the school district. When asked about two thousand dollars in checks to subcontractors for excavations, ground leveling, sidewalks, and installation of a sprinkler system, Vaello said he knew of no other contractors working on the site and the jobs described had never been done.[13]

Laughter broke out in the courtroom when Renaldo A. Maldonado testified. Wilkey asked him about a $589.50 check issued in 1950 to a person with his name for installation of a sewer line for the school district. He denied receiving such a payment and hadn't performed any work for the school district. On cross-examination, Foreman asked, "Are you sure you weren't in the sewer business in 1950?" At the time the check had been issued, Maldonado was eleven years old.[14]

The jury then heard testimony that checks remitted by various companies to pay their school taxes had never been deposited in the school account. Former tax office employee Ramiro Morin testified he was instructed by the defendant D.C. Chapa, former tax assessor-collector for the school district, to cash tax checks totaling fifteen thousand dollars at a local bank and bring the money back to the tax office. Under cross examination, the best Foreman could establish was that Morin did not know who received the money after that.[15]

Payroll checks drawn on the school district account for Nita Alva Garza and Maria Elva Garcia, daughters of two defendants, were introduced as evidence. The government then brought a Catholic nun, registrar of the Incarnate Word College in San Antonio, to testify that Ms. Garza was a student at the college during the time she was on the school district payroll. The director of the Breckenridge Hospital School of Nursing in

Austin testified that Ms. Garcia was a student at the nursing school while receiving a paycheck as an employee of the school district.[16]

Although Parr's name had been mentioned only a few times, Wilkey was methodically closing in on him, attempting to fit together pieces of the conspiracy puzzle. Microfilmed records of checks processed at Parr's San Diego Bank were the next topic to be discussed. A former bank cashier testified that records, kept in the vault with the bank's cash, were missing. Among missing records were copies of school district checks handled by both Parr banks.[17]

Checks drawn on school district accounts weren't the only way funds were diverted, Wilkey contended. He brought in two gas station attendants who testified pumping gas into vehicles owned by persons not employed by the school district, who then charged it to the school district's account. When asked who authorized the charges, both said: "Oscar Carrillo Sr." former secretary of the school board and one of the defendants.[18]

The prosecution inched closer to Parr's involvement when his brother-in-law B. G. Moffett took the stand. His testimony lasted only a few minutes, but it painted a picture of nepotism within the Parr empire. Moffett testified he received fifteen thousand dollars from the school district for legal services between 1948 and 1950. During that period, Parr was school board president. Further questioning revealed that Moffett never attended a school board meeting, never discussed legal matters with board members, and could not recall doing any legal work for the school district. Moffett said he had drawn the salary for several months while at the same time serving as judge of county court at law in Corpus Christi. The prosecution presented evidence of other schemes to bilk the school district, including carpentry and sheetrock work that was never done and furniture that was never delivered to any school.[19]

Microfilms of checks processed through Parr's two banks were missing, but records from other banks were intact. Some defendants had accounts at various banks throughout the area, allowing the prosecution to piece together damaging evidence. Defendant Octavio Saenz held an account in nearby Hebronville. It showed fifty-three checks—totaling $3,530 drawn on school district funds—deposited by him. Several checks introduced into evidence bore Parr's countersignature and one was signed only by him.[20]

The prosecution's main witness was Diego Heras, deputy tax assessor for the Benavides school district who had provided J. L. McDonald with sworn affidavits that had started the inquiry. He repeated under oath that he had been writing checks on school accounts and turning them over to Parr or William Benson, auditor for the school district. When Heras was asked to identify Parr's signature on sixteen checks totaling more than ten thousand dollars, "a small vein in George Parr's forehead began to stand out noticeably."[21]

Under a relentless, lengthy cross-examination by Foreman, Heras admitted taking sixteen checks from the tax office "for my own protection." For seven hours Foreman bore down on Heras, choosing to discredit him personally instead of attempting to dispute damaging evidence he had given. Although the following day was Thanksgiving, Judge Hannay ordered an all-day session, saying he was a "Texan who will observe the Texas Thanksgiving next week."[22] With Heras being grilled in the hot seat, Foreman tried painting a damaging picture of the witness's character. Isabel Brown reported in the *Houston Post*:

"Did you ask a woman employee of the school district to steal
some checks for you in 1952 after you had been fired?
"Did you retain any of the money you received from the fraudulent
checks you said you cashed?
"Have you ever practiced signing George Parr's name and
boasted that you could sign it perfectly?
"Did you frequent El Caliche, El Ranchito and other bars, dance
halls and bawdy houses?
"Did a Galveston psychiatrist diagnose your condition as a manic-
depressive psychosis in April, 1953?
"Did you go to old Mexico in April, 1953, to see a doctor and
get him to prescribe magic powders?
"Did you ever tell an infamous lie by saying that George Parr had
sent you with $15,000 to bribe an FBI agent?
"Did you ever have a courtesan at a San Diego bawdy house
followed constantly and give her money from time to time?"[23]

Each question was answered "No" by Heras, but astute courtroom observers knew that Foreman was only laying groundwork for rebuttal witnesses who would follow.

Having circled around Parr's involvement in the mail fraud scheme, the prosecution closed in by calling William M. Benson to the stand. Former Benavides school district auditor and Parr's personal auditor at one time, Benson was in a position to offer damaging, firsthand testimony of how the system of graft worked so well for years. Totaling the amount diverted from school funds, Benson arrived at a figure of at least $220,000 taken over a four-year period. Even more insightful was his testimony relating to conversations he had with Parr. Recalling when indictments were handed down against Hidalgo County officials, Benson was worried.

"Nothing's going to happen in Duval County," a confident Parr had told the auditor. "I've got control here."

During his testimony, Benson said Parr had accused him of "making some money" on a school-building project in Freer. "He told me he didn't mind my making some money, but he wanted to know about it."[24]

According to the *San Antonio Express*, when Foreman pressed for details under cross-examination, Benson added that "[Parr] said I was making some money on the side at Freer—good honest graft, in other words. What I made I made honestly and paid taxes on it."

"You don't call graft stealing?" Foreman asked.

"Not good honest graft like that," Benson replied. "Everything I made for 20 years I made honestly and paid taxes."[25]

When Foreman reminded Benson that he could be indicted for his "honest graft," the courtroom burst into laughter with the auditor's reply: "If they indicted everyone who is connected with the political machine down there, who would they get as witnesses?" Before leaving the witness stand, Benson stated that Parr paid taxes on a reported annual income of fifty thousand dollars, most of which had come from oil royalties.[26]

Before resting its case, the prosecution called FBI handwriting expert Earl Williams to the stand. Foreman offered to stipulate that signatures on school district checks were those of Parr, but Wilkey refused the offer. Foreman then tried to disqualify Williams as an expert, but he was overruled. Foreman objected more than two hundred times during the trial—every time he was overruled by Judge Hannay, except for the Duval map issue and a visual display with paper strips. After testifying that twenty school district checks issued to non-existent persons were countersigned by Parr, Williams was asked by Foreman if Diego Heras had signed any. "I was not able to determine whether he did or not," Williams answered.[27]

Concluding that the chief witness against Parr had been Heras, Foreman stayed true to his motto of "trying anyone but the defendant." His first witness, former San Diego bar operator Diego Navajar began discrediting Heras by calling him a drunk and an active participant in the check-cashing scheme. He said Heras frequented his bar so often—and drank to excess on each occasion—that he was labeled *El Borracho* (The Drunkard) by patrons. Shifting blame to Heras for missing school district funds, Foreman got Navajar to admit he had regularly been paid from twenty-five to forty dollars for cashing school district checks for Heras.[28]

Deputy school district tax collector Hilda Gonzales testified next. The previous year she testified to the grand jury that when tax checks came by mail to the office nobody touched them until D.C. Chapa arrived. After opening the mail, Chapa would handle the check deposits. Now she told a different story. She endorsed checks, made out bank deposits, and cashed some checks, keeping the cash in the tax office—at times as much as fifteen thousand dollars. She also said Heras was "very good" at forging signatures. Under cross-examination, Gonzales said she "couldn't remember" anything she told the grand jury because she was pregnant at the time.[29]

Continuing to focus on the probability that Heras may have been the culprit all along, Foreman brought Velia O. Bridges, another former tax office worker, to the stand. Her testimony mirrored that of Gonzales's when she said Heras often signed school district checks with another person's name. Her testimony also conflicted with what she had told the grand jury. Once again, the phrase "I don't remember" was repeated during cross-examination. Bridges said it was easy to open the school district post office mail box. "You could fool around with it a little and it would open," she said. In addition, she said the combinations to the mail box and the tax office vault were "written on the wall of the school district office."[30]

The only defendant to take the stand was O. P. Carrillo. He wanted to explain why the school district paid for his law office furniture. He said the school district hired him to collect delinquent taxes. "They simply paid my salary checks to the furniture store until the debt was paid off," he explained. After his testimony the defense rested, and Judge Hannay allotted each side six hours for final arguments.[31]

Even the government's closing arguments became a bone of contention for Foreman, who continued raising objections to disrupt the
rhythm of the prosecutor's presentation. When a six-by-three-foot board
with strips of paper tacked on it, each to be removed as the prosecution
gave its ten-point outline, was brought into the courtroom, Foreman was
on his feet. "The removal of the strips of paper one at a time during the
government's arguments is a sort of verbal strip tease," he argued. "We
would like to have more time to prepare a motion picture to use in our
arguments, and perhaps have a band for the finale." Hannay ordered the
strips removed, took one look at the board, and ruled it could not be
shown to the jury.[32]

Having targeted Diego Heras as the individual who should have been
on trial instead of his clients, Foreman used his closing arguments to
vilify persons he considered behind the plot to persecute Parr and his
associates. "Why are we here in this federal court after five weeks of
testimony?" he asked. "We are here because Johnny Benny Shepperd,
within the term of his office, hasn't been able to put any of these people in
jail. For the last three years, Shepperd has been traveling around the state
and singing like Elvis Presley, 'George Parr ain't nothing but a hound
dog,'" he said, bringing a smattering of giggles from the jury. "John Ben
Shepperd wanted to make a reputation for prosecuting Parr so he could
get elected to the U.S. Senate. But at the end of this time . . . , Shepperd's
name isn't on any ballot."[33]

Foreman's attack continued against those he accused of being responsible for the "political persecution" resulting in "about 450 of the best
people in the county" to be indicted. None of them was in jail, he
concluded, "Because these cases, these facts, stink." Picking another target for the jury to consider, he said, "Jake Floyd's offices have been the
headquarters for the prosecution."[34] With that remark, Wilkey sprang
to his feet and objected. "This is false," he shouted. "I resent his sly
implications."[35]

Sensing a full-pitched battle ensuing, Judge Hannay ordered the jury to
leave the room, but Wilkey was so hot under the collar that he began arguing before the jurors left. "Will you wait until the jury retires?" Foreman
demanded. With the jury gone, Wilkey vehemently protested that Foreman was being allowed to make false remarks concerning the state cases
against two of the defendants—D.C. Chapa and B. F. (Tom) Donald Jr.—

both of whom had been convicted and sentenced to five years.

"Like the dog that lost his tail, Mr. Wilkey is jumping at conclusions," Foreman said.

"All I said was that little Johnny Ben Shepperd hadn't been able to put any of them in jail."

"The cases are on appeal," Wilkey told the judge, "and they're out on bond."

"Well, all right, they're not in jail," Foreman shot back. "Sit down."[36]

When the jury returned, Judge Hannay instructed them to disregard Foreman's remarks that prosecution of the defendants originated in the Texas attorney general's office and to disregard any references to state cases against the defendants. Foreman, however, picked up where he had left off by continuing the attack.

"Let's see where the stench is blowing from," he offered, "the offices of the Benavides school district or from the prosecutor who started this persecution—Little Johnny Shepperd? We're not far this side of '1984' and the 'Animal Farm' and Little Johnny Shepperd is Big Brother."[37]

"He's going right back into it again," Wilkey protested, quickly jumping from his seat. "It is contemptuous."[38]

Judge Hannay managed to settle both attorneys down once again and bring order to the courtroom, but Foreman stuck to his tactic of blaming everyone except the defendants. With Wilkey continuously objecting throughout Foreman's summation, the session dragged on until five o'clock when court adjourned for the weekend.[39]

When court reopened, final arguments were still being presented and would consume the entire day. Foreman hadn't finished pointing the finger at others, including Governor Shivers, whom he accused of trying to cover up a scandal of his own. The governor and the attorney general "knew if they started a big fire down in Duval County, nobody would see the State Treasury get robbed in Austin," he claimed. Summing up, Foreman agreed money had been stolen from the school district, but the evidence against his clients was thin.[40]

"The government's case is like the man who said he killed a bear," he said in a folksy manner, "and if you didn't believe him, he'd show you the very tree he killed it under."

Wilkey's closing remarks were straightforward and to the point. "There are two elements involved in mail fraud," he told the jury. "The first is a scheme to defraud, and second is the use of the mails to further that scheme. We think we have proved the scheme to defraud."[41]

The following day, Judge Hannay charged the jury. No one expected a quick verdict due to the complexities of the case and the number of defendants involved. Each charge against the eleven defendants had to be considered, resulting in the jury having to vote a minimum of 220 times. After six hours of deliberation, the jury retired for the night. The following morning, the fourth day of deliberation, the hour-long charge by Hannay was read again and the jury retired to continue their task.[42]

At the end of the fourth day the jury was still out. "We haven't arrived at a verdict yet, your honor, but we're making some progress," Jury Fore- man Oscar Breeding told the judge. Because one of the jurors had an illness in his family, Hannay excused the jury for the weekend. "It's the longest time a jury in a criminal case stayed out that I can remember," remarked Kathryn Matthews, chief deputy marshal with twenty-five years of service in the federal district.[43] The jury foreman revised his opinion on Monday. "Your honor, I reported last Friday that we were making some progress toward a verdict. But we've been in there all day today, and we haven't done a thing in the world." Although the judge told them to come back the next morning and continue deliberating, when the jurors left, he instructed defendants and attorneys to be in court at noon.[44]

According to the *Alice Daily Echo*, at noon on the sixth day of deliber- ations, the jury asked Hannay for a little more time, but near the end of the day the jury foreman announced they still hadn't reached a verdict. He said the first vote was taken on the third day of deliberations. Two jurors were for acquittal of all defendants on all counts; the other ten voted guilty on some of the counts. "I held out for five days in an effort to get them off free," he said. "On the sixth day I offered a compromise. I was willing to convict Parr on one count but the other 10 men on the jury didn't want to free anyone." The lone holdout was Joe Grimes, a Linotype operator from Houston. "Well, that's the way I saw it—and that's the way I had to vote," Grimes said. "I just couldn't tell who was lying, and who wasn't."[45]

Although the trial ended in a hung jury, some defendants had been found not guilty on fifty-nine charges. However, none had been cleared on all counts. The jury could not reach a decision on any of the counts against Parr. After a six-week trial, during which eighty-one witnesses had been called by the government, another twelve by the defense, and at a cost of seventeen thousand dollars in jury and witness fees, very little had been accomplished. Disappointed, Wilkey announced that when a date could be arranged on the court calendar, the defendants would be retried. "If this case is ever tried again," Foreman said, "It will take six months instead of six weeks." Displaying a beaming grin, Parr was asked if he felt he had received a fair trial. "He still speaks for me," Parr said pointing to Foreman. "I've got no comment."[46]

A second trial date in Houston was set for January 28, 1957, but Foreman asked for a delay because of a scheduling conflict he had with a state case. Federal judge Joe McDonald Ingraham granted the motion, setting March 11 as the new trial date.[47] The conflict Foreman referred to was that his client, George Parr, was about to face trial on state charges of stealing school funds. Transferred to New Braunfels, Comal County (a conservative, mostly German descendant district tending to frown on political bosses controlling the electorate), Parr's trial would be the toughest test his attorney would face in defending the Duval boss.

CHAPTER 18
POLITICS AND TRIALS

Indictments piling up in Duval County back to 1954 began entering the next phase—getting to trial. As 1956 began, pending cases included charges of misappropriation of county funds against former Seventy-Ninth Judicial District Attorney Raeburn Norris, the same against former Duval County treasurer Frank Saenz Jr., forgery and theft charges against former Duval County auditor C. T. Stansell Jr., and conspiracy to commit theft charges against Givens Parr, D.C. Chapa, B. F. Donald Jr., and George Parr. Attorney General Ben Shepperd was worried that indictments against George Parr, Donald, Chapa, and Givens Parr might be jeopardized by the statute of limitations. The Adame case had been overturned when the court of criminal appeals held that the original indictment had been handed down by an improperly constituted grand jury. What bothered Shepperd was the four defendants claimed that since their alleged offenses occurred on September 1, 1951, and those indictments had been thrown out as a result of the Adame decision, then the three-year statute of limitations barred them from being re-indicted. In an unprecedented action, Sheppard requested a ruling on the matter in advance, but the court of criminal appeals felt it did not have the authority.[1]

The ruling was a minor setback, but it may have influenced Shepperd to try Norris first. With the trial scheduled for April 30, both prosecution and defense asked for a postponement. Foreman needed another day to finish up a case in Houston, but the prosecution wanted even more time. They had been unable to serve subpoenas on three state witnesses (Nago Alaniz, C. G. Palacios, and George Parr), all of whom had taken "Mexican vacations." Parr was being asked to appear as a former San Diego State Bank director and to produce records of notes signed by Norris. District judge Owen Thomas, already frustrated over previous delays, set a new trial date for September 7. With his wife recovering from an operation and his trial delayed, Norris announced he was filing as a candidate for the Seventy-Ninth Judicial District attorney. He would be opposing the reelection of Sam Burris, who had defeated Norris in the 1954 election.[2]

Parr and three other codefendants were given a trial date of June 8 in San Marcos where their conspiracy to commit theft case had been transferred. Another crowded court docket resulted in the cases being transferred to New Braunfels in Comal County and the date pushed up to June 18. Parr took advantage of the delay to stir up the opposition. He filed a legal complaint against Assistant Attorney General Sidney P. Chandler for malicious prosecution arising from a perjury indictment. "Those indictments [against Parr] speak for themselves," Chandler responded.[3] Parr's complaint was "a pretty good-sized joke," he added.[4]

The business of politics was always paramount to Parr. The game had to be played every day, never letting up for a moment. Getting candidates elected was the crux of his power, and he never sat on the sidelines. In the 1956 city elections in Benavides and San Diego, Parr candidates won every race except a San Diego alderman post.[5] Celebrations were put on hold because school elections in both districts were approaching and a serious challenge awaited. Parr managed to get his candidates a win in the city elections by splitting the vote against the two anti-Parr slates, but the school elections would be a different matter.

The Dan Tobin faction and the Freedom Party finally agreed to combine efforts and offer one slate of candidates to oppose Parr's Old Party. Making it difficult for Parr to control voting, District Attorney Sam Burris obtained a court order to impound election ballots. Although anti-Parr factions did not succeed in Benavides, two Parr-supported school trustees were defeated in San Diego. It was a major defeat for Parr, not only because his candidates lost but because it demonstrated that, by joining forces, the opposition could win. After the school elections, both anti-Parr factions met to work out a semi-merger to keep their individual identity while joining together to support one slate of candidates.[6]

An agreement was reached and they united behind one slate of candidates to oppose Parr's Old Party in the primary. With a united front against him, Parr would be facing stiff opposition over his control of several county offices, including sheriff, tax collector, and county attorney. To counter the coalition, Parr announced he was running for Duval

County sheriff. He had already held the position in 1952 and 1953, but he had resigned and appointed his nephew, Archer Parr. When Archer left to attend law school, the incumbent J. P. Stockwell was elected.[7]

While Parr fought to keep control in his bailiwick, another battle was brewing on the larger statewide stage. Lyndon Johnson was considering a serious run for the presidency in 1956 and needed control of the Texas Democratic delegation. Competing against Johnson was Governor Shivers, who vowed an "uphill fight" to keep Johnson from the leadership role. Although Parr hadn't taken part in precinct conventions in the past, this time he decided to join the fray by announcing support for Johnson. Reaction from Parr foes was immediate. The Spanish-English newspaper *New Duval* printed a scathing editorial: "If Johnson is elected president, George Parr would be secretary of the treasury."[8]

Not one to back down from a good fight, Shivers chided Johnson for accepting Parr's backing. Reminding voters that Johnson "owes his U.S. Senate 87-vote election to George Parr, the duke of Duval," Shivers said he regretted Johnson was so desperate. "I can assure him George Parr will not count the votes of the state convention."[9] Having watched the anti-Parr factions gain inroads, Shivers was confident that opposition to Parr would split the precinct vote and send anti-Johnson delegates to the state convention.

Nothing in Duval politics could ever be taken for granted, however. With a nod to the old adage that "politics makes strange bedfellows," county judge Dan Tobin Jr. broke with the Freedom Party to join forces with Parr to back Johnson, despite the fact he was backing anti-Parr candidates in local elections.[10] Unpredictable Duval politics then took another strange turn. A group of Freedom Party delegates bolted. They held their own convention on the courthouse lawn where they selected their own delegates and endorsed Johnson. Their only reason for splitting was to go on record as an anti-Parr group.[11]

Both delegate groups took their battle to the Texas Democratic Convention in Dallas where they petitioned the credentials committee to seat them as the legitimate delegation from Duval County. After listening to allegations from both sides, and realizing that hearings would have to be held to settle the matter, the credentials committee took a Solomon approach. Both groups were granted equal recognition, splitting Duval's convention votes between them. "It's time the state people realize that the anti-Parr forces in Duval county are strong enough to be recognized state-wide," said Freedom Party delegate Donato Serna.[12] Gaining recognition was one matter, of course; ousting Parr-backed candidates at the polls was a more difficult task.

Tending to political matters in his own backyard, Parr also had his eye on the governor's race. Shivers was not running for reelection, giving Parr the opportunity to back a candidate who might call off the Duval witch hunt. He had backed Ralph Yarborough in 1954 against Shivers, but this time he decided to switch support to Price Daniel. "Our vote then was against Allan Shivers," Parr commented on his 1954 backing of Yarborough. "We would have been for anybody besides Shivers."[13] Daniel, a U.S. senator, however, did not want Parr's endorsement. "I have said repeatedly that as governor I would continue the investigation of corruption in Duval County and I shall do so with all the vigor at my command," he declared. "I hereby decline his support." Daniel was commended in newspaper editorials for rejecting Parr and showing "a genuine sense of public responsibility." But it was difficult for him to distance himself from Parr as other candidates were quick to pair the two together. Parr, stunned by Daniel's reaction, tried to recover by offering to switch his support to any other candidate who wanted it.[14] None seemed interested.

Yarborough wouldn't let Daniel off the hook so easily. "George Parr must be surprised that his bosom friend, Price Daniel, now says: 'I know not the man.'" Daniel's campaign manager Joe Greenhill fired back. "The people of Texas will be greatly amused by Mr. Yarborough's attempt to conceal the fact that he has been, and continues to be, the favorite candidate of George Parr and all other bosses with whom he has made deals."[15]

Daniel and Yarborough were the frontrunners, and their back-biting, finger-pointing statements on Parr were fodder for the other candidates seeking media attention. "Parr's disreputable running irons are on them both," declared the longshot James Evetts Haley, a rancher and author of West Texas history. Reuben E. Senterfitt, another slim-hope candidate, labeled the Parr-support controversy a "smokescreen to cloud the real issues in the governor's race," but he was quick to add the two front-runners desired Parr's backing "privately, but not publicly."[16]

To assure voters he wanted nothing to do with the Duval political boss, Haley went to San Diego to meet Parr face-to-face. According to the *Dallas Morning News*, when he arrived in town Haley issued a signed, public statement on the courthouse steps: "I guarantee to pay Mr. Parr off by putting the full authority of Texas behind a move to clean up Duval and put him permanently where he belongs." He then walked across the street to deliver a copy of his statement to Parr at his private office.

"Glad to see you," Parr greeted the candidate, "but I could not support you because you would cut my throat."

"That's exactly what I would do," Haley replied. After thanking Parr for the reverse endorsement, Haley said he would return to Duval County after being elected governor and carry out his pledge to cleanup the corruption.

"Be glad to see you, with bells on," Parr said with a smile.

After passing out campaign literature in front of Parr's office, Haley traveled to nearby Alice to meet with Freedom Party leaders.

"The strongest recommendation for governor that I have had," Haley told them, "comes from the most notorious political figure in Texas, George Parr, the gun-toting Duke of Duval."[17]

The confrontation was an amusing diversion for Parr, but the primary was approaching, and there was little time to waste because of the bona fide threat from the slate of Freedom Party candidates. Unification of anti-Parr political factions meant that Parr's power base would finally be facing a serious challenge. In addition, this time his name would be on the ballot. Three men were running against Parr, but only one offered any hope of winning—the incumbent, Julian P. Stockwell, who was supported by the Freedom Party and the Dan Tobin faction. Having broken ties with Parr the year before, Tobin was vehemently opposed to Parr being elected. In a statement released to newspapers he expressed disdain for the political boss: "His naked nerve in asking the good people of the county to vote for him for sheriff is beyond the concepts of the human mind. His only desire to want to be sheriff is for political revenge, to promise a few of his flunkies deputies jobs and to be able to wear that $100 Stetson hat he once wore when he was sheriff. George Parr has no love for the future of our county outside of his only love and that is to dominate the political machine that is rapidly slipping away from him." Tobin's remarks were intended to rally voters against Parr, but with his political base challenged, Parr took no chances. For the first time, he was going door-to-door to round up votes.[18]

When the polls closed, the unofficial count gave Parr a slim 164 vote lead, but absentee ballots hadn't been counted. When the final tally was made, Parr won, avoiding a runoff by only 73 votes. Judge Laughlin had election officials join him behind closed doors to inspect the impounded absentee ballots for irregularities. Lawyers for the Old Party objected to the secrecy, calling it a "star chamber proceeding," but a Texas Ranger stood post outside the room to prevent anyone from entering. Nothing out of the ordinary was found and the vote stood—Parr was the Democratic nominee for sheriff, which virtually assured him a win in the November election.[19]

But this was Duval, and nothing could be taken for granted in politics. Stockwell filed suit contesting the primary, asking the court to throw out all absentee votes. He also wanted 347 contested votes subtracted from Parr's total and added to his. Parr's attorneys argued that only the state is permitted to intervene in an election dispute, so the attorney general's office petitioned the court to allow the state to pick up the suit. When Judge Laughlin denied the petition, the state asked for an injunction to keep Parr's name off the November ballot. Laughlin agreed to hear arguments on the motion.[20]

At the conclusion of the hearings, Laughlin ruled that Stockwell hadn't produced evidence of enough illegal votes to change the outcome. Parr was ruled to be the Democratic nominee for sheriff. Bolstered by a strong showing of anti-Parr votes in the primary, the Freedom Party met with the Tobin group to consider running Stockwell as an independent in November.[21] Stockwell kept the election close with the vigorous write-in campaign, but after tabulating absentee ballots, Parr won by 396 votes. Not willing to concede, Stockwell said he might "wind up sitting in the sheriff's office anyway. . . . George just has too many criminal matters pending against him."[22]

Continuing to keep Duval politics on its radar screen, the attorney general's office sent a letter to the county commissioners advising them not to certify Parr for sheriff. The letter quoted a section of the Texas Constitution barring anyone from public office "until he shall have obtained a discharge . . . for all public moneys with which he may have been entrusted." They contended Parr had been a bank officer where the misappropriated school funds were kept. The letter added that the judgment against Parr in the Dobie Ranch civil suit was another public money debt that hadn't been discharged. It was a slim interpretation of the Texas Constitution, but enough for the majority anti-Parr commissioners to deny certification.[23]

Parr was in the middle of his Houston mail fraud trial, but this didn't prevent him from acting on the commissioners' decision. Raeburn Norris filed for a writ of mandamus in Judge Laughlin's court to force certification of Parr as the duly elected Duval County sheriff. After hearing arguments Laughlin dismissed the suit, leaving Parr stalemated—but not finished. His attorneys immediately filed an appeal with the Fourth Court of Civil Appeals at San Antonio. Before the case could be heard, Duval County commissioners took matters into their own hands by appointing Stockwell as sheriff and swearing him in on New Year's Day.[24]

Arguing before the appeals court Parr's attorney Gerald Weatherly accused the Duval commissioners of running a "dictatorship," citing their action as showing "how far so-called reforms can be led to go." Standing before the three justices, Assistant Attorney General Sidney Chandler commented: "I appreciate why George Parr can't understand how his county became a democracy." Chandler stuck to the right of the commissioners to hold that Parr was ineligible to be sheriff because he hadn't accounted for the misappropriated county funds. Without ruling on the merits of the case, the appeals court reversed Laughlin's dismissal of the mandamus suit, ordering the case to be heard in the lower court.[25]

Battling for the sheriff's post would keep Parr in the courts over the next few years, but the fight was only a minor diversion for him. Winning local elections was the mainstay for political power to keep his empire intact, but staying out of prison was a more serious concern. If sent to prison, Parr and his cronies would lose everything. As trial dates neared, the question of who would be first was on everyone's mind. After two years of delays, most of the pending indictments hadn't been to trial, but time was running out. Someone had to face a jury.

The trial of D.C. Chapa, on charges of theft and embezzlement of school funds, finally began on June 5, 1956, with Percy Foreman leading the defense. Although the trial was moved to Fort Stockton on a change of venue, District Attorney Sam Burris prosecuted the case. Because of a crowded docket, Judge J. C. Langdon announced night sessions would be held.

Laying the groundwork for the state's case, Burris called witnesses connected with the Benavides school district to testify that Chapa had never been authorized to collect school district taxes. Former school board members said they never heard of a contract giving Chapa a salary and 4 percent commission to collect taxes. Other witnesses told the jury that Chapa did not have the authority to withdraw money from the school account to cover his expenses.[26]

Getting witnesses from Duval County to testify wasn't easy according to Burris. "One witness told me he was afraid he would get a knife in his back when he returned home," he said. "Others told me they still have to live in Duval County after the trial is over." Despite their fears, some witnesses gave details of how tax money came through the school district office and was often diverted for Chapa's personal use. One former tax office employee said he cashed three tax checks totaling ten thousand dollars and gave the cash to Chapa. Bank tellers at the two Parr-owned depositories for school funds testified to never having seen cash deposits being made for the school district.[27] The unanswered question was— Where did the cash go?

Burris called U.S. postal inspector William E. Main who testified he had great difficulty in finding records while conducting an investigation for the federal mail fraud case against Chapa, Parr, and six others. When Main first approached Chapa for the records, Chapa said he could not speak English. Main said Chapa hired a lawyer as a spokesman, and any questions had to be posed to the lawyer, not Chapa. Corpus Christi accountant Ed Ponder, hired as school board auditor, testified there were no formal records in the tax office. To establish a set of books for an audit, Ponder said he built a set based on bank statements he could find. In his cross-examinations, the best Foreman could do was show that with lax record keeping in the tax office, it would be impossible to know exactly where the missing funds went.

William Benson, a certified public accountant who prepared Chapa's income tax returns, was asked details on "$19,000 miscellaneous income" reported on one of the returns. Foreman asked that Benson's testimony be considered hearsay because he was using tax return forms to refresh his memory, which the judge sustained. Although there was no specific way Burris could tie Chapa's extra income to the missing school funds, he led the jury to wonder what other source could account for that amount of money.[28] Chapa's son O. P. Carrillo testified that the money came from the sale of hunting fees on his ranch and the sale of fifteen registered bulls shipped to Cuba. However, a state livestock commission member was brought in to testify that no official record existed, which would have been necessary for any livestock shipped from a Texas Gulf port. The witness said a blood test for Bangs disease (Brucellosis) would have been taken if the animals were six months old, but no such records were on file.[29]

In his closing argument, Foreman described his client as "an outdoors man, a hunter, not a pen pusher" who could have orchestrated such an elaborate scheme to embezzle school funds. Any missing funds, he argued, could have been taken by anyone in the tax office, but without proper records, the culprit would never be found. After Burris gave his closing remarks, the judge charged the jury, which received the case at 10:30 at night.[30]

After deliberating for an hour, the jury retired and resumed the next day, returning with a verdict that afternoon. Standing with his three sons by his side, Chapa heard the verdict returned by the seven-man, five-woman jury. Guilty as charged. Judge Langdon immediately sentenced Chapa to five years in prison, and Foreman gave notice his client would appeal.[31]

While the state case against Parr was being delayed, the trial of former district attorney Raeburn Norris on a charge of misappropriating Duval County funds opened in Anson. The charges against four others in the indictment were dropped because of insufficient evidence, leaving Norris to face a jury alone. Once again, Foreman appeared for the defense.[32]

The core of the prosecution's case was a five-thousand-dollar check dated July 15, 1953, and drawn on the Duval County Road and Bridge Fund. The state contended the check was applied to a note of Norris's held by the San Diego State Bank. Dan Tobin Jr.—named in the original indictment but the charges were dropped—testified he could not recall the county commissioners authorizing the check, which had a penciled notation on it reading "for labor." Under cross-examination, Foreman maintained the charges against Tobin had been dropped because he agreed to testify against Norris. Tobin denied the accusation.

To account for the five thousand dollars Norris used to repay the bank loan, Foreman took the stand to testify. Foreman said he received three payments of five thousand dollars each, drawn on the San Diego State Bank from Nago Alaniz, whom he had defended in the murder of Buddy Floyd. Alaniz followed Foreman on the stand, testifying that friends had raised money for his defense and Norris was custodian of the funds. A San Diego State Bank employee testified that the Norris loan had been paid off on July 17, 1953. Another bank employee said a check had been received that same day from the First State Bank at Alice, depository for Duval County funds. Donato Serna, the new Duval County auditor, identified the check as being the same one drawn on the county road and bridge fund.[33]

If Foreman's tactic was to raise doubt as to where the money came from to pay off the Norris bank loan, the jury didn't appear to be confused. At the end of the three-day trial, the jury took its time deliberating and returned with a guilty verdict. Judge Owen Thomas quickly assessed a two-year sentence in the state penitentiary. Luther Jones, one of the attorneys for Norris, said his client would file an appeal and Norris was released on a five-thousand-dollar appeal bond.[34]

Having garnered two back-to-back convictions against George Parr's pals, the state was ready to take on the boss himself. Four defendants, George Parr, B. F. (Tom) Donald, Givens Parr, and D.C. Chapa, were all scheduled to be tried together in New Braunfels on October 22, 1956. Foreman tried to get the case transferred back to Duval County, but Judge Johannes "John" Rohmberg Fuchs denied the motion. The state was ready, and the judge would not tolerate further delays. After nearly half of the veniremen were dismissed by the judge for various causes, Fuchs took under advisement a motion to quash the indictments under the statute of limitations.[35]

The next day Fuchs handed down rulings that completely changed the proceedings. First, he ruled the defendants should be tried separately. Next, he dismissed charges against D.C. Chapa since he had already been convicted on similar charges. Givens Parr was ill at the time, so the judge ruled out having him stand trial for now. That left Tom Donald or George Parr to be the first. Fuchs chose Donald and ordered the trial to begin immediately.

After jury selection was completed, the prosecution led off with Jewel Mayfield, assistant cashier at the Texas State Bank at Alice where Donald was the head cashier. She identified checks drawn on the school district's account, presumably paid for construction work. School district trustees testified that no authority had been given by them to issue the checks. More witnesses followed, each claiming that, although their name appeared on school district checks, they hadn't done any work for the school district and hadn't received any money after the checks were cashed.[36]

Up to this point, the prosecution hadn't mentioned Donald's name in connection with the checks. The link was made by the prosecution's star witness—Diego Heras. Having relocated to Houston, the former acting secretary of the Benavides school district testified that he signed and cashed between one hundred and twelve hundred checks drawn on the school district's account. He said he cashed most of the checks with Donald at the bank on orders from George Parr. The best Foreman could do was verify that Heras was testifying under immunity, hoping to cast doubt on his veracity. The defense called only two witnesses, both of whom were asked to testify as to Donald's good character and solid reputation in banking circles.[37]

After deliberating for only two hours, the jury returned with a guilty verdict. Judge Fuchs sentenced Donald to five years in prison but allowed him released on a twenty-five-hundred-dollar appeal bond. The state had gotten another conviction, but the big fish still avoided the hook. Parr's trial was reset for December 10, 1956, but as that date approached, it seemed unlikely his trial would begin. Foreman, handling Parr's mail fraud case in Houston, requested a continuance. The trial date was rescheduled for January 21, 1957.[38]

The prosecution's steamroller was crushing the opposition as convictions piled up. They still wanted a shot at Parr, but more importantly, they had to make sure the convictions already handed out would stick. While Parr was facing federal and state juries, the appeals for Raeburn Norris, D.C. Chapa, and Tom Donald were being heard in the higher courts.

Foreman argued Chapa's case before the Texas court of criminal appeals. "The state tried to make its case by showing that Chapa received the money but it never was deposited to the school fund account," he told the court. "They never did show that he took it." He contended state witnesses said anyone in the tax office could have stolen the money. Aside from the lack of evidence, Foreman objected to the severance of defendant Oscar Carrillo Sr., who had been indicted on similar charges. He argued Carrillo should have been tried first.[39]

The court agreed that the lower court ruling to sever the two cases should be reversed. Without commenting on the merits of the case, Judge Lloyd Davidson threw out Chapa's conviction and ordered a retrial. Burris was furious: "the district attorney's office will keep on trying the Duval county cases until they wear these defendants out—or the Court of Criminal Appeals follows the law and upholds our convictions."[40] More bad news for Burris was soon to arrive.

Foreman had been busily preparing an appeal for the conviction of Raeburn Norris. At the same time, Foreman was handling Parr's conviction for threatening the life of Tomas Molina at the Duval County courthouse. Presenting back-to-back arguments before the Texas court of criminal appeals, Foreman began with Parr's case. "At no time did George Parr say he planned to kill anyone," he told the court, "he only said he wanted to." It wasn't much of a defense, but it was all Foreman had. Speaking on behalf of Norris, Foreman argued "the evidence does not show or even indicate conspiracy." He contended the state erred in trying to connect the five thousand dollars allegedly stolen from county funds to Norris. "We have public officials taking public money to pay private obligations," said Assistant Attorney General Sidney Chandler, representing the state. "It doesn't make any difference whether the $5,000 was used to pay an attorney or whether it was used to pay off a Raeburn Norris note at the bank."[41]

In a two-to-one decision, the appeals court reversed the conviction of Norris, remanding the case for a new trial. The majority opinion found "there was no conspiracy as alleged," adding that "the evidence shows only circumstantially" the five thousand dollars had been applied to Norris's bank note. In his dissent Judge K. K. Woodley felt the record clearly showed five thousand dollars was "falsely" drawn on the county account and misappropriated by Norris.[42]

Although the court upheld Parr's threat conviction, the Norris ruling didn't sit too well with Sam Burris. He said he had remained silent in the past but, "I cannot any longer. I must let the people of Texas know what a sorry mess they have in Austin." He complained that the Chapa and Adame convictions had been thrown out by the appeals court, but "to appear judicious and non-partisan, affirmed a $1,500 fine against George

Parr." As for the Norris case, Burris felt robbed. "Twelve jurors and one trial judge thought that there was enough evidence to convict Norris— yet those people in Austin act as God and reverse it." Burris predicted the five-year sentence of Tom Donald would also be reversed.[43] He wasn't wrong.

In another divided opinion, the appeals court threw out Donald's conviction, this time ordering further prosecution attempts should be dismissed. Texas law had no limitation on felony conspiracy charges, so the court applied the rule that, "An indictment for any other felony may be presented within three years from the commission of the offense." Since the conspiracy was alleged to have been entered into on September 1, 1951, and Donald wasn't indicted until November 4, 1955, they reversed the lower court judgment. Judge Woodley, again offering the dissenting opinion, argued that the alleged offenses had been continuous, with several of the school fund thefts occurring within the three-year limitation. Asked by journalists to comment on the ruling, Burris declined. "I've made all the statements that I'm going to make about the court," he said. "It would just end by my getting disbarred if I make any more statements."[44]

While his associates were battling to have their convictions overturned, Parr faced trial for the long-delayed case of conspiracy for the misappropriation of school funds. With the retrial of the federal mail fraud case set on hold, Percy Foreman geared up to defend his client against the state charges. With defendants being tried in several jurisdictions, and Foreman appearing as counsel in the trials as well as for the appeals, the Houston attorney was conducting a traveling road-show marathon of court appearances to defend Parr and his fellow codefendants.[45] The state hadn't fared too well in prosecuting the cases so far, but Parr was their main target. Getting him convicted and making it stick, would be their ultimate goal.

CHAPTER 19

TEXAS TRIES PARR

The year 1957 had hardly begun when Parr was back in court to start the New Year. The Duval grand jury had just indicted him and two associates on charges of forging checks drawn on the Benavides school district account. Parr was facing seven counts, as was Tom Donald, while former Duval County treasurer F. Saenz Jr. was named in four. After each posted a fifteen-hundred-dollar bond, Judge Laughlin ordered the cases transferred to nearby Jim Wells County, with trial dates to be determined sometime after the new court term began in March.[1] Parr's immediate concern was the upcoming trial in New Braunfels for conspiracy to steal school funds.

Delay after delay had postponed the trial, which Judge Johannes Fuchs now ordered to begin. Percy Foreman attempted further delay by submitting a motion that Parr and his brother Givens be tried separately. In a surprise counter-move designed to get the trial under way, the state requested charges against Givens be dismissed. The motion was granted, and jury selection began as George Parr stood alone in the docket.[2] After two days of jury selection the trial began with the state calling its first witness.

Earl Delaney, partner with Parr in the oil business for twenty-four years and former member of the Benavides school board, said Parr attended school board meetings in the capacity of a "legal advisor." Fuchs overruled several objections by Foreman to the introduction of evidence, as Jewel Mayfield, former assistant cashier at the Texas State Bank of Alice, showed canceled checks and financial statements of the school district's account. Foreman continued objecting, with Fuchs overruling each time, as more witnesses filled in details of how Parr got his hands on the funds.

Referring to the school district's financial statements, school superintendent W. F. Reed said the actual expenses were far less than those indicated in the reports. He added that many of the names appearing on checks issued to teachers were unknown to him. Others testified many of the names on the checks were nonexistent persons. Former teacher John Ballard had been informed checks had been issued to him after he had left the district, but he said he never saw any.[3]

Once again, Diego Heras was the prosecution's star witness. Parr displayed little emotion as he listened to Heras describe how funds were diverted. He had been instructed by Parr to endorse checks made out to fictitious persons, cash them at the bank, and bring the money back to Parr. Under cross-examination, Foreman pressed for details of the immunity agreement. He asked Heras how many years in prison he might have received if not for the immunity. No matter how hard he grilled him, Foreman could not shake Heras. Although an accessory to the acts, Heras seemed a credible witness.[4]

Joe Vaello was awarded a contract to build a new cafeteria at the Benavides school in 1949. Shown checks drawn on the school account issued for electrical and roof repair work during the time he was constructing the cafeteria, Vaello said he knew of no other work being done while he was on the job site. He was then shown a forty-thousand-dollar school fund voucher dated November 9, 1949, which was payment for a new school football stadium. Vaello said the stadium existed but had already been built and paid for in 1946.[5]

In an effort to speed up the trial, Fuchs called a night session. Moving closer to showing Parr's direct involvement in the thefts, the state called Parr's personal accountant, W. M. Benson. Having testified in Parr's aborted mail fraud trial, Benson repeated the same information concerning his dealings with Parr. He told of a conversation with Parr concerning school funds. Parr implied Benson was taking some of the money for himself, which Benson denied. "I don't mind your taking money," Parr had said, "but I want to know about it." The prosecution implied that if Parr didn't mind Benson putting his hand in the cookie jar, then Parr was probably taking some for himself. To dispel this theory, Foreman questioned Benson as to the source of Parr's income. Never mentioning school funds, Benson, who prepared Parr's personal income tax returns since 1935, said Parr's income, reportedly one hundred thouand dollars a year, came from oil royalties and various business interests.[6]

After several bank employees and county tax office staff testified to amounts of money being handled in the scheme to divert school funds, the prosecution rested its case. The eleven-man, one-woman jury had been sequestered since being sworn in, and Fuchs was hoping to end the case before the weekend. In a Saturday session, Foreman offered rebuttal witnesses, all aimed at discrediting Heras. Repeating testimony given at Parr's mail fraud trial, they described Heras as a "drunkard," who bragged he could forge Parr's signature.[7]

Fuchs considered holding another night session with the hope of sending the case to the jury but was informed by Foreman that the defense still had more to offer. Before the trial resumed on Monday, another news item diverted everyone's attention. With his nephew Archer Parr acting as his attorney, George Parr had filed a petition for bankruptcy on Saturday.

Federal judge James V. Allred in Corpus Christi, who received the petition on Monday, immediately decreed Parr bankrupt. The petition stated Parr's debts were "extensive," and his properties and business interests have been "continuously involved in law suits and legal proceeding" for the past three years. Liabilities were listed as $1,925,093 and assets totaled $532,106. Among the liabilities, under "disputed obligations," Parr listed $654,697 in federal, state, and county taxes owed. The only exempt asset claimed was $74,569 in homestead property and personal household goods. Allred granted Parr a twenty-day extension to file additional debts and assets that might have been overlooked during the hurriedly prepared petition.[8]

Parr held off his creditors, but this had no effect on his criminal trial. To raise reasonable doubt as to who had taken the money, Foreman called former school board member Jesus G. Garza. Foreman's new target was former school auditor W. M. Benson. Garza, indicted along with Parr for mail fraud, said that Parr told school board members in 1950 that the school bond building fund was one hundred thousand dollars short. "We decided Benson would have to quit signing them checks," Garza said, adding that the board authorized Parr to sign school fund checks from then on.[9]

Closing arguments lasted until midnight. As Parr sat in the courtroom the next day, he predicted the jury would be out for only two hours. He was off by five minutes. Waiting for the verdict, Parr sat expressionless, showing no emotion. "Guilty," announced the jury foreman. The jury

also had the duty to assess the sentence. They gave Parr the maximum—
five years in prison.

Asked if the verdict was what he had expected, Parr quipped he "lost
the case when they read the indictment." Foreman quickly gave notice of
appeal, and Fuchs set the appeal bond at three thousand dollars. After posting the bond, signed by George and his brothers, Atlee and Givens, they
headed back to Duval County.[10] There would be no time to relax because
George had several unresolved matters. The second mail fraud trial was
being scheduled, the federal income tax evasion charges were still looming,
and Texas still wanted to try him for forging school account checks.

Now that Parr was under the protection of bankruptcy laws, District Attorney Sam Burris was appointed by the Duval commissioners to
ensure that when the pie was cut Duval would receive its fair share. Having already received a $273,000 judgment against Parr for oil royalties,
rental, and interest on the Dobie Ranch, the county had more civil suits
pending. The court appointed James M. Easterling to act as referee in
bankruptcy to oversee the complexity of Parr's financial affairs. Seeking
to sort out the myriad issues and to prevent any state or federal agency
walking off with assets from Parr's estate, he issued an order to stay the
sale of the Dobie Ranch. Duval County had a judgment against the ranch
and the federal government had a tax lien on the property, but Easterling
felt that, if the sale proceeded, Parr's unsecured creditors might be dam-
aged if the property realized less than market value from the auction.[11]

While awaiting a hearing to set aside the stay order, Duval County
officials went ahead with plans to auction off the Dobie Ranch. Adver-
tisements were taken out in newspapers and national magazines, hoping
to attract bidders willing to pay more than one million dollars for the
ranch. It was anticipated that the federal tax liens would be settled before
the auction date.[12]

Always enjoying a good court battle, Parr added another roadblock to
the disposition of his holdings. Filing an amendment to his bankruptcy
petition, he increased his assets to include a 40–45 percent interest in the
Dobie Ranch, valued at $250,000. Judge Allred ruled the stay order would
remain in effect. Nevertheless, Burris said he was going ahead with the
civil suit for the $172,500 he claimed Parr had taken from county funds
to pay his 1946 income taxes.[13]

While Burris pushed for a trial date on the civil case, Parr's creditors held their first meeting to sort out the complex holdings. Adding to their task, Parr filed another amendment to his bankruptcy petition. He added the thirty thousand dollars he claimed was due for his salary as sheriff in the yet-unresolved contested election. Trying to sort out the constantly changing assets, the creditors asked Parr to explain numerous transactions and lawsuits. "I have been in so many lawsuits I can't say right off what is involved in each," Parr said on the witness stand. He testified to a thirty-thousand-dollar note given to one attorney to represent him, the bank stock assigned to Percy Foreman to pay some of the legal bills, and oral agreements for fees to other attorneys, including fees to represent some of his fellow accused. "They never have [the money], so I foot the bill," he said.[14]

When Burris questioned Parr, the mood of the political boss suddenly changed. Parr invoked the Fifth Amendment, refusing to answer any questions put to him by Burris. But Parr wasn't silent on one issue. He accused Burris of "buying" the court decision in which Duval County was awarded the Dobie Ranch. He contended Burris subsequently rewarded Judge H. D. Barrow by getting him a seat on the Fourth Court of Civil Appeals in San Antonio. There was no basis for Parr's accusation, but when the Dobie Ranch appeal reached the Fourth Court of Civil Appeals, it was transferred to the Eleventh Court at Eastland.[15]

Being under the protection of the bankruptcy laws, Parr was helpless to prevent having his assets sold off to satisfy creditors. The first to go was the Parr Cattle Company, which was dissolved. Thelma Parr, a shareholder in the concern, received $60,000. She immediately turned the money over to Duval County to reduce her $388,000 debt. George's $10,499 share was paid directly to the bankruptcy trustees. Anxious to pay her debt, Thelma agreed to turn over her $7,000 a month share of profits from the Parr-Delaney Oil Company. As a result of receiving these funds, Duval County reduced the tax rate levied to pay off road bonds by twenty-seven and a half cents.[16]

Continuing to liquidate Parr's assets, the bankruptcy referee ordered Parr's oil holdings to be auctioned off. Consisting of Parr's interest in the Parr-Delaney Oil Company, royalty holdings, and a forty-acre lease operated by Shell Oil, the assets netted Parr more than $5,000 a month. Both Duval County and the IRS agreed to clear all liens against the properties, which were being offered with a minimum bid of $185,000.

Only four bids were received, with the winning offer of $216,000 going to Cicada Oil Company of Dallas.[17] Three weeks later, Cicada Oil turned around and sold their interests in the property to a group headed by Parr's former partner Earl Delaney. The "others" in the group were not disclosed, nor was the sale price.[18]

Knowing he was dealing with a slippery eel, Burris requested a hearing in bankruptcy court to determine if Parr had disclosed everything about his assets. According to the *Corpus Christi Times*, Parr swore under oath that he hadn't received any money from assets placed under bankruptcy protection. He denied having money hidden in Mexican banks or any other assets or property in Mexico. When asked about the operations and transactions of his cattle, oil, and bank interests, Parr claimed he had let his auditors handle his business and he couldn't recall any details.

"I don't understand audits," Parr responded when pressed for more information. "When I try to read one I don't know whether I am afoot or horseback."

Folksy humor couldn't sidestep the fact that, since filing for bankruptcy, Parr still managed to live the same lifestyle. How was this possible, Burris asked? Easy, Parr responded—he borrowed. Listing those he had borrowed from, Parr said the loans had all been made without putting up collateral. Asked about the amounts, he rattled off a list varying in size between one thousand dollars and twenty-five hundred dollars. He said the lenders were keeping track and he intended to repay in time.[19]

The nibbling away at Parr's assets continued. He held a 32.5 percent interest in the Oil Belt Chevrolet Company of San Diego with his partners J. C. King (35 percent) and Thelma Parr (32.5 percent). King made an offer to the bankruptcy referee to purchase George's share for eight thousand dollars, which was approved, despite objections by Burris that competitive bids should be accepted. Parr also held an interest in the Duval Motor Company in which Thelma held a one-sixth share. She filed a petition asking for a receiver to be appointed to protect her interest, claiming that no accounting of the company's profits had been made since George filed for bankruptcy.[20]

Criminal and financial problems continued to plague Parr, but to him the most important matter was to maintain political power. Anti-Parr forces had succeeded in ousting Duval County Democratic chairman J. C. King, but the Old Party still seemed to be calling the shots. Taking their case to the State Democratic Executive Committee in Austin, the anti-Parr group demanded to be recognized as the true leaders of the Duval County Democratic Party. The state committee ruled that King had been ousted illegally, but the anti-Parr faction wouldn't quit.[21]

Freedom Party members along with Dan Tobin's faction filed suit in Judge Laughlin's court to have two of their members seated on the local committee. A compromise prompted by Laughlin was reached in which committee membership would be divided. The Old Party, with King at the helm, would seat five members, while the combined forces of the Freedom Party and the Tobin faction would also have five. In effect, the compromise would allow each side to offer their own slate of candidates, which suited Parr. Splitting tickets was his forte, especially if he could get the two Anti-Parr factions to put up separate candidates.

As if orchestrated by the Duke of Duval, the two anti-Parr groups did just that during the July 1958 primary. The Old Party slate, headed by Archer Parr running for Duval County judge, was matched against two other lists of candidates. The Freedom Party backed four, including Horatio R. "Lacho" Canales for county judge, while the Tobin faction gave voters a third choice with Tobin at the top for the judgeship. Tobin's slate came in dead last, but the Freedom Party fared better. Their candidate for county treasurer garnered the most votes, but not enough to avoid a runoff against the Old Party candidate. In the other three races, Old Party candidates polled the most votes, but they too had to face runoffs.[22]

In a surprise move, Tobin threw his support behind all four Old Party runoff candidates. "There will still be a Tobin Faction," he vowed. "We just think the Old Party candidates are better qualified than the Freedom Party hopefuls." The Freedom Party attacked Tobin for his decision. "Dan Tobin has always been a Parr man in disguise," said H. L. Canales, opponent of Archer Parr in the runoff. Canales had reason to be irate because Tobin was his cousin. Not being elected was one matter, Freedom Party leader Walter Purcell said about Tobin, "but to sell his supporters down the river—I cannot understand."[23]

When all four Old Party candidates won their runoff elections, the Freedom Party cried foul. Headed by Burris, with assistance from the state attorney general's office, a full-blown investigation began looking into voting fraud. Convening the grand jury, Burris conducted the probe behind closed doors. Indications of what they were investigating came only from what observers saw on the outside. Ballots from the runoff were subpoenaed, but no witnesses were called. Neither side in the dispute had any idea of what was happening in the grand jury room.[24]

After the grand jury session ended, they issued a report charging that Burris had been a "stumbling block" during the investigation. Burris was furious: "That is a lie!" He countered with charges of his own, accusing the outgoing grand jury of having eleven "Parr men." Adding that the majority of the jurors served as election judges, supervisors, or clerks in the runoff, Burris questioned how it was possible for them to conduct an investigation of themselves. With no evidence of election fraud found, the results of the runoff and general election stood. The Old Party maintained power, but Parr was still being denied the sheriff's job he wanted.[25]

Throughout his criminal court battles, and the seemingly endless dwindling away of his estate in the bankruptcy court, Parr continued to fight for the post of Duval County sheriff. He had a battery of lawyers filing motions to have the appointed sheriff, J. P. Stockwell, removed so he could assume the position he had won in the election. The legal maneuvering reached a climax on April 17, 1957, when the Texas Supreme Court refused to review the Civil Appeals decision, which had ordered a new trial to decide who would be sheriff. Assistant Attorney General Sidney P. Chandler, who after leaving office signed on as Stockwell's attorney, relished the opportunity to shed light on Duval, saying he would "open the book and take a look at every page." He was particularly looking forward to getting Parr on the stand. "I'll probably take a full 10 days just to examine him," he said. "I'm planning to start with his birth certificate and bring him right up to date."[26] Because this was a civil case, as plaintiff, Parr would be required to answer every question. He never got the chance, however, because Laughlin granted a summary judgment against Parr, effectively denying him the sheriff's post. Both sides immediately filed appeals, placing the question once again in the hands of the appellate division.[27]

In his appeal to the court of civil appeals, Parr admitted he owed Duval County money that he had borrowed to purchase the Dobie Ranch, but the funds hadn't been "entrusted" to him—the reason the commissioners had given for him to be ineligible to hold office. The court agreed and reversed the lower court, but not before offering comment: "It may seem strange to say that if a person is entrusted with funds and fails to account properly for them he is ineligible to hold public office, but that if such a

person wrongfully takes public money he is not thereby rendered ineligible to hold public office."[28] The matter would now be placed before
the Texas Supreme Court, but there were other problems concerning the
question of who would be sheriff.

Because Stockwell had been appointed to the position, and state law
provided that appointments cannot run past a general election, the post
of sheriff would be considered vacant after January 1, 1959. On the other
hand, since Parr had been elected to serve through 1960, if the courts
decided he should be certified as sheriff, then no vacancy would exist and
no election would be held in 1958. Parr had succeeded in creating a quandary in Duval County politics, which must certainly have delighted him.[29]

Parr's battle to become sheriff kept his political juices flowing, but he
received a personal blow when his ninety-one-year-old mother passed
away on April 23, 1958. Elizabeth Parr had been living in her Corpus
Christi home since the death of her husband in 1942 and had been content to lead a quiet life. The previous year, at the age of ninety, in one
of her rare public appearances she testified at George's mail fraud trial
in Houston.[30] His last link with the past had died. Although still facing
the possibility of spending several years in a federal prison and losing the
dukedom he had inherited from his father, he still wanted to be sheriff.

The county commissioners' appeal to the Texas Supreme Court was
based on three grounds: Parr took money from Duval County and school
district accounts in the bank he owned; he borrowed money from the
county and had not repaid it; and he had taken twenty thousand dollars
from the county to induce Dan Garcia to resign as Duval County sheriff.
The court upheld the court of appeals ruling but ordered a trial to hear
the case on its merits.[31]

Before a trial date was set, Parr attempted a little backroom dealing to
be certified as sheriff. An unusual pact was formed when Duval County
judge Dan Tobin Jr. lost his bid for reelection in the primary to Archer
Parr. Swinging support to the Old Party, Tobin's first step was to call for
a commissioners' court meeting. A Parr-man would call for a motion to
certify George Parr as sheriff, followed by a Tobin-man, who would second the motion. Two Freedom Party men were expected to vote against
the motion, but the Tobin and Parr men would vote "Yes," making it
a tie vote. Tobin would then break the tie by voting in favor of Parr.[32]
When the commissioners' court met on October 13, 1958, the motion

to certify Parr as sheriff was again raised. Proceeding with the motion, the commissioners voted to cancel their civil suit against Parr, dismiss Chandler as their attorney, and seat Parr in office. Each vote was decided by Tobin, who cast in favor of all motions.[33]

After posting the required bond, Parr was sworn in as Duval County sheriff. "When do you take over?" a reporter asked. "Right now," Parr said. Pushing past the crowd of well-wishers and curious spectators, Parr made his way from the commissioners' courtroom, down the long corridor leading from the old section to the sheriff's office in the new part of the building. Within a half hour of being sworn in, George Parr was served with a restraining order issued by Judge Laughlin at the request of Burris.[34] Once again, the matter was back in court.

Two days later, at the hearing to decide whether to keep the injunction in force, Laughlin ruled against it. According to the *Alice Daily Echo*, after making his decision Laughlin said that Parr could ask Stockwell to give up the sheriff's office, but if he refused, it would be another matter. "I want it to be peaceful, though," Laughlin added, "and I certainly hope no guns are involved."

Once again, Parr took the long walk to the sheriff's office, but this time he had company. Texas Ranger Captain Allee, who may have been thinking back to his altercation with Parr four years ago, was prepared to step in if any disturbance occurred. Arriving at the sheriff's office, Parr was met at the door by Stockwell, who refused to vacate the post. "That's alright, Julian," Parr told Stockwell as he patted him on the back. Grinning to a reporter, Parr said, "I don't give a damn. If he turned over the office I'd have to go to work."[35]

While awaiting the appellate decision on Laughlin's ruling to refuse an injunction to prevent Parr from assuming the sheriff's job, Burris filed a petition on behalf of Duval County to have Tobin and the two commissioners who voted to install Parr as sheriff to be removed from their posts. He alleged the three had conspired with Parr to accomplish the deed while the suit determining Parr's qualification was pending. Furthermore, he contended "widespread confusion" in the county had resulted in uncertainty as to who was authorized to make legal arrests, serve warrants, or issue marriage licenses.[36]

The suit was eventually withdrawn, and on December 3, 1958, the Texas Supreme Court turned down Stockwell's request to be reinstated as sheriff. The next day, Parr's attorney filed for an injunction to prevent Stockwell from interfering with Parr in carrying out his duties as sheriff. Laughlin denied the request, but it was moot anyway. Just when everyone in Duval felt the sheriff's position had been settled, the appellate division handed down a ruling barring Parr from assuming office until after the first of the year.[37]

When the New Year began, everyone expected to see Parr sporting a sheriff's badge, but that was not to be. The Duval County commissioners' court, now stocked with Old Party members as a result of the November election, held their first session at one minute after midnight on the first day of the year. Their first order of business was to fire every salaried county employee except four. Next, they issued an order appointing San Diego service station owner Vidal Garcia as the new sheriff. After naming ten deputies, Garcia, his new deputies, and newly installed county judge Archer Parr appeared at the sheriff's office to take over. Stockwell refused to relinquish the post without a court order, so Garcia left without incident.[38]

The order came. Judge Laughlin issued a restraining order to prevent Stockwell from blocking Garcia taking over as sheriff. A week later, Laughlin issued a temporary injunction, which in effect solidified Garcia's right to be sheriff. Stockwell was at a dead end, but Parr wasn't finished. Taking the matter to the Texas Supreme Court, Parr managed to get a hearing on a writ of error. The high court considered the matter and then dismissed the motion. They said the restraining order on Parr had been effective until the end of 1958. Since Garcia had been appointed to the post after the order expired, the court ruled the point was moot.[39]

Two more decisions sealed the sheriff's position for Garcia. The Fourth Court of Civil Appeals upheld Laughlin's injunction to keep Garcia in office. The second decision came from Laughlin, who granted Parr a non-suit in the matter, effectively dismissing his claim to be sheriff. Following on the heels of the decision, Parr filed a suit for back wages due from the time he had been duly elected. His claim for a little over seventeen thousand dollars remained on the court calendar until May 30, 1961, when Laughlin ruled against him.[40] The controversy over Parr's bid to become sheriff had taken more than six years to reach a conclusion. Except for a brief moment when he was sworn in, he never held the post and never collected a penny in wages.

CHAPTER 20
MAIL FRAUD REDUX

In the spring of 1957, the federal government began its second try to convict Parr, eight associates, and Parr's two defunct banks on the mail fraud case, but there were problems right from the beginning. Judge Joe Ingraham, who in 1967 would preside at the draft-evasion trial of Mohammed Ali, declared one mistrial due to a juror's residency, and another due to a juror's criminal record. The process began once again on May 6, 1957.[1] Excluding the expense of the two-year investigation, prosecuting Parr for mail fraud had already cost the government more than thirty-five thousand dollars.[2] At this point, it seemed the government would spend whatever amount of money it would take to convict the Duke of Duval. Finally, an all-male jury was impaneled and the trial was underway.

To lay the groundwork for its case, the government called a former school district trustee to explain how the school board functioned and financial records were kept. Under cross-examination by Percy Foreman, it was revealed that no school records audit had been made, no shortage of funds reported, and no suits had been filed against any of the defendants during the time the government claimed Parr and his associates were raiding school funds. Seven South Texas postal workers testified they had scoured the area around Duval County searching for three hundred individuals who received checks drawn on the school district's account. Utility companies, tax records, county clerks, and the sheriff's office were all checked during the investigation, but no names were ever identified as belonging to actual persons.[3]

The prosecution's case was a rewrite of the script used in the first trial with the same cast of characters repeating their lines. Former cashier at Parr's bank Karl Williams testified he cashed numerous "bundles of checks" presented to him by Diego Heras but refused to use his teller's stamp on the checks. Foreman pressed for details, each question aimed at bolstering his defense strategy that Heras, not Parr, was the real cul-prit. He had difficulty with this tactic when another witness, bank teller Edna Fitch, said that Parr would enter her teller's cage, cash a handful of checks—some drawn on the school account—and walk out with the cash in hand.[4]

The second week of the trial began with a lineup of witnesses testi-fying they had never received school checks made out to them, nor had they ever done any work for the school district to merit compensation. Parr's brother-in-law Corpus Christi attorney B. G. Moffett rehashed his previous testimony, telling jurors he had received five hundred dollars a month for more than two years from the Benavides school district but never performed any legal work for the schools. Foreman asked only one question on cross-examination: "Was there a licensed attorney residing in Benavides at that time?" Moffett replied there wasn't.[5]

Several representatives of oil firms doing business in Duval were called to identify tax checks they mailed to the school district office after receiving tax statements in the mail. Their testimony was the foundation of the government's claim that Parr and the other defendants had used the U.S. postal system to carry out their conspiracy. Sending tax statements by mail and receiving checks from taxpayers by mail, which were then cashed to benefit the defendants, the prosecution reasoned mail fraud conspiracy had been committed.[6]

According to the *Alice Daily Echo*, while questioning school district tax assessor-collector R. R. Gonzales, Wilkey asked what appeared to be an innocent request, but Foreman saw a more sinister meaning he felt was sufficient ground for a mistrial. Gonzales had stated that certain school records covering the period of the alleged conspiracy were miss-ing. When Foreman asked if he still had any records, Gonzales said he still had "a room full of records." Wilkey asked if he would be willing to produce them "at the request of either the defense or prosecution if we specify the records."

It was a subtle legal point that Foreman raised, but enough to delay the trial while Ingraham considered a mistrial motion. Under federal rules of procedure the prosecution is prohibited from commenting on failure of the defense to produce witnesses or evidence when either is equally avail-able to both sides. Ingraham had to consider if the jury had also picked up on the fine point of law. "My own feelings are that no actual damage was done," Ingraham said, but he would halt the proceedings while he considered if any legal damage had been caused. After deliberating over a four-day weekend, Ingraham ruled that the question was not prejudicial.[7]

Before the trial resumed, assisting defense counsel Thomas Gilbert Sharpe Jr. of Brownsville reported that his father had died. Ingraham called for a two-week recess until June 3. After the hiatus the government presented evidence that destroying microfilm records was a regular practice at both Parr-owned banks. Special IRS agent William Dimler testified that during his investigation he discussed the matter with Tom Donald, the former cashier at the Texas State Bank of Alice and one of the defendants. When Dimler asked who destroyed the records, Donald said "he did not know when the records were destroyed and that anyone in the bank could have destroyed them."[8]

U.S. postal inspector William E. Main testified that during his investigation he encountered difficulty getting to see school district records. Foreman ignored Main's testimony, preferring to attack the government for methods used to gather evidence. According to the *Houston Post*, when Main said he had taken some Duval County grand jury transcripts to Wilkey's office, Foreman cited statutes making it a felony to use state evidence in a federal case. "These are purely political machinations engaged in by the prosecutors all the way to Washington," he charged. Wilkey was immediately on his feet vehemently protesting and initiating a heated verbal exchange between the two until Ingraham brought order to the courtroom.[9] Although Ingraham sustained Wilkey's objections, Foreman had made his point—it's not Parr who should be on trial—the finger should be pointed at the government for underhanded tactics in seeking a conviction.

Wilkey called former assistant state auditor Grady C. Starnes, who said an audit of school district records would be "impossible" because of missing records. "No auditor would sign an audit unless he had documented records to back up his figures," Starnes firmly said. When he questioned Starnes, Foreman ignored previous testimony and chose to take another opportunity to attack the government. This time the target was Texas attorney general John Ben Shepperd.[10]

According to the *San Antonio Express*, Starnes stated that the state auditor was independent of Shepperd's office, but Foreman wasn't satisfied. He asked if the audit would have been conducted if Shepperd had requested it. "No," Starnes replied. He described state auditor C. H.

Cavness, as "an extremely cautious and conservative man" who wouldn't act until after a closer examination of the reasons for the audit.

"In other words," Foreman asked, "he wouldn't take part in a political crusade to pull someone's chestnuts out of the fire . . . is that what you mean?"

"That's exactly what I mean," Starnes answered.[11]

Once again, the main witness for the prosecution was Diego Heras who repeated most of his testimony given at the first trial. He described how Parr took school funds on a regular basis. On instructions from Parr, he made out checks against the school district account to fictitious persons, cashed them at the bank, and handed the money to Parr.[12]

Foreman received a bit of luck from a recent U.S. Supreme Court decision (June 3, 1957) indirectly related to his case. Union official Clinton E. Jencks was convicted of falsifying an affidavit that he wasn't a Communist. The appeal centered on the defense not having access to government files they felt were necessary to prepare their cross-examination of government witnesses. In dismissing the conviction, the high court ruled that "relevant statements" made by government witnesses "touching the subject matter of their testimony at the trial" should be made available to the defense.[13]

With the jury out of the courtroom, Foreman asked for the same consideration. Citing the Jencks ruling, he wanted copies of all statements Heras had made to the government. According to the *Corpus Christi Caller*, Wilkey objected, quoting the *New York Times* article on the Jencks case saying the ruling applied to producing statements only after a witness had given direct testimony. "I might say this is the first time I've ever seen lawyers and the court working from a newspaper," Ingraham quipped. One step ahead, Foreman gave the judge a copy of the Supreme Court decision that he had just received by air mail. After reading the decision, Ingraham made his ruling: "I think the government is within its rights to withhold the statements until the testimony is given."

Heras returned to be grilled by Foreman, who attempted to trip up the evasive witness. He came right to the point, asking Heras if he had ever made a statement that Parr had given him fifteen thousand dollars to deliver to an FBI agent back in 1950. Heras denied making the statement.

"Did you ever make a statement that you had ever made such a statement?" he asked.

"I did," Heras replied.[14]

Foreman then turned to Wilkey, asking the prosecutor if he had ever seen any statements by Heras, including the remark about the fifteen thousand dollars. Wilkey said he had, but he didn't know where it was at the present time. That was all Foreman needed to hear. He asked the judge to order the government to produce all past statements given by Heras. He wanted statements made to the FBI, copies of testimony Heras gave to the federal grand jury, his Duval grand jury testimony, and copies of interviews given to District Attorney Sam Burris.

Ingraham ordered the statements turned over to the defense, except for federal grand jury transcripts. "It is my opinion it is privileged and secret and I so rule at all risks." He deferred a ruling on the statements that Heras had made to the FBI until he had an opportunity to inspect them and determine their material value to the trial. Wilkey objected, saying the FBI documents were not in his possession. Ingraham overruled the objection, ordering Wilkey to contact the FBI and have them submit to the court the next day any statements by Heras made to them in the past.[15]

After reviewing the documents, Ingraham allowed limited use of them by the defense. Foreman would be permitted to ask Heras if he had pleaded the Fifth Amendment while giving a deposition during a libel suit brought by Parr, but he was restricted in using statements Heras gave in depositions taken by the FBI. Specifically, Foreman could not ask if Heras made the statement about Parr giving him fifteen thousand dollars to bribe an FBI agent. However, Foreman was allowed to use a portion of a statement Heras made during his second FBI deposition. The damaging statement read: "I wish to state under oath that much of the information I gave in my statement to FBI agents in Galveston on April 9 [1953] was false and I knew at the time that it was false."[16]

Armed with new ammunition, Foreman went after Heras with renewed vigor. He began by asking about his reported income during the time covered by the indictments. Heras said he had been receiving $275 a month salary, $200 a year for preparing tax rolls for an accounting firm, and $60 a year from rental property. Waving copies of bank records, Foreman asked how he had been able to deposit over $12,000 to his personal account on such income.

"I believe it was advances and loans—loans from banks and by the school district."

"Did the school district know it was loaning you money, or did you just do it yourself?"

"Someone knew or else I was told to get the money from some source," Heras answered. "It was common practice. I would be told by Mr. Parr or Mr. Benson to take care of some person, perhaps a janitor or a bus driver. I'd get the money on a loan, and then they'd tell me to get the money to pay the loans."[17]

The trial entered its fifth week with Heras still on the stand and Foreman still bearing down. Dramatic as ever, Foreman dubbed Heras as "Lord Bountiful, using the funds of the Benavides school district," but now he wanted to know if Heras had used school funds to benefit himself.[18]

Focusing on three checks drawn on the school account in September 1949, each for $225, and all made out to Heras, Foreman quipped, "perhaps you worked extra hard that month."

"One was a salary check and the others I considered advances and travel expense checks," Heras calmly replied.

"How did you arrive at how to mark these checks—advance or salary—what was the distinction made in your mind?" Foreman asked.

"Well. I called anything that was not my salary an advance."

"You mean anything you got caught stealing was an advance," Foreman accused.[19]

Before asking about the FBI affidavits, Foreman wanted to establish a motive for Heras having turned against Parr. According to the *Corpus Christi Caller*, he asked what happened when the tax office was moved from Parr's building in San Diego to Benavides. "I had talked to Mr. Parr months before and he assured me I would remain in San Diego and that's all I wanted," Heras said.

Pressing for more details, Foreman asked Heras where he was when the school's tax records were being moved to Benavides.

"I left town that morning and did not return to work for about a week or 10 days."

"You were mad at George Parr?"

"Yes sir."

During the first mail fraud trial, Foreman hadn't asked Heras questions concerning his personal bank account because the defense didn't have the records. Handing Heras photostatic copies of checks drawn on the school account and made out to several individuals, Foreman asked how these checks came to be deposited in Heras's account.

"Yes, because it is one of those checks I cashed for those people," Heras said. "The banks closed at 2 o'clock. I had a steel box where I carried a little cash of my own."

"Was that spelled s–t–e–e–l?"

"Yes, sir, s–t–e–e–l," Heras replied. "It was a gunmetal gray box with a lock. I kept my personal cash and also I had some American Red Cross money."

"American Red Cross?" Foreman exclaimed, performing for his audience. "You weren't stealing from them, too, were you?"[20]

Heras had been squeezed through the wringer, but the grueling ordeal wasn't over. The following day, Heras was continuously subjected to a barrage of questions concerning affidavits he signed and the immunity from prosecution he received to testify against Parr. Delving into the affidavits, Foreman quoted freely from them, using the statements to refute testimony Heras was now giving. Backed into a corner, Heras could only answer: "I don't recall," or "I'm not sure." Reading several questions and answers from the affidavits, Foreman attempted to show that Heras had allowed District Attorney Sam Burris to mold the answers to fit his purpose.

Foreman read from an affidavit: "And let's see, Sam, if this is answering the way you wanted it. I want my answers to be in the right way." When asked what he had meant, Heras said, "I wanted to answer the right way. It was not that I was hoping to please him." Foreman then read a portion referring to the break-in at the tax office. Heras said Parr had broken the office desk open with a sledge hammer during the night. Burris asked Heras if he had personally witnessed the act. "No," the affidavit read, "but I'd say he did if someone asked me."[21]

Keeping up the pressure, Foreman asked if Heras had been granted immunity in exchange for testifying against Parr. Heras said repeatedly he had never been offered immunity. At this point, Foreman turned to the jury: "I intend to offer a certified copy of the order granting him immunity."[22] Contrary to his promise, Foreman never produced the document.

Continuing to play a cat-and-mouse game, Foreman rehashed statements Heras made in affidavits and during the first mail fraud trial. Each time Foreman seemed to have him trapped in a discrepancy, Heras would simply say, "I don't know," or "I don't recall," slipping out of the noose. By the end of his sixth day on the stand, Heras, though weary from the ordeal, showed no signs of wavering. According to the *Houston Post*, after excusing the jury for the day, Ingraham expressed his impatience.

"Mr. Foreman, you have been cross-examining Government Witness Diego Heras since last Friday. Is there an end in view?"

"I'm sure the jury is tired of hearing this testimony," Foreman replied, adding that he hoped to finish the next day.

"The jury?" Ingraham said with a smile.[23]

Back on the stand Heras was confronted on the sworn affidavit he made about bribe money he delivered from Parr to an FBI agent. Reading from the first affidavit Heras gave to the FBI, Foreman quoted him as saying that, after Parr ended a phone conversation with an FBI agent in Corpus Christi, Parr handed Heras an envelope filled with cash and instructed him to deliver it to "that man." Turning to the second affidavit, Foreman again quoted Heras, this time talking about his previous affidavit. "I knew at the time I made it that it was false," the statement read. "The details I gave about the FBI agent were made up by me."[24]

According to the *Corpus Christi Caller*, Foreman pressed Heras on which version was the truth. Choosing neither, Heras now offered a third version he swore was the truth. He now claimed he received a call from someone saying he was an FBI agent from Corpus Christi who was trying to contact Parr. Heras said he gave the message to Parr, who then placed a call to the man, but Heras didn't hear what was said. Parr then gave him an envelope that felt as if it contained cash and instructed him to deliver it to another man—not an FBI agent—at a finance company in Corpus Christi.

"Then the affidavit of April 11 is a bunch of lies?" Foreman asked.

"I think it inconsistent with the facts as I knew them," Heras replied.

Offering an explanation for his flip-flop version in the affidavits, Heras said he had been sick at the time, having been released from a hospital and not having had solid food for days. "I had been having convulsions and spasms," he said. "I was very ill." When Foreman suggested the illness had resulted from a "diet of liquor," Heras denied the accusation. Continuing to hammer away, Foreman kept grilling Heras right up to the end of the day's session. Ingraham called a halt, recessing for the weekend, but Foreman wasn't finished with Heras yet.[25]

Heras was on the stand for his ninth consecutive day as the trial headed into the sixth week. After questions about deposits made to personal accounts, Foreman turned Heras back to the prosecution. Wilkey attempted to clarify some of Heras's testimony by showing Foreman had taken many of the statements in the two affidavits out of context. Foreman took another stab at Heras on redirect by asking him again if he had been granted immunity for testifying. The best Foreman could get Heras to admit was that he could have been indicted for misdeeds he had disclosed during his lengthy testimony. To his relief, Heras was finally excused.[26]

Parr's former personal accountant William Benson was the next government witness. His testimony was almost a verbatim rehashing of his testimony in the earlier, hung-jury mail fraud trial, delving into Parr's control of the school district and its funds. Having also prepared income tax returns for D.C. Chapa and Oscar Carrillo Sr., Benson was asked about reported income on both returns that hadn't been identified as to their source. He stated that he had no idea where the money came from. Furthermore, he couldn't link the income to missing school funds because he hadn't learned about fictitious checks being drawn on the school district account until after the Duval investigation began.[27]

The government had already called over seventy witnesses, but a few more were needed to tie up loose ends. Two bank employees who testified in the hung-jury trial were called to verify bank documents and implicate other defendants in the conspiracy. The prosecution finished by calling its last witness—FBI handwriting expert Earl Williams. He said he was assigned the task of determining who signed many of the checks drawn on the school account and made out to fictitious persons. Comparing signatures stipulated authentic by the defense with those on the checks, Williams concluded they were written by the same person—George Parr. He also identified signatures of three other defendants on some of the checks.[28] With the jury excused, Foreman made a futile motion that the jury should not consider Williams's testimony.[29]

Before the prosecution ended its case Foreman submitted another motion. The defense wanted all statements made to government agencies by every prosecution witness who had testified turned over to the defense. If this motion were granted, Foreman could then call all the witnesses back, picking apart their testimony by comparing it to their earlier affidavits. Basing his ruling on the Jencks decision, Ingraham granted the request. Wilkey protested on the ground that "the witnesses then become defense witnesses," but reluctantly agreed to comply.[30]

After Wilkey turned over an additional 121 documents, obtained from ongoing Justice Department investigations of perjury and income tax and Federal Reserve violations, he asked the court to enjoin the defense attorneys from keeping any copies when the trial ended. "Some of them contain matters not even yet presented to the grand jury," he explained.[31] Ingraham agreed, asking the four defense attorneys to stand. "Each of you is enjoined that when the documents have served their purpose, every copy will be returned to this court and no copy will be retained by you," he ordered. "The copies are not for your continued use and not for your files." But Wilkey wanted more. Not only did he want the documents back, and any copies made by the defense, he also wanted all notes made by the attorneys in perusing the material. Once again, Ingraham agreed, ordering the defense team not to destroy any notes and to turn them over to the court clerk. Foreman, thinking ahead to federal tax cases and state criminal cases his clients still faced, questioned the ruling.[32]

According to the *Alice Daily Echo*, he asked "Can we later make notes from what we may recall having seen in the documents?" It was a delicate point, but Ingraham was not moved. "The attorneys, all four of them, are admonished not to make any notes based on information obtained from matters described as privileged and confidential," he ruled. Foreman raised another point.

"If I get in state court I may recall something in one of the documents."

Ingraham was now put on the spot. "By order of this court I cannot restrict your memory but I do believe we can restrict what you may keep," he replied.[33] Left unsaid was what would happen if the defendants were found guilty. To prepare an effective appeal, the defense might need the sensitive documents returned to them. In addition, when Parr was tried on pending charges, it was almost certain that Foreman would submit motions to have the paperwork back.

With the rulings granted, the government rested its case. Foreman estimated it would take only a week to present his case, but most veteran court observers felt he was being optimistic. Quickly establishing a counterattack, Foreman called witnesses to refute testimony given by Heras. A former tax office employee said she saw Parr sign several blank school checks at the request of Heras, contradicting his statement he had

refused to countersign checks until they were made out in full. A grocer
from Benavides denied receiving two hundred dollars in cash from D.C.
Chapa to settle an account. This conflicted with Heras's testimony he had
been with Chapa when the transaction was made.[34]

Foreman then launched a surprise attack by calling Wilkey to the
stand. Questioning him about conferring with U.S. attorney general
Herbert Brownell, Foreman asked: "Did Mr. Brownell tell you this was
a good way to get even with Lyndon Johnson because Mr. Parr helped
elect him?" Wilkey said, "Mr. Johnson's name was never mentioned."[35]
Pressing further, Foreman attempted to establish that the case really
began with Governor Shivers, but Wilkey remained calm and said he
never discussed the case with the governor and the indictments began
with his predecessor. Foreman then questioned the validity of Heras's
sworn affidavits:

> Foreman: *Did you read that statement before you called Heras as a*
>   *government witness in this case?*
> Wilkey: Yes, I did.
> Foreman: *Then you knew Heras was a certified liar when you called*
>   *him as a witness; isn't that right?*
> Wilkey: The government doesn't pick its witnesses. We take no
>   position of vouching for any witnesses.
> Foreman: *Then you, yourself, have doubts as to the veracity of the*
>   *witness?*
> Wilkey: I make no statement as to the veracity of that or any
>   other witness. The jury will have to be the judge of veracity.[36]

Wilkey survived the verbal barrage without faltering, but Foreman
had made his point—Heras was an unreliable witness. To bolster his contention Foreman offered more defense witnesses, each casting aspersions
on Heras. Depicted as a drunkard, known to drink "after, before and
during office hours," Heras was also characterized as a big spender who
always carried around wads of money in his pocket. Others testified to
having seen Heras leaving through a window on the night of the tax
office break-in.[37]

The lengthy trial took a toll on the jurors, many of whom could
ill afford to take time away from their jobs. Sympathizing with their
plight, Ingraham announced he was giving them a raise. Instead of seven

dollars a day, they would be getting ten dollars, but some jurors had more pressing problems. "One man is being pressed for a $51.72 furniture note and another is about to lose his automobile," the judge said. Ingraham wrote letters to the creditors asking for patience, but it was becoming evident that the jury was getting anxious to end their ordeal and render a verdict.[38]

In presenting the case for the defense, Foreman called only one of the nine defendants to testify—O. P. Carrillo. A practicing attorney and former school board legal counsel, Carrillo may have been considered by Foreman to be a witness who could remain cool under cross-examination. When asked if he knew taxes were being collected by mail, Carrillo replied, "I'm telling the jury exactly what I know. I can't tell them anything I don't know and didn't see."[39]

Character witnesses followed as the defense neared completion. Government rebuttal testimony was then heard, after which charges the judge would make to the jury were taken up in conference. Asked if he reviewed the defense's requests of charges, Wilkey said he had. "I have weighed them carefully," he told the judge, "and found that papers containing the defense's charges weigh 2 pounds 11 ounces and ours weighs 2½ ounces." Final arguments were limited to six hours for each side. Foreman used every minute to convince the jury Heras couldn't be trusted, having been "turned into a talking machine" for the prosecution.[40]

After a two-month trial, the case finally went to the jury on July 12. It took them until July 17 to evaluate the multitude of evidence, but they reached a decision. Out of 161 counts, only 4 were returned not guilty—the remaining 157 counts were all for conviction. During reading of the verdicts, Parr remained impassive as the jury foreman read each count, pausing slightly after each before saying "guilty." After all of the verdicts had been read, Wilkey said none of the defendants had been fingerprinted, which Ingraham then ordered. While being processed, Parr was asked his occupation. "Just say I'm unemployed," he quipped, seemingly in a jovial mood. "No, just write down 'rancher.'"[41]

On July 30, 1957, Parr and his codefendants received their sentences from Ingraham. Guilty of twenty counts, Parr's maximum sentence could be as much as one hundred years in prison and twenty-nine thousand dollars in fines, but it was unlikely he would receive either. Before he gave out the sentences, Ingraham listened to oral arguments from both sides. Wilkey attacked Parr by summarizing the Duke's control over the south Texas community: "The actions of the defendant Parr over a period of some 23 years reveal the actions of a man whose character is completely amoral—no higher consideration for the rights of other humans, no consideration for the obligations of honor or faithfulness in public office or public trust, no differentiation between the money of others and money of his own, no rule of action or conduct during those years except what he considered at the moment desirable for himself."[42] When Foreman spoke, he continued his attack on Wilkey, accusing him of offering into evidence matters not pertaining to the trial. He asked Ingraham to disregard the "odiferous insinuations" made against his clients when rendering his decision.[43]

Ingraham adjourned for a three-hour recess before returning to pass sentences. School board attorney O. P. Carrillo received a suspended two-year sentence. School board members Jesus Garza and Santiago Garcia received suspended three-year sentences. School board president Octavio Saenz received a three-year prison term; school board secretary Oscar Carrillo Sr. and Alice bank cashier B. F. Donald both received four-year prison terms; and tax collector D.C. Chapa received a five-year prison sentence. Alice bank director Jesus Oliveira was fined seven thousand dollars; the Alice bank was fined two thousand dollars; and the San Diego bank nine hundred dollars.[44]

Then it was Parr's turn. Standing before Ingraham, he was sentenced to five years on each of ten counts, all to run concurrently, and sentenced to another five years on the remaining counts. Including a twenty-thousand-dollar fine, Parr was sentenced to a total of ten years in prison. After leaving the courtroom, he smiled for the photographers, telling them they could take all the pictures they wanted. Asked for a statement, Parr said: "No comment. That's what I have a lawyer for." No one doubted Parr would appeal his conviction. Foreman began immediately by requesting the six-thousand-page sixteen-volume trial transcript (at a cost of fifteen thousand dollars). "This was only the first round. We have nine more rounds to go," Foreman told reporters.[45]

Two days later, the Justice Department announced it would await the outcome of the appeal process before going ahead with the tax evasion case against Parr. "We are not dismissing the income tax case," Wilkey declared. "We're just waiting for the prison doors to close on George

Parr before acting on it." Sam Burris, who still had state charges pending against Parr, came forward with a deal. Burris wouldn't dismiss the charges, but he would consider a state sentence running concurrent with Parr's federal sentence. However, the offer would not remain open while Parr pursued a potential lengthy appeal process in the federal courts. If Parr wanted the deal, he would have to accept it now. Parr refused, intending to fight to the bitter end.[46]

Thelma Parr received good news from the IRS when they announced they were relieving her of the $441,000 tax claim against her. It was being dismissed because the IRS felt she had not taken part in the tax evasion scheme. The IRS also removed the property lien and refunded $112,000 she had already paid against the lien.[47]

Thelma was off the hook, leaving George to fight on his own. The pending IRS case was a minor concern at this point; what really mattered was staying out of jail. After Tom Donald had his state case overturned by the appeals court, Foreman reasoned that Parr's state conviction should follow the same course. The court of criminal appeals agreed. On November 20, 1957, the higher court reversed and ordered prosecution dismissed on Parr's conviction.[48] Parr had dodged state prison, but his legal problems weren't over.

The federal government was still breathing down his neck. On March 10, 1958, the IRS filed a $754,645 tax lien on his property for income taxes owed from 1949 to 1956, bringing the total claims to $1,340,249. George didn't seem overly concerned with tax problems because his first priority was the appeal for his mail fraud conviction. But the trustee in bankruptcy for Parr's estate, George Clower, was concerned about the IRS claim and challenged it. The dispute led to a hearing in Corpus Christi where more disclosures of the Parr empire were revealed.[49]

The main contention was whether money Parr obtained from Duval County to purchase the Dobie Ranch and pay his 1946 income taxes had been in the form of a loan. If it was, then the money was not taxable income. Testifying at the hearing, Kenneth Bennight, the court-appointed accountant for Parr's estate, said he traced the county funds to the Wilder Construction Company, and from there to Parr. Examining Parr's account books, Bennight said the money had been listed under "mortgage payable." Another entry in the ledger showed a payment on the principal of ten thousand dollars and eighteen thousand dollars in interest toward the loan.[50]

The well-traveled Diego Heras was back again to offer his recollection of Parr's handling of school funds. Once again, he described how Parr gave him lists of names and told him to write out checks payable to those on the list. Heras repeated his previous testimony saying he had cashed the checks and turned the money over to Parr. Under cross-examination by the attorney for the trustee, Heras remained steadfast in denying that any of the money went into his own bank account. The money went to Parr, he insisted.[51]

Delving further, the government called Dan U. Garcia. A former Duval County sheriff, Garcia testified that he resigned the position in 1952 after reaching an agreement with Parr, who was appointed sheriff after Garcia stepped down. Garcia said he met with Parr on two occasions to discuss the matter, both times on a country road outside of San Diego. He told Parr he was willing to resign, but he needed money. Parr agreed to pay him twenty thousand dollars and the pact was sealed. Garcia said he resigned and later received an envelope containing twenty thousand dollars in cash from W. C. Johnson, a former partner of Parr and Garcia in the Duval Motor Company.[52]

The hearing continued with an IRS agent testifying he had been unable to determine if the money Parr had received from the county was a loan. His investigation was incomplete because of missing records, he said. County records were missing, microfilm bank records had been destroyed, and six hundred Duval County checks had mysteriously disappeared from the county auditor's vault, all of which hampered his inquiry.[53] The testimony being offered had shed light on Parr's manipulating county funds, but very little was learned about the so-called loans.

The hearing came to a sudden halt when an announcement was made that a tentative out-of-court agreement had been reached between the federal government and the trustee of Parr's estate. Over the next eight months, both sides attempted to finalize the agreement, but when it failed to receive Justice Department approval, the contest went back to the bankruptcy court.[54] Fighting for claims against Parr's bankrupt estate became a full-time job for some over the next two years. While George had little to say concerning the dragged-out proceedings, he must have privately chuckled to see the combatants arguing over the spoils.

On April 13, 1961, bankruptcy referee James M. Easterling handed down a fifty-page decision. Citing failure of the federal government to prove fraud when Parr obtained county money, he added that the government had failed to file its claim within the required three-year period when the taxes were due. As a result, the government's claim for $1.24 million was reduced to a paltry $68,000. That claim, however, was wiped out when Easterling determined that the bankrupt estate was entitled to an offsetting credit for the same amount.[55]

On appeal by the government, the district federal court ruled "that the moneys were illegally obtained with no intention on the part of the bankrupt of ever repaying them." In reviewing the manner in which the loans had been given, the court viewed them as "diversion tactics to draw attention away from the true illegal nature of the transactions" and accused Parr of having "simply helped himself to the money." However, even though the court determined the loans were taxable income, it ruled that since the government had failed to prove fraud, the income tax due was to be considered part of the debt to Parr's creditors.[56]

The government continued fighting its claim until an agreement was made in November 1963. In the compromise, the $68,000 offsetting credit was abandoned and the IRS was granted a $147,393 claim on Parr's bankrupt estate.[57] It had taken six and a half years since Parr had filed for bankruptcy for the parties to reach a settlement. In the interim Parr's creditors were forced to await the outcome before any hope of receiving their share. Parr could care less, knowing that whatever settlement was made, he wouldn't receive a penny. His primary worry was the outcome of his criminal conviction appeals.

The appeal was heard by three judges from the Fifth Circuit Court of Appeals of New Orleans, meeting at the federal court in Fort Worth.[58] On April 6, 1959, the court handed down its ruling and the news wasn't good. After reviewing trial transcripts, they determined Parr was the controlling figure in the scheme to defraud the school district. They noted that, although he wasn't a school board member, he "completely dominated its activities," and "he personally countersigned substantially all the Board checks." Defending Parr on the merits of the case was virtually impossible due to the enormous evidence against him, so the main argument presented by Foreman was that the U.S. postal system was not used in furthering the scheme. The appeals court found no merit in this claim. Foreman also attacked the testimony of Diego Heras, whom the court recognized as a man who had "feathered his own nest at the expense of the board," but, according to the court, the jury had an opportunity to discredit his statements and chose not to. A petition for rehearing was denied on August 12, 1959. The conviction against George Parr was affirmed and he was down to his last legal straw—the U.S. Supreme Court.[59]

CHAPTER 21

REGAINING POWER

Down to his last straw, Parr filed an appeal with the U.S. Supreme Court on September 15, 1959. In addition to both banks Parr was joined by his eight mail fraud codefendants in petitioning the high court to overturn the convictions. The brief centered on two points: Parr was not allowed to see grand jury testimony of the government's star witness Diego Heras; and the case should have been tried as local embezzlement, not a federal mail fraud charge. In answering the appeal, James Lee Rankin, U.S. solicitor general, and Wilkey, now assistant attorney general, the government cited a recent Supreme Court ruling holding that grand jury testimony did not always have to be disclosed to a defendant.[1] As for the case being "local," they contended: "The mails were used here as an integral part of the scheme to defraud."[2]

In 1960 Lyndon Johnson was becoming a serious candidate for the Democratic presidential nomination, and the last thing he needed was any publicity connecting him with Parr. He called upon his friend Abe Fortas to handle Parr's Supreme Court appeal and take the case pro bono because George was having financial problems. Assisting Fortas was Paul A. Porter, who was told to keep Johnson informed by phoning Walter W. Jenkins, Johnson's friend and adviser. Distancing himself from the situation, Johnson became paranoid about anything connecting him with Parr, telling Jenkins to "burn your memos on phone calls."[3]

Getting heard by the highest court was no easy matter, even for an experienced attorney of Fortas's reputation. For an appeal to be granted a hearing, a writ of certiorari had to be issued, which was applied for on September 15, 1959, and granted on December 7, allowing the appeal of Parr and his codefendants to be heard.[4] During oral arguments before the court on April 28, 1960, Wilkey admitted he had made a "flat misstatement, unintentionally" at the trial. Three times during the mail fraud trial he stated that a transcript had been made of Heras's grand jury testimony. He later discovered it had not, but he insisted "there was no need for a transcript" because "we had all the written statements from him we needed." Fortas pounced on Wilkey's admission, saying that withholding the transcript was one of two issues in his argument. The second point being made was that no mail fraud ever occurred because the county was required by law to mail out tax statements.[5]

The U.S. Supreme Court rendered its decision on June 13, 1960. The twenty-four-page majority opinion written by Judge Charles Evans Whittaker, in which he was joined by five other judges (Warren, Black, Douglas, Clark, and Brennan), began with where school funds came from and how the defendants "devised and practiced a scheme to defraud" the school district and "obtain their money and property for themselves and their relatives." The court said the facts had shown that the defendants sent out tax statements through the U.S. mail and received payments from taxpayers to be credited to the school district in the authorized depository bank, "against which [the defendants] would issue district checks payable to fictitious persons." The checks were then cashed "upon forged endorsements or without endorsements," and defendants would "keep the proceeds." The defendants would "obtain merchandise for themselves . . . at the expense of the District" and prepare "false Annual Reports" and "conceal their fraudulent misuse of district funds by destroying canceled checks, bank statements . . . and the microfilmed records."

The opinion detailed how the evidence had shown various methods by which large amounts were "misappropriated, converted, embezzled and stolen" by the defendants. The court had no doubt "the evidence tended strongly to show that [the defendants] devised and practiced a brazen scheme to defraud by misappropriating, converting and embezzling the District's moneys and property," and the defendants' own counsel conceded it as fact.

But the court was more concerned in how the government based its case on the defendants' using the U.S. mail to perpetrate their conspiracy. This was the crux of Fortas's argument: the mails had not been used "for the purpose of executing such scheme." Because the school board was required by law to collect taxes and to perform its duty, its members were compelled "to cause the mailing of the [tax statements]." Wilkey argued that once fraud was shown to exist, the mailings "constituted essential steps in the scheme," and they "falsely represented that the tax moneys would be used only for lawful purposes."

Justice Whittaker concluded "there was no evidence tending to show, that the taxes assessed were excessive, 'padded' or in any way illegal." He dismissed the Court of Appeals opinion that "the assessments were designed to bring in not only 'enough money . . . to provide for the legitimate operation of the schools [but also] enough additional . . . to provide the funds to be looted.'" He added that the government didn't question that the school board was required by state law to use the mails in collecting taxes, thereby compelling the defendants "to cause and causing those mailings planned to steal an indefinite part of the receipts." The court could not find the mailings "criminal under the federal mail fraud statute." The opinion also dismissed the charge that mailing checks to oil companies for payment of fraudulent use of gasoline and services constituted using the mails for fraud. The majority opinion concluded with an expression of displeasure in overturning the conviction:

> The strongest element in the Government's case is that petitioners' behavior was shown to have been so bad and brazen, which coupled with the inability or at least the failure of the state authorities to bring them to justice, doubtless persuaded the Government to undertake this prosecution. But the showing, however convincing, that state crimes of misappropriation, conversion, embezzlement and theft were committed does not establish the federal crime of using the mails to defraud, and, under our vaunted legal system, no man, however bad his behavior, may be convicted of a crime of which he was not charged, proven and found guilty in accordance with due process.[6]

With this closing statement, Parr and his codefendants had won—but not without hearing the blistering dissent written by Justice Frankfurter (joined by Harlan and Stewart). "Through their control of the District's fiscal affairs they looted it of at least $200,000 between 1949 and 1953," he wrote. Frankfurter outlined evidence not mentioned in the majority opinion—the defendants acted in collusion to raise the tax rate to the maximum allowed by state law, and, "pursuant to a scheme devised in 1949, they regularly spent less than the amount collected on the schools, created no reserves, and appropriated a portion of the proceeds to their own uses. When their domination of the District ceased in 1954, school expenditures sharply rose, while tax collections remained substantially unchanged." The dissenting Justices were incensed the majority had said that because the state mandated tax statements are sent by mail, the defendants were immune from the Mail Fraud statute: "It bespeaks an audacious lack of humor to suggest that the law anywhere under any circumstances requires tax collectors who send out tax bills, and who also have complete control over the returns, to send out bills to an amount which they predeterminedly design to put in part to personal uses." The argument continued that the majority opinion would have everyone believe the mails "were not used in the fraud because the wrongdoing only arose after the mails had fulfilled their function by bringing the returns." Before closing his opinion, Frankfurter added: "If the fraudulent enterprise of which this record reeks is not a scheme essentially to defraud the taxpayers who constitute the District rather than a disembodied, abstract entity called the District, English words have lost their meaning."[7] No matter how strongly Frankfurter worded the dissenting opinion, the final result was unchanged—Parr was a free man.

Percy Foreman, commenting on the decision said: "Out of those 454 indictments, not one person has been mugged, printed [incorrect], or served a minute in jail." Six months after the Supreme Court decision, the federal government filed a motion to dismiss all charges in the case.[8] It had taken almost six years in one court after another, but in the end Parr and his codefendants had emerged after 656 counts of federal and state indictments without one conviction among them. The mail fraud case was over, and the state criminal charges against him had lost steam after the Supreme Court decision. Heading into 1960, Parr still had the federal income tax evasion case pending and was facing an assault on his dukedom from the increasing strength of the reform party. The power he once held would never be the same.

The Freedom Party was dealt a blow with the untimely death of their leader Horacio R. "Lacho" Canales. Running for sheriff in the 1960 Democratic primary, he had just finished giving a speech at a campaign rally when he suffered a heart attack and died on the way to the hospital. His name remained on the ballot and voters were asked to cast their ballots for him as a tribute. Under Texas election laws, if Canales won, the dead man would be certified the winner and the Democratic committee (eight-to-five anti-Parr) would name a successor.[9]

Incumbent sheriff Vidal Garcia won the primary by a narrow margin, but three other county offices were taken by anti-Parr candidates, and Atlee Parr was forced into a runoff for county commissioner. He won the runoff by forty-three votes, giving the Old Party complete control of the commissioners' court, but three anti-Parr candidates who won the primary forced the Old Party to run as independents in the November general election.[10] Switching the three Old Party candidates to an independent ticket proved to be a success as all three won.

In the presidential race, Parr did his part for the Democrats by bringing in 3,803 votes for the Kennedy-Johnson ticket to 809 for Nixon-Lodge. Earlier that year, two longtime supporters of Parr—C. O. Foerster Jr. and Asher Neil—circulated a petition to get Parr on the ballot for governor. The organizational director for the Democratic Party, Jake Pickle, informed them that Parr's consent was required, which they tried to secure, but he wasn't interested.[11] Parr was running for office, but wasn't setting his goal as high as the governor's seat.

In his first bid for an elected position since running for sheriff in 1956, Parr ran for chairman of the Democratic Executive Committee in the May 1960 primary and defeated Santiago Cantu by a narrow margin.[12] It was an important post because, not only would he be presiding over committee meetings but any candidate seeking office would be required to file with him to get on the ballot and qualify for campaign funds from the party's coffers. Charges of voting irregularities came from both sides after Cantu filed suit in Judge Laughlin's court.

At stake were 637 absentee ballots that Cantu wanted invalidated. According to the *Alice Daily Echo*, witnesses testified how their ballots had been marked. Ernesto Alvarado—assisted in marking his ballot by Old Party member Berta Guerra—was asked how he knew his ballot was marked properly.

"They told me my ballot was marked the way I wanted it," he testified, raising laughter in the courtroom.

Mrs. Francisco Madriano, unable to read or write, was offered aid to obtain citizenship papers so she could receive welfare rations if she would vote the Old Party ticket. "They told me to vote and I voted," she told the court. Again, it was Berta Guerra who helped mark the ballot. After hearing the evidence, Judge Laughlin ruled all 637 absentee ballots valid.[13]

Filing a petition in Jim Wells County, Parr asked that three commissioners be appointed to recount the votes. He was declared the winner by 332 votes, whereupon Cantu filed with the court of civil appeals to contest the results. The higher court ruled against the lower court's decision, and Cantu was declared the winner as the new Duval County Democratic Party chairman, marking the first time that Parr's ability to be elected to any position he desired was thwarted. In an appeal to the Texas Supreme Court, the appellate decision was upheld based on a provision of the Texas election code that "The Supreme Court of Texas shall have no jurisdiction to review any election contest filed under this Act."[14]

Two days before the Texas Supreme Court decision, the Dobie Ranch was sold at public auction to satisfy judgments against Parr. It had taken four years after Duval County had taken possession of the property to reach an agreement for the ranch to be sold. In May 1959, an offer of one and a half million dollars was made for the property, but it was turned down. Oscar Spitz, attorney for the trustee in bankruptcy for Parr, and George Clower, trustee of the bankruptcy, and the commissioners for Duval County reached a compromise whereby the first 20 percent from the sale would go to the bankrupt Parr estate and the rest to Duval County. During the time the county maintained control of the property, it had cost Duval taxpayers close to two thousand dollars a month to guard it and keep it in repair. The auction notice was advertised in 165 newspapers across the nation, but only six bidders submitted the required one-hundred-thousand-dollar certified check to participate in the bidding.[15]

The auction took place on the lawn of the Duval County courthouse. The opening bid was $1,015,000 but like a six-handed, no-limit poker game, the players kept raising the stakes. Never flinching, they kept pushing the price up in thousand-dollar increments. With only two players still bidding in an auction lasting twenty-five minutes, James Oliver "J.O." Walker, a seventy-three-year-old cattle man from Laredo outbid his last opponent by offering $1,575,000. Media interest had brought newspaper and magazine reporters from six states, including a *Life* magazine photographer. Parr's comment was that he had made a wise investment of the county's $622,000 he "borrowed" for the purchase.[16]

With the sale of the ranch, Judge Laughlin dismissed a $172,500 suit against Parr and his former wife, Thelma, for recovery of money illegally withdrawn from Duval County funds. Parr had used the $172,500, along with the half-million-dollar "loan" to purchase the ranch.[17] Parr still retained his San Diego mansion, and his nephew Archer purchased some of the real estate holdings from the bankruptcy trustee, which in turn he sold to George for nominal prices, but George's massive holdings, including his beloved Dobie Ranch were gone.

Duval County had changed, and so had the political game. "George never will be the man that Archie was," said John Sutherland, a long-time community resident named after his grandfather who served as a physician at the Alamo. On a scouting expedition, his grandfather had galloped back to the Alamo, but when his horse slipped he fell and broke his hip. He was ordered by Colonel Travis to accompany another man to enlist reinforcements and thus escaped the fate of the remaining Alamo defenders. The grandson was very outspoken about the Duke of Duval. Young people were leaving the county he sadly noted. "They don't have to put up with all this politics. They leave and the county grows smaller." An even more acute observation was made by a close associate of Parr. "He's bull-headed. . . . There's no reasoning with him. . . . He's willing to lose every penny he has to keep his political power."[18]

Parr must have regained his political confidence because he decided to run again for public office—once again as chairman of the Duval County Democratic Executive Committee. His announcement came one month after his brother Atlee had resigned his post as trustee of the Benavides school district—a position he had held for nine years. Not the political animal his brother was, Atlee said he wanted to take a vacation of several months in California, but local observers felt he had tired of being part of the Parr machine and wanted out.[19]

George won the chairmanship against Progress Club candidate Juan Garcia in a landslide, but Garcia petitioned U.S. attorney general Robert F. Kennedy to impound the ballots in a neutral county, because "irreg-ularities of past made secrecy of ballots questionable and violated civil rights of opposition voters." The Justice Department ignored the local political squabble, and Judge Laughlin impounded the ballots in Duval County.[20]

Although much of Parr's control over Jim Wells County politics had waned during the last decade, he continued to be a dominant influence in local elections. The *Alice Daily Echo*, in a precedent-setting front-page editorial, denounced tactics of Jim Wells County candidates who tagged "their opponent or opposition as a 'Parr man.'" The local newspaper prided itself on never endorsing candidates for public office but called for the electorate to keep "outside influence" where it belonged—"Outside and in the past."[21]

With the mail fraud conviction behind him and bankruptcy claims settled, George also escaped additional state charges when District Attorney Sam Burris dismissed the last of sixty-one indictments against Parr and his codefendants. The income tax evasion case, placed on the back burner pending outcome of the mail fraud appeal, was also dismissed after a "thorough review" by order of the new U.S. attorney general, Robert F. Kennedy. Filing the dismissal motion, U.S. Attorney Ernest Morgan said the decision was based on Supreme Court decisions restricting prosecutions for "failure to report misappropriated funds for years prior to 1961." A second factor was that a key government witness, W. M. Benson, had died.[22]

In early March 1963, two identical bills were introduced in the Texas House of Representatives and the Texas Senate. They called for creation of the Duval County Conservation and Reclamation District, a title belying its true purpose—to consolidate county water districts, with the exception of Freer, under one commission. The board of directors would be appointed by the Parr-controlled Duval County commissioners' court and empowered to use county tax funds for its management. Section 4 of the bills stipulated "no election shall be necessary for the purpose of confirming its organization and no hearing shall be necessary to determine whether any land should be excluded from the district."[23]

Two years later, a $2.5-million bond issue was approved by Duval voters. Funds received were earmarked to purchase municipally owned water, sewage, and gas plants, placing them under one jurisdiction.[24] The formation of the consolidated water district would later prove to be a financial boon for Parr—but it would also lead to his downfall.

The death of President John F. Kennedy on November 22, 1963, shocked the nation and brought more controversy upon Parr. Political observers remarked that Lyndon Johnson would never have ascended to the Oval Office if it hadn't been for the 1948 senatorial election that catapulted him into the national political arena. Three days after the assassination, reports began to surface connecting Parr with the conspiracy.

John C. Askew—brother of Florida state senator Rubin Askew, and a former sign maker in Alice, Texas, who moved to Florida in 1954—contended that "Parr may have been behind the assassination of President Kennedy so that Parr might control Johnson politically." To add credence to his allegations, Askew linked Parr with the Bill Mason and Buddy Floyd murders. Rubin Askew claimed his brother was an alcoholic, "and not reliable," and the FBI discredited the rumor.[25] In another report filed with the CIA, Hal Keese, a rancher from Medina, Texas, stated "he knew for a fact" that Lee Harvey Oswald had spent the night before the assassination at Parr's ranch and that Parr and Lyndon Johnson had Kennedy assassinated. Following up on the CIA report, the FBI established that Oswald and his wife, Marina, had "definitely" spent that night at the home of Ruth Paine in Irving, Texas.[26]

At one o'clock in the morning on July 31, 1967, the FBI San Antonio office received a call from Mrs. Pat Luby of Los Altos, California, advising them she had information concerning the Kennedy assassination. She learned that former Alice district attorney Sam Burris was being held at Corpus Christi Spohn Hospital against his will. Mrs. Luby stated she was told by Burris's wife, Dorothy, a friend of hers, that Dr. Fitelli and Dr. Paul Gutman were keeping Burris and a man named Lester under narcotics and being paid by George Parr to "keep them quiet" because they had learned something about the assassination. Mrs. Luby said it was all part of "a political matter headed up by President Johnson and is directed through the George Parr machine." Apparently the FBI found no basis of the allegations because they recommended "no investigation be conducted" concerning the reported incident.[27]

Two other reports connecting the Kennedy assassination with Parr didn't specifically name him but indirectly associated him with the conspiracy. In the first, Lee Harvey Oswald was reported to have stopped in Alice, Texas, on his way back from Mexico City on October 3, 1963, to apply for a job at radio station KOPY. Mike Rioa, an announcer at the radio station, said Oswald came in around 6 P.M., but was told to come back the next day to see the manager.[28]

The following day, Oswald returned to the radio station at 1:30 P.M. and talked to L. L. "Sonny" Stewart, the station manager. Stewart said Oswald was driving in an old model car with a woman passenger, but when Stewart invited her in, Oswald said she couldn't speak English.

Oswald told Stewart he had been traveling from Mexico and spotted the station from the highway. Oswald told Stewart he had no radio experience and Stewart told him there were no openings at the station. "Most of the interview was spent discussing radio stations where Oswald might have a chance of getting a job," Stewart said, adding, "There was a strange quality about him that would have made me hesitant about hiring him." After jotting down the man's name as "Lee Oswald," Stewart told him to check out a radio station in Pleasanton, Texas. The Warren Commission determined Oswald traveled by bus from Mexico City and applied for two jobs in Dallas that day, but the bus never passed through Alice.[29]

The second report surfaced in 1977, when Ronald Smith told the FBI he had read a report in a newspaper about police in Waco stopping teenagers who were carrying five hundred thousand dollars in cash they claimed they had found on a ranch in Alice. Smith added he heard that Oswald had spent the first night upon returning from Mexico City at an Alice ranch. After investigating, the FBI discovered the bills found in the possession of the teenagers were mostly from the 1969 or 1974 series, ruling out any connection with the Kennedy killing.[30]

Having survived state and federal criminal trials, Parr continued his political comeback. Already chairman of the Duval County Democratic Executive Committee, which he used to fill county posts with hand-picked officials, he sought to expand his control. In April 1964, he ran unopposed for trustee of the San Diego Independent School Board. Because Texas law forbade him from holding both positions, he resigned as Democratic Executive Committee chairman to be replaced by J. C. King, who had held the position from 1936 to 1956. Parr still exercised control over the Old Party, but now he held the school district reins as well.[31]

Controlling Duval County meant more to Parr than just being a political boss. He acted as though the county was his fiefdom, allowing him to do whatever he wanted, including illegal hunting. On the night of October 22, 1969, Game Warden James Stinebaugh approached a car parked along the side of a road. The occupants had rigged a handheld spotlight connected to the car battery and were using it to attract wild game. Hunting at night with an artificial light is a violation of Texas hunting laws. Well aware of their transgression, when the hunters spotted the game warden, they jumped into their car and sped off into the night.

Radioing ahead for a deputy sheriff to help, Stinebaugh gave chase. After a wild twenty-mile pursuit, he stopped the car a few miles outside San Diego. A seven-millimeter rifle and the spotlight were confiscated as evidence. The sole occupant of the car, George Parr, was arrested, taken to the Duval County courthouse, and released on his own recognizance.[32]

The following day, the deputy sheriff who had helped in the chase was fired. Stinebaugh was transferred to another area, leaving one game warden based one hundred miles away in San Antonio to enforce hunting laws in Duval County. Parr was never brought to court on the charge. In a front-page editorial Bob Parker, editor and publisher of the *Texas Observer*, likened the incident to medieval times when the king hunted wherever he chose. "The divine right of one man to kill game animals when and where he pleases is no longer recognized," Parker wrote. "Except in one place, Duval County."[33]

On April 5, 1968, Elizabeth Frances Parr filed for divorce against Archer Parr in the Court of Domestic Relations of Nueces County. Elizabeth claimed she had been living with her husband in Corpus Christi for two years prior to the filing. Archer answered the divorce suit on May 23, 1968. He subsequently filed his own suit on August 14, 1968, but in Duval County where he knew he would find a friendly judge. Seeing that she would be arguing her case before Judge Laughlin, Elizabeth filed an appeal to have her suit heard back in Nueces County where the original divorce suit had been filed. Claiming fraud and naming Laughlin in her appeal, she had her date in court before the Court of Civil Appeals of Texas in Corpus Christi, but the judges ruled against her and the divorce case took place in Duval County.[34] It came as no surprise to anyone that Archer was awarded the divorce on favorable terms.

Unlike his uncle, Archer was a world traveler and enjoyed being a playboy in Corpus Christi society where he was often seen wearing a mink coat, custom-designed for him by Anamorena Furs on North State Street in Chicago. Although he vacationed in Spain and Africa and was a member of the Corpus Christi Yacht Club, he lived in a concrete-block ranch house and raised South Texas–bred Beefmaster cattle, a prized breed in the area. At one cattle auction, Archer purchased eleven thousand dollars' worth of prize beef, including the top Beefmaster bull. Archer also raised twelve hundred Spanish goats on his ranch, prompting one observer to say, "He can't even make up his mind whether he wants to be a cattleman or a goat herder." Although eccentric in some ways, Archer still managed to keep his mind on Duval County politics as county judge and, in 1964, as a Texas delegate to the Democratic National Convention in Atlantic City.[35]

On July 12, 1969, Archer married his fourth wife, Jody Martin, a tall, strikingly beautiful blonde who was a member of the jet-set crowd in Corpus Christi. A former model and onetime boutique owner, Jody viewed Archer as the means to provide for her expensive appetites (beginning with a seven-carat engagement ring), but she failed to consider the price to be paid. She began her second marriage by moving into Archer's sixteen-hundred-acre ranch a few miles west of San Diego, but in July 1971, they bought a luxury townhouse in the fashionable Santa Fe Street section of Corpus Christi.[36] The marriage would eventually end up in divorce court, but the final outcome, like anything connected to the Parr family, would make newspaper headlines.

PART V

END OF THE DYNASTY

CHAPTER 22

A ROUTINE TAX AUDIT

The political empire of George Parr appeared to have weathered the worst of times. The criminal and civil cases were behind him, and although the reform party had gained inroads, he was still the power to be reckoned with in Duval County. Parr-supported candidates continued to win, although not by the vast pluralities of the past. Parr was content to spend most of his time close to home in the company of his young wife and poker-playing cronies, but in Austin, ominous events were taking place that would lead to his eventual downfall.

It began in the early fall of 1971 with a routine IRS tax audit of Carl H. Stautz, sole proprietor of the Triangle Construction Company. In examining his records, the IRS auditor noticed that Stautz had been paid $2,500,000 over a three-year period by the San Diego and Benavides Independent School Districts for construction and remodeling contracts. In addition, records showed checks drawn to cash amounting to over $350,000, but Stautz hadn't claimed any business deductions on the amounts. When questioned by the auditor as to the nature of the withdrawals, Stautz became nervous and had difficulty in providing convincing answers. Suspicious that there might be a connection between the income from the school districts and the $350,000 cash payouts, the IRS auditor turned the files over to the IRS Criminal Investigation Division in Austin.

Stautz was represented by one of Austin's most powerful lawyers who argued there was no justification for a criminal investigation because Stautz hadn't declared business deductions for the cash withdrawals. Since he had paid the proper taxes on the income, no tax laws had been violated. Whether Stautz had a guilty conscience or was bothered by personal problems (his wife had died, his mother was ill, and his son had moved away), against the advice of his attorney he insisted on baring his soul to the government agents.

His attorney offered to explain the cash disbursements in return for full immunity from prosecution. Enticed by the prospect of a bigger fish, the agents listened as the attorney told them the $350,000 had been used for kickbacks on the school construction contracts Stautz had been awarded in Duval County. More importantly, and what made the hairs on the back of the agents' necks stand up, was that the payments had been made directly to George Parr.

Going after the Duke of Duval was risky because he had eluded charges of mail fraud and income tax evasion, and any prosecution aimed at him had to be carefully and meticulously planned. "Nobody wanted to rush into another one on George Parr without being pretty sure they were on solid ground," an IRS agent noted. Spearheading the inquiry was William Sessions, an Arkansas native and law graduate of Baylor University who would later become director of the FBI. Assisting him was John E. Clark, a Texan with a degree in business administration from Lamar University and a law degree from the University of Texas. Clark would write about his experiences with the Parr case in a well-documented book—*The Fall of the Duke of Duval*.[1]

The investigators had two immediate problems placing pressure on the probability of a successful outcome. Stautz was a reluctant witness who feared for his life. "He's convinced Parr has so much influence in Austin and Corpus that he could find out what Stautz said to a federal grand jury in either place," said George Stephen, IRS chief of intelligence in Austin. Parr's history was fraught with violence, giving Stautz a genuine concern (he received telephone death threats and someone shot at his window during the 1971 Christmas holiday).[2]

The second problem was the statute of limitations. Stautz came forward in late 1971, and the case had barely begun by March 1972, when the Justice Department finally granted him immunity. Any tax evasion case of such importance had to be reviewed and approved through a slow and tedious process. If they used evidence of illegal kickbacks from 1966, an indictment had to be forthcoming prior to April 1973 to avoid being barred by the statute.[3] The first priority was to interview Stautz and garner necessary information with particular attention to details leading directly to Parr's involvement.

Stautz was cooperative, but his main concern was the threats he had received since coming forward. How Parr had discovered Stautz was about to spill the beans was never detected, but it was obvious that some-how he knew. Stautz was concerned for his safety and kept detailed notes on threats he received. *"Your days are numbered if you talk to the tax people,"* read a note from January 1972. *"This is your second warning. Don't talk,"* was noted in February, and in March, *"This is the last warning not to talk to anyone about South Texas. Tell your lawyers to lay off. This is the last warning, Okay?"*[4] Investigators waited patiently for Stautz to discuss the cash pay-ments they needed to know about for their criminal inquiry.

Representing Stautz during the interview was Sander W. Shapiro from the Austin law firm representing Lady Bird and Lyndon Johnson in their personal legal matters. When Shapiro was confronted with the possibility of his client's immunity being voided and prosecutors hauling Stautz before a grand jury, the tone of the interview changed. Stautz began explaining the disbursement of cash payments he made in 1966, 1967, and 1968.

He identified $10,000 paid to Benavides school district superintendent Eunice Powell; $53,500 paid to San Diego school district superintendent Bryan Taylor; and a single cash payment to Parr in 1966. Stautz kept turning back to the death threats, saying he would disappear if called to testify before a federal grand jury. Despite his fears, Stautz provided agents with enough evidence to begin investigating Parr and the two school superintendents. Stautz had records showing twenty-two checks, amounting to $353,500 during the three-year period, being cashed for payoffs to the three men.[5]

Cash withdrawals alone were insufficient evidence; corresponding deposits by the recipients or eyewitnesses corroborating payoffs were needed. Two teams consisting of two agents each were assigned to investigate the two school superintendents. I. A. Filer and Charlie Volz, along with IRS agent Edwin Watts, were assigned the task of digging up evidence on Parr.

The first order of business was to pay a call on Parr to serve the required notice that he was the subject of an IRS investigation. Watts and Filer drove to San Diego to visit Parr, who appeared at his home just as the agents arrived. Parr invited them inside and was advised by Filer of his rights in the criminal investigation. Parr listened before saying, "I understand all of that and I'll talk about anything else, but I'm not going to talk about my business." The friendly conversation turned from his marriage to Eva Perez to small talk about the house and Parr's younger daughter, Georgia, before the agents left. "I want to wish you gentlemen good luck," he said as they were leaving, "but not on me."[6]

After careful review of Parr's tax returns from 1966 through 1969, the agents visited Norman H. Ransleben, a Corpus Christi CPA who handled Parr's tax returns for those years. Two items struck their attention: a long-term capital gain of forty thousand dollars on the 1967 return for the sale of City of Benavides bonds, and two transactions totaling fifteen thousand dollars from the Duval County Conservation and Reclamation District, noted as tax-free "loans and salary advances" and therefore not reportable income.[7] Ransleben told the agents that information used to prepare the tax returns were supplied by Parr in various forms—Parr's own records or statements provided by third-party records. The forty thousand dollars in bonds were acquired in 1939 and declared worthless in Parr's 1957 bankruptcy filing. The fifteen thousand dollars from the reclamation district were described as advances or "check swaps" on loans to Parr as the district's legal counsel—both sums and the circumstances surrounding their acquisition led the agents to investigate further.

Parr had been expecting trouble from the federal government ever since Republicans had taken control in Washington. He knew it was only a matter of time before they tried wrestling South Texas from the Democrats and rid the area of Parr politics. What was not expected was trouble within his family that would split his power. It was Archer and his trophy wife, Jody, who brought woes into his life at a time when he needed the support of family more than ever.

Archer's marriage to Jody was a battle of opposites: the volatile and heavy drinking Archer who readily raised a hand against his wife, at times causing her to check into a hospital (on New Year's Eve 1972 she was in a Corpus Christi hospital as a result of his choking her), and the proud, beautiful Jody who tried reviving her marriage with a pregnancy (but miscarried in May 1973 at the age of thirty-nine).[8] The quarreling came to a head on June 24, 1973, at their Corpus Christi home when Jody refused to sign the joint income tax return Archer had prepared because she knew her husband received five thousand dollars in cash every month from assistant Duval County treasurer Sylvester Gonzalez that wasn't included in the tax return. Jody decided she had had enough. The following day she filed for divorce in Nueces County, and on July 3, Archer filed in

Duval County (repeating the same scenario as when he was divorcing his third wife, Elizabeth).[9] The stage was set for an acrimonious court battle affecting not only their personal lives but the continued existence of the Old Party in South Texas politics.

George Parr was well aware the IRS was closing in on him. The inquiry into the sale of the forty thousand dollars of worthless bonds led investigators to Harris R. Fender, a wheeler-dealer from Tyler, Texas, more than four hundred miles away from Duval. The investigators wondered how Fender managed to have any dealings with Parr, but after delving into Fender's background it became readily apparent why Parr would trust him. Fender ran an investment banking firm (James C. Tucker and Company) in which his principle business was underwriting municipal bonds throughout Texas. He handled every Duval County bond issue since 1962, except one. He was also the majority stockholder (77 percent) in Parr's old bank—the First State Bank of San Diego.[10] During an interview, the agents quickly learned it was Fender who bought the worthless bonds from Parr and he had a plausible explanation.

Fender said he found it necessary to buy up the bonds of the City of Benavides, which had gone through bankruptcy in the 1950s, in order to issue new bonds for the Duval County Conservation and Reclamation District (the other entity agents were interested in). Without the bonds being purchased, the reclamation district could not hold title to the Benavides water and sewer systems, and since the municipality had no funds, Fender purchased them himself. He explained that he would later recoup his outlay once the reclamation district made money and could buy back the old bonds from him. Although it sounded reasonable, the agents were not that gullible—the forty-thousand-dollar check issued on May 24, 1967, was in reality a payment Fender made to Parr for the privilege of dealing with the reclamation district's new bonds.[11]

In his notes from the interview, agent Filer wrote that Fender said "Duval County, Texas is like a foreign country in that things are done differently," and Duval records are synonymous with Parr's records "because he is the county." Although the agents garnered information from Fender, they knew that to acquire any records from him would necessitate a civil summons issued by a federal court. After the summons were served at the First State Bank, it didn't take long before they heard from John G. Heard, a high-powered Houston attorney in the Vinson

and Elkins Law Firm (John Connally, former governor and Nixon's secretary of the treasury, was a former partner). Heard advised the agents
he had instructed the bank not to comply with the summons.[12] Getting
bank records would now require a protracted court battle, long enough
for Parr to avoid prosecution before the statute of limitations had run out
on records for the crucial year of 1966.

Continuing with another aspect of the case, the prosecution team
issued a subpoena for Stautz to appear before the federal grand jury in
San Antonio on May 9, 1972.[13] A federal grand jury not only had broad
powers in its scope to bring indictments; it also had federal resources
(FBI, ATF, and Secret Service) to help in the investigation. Jury members
also had authority to issue subpoenas to anyone within the United States
or its territories and possessions. The U.S. attorney's office in West Texas,
headed by William S. Sessions, could "lead" the grand jury by steering
it in the direction that would indict Parr, although the grand jury could
broaden its scope in any manner it chose.

According to Clark, in *Fall of the Duke*, Sessions spoke to the grand
jury and first gave them background information concerning the investigation into school construction contracts in Duval County and how
IRS agents initiated their inquiry after questioning Stautz's tax returns.
The stage was now set for the prosecution's star witness to tell his story. It
was apparent from the very beginning that Stautz was a frightened man.
When it came time for Stautz to discuss his relationships with officials
and other persons from Duval, he refused until he was formally granted
complete immunity. After a brief session with his attorney outside the
grand jury room, Stautz returned and was notified he would be granted
immunity.[14]

The testimony he now gave, however, turned to the threats he had
received on his life. He told a bizarre tale of being stalked by "a dark car
with a light top" near his home in an exclusive section of Austin. The
car kept circling the block, slowing down as it approached his home, but
continued without stopping. Remembering the Buddy Floyd murder of
twenty years ago, Stautz decided to leave town and hide out at his son's
home in Dallas. Instead of a direct route, he took back roads and kept
changing direction to shake off anyone following him before connecting
with the interstate highway twenty miles away for the trip to Dallas. It all
sounded a bit cloak-and-dagger, but Stautz said that, when he got onto

the interstate, the same car followed him for one hundred miles until he managed to shake it off his tail by leaving the interstate just outside Waco.[15]

Stautz took a circuitous route from Waco to Dallas but felt he had eluded his pursuers. After a week at his son's apartment in Dallas, he went out for a walk one evening and saw the same car again. He said the car made a U-turn and headed back toward him. "I ducked between some of the apartments . . . and finally got myself back to my boy's apartment." Nine days later he went out again in the evening, and this time the same car pulled to the curb and the men inside told him to get in. Both wore nylon stockings to cover their faces. When he refused to get in the car, one of them opened the glove compartment, allowing Stautz to see an automatic pistol lying inside. Realizing he had no choice, Stautz got into the vehicle and it sped off into the night.[16]

The grand jury was captivated by the hair-raising tale as Stautz recalled the two-hour ride that night. During the trip the two men kept reminding Stautz he had been given plenty of warning about talking to the IRS, but Stautz kept insisting he had only been answering questions about his late wife's estate. "That's not the only reason," they said, but Stautz kept insisting it was. "What we're talking about is stay out of the business of South Texas," they said. Visibly shaken from the experience, Stautz told the grand jury that the men spoke with Mexican accents and he knew they were the same men as were following him in Austin because they told him, "We have been hunting all over for you, and we finally found you."[17]

His adventure was an interesting story, but Sessions was more concerned about getting testimony about his South Texas dealings, particularly those with Parr. When questioning resumed, Stautz suddenly had a lapse of memory about the cash payments he had previously mentioned to the investigators. Sessions tried leading Stautz through personal records the contractor kept on payoffs to Duval County officials, but each time Stautz hedged his answers.

Sessions: *Do you remember any occasion between January 1, 1966 and December 31, 1969 when you delivered any amounts of money to George B. Parr in Duval County?*
Stautz: Yes, sir, I remember one occasion. I received a phone call from Bryan Taylor [San Diego school superintendent] that Mr. Parr needed a couple of thousand dollars. . . .

Sessions: *There must have been some other payments to Mr. Powell,*
   or Mr. Taylor, or Mr. Parr, or to somebody. I want you to tell me
   frankly, the occasions when you paid money to any of those people.
Stautz: I can't remember.[18]

The testimony he was giving wasn't matching his earlier affidavit ("I
gave him [Eunice Powell] some money, some cash"), so the grand jury
hearing was brought to a halt to allow Stautz the opportunity to gather
his thoughts.[19]

Behind the closed door of Sessions's office, Stautz was reminded by
agents that immunity from prosecution was only guaranteed if he testified truthfully to the grand jury. Seeing that Stautz was visibly shaken
(he had vomited), Sessions offered him twenty-four-hour protection, on
the condition that he spent the time going over his records and that he
returned to the grand jury ready to explain the cash payments to South
Texas school officials and Parr in minute detail, leaving nothing out.

From the moment he left the U.S. attorney's office, Stautz was always
with one or two armed IRS agents. He may have felt relieved for the
moment, but a late-night disturbance by two Travis County deputy sheriffs set him back on edge. They claimed they were there to serve him
with a subpoena to appear for the First State Bank's hearing to enforce
the summons for bank records. It was suspected that Parr had orchestrated
the incident so as to remind Stautz he was still being watched, and it upset
him enough that he was moved to an apartment in downtown Austin.[20]

Prosecutors knew that getting the court to enforce the summons for
bank records would take time. No matter what the outcome at the hearing, the government would still face an endless round of appeals, so it was
decided to petition the court to dismiss the summons and to issue a grand
jury subpoena for the same records. Prior to the hearing, a motion was
filed by lawyers representing Parr and the two school superintendents to
allow the three men to be heard at the hearing on the ground that their
civil rights were being violated.

What the prosecutors found interesting in the motion was that Parr
and his lawyers already knew Stautz had been granted immunity to testify before the grand jury. When attorney Marvin Foster, representing
school superintendent Bryan Taylor, was informed that the government
was withdrawing their motion to enforce the summons on the bank, he
pressed Judge Owen DeVol Cox for information as to whether the issue

would be continued in another venue, but Cox wouldn't be pressured. Later that same day, subpoenas were issued for the same bank records to be handed over to the grand jury in Austin.[21]

When the grand jury reconvened, Stautz was ready to cooperate after signing a twenty-three-page affidavit attesting to cash payments to various persons in Duval, including Parr. The second witness that day wasn't as cooperative—Karl Williams, cashier at the First State Bank, who was subpoenaed to bring all original documents held by the bank covering any transactions with Parr, Taylor, and Powell. Williams complied, however, only to the exact wording of the subpoena. He appeared with just the *original* documents, not microfilm records kept by the bank. It became apparent that Williams was attempting to sit on the fence; he wanted to provide the records, but at the same time, he didn't want to suffer consequences from Parr for having provided any unsolicited information.

A cat-and-mouse game began with Sessions wanting all bank records and Williams desperately trying to avoid handing them over. He claimed the bank had insufficient manpower to go through the microfilms. John Heard, the bank's counsel, had concerns of compromising the privacy of depositors by allowing the government to handle the microfilms. Sessions offered a compromise. The grand jury would provide the bank with microfilm readers, and Williams would supervise bank employees in copying subpoenaed records.

Now it was Stautz's turn to be grilled by Sessions. Stautz was more forthcoming this time as he described the ways and means of doing business in Duval. A scheme was devised to award almost every school construction contract to him in a system requiring competitive bidding on all projects. Stautz would submit a bid ("[normally] I tried to figure in a . . . six or seven percent [profit]"), but it had been arranged for a select group of construction firms to submit intentionally higher bids. "It was necessary for me to increase my profit percentage by approximately five to ten percent," Stautz testified, in order to allow for cash kickbacks he was expected to make.[22] He described in detail the cash payouts he gave to the two school superintendents, but Sessions was more interested in the payments to Parr.

With the aid of his business diary, Stautz recalled two payments. On May 5, 1966, he delivered twenty thousand dollars to George in the backyard of Parr's home in San Diego. The second payment was on July 11, 1966. Stautz received a call from a man telling him "the Papacita [Little Papa] wanted $40,000" and would be waiting outside the courthouse at 9:30 that night. Stautz said Parr met him on the sidewalk "and I handed it to him in a brown grocery sack." Parr stuffed the bag in his shirt, and Stautz recalled mentioning it was a lot of money to be walking around with at night. "I don't have to worry around this part of the country," Parr told him.[23]

After further questioning by Sessions on details concerning the construction contracts and kickbacks (Stautz proved to be a businessman who kept meticulous notes), he was excused. Now that the grand jury had heard his testimony, it was imperative they receive microfilm copies of bank records to corroborate the transactions had actually taken place. When bank cashier Williams returned to face the grand jury again, he brought with him the requested copies of the bank's microfilm records, but they were of such poor quality that they were useless. Williams attempted to place the blame on the copier the government had supplied, but the grand jury wasn't buying his explanation. New rounds of subpoenas were issued in which the grand jury demanded the microfilms to be delivered by Williams to any other bank of his choice where copies could be made.

John Heard, the bank's attorney, filed a motion to quash the subpoenas because it would be disruptive to the small bank and privacy of depositors would be violated. On June 23, Judge John Howland Wood Jr. heard the motions.[24] He denied the motions and ordered the microfilm to be delivered to the Frost National Bank in San Antonio to be copied.[25]

While bank records were scrutinized, investigators turned their attention to records of the San Diego and Benavides school districts and the reclamation district. Subpoenas were served on Dan Tobin Jr., president of the San Diego school board and D.C. Chapa, president of the Benavides school board, who also served as president of the reclamation district. When Tobin appeared before the grand jury, he brought very little paperwork with him and none of the payroll or fund disbursement records. Chapa was even more recalcitrant, having brought nothing and requesting an interpreter to aid him during the interview. This request surprised agent Filer, who recalled talking with Chapa in English when he served the subpoenas ("we had a twenty-minute conversation about his sons, and his hunting trips to Wyoming").[26] Tobin and Chapa were ordered to find the requested records and make a second appearance before the grand jury.

Among tax return records that agents received from Parr's accountant were $250 rent payments (half went to George, the other to his former wife, Thelma) from Oil Belt Chevrolet, a small San Diego dealership. Not expecting to find anything more than background information, the investigators were surprised when Oil Belt Chevrolet owner J. C. King said he had bought the gas and water systems of Benavides in 1967 for $717,478.21, even though bank records showed only a few hundred dollars in his account at any one time. King was issued a subpoena to appear before the grand jury to get his story on record, which turned out to be the tale of a man who had merely been the front man in the transaction.

"They called me from the bank to come over and sign some papers," King testified. After leaving the bank, King was told he was now owner of the Benavides water and gas systems. Archer Parr was at the five-minute meeting at the bank, so King was under the impression that George Parr had something to do with the deal. King lent his name to an oil royalty deal with Parr in 1949 and had expected the water and gas system purchase was pretty much the same: "I've done that before, and I made money out of it, and I thought I was going to make some money out of this too."[27] Although King made forty-nine hundred dollars on the oil royalty deal, he didn't make a dime on the water and gas transaction and was relieved when ownership was transferred to one of Parr's cronies.

Tobin and Chapa reappeared before the grand jury without the requested records, but with explanations. Tobin said school records for 1966 through 1969 were missing. Chapa had a better story—the water district records were stolen during a burglary of the office and the Benavides school records had been thrown out when the school where they had been stored had been torn down. Meanwhile, the bank microfilm search turned up deposit records of Taylor and Powell, corresponding with dates of cash payments Stautz had told the grand jury about, but nothing could be found to indicate what Parr had done with his payments.

The case against Parr so far was thin, but investigators kept digging even as John Heard was back in court filing another motion on behalf of the bank to have its microfilms returned. Referring to the two school districts and the water district's records, Judge Wood remarked it was "an unusual circumstance" that records of three public corporations "have become lost, stolen or perhaps even destroyed." He ordered the micro-films to remain in San Antonio until the government was satisfied they had completed their search.[28]

Tobin and Chapa appeared again before the grand jury after being instructed to search further for the missing records or come up with a reasonable explanation for their disappearance. Tobin said he had con-tacted school district tax assessor A. V. Barrera but was told the records couldn't be found. Chapa insisted that the school records were "acciden-tally" destroyed when the old school had been razed. "There is no school there," Chapa said. "They knocked it all down, made it into little pieces, about a year ago." His testimony on the water district's records being stolen was much the same. "Where I looked in there, there was nothing. There was not even a pencil."[29]

Water district bookkeeper Leopoldo V. Sepulveda was next before the grand jury. An unimposing man with a slight figure, Sepulveda seemed cooperative, even though he had little to offer. He testified he kept the books and worked on checking accounts reconciliation at the First State Bank where the records were kept. The nervous bookkeeper said he wrote checks but wasn't authorized to sign them. He testified that Parr received a one-thousand-dollar monthly salary check as the water district's lawyer, but he couldn't recall Parr doing any legal work for the board.

When confronted with a photocopy of a twelve-thousand-dollar check made out to Parr from a "Special Account" fund and marked "advance salary," Sepulveda denied any knowledge of its existence. Further ques-tioning by Sessions established that Parr had not missed receiving any of his one-thousand-dollar monthly retainer checks, raising the question as to why he had received an "advance" on his salary. Chapa, whose signature was on the twelve-thousand-dollar check, was asked to explain. "I don't remember," he said. Another revelation in Sepulveda's testimony was that, although required by law, the water district's books had never been audited since the day it had been organized.[30]

Since Sepulveda hadn't been allowed to remove the water district's account statements from the bank during the normal course of business, it was unlikely the bank would permit him to bring the records before the grand jury. The prosecutors decided they would save time if Karl Williams, the reluctant bank cashier, was subpoenaed to bring the water district bank records. Surprisingly, Williams showed up before the grand jury on July 19, with all the water district's bank records—including those of the "Special Account" from 1966 through 1969.

His explanation for not producing the records earlier didn't sound plausible, but his excuse wasn't a concern because the prosecutors now had something substantial that could possibly lead to an indictment. Marvin Foster would later acknowledge that, "When y'all finally got hold of the Special Account, I knew y'all had done hit the mother lode."[31]

CHAPTER 23

CLOSING IN ON THE DUKE

The break in the investigation came in July 1972 when Corpus Christi police received a mysterious telephone call that the missing water district records had been found. Two young Hispanic men reported accidentally stumbling across them on a dirt road just outside San Diego. After looking through the ledgers, the young men realized what they had found but were frightened about getting involved. Living in Duval and knowing what it meant to go against the Parr machine, they waited several days before reporting their discovery. Although some records were still missing, there were enough to shed light for the probe; it was all there—check stubs and journals recording matching disbursements from the water district's operating fund.[1]

Delving through the records that Karl Williams had delivered to the grand jury unearthed an interesting item. Hilda Parr, Atlee's widow (he died in January 1967), lived on a fourteen-thousand-acre ranch with her son, but George Parr ran it as if he owned it. According to disbursements in the water district's account, more than $166,000 had been spent for an irrigation system installed on the ranch (George cleared the land to grow grass to feed his prize cattle). The list of equipment purchased was extensive, including eight miles of aluminum pipe, several dozen seventy-six-inch wheels propelled by ten-thousand-dollar diesel engines and several hundred sprinkler heads. All together, the sophisticated self-propelled watering system, described by the company handling the sale as being the largest they had ever installed in South Texas, covered two square miles of cleared acreage. All of it had been billed to the Duval County Conservation and Reclamation District.[2]

Barney O. Goldthorn, president of the First State Bank, was called by the grand jury to explain the water district's accounts. He was asked for details on the bank's handling of several accounts that Parr and his associates appeared to be raiding. A nervous and unwilling witness, Goldthorn knew all the players in the scheme to defraud the water district. When questioned about the special account, Judge Archer Parr's name popped up for the first time in the inquiry. "Archer Parr said he was due a $14,000 legal fee from the Conservation District," Goldthorn told the grand jury. In checking disbursements of the special account, investigators noticed that Archer had been given $28,000 in 1968 and $38,700 in 1969.[3] Goldthorn said he did only what Jose Tovar, water district board secretary, had instructed him to do. Unfortunately for investigators, but convenient for Goldthorn, Tovar died shortly before the grand jury convened. Nevertheless, investigators were amassing sufficient evidence to indict everyone who received money from water district funds for personal use.

Before word leaked out of testimony being given to the grand jury and before George had time to remove it, the investigating team decided to photograph the irrigation equipment at Hilda Parr's ranch. During an aerial helicopter flight over the property agents were concerned that Parr, who owned a Bell helicopter and kept it on the property, might have a mind to engage them in some form of air-to-air combat. It was a real concern because he was known to shoot coyotes and deer while aloft. "George would just shoot the deer and cut their heads off, and put the heads in the helicopter," his pilot said. George had also taken a few shots at intruders nosing around the property. Fortunately, the aerial photo mission went off without any problems, and investigators had corroborating evidence to match records of irrigation equipment purchased for the ranch.[4]

Meanwhile, the grand jury was uncovering more evidence of dealings Parr had with water district funds. It was like pulling teeth to get witnesses to testify, but through direct questioning by prosecutors more and more disclosures were made that led the investigation in other directions. One hundred tons of bagged fertilizer delivered to Parr's ranch were charged to the water district.[5] Other supplies and rented equipment were charged to the Zertuche General Store, which prosecutors dubbed "The Phantom Store," as no one had ever heard of it.

There were other shady deals siphoning off county funds, including the purchase of a snow plow for the road department. "Why would George Parr buy a snow plow?" Mike Wallace asked Texas Ranger Captain Wood in a *60 Minutes* interview focused on Duval. "Well, the only reason I can figure out is because he wanted to help his self to getting a kickback," Wood replied. Wallace also questioned about five Caterpillar tractors sitting on Parr's ranch, "at an average cost of about $50,000 apiece?" Wallace, who conducted the interview in 1976, after Parr's death, added, "local reporters didn't write much about Duval County. Maybe that's because one reporter who nosed around was shot and killed."[6]

One worry IRS agents had was the memory of failed prosecutions of Parr in the past. Their income tax evasion case hinged on whether money that Parr had drained from the water district's accounts would be considered "loans," as they had been deemed when he purchased the Dobie Ranch. In that event, Parr may have violated Texas state laws in obtaining funds, but the funds wouldn't be considered income and therefore taxable. It was a fine distinction and the only way to eliminate that possibility was to continue gathering solid evidence that Parr had simply taken the money for his own use. In addition, time was running out for issuing indictments that would beat the statute of limitations for the crucial 1967 tax year.

According to Clark in *Fall of the Duke of Duval*, in August 1972, the grand jury recalled Leo Sepulveda to explain invoices paid from the water district Special and Reserve Accounts. Considered "only a pencil-pusher" who paid the bills and didn't want to be unfaithful to the Parr machine, Sepulveda sweated on the stand but wouldn't go so far as to perjure himself. When asked how much weed killer the water district used annually, he replied, "about $600 worth," but when shown invoices totaling 1,045 gallons he acted surprised. An invoice for $21,925.14 for "transfer of funds to George B. Parr in payment of aluminum pipe sold to district" also brought a wide-eyed look from the witness. Parr had managed to "double-dip" the water district by having them buy the pipe and then he bought it back in a separate transaction. The pipe ended up at Hilda Parr's ranch.[7]

It was time to get even closer to Parr by calling his sister-in-law to appear before the grand jury. Nervous and seemingly intimidated, Hilda wanted nothing better than to answer questions quickly and end the ordeal. The prosecutors hoped to establish irrigation equipment at her ranch was actually owned by Parr, thereby making the purchase to improve the land taxable income.

"When my husband died, my brother-in-law, George Parr, agreed to take over the operation of the ranch," Hilda testified.

"If he buys equipment and uses it there, then it's his equipment, is that right"? She was asked.

"Yes, sir."[8]

The grand jury now had testimony that irrigation equipment installed at Hilda's ranch and paid for by water district funds was owned by George Parr. In addition, Hilda said her late husband had a fifty-thousand-dollar note payable to the First State Bank, but the water district board purchased the note.[9] It was a clever maneuver to remove a property debt that bank examiners would insist on being collected and place the note in the water district's debit where it would remain unnoticed and noncollectable. But it was also considered taxable income for George.

Hilda also said that more than seventy thousand dollars in property taxes hadn't been paid, which came as no surprise to the prosecutors. Digging through tax rolls, agents discovered that taxes on Parr's San Diego mansion had been lowered to practically nothing. The county tax assessor appraised the $250,000 home at $1,210, requiring a $43 property tax, which Parr never even bothered to pay. When questioned as to the reason for such a low assessment, the county assessor said, "Because Mr. Parr asked us to; but it doesn't make any difference, because he doesn't pay taxes anyway."[10]

Further revelations to the grand jury showed a regular pattern of looting water district and county funds, and of those funds' going to George Parr, Judge Archer Parr, or recipients of their political largess who took what was given them and kept silent. Debit memorandums "to transfer funds [$32,000] to City of Benavides per instructions from [water] district" never reached the city, said Santiago Garcia, treasurer of Benavides. Mrs. F. C. Perez, San Diego treasurer, said the same about $120,000 her city was to have received in 1971 and 1972.[11]

Another mystery was—if George Parr was the water district's attorney—why was Judge Archer Parr receiving more than fifty thousand dollars for "legal fees" at the same time? When asked by the grand jury, Archer at first said he hadn't done any legal work for the water district, but when confronted with checks payable to him with notations for "legal services rendered" he did an about-face. He had done, "Budget work, studying up books. Just general legal work."[12]

In his grand jury testimony, Benavides mayor Octavio Saenz, a code-fendant in the Parr mail fraud case, couldn't explain why he had received five thousand dollars from the water district. Nor could water board chairman D.C. Chapa, another mail fraud defendant, explain why Archer Parr had received compensation for legal services. Chapa was granted immunity with the hope he might shed more light on the special account disbursements, but he denied any knowledge of what had happened to the money. Both Archer Parr and Octavio Saenz would later be indicted on charges of perjury for lying to the grand jury.

The search for the phantom Zertuche General Store continued. When asked for its location, a post office clerk pointed and said, "As far as I know, it's that post office box right there." Further inquiries revealed that Arturo R. Zertuche was a teacher and coach in the Freer public schools and had operated the store for four years out of a dilapidated building across from City Hall. "We get invoices from the Zertuche General Store," Leo Sepulveda testified, but aside from paying bills as instructed by D.C. Chapa, he couldn't offer any more information.[13]

The investigators discovered that bills paid by the water district, including invoices from the phantom store, were hand delivered and paid by checks (also hand delivered)—more than likely to avoid recurrence of mail fraud charges. Subpoenaed by the grand jury, Zertuche invoked his Fifth Amendment rights, but he did testify that records from his store were destroyed by a hurricane in 1970. An examination of his federal tax returns showed deductions for expenses from operating the store, but they were strangely inconsistent, showing no inventory and very little documentation to support his claims. This led prosecutors to believe Zertuche had left himself wide open to criminal liability for filing false tax returns.[14]

Cleofas Gonzalez returned for further questioning before the grand jury about his work at the Farm and Ranch Supply store, which had sold the large quantity of fertilizer to George Parr. His testimony revealed the business was owned by County Commissioner Ramiro Carrillo and his brother, district judge O. P. Carrillo. Gonzalez furnished the connection that prosecutors had been seeking when he told them, "everything I sold to the county, or the school district, or the water district, or the city, that I had to sell it to the Zertuche General Store first, and then the Zertuche General Store would sell it to them."[15] Gonzalez was told it was a way around the nepotism law, but conflict of interest avoidance was more probable—because Ramiro Carrillo, his brother O. P. Carrillo, and their father, D.C. Chapa, were all elected government officials who needed to hide business dealings with public entities.[16] By routing invoices to the county and water district through the phantom store and then cashing the checks, Ramiro and O. P. Carrillo hid close to eighty thousand dollars a year in unreported income.

Evidence was piling up, but prosecutors now needed to sort out charges for the grand jury to issue indictments. School superintendents Bryan Taylor and Eunice Powell hadn't received money directly from water district accounts, but both had increased their net assets during the years being investigated—none of which could be explained by their reported school district incomes. Everyone else, including Parr and his associates, had direct dealings in the scheme to drain county, school district, and water district funds. Records existed to indicate that tax evasion charges were supportable. Armed with bank records and canceled checks, along with nineteen hundred pages of testimony, the evidence was carefully presented to the grand jury.

On April 6, 1973, the indictments were handed down. George Parr received eight counts, two for each year from 1966 to 1969; Bryan Taylor and Eunice Powell each received six counts, two for each year from 1967 to 1969. On November 6, 1973, the grand jury indicted Archer Parr on six counts of perjury and Benavides mayor Octavio Saenz with one count of perjury.[17]

Parr's indictment came on a Friday, and on Saturday he was reelected member of the San Diego school board against no opposition or any write-in votes. At the bail bond hearing, Parr was represented by Nago Alaniz (the attorney who had warned Jake Floyd he was to be killed) and Anthony Nicholas of San Antonio.[18] Marvin Foster appeared for school superintendents Bryan Taylor and Eunice Powell. Taylor's bond was set at twenty-five thousand dollars, Powell's at twenty thousand dollars, and Parr's at fifty thousand dollars, which was signed for as surety by Clinton Manges. A wealthy wheeler-dealer, Manges owned the largest ranch in Duval County and had designs of his own to fill the political power vacuum if vacated by Parr.[19]

How Manges came into money remains a mystery. He had gone broke in 1961 operating a cotton gin, but his fortunes changed over the next few years. He came to prominence in 1968 when he purchased an interest in the M. Guerra & Son ranching and banking partnership. Virgil and J. C. Guerra, two of the six partners, sold him their shares over objections from the other four partners. Assets of the partnership included a seventy-two-thousand-acre ranch and the First State Bank and Trust Company of Rio Grande City.

To break up the partnership, Manges petitioned the courts to appoint a receiver. The case was dismissed in federal bankruptcy court in 1971, returning jurisdiction to Starr County. One month earlier, Manges had stacked the board of directors of the Guerra-controlled bank with friendly faces. O. P. Carrillo, judge of the 229th Judicial District, along with his brother Ramiro, a Duval County commissioner, sat on the board. Both were members of the powerful Carrillo family that was headed by D.C. Chapa and that included State Representative Oscar Carrillo Sr.[20]

If Parr lost his political power, Manges and the Carrillos would fight to fill the void. But the Carrillos faced problems of their own. U.S. Attorney William Sessions issued a subpoena on March 27, 1973, for bank records of O. P. Carrillo, Ramiro Carrillo, and Oscar Carrillo Sr.[21] The widening probe in Duval was of little concern to George Parr, who was readying his own battle with the government.

The defendants sought to have the charges dismissed due to a matter of jurisdiction, and Judge Dorwin W. Suttle, unwilling to try a case that might be overturned on a technicality, dismissed the indictments.[22] Undaunted, federal prosecutors filed a motion to have the San Antonio grand jury testimony and evidence transferred to a Corpus Christi grand jury where new indictments were issued against the three defendants—this time within the district where their tax returns had been signed. Parr and the two school superintendents were arraigned again on July 30, this time before Judge Owen Cox of Corpus Christi.[23]

Parr's tax evasion case was news—but he was also generating news of his own, first by resigning as Duval County deputy sheriff and then for firing a weapon within San Diego town limits. When a grand jury convened to investigate the shootings, nine persons came forward to testify that Parr had shot at them with a high-powered rifle. They complained that when they reported the incidents to local officials, nothing was done. The grand jury refused to indict Parr, but this didn't prevent him from getting even with one of the witnesses.[24] J. S. "Checo" Garcia, owner of

Duval County's only Ford dealership, found his water shut off, forcing him to haul tanks from his ranch to wash the cars on his lot.[25] Facing prison, Parr was letting everyone know he still had power in Duval County. In the meantime, Archer Parr had his hands full in divorcing his wife, Jody.

Jody knew that attempting to divorce Archer meant taking on the established power in the area. Hoping to prevent her husband from taking any of their community property, on August 2, 1973, Jody deeded or transferred a portion of the couple's property to her sister, Bonnie M. White. Jody underestimated the power Archer wielded.[26] As in his last divorce, proceedings were transferred to Duval County, where Archer arranged for creditors to file against the couple's community property. With twelve attorneys present in the courtroom, many representing creditors, Jody took the stand during a hearing to determine if an injunction should be ordered to freeze the couple's assets. Reading from a sworn statement, she accused Archer of bragging about his political power and that "he can control the outcome of any judicial matter he is personally involved in, in Duval County." Citing examples of how her estranged husband held power, Jody dropped a bombshell when she said "many of the ranch hands, the cook, and the handymen supposedly employed by [Archer] are in fact paid by the County of Duval."[27]

District judge O. P. Carrillo immediately called a recess, much to the relief of "visibly shaken" attorneys on both sides. When the session resumed, questioning continued with Jody not seeming to care about the legal implications of her statements. With accusations hurled by attorneys from both sides, Carrillo had all he could do to maintain order. Late in the session, he said, "It would appear from the testimony we need a receiver right now while this hearing is going on." He granted a temporary injunction freezing Jody and Archer's estate. He also appointed Laredo attorney Emilio Davila as the receiver to oversee their joint assets.[28]

To keep the case in Duval County, Archer's attorneys filed to subpoena the Mexican consul so as to produce a Mexican tourist card Jody filled out several months earlier in which she listed her home address as Duval, not Nueces County. Jody's lawyer objected on the ground that serving a subpoena on a foreign consulate violated diplomatic immunity. The controversy was thrown into the federal courtroom of Judge Owen Cox, who granted a temporary injunction until the matter could be heard.[29]

The case was further complicated when Jody's attorney filed a motion to disqualify Judge Carrillo from presiding over the matter. In the brief Jody contended the judge was "friendly" with Archer, and her estranged husband "exercises political and financial control over all officials" in Duval County. Another twist was added when Carrillo announced he would preside over the hearing to determine if he should be disqualified.[30] No one seemed a bit surprised when Carrillo denied the motion to recuse himself.

Based on her hell-hath-no-fury testimony when accusing Archer of using county employees for personal use, Jody was issued a subpoena to appear before a federal grand jury in Corpus Christi. Already being investigated by the U.S. attorney for income tax violations "and other federal criminal statutes," Archer tried keeping Jody from the grand jury by filing for a temporary restraining order. Citing any information Jody had concerning his finances as being privileged and protected by the Fifth Amendment, Archer petitioned the court to prevent Jody from testifying. Judge Owen Cox refused to grant the order, leaving Jody free to tell all.[31]

The divorce soap opera plot thickened when Jody, along with her lawyers as plaintiffs, filed a two-million-dollar suit against creditors in the case. They claimed the creditors had joined in a conspiracy to harass Jody and her lawyers in an effort to deny her a fair share of the community estate. The petition also listed assets Archer excluded from his divorce filing, among which were land, a racetrack, cattle, horses, and a boat. The "hidden" assets came to an additional one million dollars.[32]

To counter, Archer claimed in a restraining order request that Jody had royalties from an oil lease transferred to her sister. Judge Carrillo granted a restraining order preventing Jody from selling, transferring, or mortgaging any community property and from making any withdrawals from checking or savings accounts.[33] It was all-out war and Archer knew how to fight in the trenches, as demonstrated by an aspect of his personality that was downright nasty.

One of their jointly held properties was a small house on Louise Street in Corpus Christi where Jody's seventy-year-old mother had lived for years. "Archer had been talking around town about how he was going to have my mother out in the street," Jody recalled. Trying to stay one step ahead, Jody hired a moving truck to remove her mother's possessions from the home, but Archer caught wind of it. Showing up at the house with security service guards and the court-appointed receiver, Archer ordered the movers to put everything back in the house. Jody's mother was then prevented from going back into the home. "I sure don't know what right that damn guard has to keep my mother out of that house," Jody cried as she sat on the front steps.[34]

Archer was even more vindictive. Jody had been living in a town-house in the fashionable Santa Fe district of Corpus Christi when the receiver took control and had her evicted. Although she managed to have the furniture removed prior to the eviction, Jody was not allowed to return to pick up her clothing or personal effects. Texas law exempted personal clothing from being taken in legal actions, but Archer followed his own brand of law. "I can't really get any help; I'm at my wits end," Jody told reporters from the front steps of her mother's home. Wearing a white sweater and trousers ensemble, now her entire wardrobe, Jody complained she was stymied at every turn. "I need an injunction right now and I can't get one fast enough," she said, "no judge will sign it. I just can't afford to keep filing lawsuits."[35]

Getting Jody out of her townhouse was a violent skirmish played out in public. Jody was so frustrated that she punched the court-appointed receiver when he arrived (accompanied by Archer) to throw her out. During the fracas, Archer was the target of an ashtray thrown by Mrs. Bonnie M. White, Jody's sister, who was incensed when Archer insisted that Jody leave the house without taking anything, even her nightgown. "She's slept naked before," he commented.[36]

Destitute and unable to sell any possessions, Jody petitioned Judge Carrillo to order Archer to pay her $20,000 a month support. Carrillo granted $2,000 a month but added he would hear arguments on a petition by Archer that the payments be reduced to $250 a month. After hearing Archer testify that his income was slightly under $900 a month, Carrillo cut Jody's temporary alimony to $300 a month. Quoting a U.S. Supreme Court ruling that it was "the duty of wives to support husbands as well as husbands to support their wives," Carrillo hinted that Jody might end up paying support to Archer.[37]

Two days later, Carrillo announced he had asked the judicial district presiding judge to appoint another judge to handle the divorce case. "I have other cases in my district which need my attention," Carrillo said, "and it is unfair to these other cases . . . for me to be spending all of my

time on this divorce case." Two show cause hearings against Jody on
contempt of court for failing to appear at previous hearings were on hold,
as well as new filings by court-appointed receiver Emilio Davila, who
charged Jody and her sister, Bonnie White, had defied court orders by
attempting to enter the townhouse where Jody lived. When Judge Magus
Smith of Edinburg was assigned to take over "the battle of papers," he put
everything on hold until he had time to familiarize himself with the case
and to confer with attorneys on both sides.[38]

Eighteen days later, Judge Smith was ready. "It is clear Mrs. Parr is in
contempt of court," he said after a hearing, "and I hereby remand her to
90 days in jail," adding that it might give Jody time to "consider some of
her actions." Seated with her attorneys, Jody replied, "I doubt that, your
Honor." The judge always has the last word, and Smith was no exception.
"And if you have blue jeans, Mrs. Parr, I suggest you should put them on,"
he added.[39]

There was a ray of hope. Judge Smith granted a delay in the sentence
so as to allow Jody to "purge herself" by providing detailed information
on the sale of her furs, jewelry, furniture, and disposal of four houses
in Corpus Christi. If she provided a complete accounting of the sales
and where the money went, he would be inclined to drop the contempt
charges.[40]

Knowing she would never find justice in Duval County, and unwilling to stand by while her assets were being depleted, Jody hired Corpus
Christi attorney A. J. "Jack" Pope to file a civil rights suit in federal court
on the ground that the Parr-controlled courts were allied against her
receiving a fair and impartial hearing. To clarify what assets remained for
Jody to pay her liabilities, Pope filed for her protection under bankruptcy
laws.[41] The divorce case was now spread out in state and federal courtrooms in Corpus Christi and San Diego.

Judge Smith was seeing his courtroom turn into a media sideshow.
In a subsequent hearing, Jody's lawyer argued that since she was now
in the hands of the bankruptcy court there was no need for the contempt order because her property was no longer under her control. Smith
would not bend and increased the penalty to five months in jail. He also
signed an order to sell several jointly owned properties of the estranged
couple, including the Corpus Christi townhouse where Jody lived. Jody
petitioned U.S. district court judge Owen Cox to grant a temporary

restraining order to keep her out of jail, but the request was denied.[42]

Fearful of her life, Jody requested to be sent to the Nueces County jail, but after the sheriff there refused, she was sent to Duval County. George Parr visited her in jail and graciously invited her to stay at his house instead, but she declined. Duval County sheriff Raul Serna received a telegram from the U.S. attorney's office in Houston reminding him that Jody was under a federal grand jury subpoena and asked for assurance of her "safety and proper treatment." After spending three days in jail, Jody was released on a writ of habeas corpus issued by the Texas Supreme Court. "I bet I'm the only Parr, even by marriage, who has spent any time in the Duval County jail," Jody quipped.[43]

On November 2, the U.S. attorney in Houston subpoenaed Jody as a federal witness against her husband. Four days later, Archer was indicted by the San Antonio grand jury on six counts of perjury, along with Mayor Octavio Saenz, who was indicted on one count (another was added later).[44] The floodgates of publicity had opened and the secret maneuverings in Duval County were being revealed to the public in nonstop newspaper articles listing graft and corruption practices carried on by the Parr political machine.

CHAPTER 24

TAX EVASION TRIAL

In November 1973, the Duval County commissioners held their first public hearing in more than a dozen years on the proposed budget for the coming year. The rare event offered a glimpse into the extent of funds taken for personal use by the Parr machine. The bill for gasoline, oil, and maintenance of county equipment alone ran to $410,000, compared to $194,000 spent by nearby Nueces County with a population twenty times that of Duval.[1] Outrageously high expenses were one matter; paying high taxes while many county officials didn't was another.

The *Corpus Christi Caller* published a list of delinquent taxpayers, many of whom were elected officials, prompting George Parr to accuse the newspaper of "stirring up a bunch of old crap." Parr was listed as not having paid property taxes for the last four years. The *Caller* also reported that former sheriff Vidal Garcia owned a gas station where Judge Archer Parr charged nineteen hundred dollars a month to the county and that Duval was also paying the lease on Archer's new Thunderbird. An examination of the charge slips revealed a man employed at Archer Parr's ranch signed as many as three slips a day—and they were all paid by the county.[2]

In January 1974, Judge Cox heard pretrial motions in Parr's tax evasion case. Nago Alaniz was still a member of the defense team, but Anthony Nicholas was replaced by Corpus Christi attorney Douglas Tinker. "It was getting to be too much of a hassle," Nicholas said, referring to Parr's refusal to discuss aspects of the case with him. Graduating from law school in 1963, Tinker would practice law for the next forty years. His most famous case came in 1995, when Tinker represented Yolanda Saldivar, killer of Tejano singer Selena.[3]

Judge Cox overruled most of the motions, some which seemed grasping at straws. Alaniz said a telephone company executive informed him that the government had placed a wiretap on Parr's phone. Another motion asked for the prosecution to produce Nixon's "Enemies List," which Alaniz claimed listed Parr as a target for Republican retribution. Released the previous summer, the Nixon "Enemies List" did not name Parr.[4] Cox decided against both motions.

Parr was not on Nixon's list, but Archer claimed both were on the "Texas List" compiled by Republicans. "It's political," Archer contended. "The Republicans are in. It's a Republican vendetta." The "Texas List," according to Archer, was created by Senator John Goodwin Tower, assisted by Will Wilson, a former U.S. Department of Justice official, and "the Republican hierarchy of the State of Texas." The charge was "utter nonsense," Tower replied. "It's the same old story," a spokesman for Tower said. "They're just trying to take advantage of a political climate."[5]

Before the trial, Judge Cox ordered grand jury testimony of all government witnesses to be turned over to the defense team. Based upon the "Jencks Act" U.S. Supreme Court ruling, the prosecution argued vehemently against any testimony or written statements being released prior to a witness being called.[6] Parr was a dangerous man in Duval County, they contended, and allowing him access to grand jury testimony in advance would place witnesses in jeopardy. Cox listened to the prosecution's argument that the law required grand jury testimony to be released to the defense *after* the witness had testified at the trial. The judge was adamant, but returning from the noontime recess, he reversed his decision and jury selection began.

During the selection process, the staid atmosphere of the proceedings broke down when Cox asked the panel if anyone had a legitimate reason to be excused. One young woman told the judge she needed to visit her doctor every week. "For what purpose, ma'am," the judge asked. When the woman stood up, spectators in the courtroom burst into laughter. The answer was obvious—she was pregnant. The expectant mother was excused.[7] After the seven men and five women were selected, Cox sequestered the jury, and U.S. marshals commandeered an entire floor of a local Holiday Inn. All news and media that reached the jurors was censored.[8]

After his opening statement, Assistant U.S. Attorney Edward B. McDonough Jr. laid the groundwork for the government's case. An IRS employee produced tax returns of George Parr, his brother Atlee, and Atlee's widow, Hilda. Norman Ransleben, the CPA who prepared Parr's tax returns, furnished details of Parr's income. According to Ransleben,

Parr received one thousand dollars a month as "consultant" for Duval County. In addition, Parr was a partner in a cattle company with his nephew Archer, but the returns showed a loss for each year during the period the government claimed Parr evaded tax payments. Three items on the returns were questioned: the sale of forty thousand dollars in bonds, a twelve-thousand-dollar salary advance, and a three-thousand-dollar "check swap." The last two items came from the water district office where Parr served as legal counsel.[9]

George Parr, who had just turned seventy-three, was beginning to show his age. Dressed neatly in a blue suit, the stocky, bald-headed political boss sat quietly during testimony, occasionally closing his eyes to nap. The proceedings were tiresome to him, he said during a recess. When the government's star witness, Carl Stautz, was called to testify about cash payments to Parr for the privilege of doing business in Duval County, Parr seemed to pay more attention.

Nervous at having to face the Duke in an open courtroom, Stautz began by telling the story of delivering the brown bag of cash to Parr and details of other payments made to Duval County officials. After Judge Cox ruled that Stautz could testify about phone threats he received, only for the purpose of determining his credibility, Stautz told the jury one caller said "my days were numbered if I talked to the tax people." At one point during his testimony, Stautz had to leave the courtroom to take his medication.[10]

Under a grueling cross-examination by defense lawyer Douglas Tinker, Stautz stuck to his tale of being awarded school construction contracts inflated to cover costs of kickbacks. Tinker managed to get Stautz to admit that, after receiving immunity, he denied to the grand jury he had delivered forty thousand dollars to Parr. Pressed for specifics on checks drawn on his construction firm's account, Stautz seemed confused at times and, on occasion, answered Tinker in an angry voice. After two full days of squirming on the witness stand, Stautz finished his testimony and was allowed to leave.[11]

Bank records were the main focus of the trial as it entered its second week. Drawn-out, lengthy testimony, first by bank cashier Karl Williams, then by bank president B. O. "Barney" Goldthorn, established that numerous checks from the water district were made out to Parr in $1,000 amounts. Other checks, some in amounts as high as $65,000 were issued to Stewart and Stevenson, Inc., an irrigation equipment company. Goldthorn also testified a note owed by Parr's deceased brother, Atlee, was paid with $57,850 withdrawn from the water district's account. Payments amounting to $21,900 from the water district account were identified as being paid to James E. Dula, a pilot from Oklahoma. Apparently, Parr found the financial testimony boring as he slept during the entire afternoon court session.[12]

Dula testified he was hired by Parr to use his helicopter to count and round up cattle and spray brush killer on the Atlee Parr ranch. Identifying deposits slips for payments received, Dula said he thought the initials "D.C.C.R.D." on the slips stood for a company Parr owned. Actually, they stood for "Duval County Conservation and Reclamation District," the official name of the water district. When Leo Sepulveda, the water district's bookkeeper, testified concerning checks he wrote and disbursements of funds, he added that Parr's salary as legal counsel had risen from one thousand to two thousand dollars and was now five thousand dollars a month.[13]

At the end of the second week, jurors heard testimony regarding $166,000 in irrigation equipment billed to the water district.[14] Other witnesses reported delivering $14,000 worth of fertilizer and weed killer to the ranch, all paid for by the water district. The irrigation system, the fertilizer, and the weed killer, all paid for by taxpayers' money, were being used for one purpose—to grow grass to fatten prize cattle raised by George on his sister-in-law's fourteen-thousand-acre ranch.[15]

The jury then heard testimony concerning the $40,000 payment to Parr for the worthless City of Benavides bonds as part of Harris Fender's participation in handling underwriting of municipal bonds in South Texas. An officer of the Dallas bank that handled the bonds said Parr was not listed as a holder of the bonds in 1966 even though Parr claimed redeeming them that year. The government claimed that Parr should have claimed the $40,000 as attorney's fees and paid taxes on the full amount. The last government witness was a special IRS intelligence agent who used a series of charts to illustrate what Parr had paid in income taxes and what he should have paid. Totaling amounts for the four years covered under the indictment, he claimed Parr understated his income by more than $287,000. By the end of the second week, after presenting twenty-five witnesses, the government concluded their case. When the trial resumed after the weekend, the defense also rested their case without calling one witness.[16]

The following day, March 19, 1974, both sides gave closing summations to a jury that had listened to Parr depicted as an iron-handed political ruler in South Texas with easy access to public funds he raided for personal benefit. The government's case, Assistant U.S. Attorney John Clark said, could be summarized in four words: "George was the boss."[17] Douglas Tinker, summing for the defense, continued to attack Carl Stautz. "Would you let him babysit with your children over the weekend? Would you let him work as a cashier in your store?"[18]

Judge Cox instructed the jury on what to consider in their deliberation before they retired to consider a verdict. Less than three hours later, they announced they had reached a verdict. None of the jury members looked at Parr as they filed into the courtroom—for good reason—they had found him guilty on all eight counts. After excusing the jury, Cox announced that Parr would be allowed to remain free on the posted bond until the day of his sentencing. "Don't worry about it," Parr said to a group of supporters while shaking hands. It was easy to say to friends, but he was facing up to thirty-two years in prison and a sixty-thousand-dollar fine. Reporters tried getting a statement, but Parr's only comment was: "I'll let my lawyers do the talking."[19]

While George waited to hear his fate, Archer Parr went on trial for perjury in San Antonio before Judge Dorwin Wallace Suttle. Having lost his case, George reminded his nephew, "Your last name is Parr. That's enough. They'll get you too."[20] With a conviction against George Parr to his credit, Assistant U.S. Attorney John Clark headed the prosecution of Archer. The case against Archer rested on his grand jury testimony and credibility of witnesses who would testify he had lied about money he received from the water district's funds.

After motions were argued as to how Archer's statements to the grand jury would be introduced as evidence, the prosecution called D.C. Chapa, recently resigned water district board chairman. Difficulties with proper translation in Spanish for Chapa resulted in his entire testimony being stricken from the record and starting all over again with a new, court-appointed translator, even though the wily old Mexican had previously demonstrated a fluency in English.[21]

Answering almost the identical questions in his earlier testimony,

Chapa said Archer Parr had been the water district's attorney during its organization, but George Parr took over handling legal services soon after. As far as Chapa knew, Archer hadn't performed any legal services during the period alleged payments were being made to him. Chapa said he was unaware of a "special or reserve account" from which funds were paid to Archer, even though Chapa's signature appeared on three checks made out to the defendant. He also admitted he hadn't attended all the water district's board meetings, and Archer may have been hired for legal advice without his knowledge.[22]

Former water board member Heberto Garza testified he did not know of any legal services Archer Parr had performed for the water district. However, under cross-examination he changed his story. Defense attorney James R. Gillespie introduced a statement signed by Garza in which he said Parr advised the water board on a project to drill water wells. Minutes of two 1967 water board meetings were introduced verifying that the board approved payment of fourteen thousand dollars to Parr for "work on water district budget." The next witness, water district office manager Leopoldo Sepulveda, testified that he prepared the budget every year since 1967, and Archer Parr never assisted him.[23]

Concluding their case, the government introduced transcripts of Archer Parr's testimony before the federal grand jury—the crux of the perjury charge. In his testimony, Archer claimed he performed "all types" of legal services for the water board and received $121,500 in six payments during a twenty-eight-month period. Later in his testimony, Archer stated he charged the water district sixty dollars an hour for his services. The prosecution pointed out that Parr would have had to put in a forty-hour week for one year to earn payments at that rate.[24]

After the prosecution rested its case, a cast of influential well-known character witnesses were paraded before the jury by the defense to testify to the honesty and integrity of Judge Archer Parr. Each depicted Parr as having the reputation of a fair and impartial jurist and a pillar of the community. Under cross-examination, each witness was demonstrated as having owed the Parrs for political favors or as having very little knowledge of what really went on in Duval County, thus discrediting their testimonials of Archer as an upright citizen being railroaded in a federal courtroom. The court session abruptly ended when defense attorney James Gillespie suddenly collapsed. Rushed to the hospital, he was treated and released to the care of his physician who had been treating him for an ulcer and high blood pressure. Recessed for the weekend, the trial resumed on Monday when Gillespie reported feeling well enough to continue.[25]

According to the *Corpus Christi Caller*, Mary Elizabeth Ellis, Archer's half sister, was called to the stand and depicted the prosecution of her brother as nothing more than a political feud between Republicans and Democrats with Archer as the poor, innocent victim selected as a target:

> Gillespie: *Were you questioned at the water district office by IRS agent Ed Watts in 1972.*
> Ellis: Yes, I was.
> Gillespie: *Did you ask him who ordered this investigation?*
> Ellis: Yes, I did.
> Gillespie: *What did he say?*
> Ellis: By executive order of the President of the United States.[26]

Under cross-examination, Ellis painted an even more lurid picture of the vendetta against her brother by saying she had the feeling of being constantly watched by federal agents wherever she went. "There are just oodles and oodles of government agencies we don't know anything about," she dramatically told the jury. IRS agent Edwin Watts was called as a rebuttal witness by the prosecution to refute her testimony, saying: "I did not make the statement."[27]

Archer took the stand to explain why he received so much money from the water district. It was simple, he said—the $121,500 received was for legal work in setting up the water district. He added that the water district owed him even *more* money for work he did. He said an agreement was made with water district board secretary Jose "Pepe" Tovar (conveniently dead), to handle legal paperwork for a $150,000 fee paid in installments.[28]

On the stand for seven hours over two days, the balding, bespectacled Archer Parr spoke in a measured, confident voice as the prosecution tried to shake his testimony. Where were the files, legal briefs, and notes he used in his work for the water district? he was asked. Parr said he looked for them but couldn't find any. He did recall Tovar had once taken two boxes full of legal notes from him, but he never learned what happened to them.

As for fees paid to him by the water district years after he performed work for them, Parr had an explanation. Most of the work was during the period when the water district was being organized. Since the district was short on revenues, Parr said he waited several years before collecting his fees. A 1968 water district check made out to Parr with the notation "for legal services rendered in 1967" was shown to him. How could he explain the discrepancy in the date if he helped organize the water district between 1963 and 1965? "I could not control . . . what the (water district) office personnel wrote on the face of the checks," he responded.[29]

In closing for the defense, Gillespie reiterated the political character assassination plot hatched "to detract from the horror and corruption of the present administration we have in Washington," but the prosecution had the final word. "Watergate is 2,000 miles from here," Assistant U.S. Attorney John Clark summed up for the government. "This case is about Archie Parr's lies to the grand jury." Linking George Parr's name to the nephew, Clark added, "No wonder taxes are high in Duval County. Look at the overhead they've got."[30]

After Judge Suttle gave final instructions to the jury on May 9, 1974, they retired to deliberate, returning in less than two hours with a verdict—Archer Parr was found guilty on all six counts. His court appearance bond was $5,000, but Judge Suttle raised it to $121,500 (the amount Archer had received from the water district) and specified it had to be cash. The verdict had been returned after five o'clock, and the U.S. magistrate's office, where the bond would be posted, was closed. Led away in handcuffs, Archer had to spend a night in jail.[31]

Exchanging his dark business suit for a pair of white jailhouse coveralls, Archer stayed one night in the Bexar County jail. Clint Manges, who had posted George's bond, arrived the following morning to sign the bond but was told it had to be cash. Three hours later he returned with a cashier's check. Archer, a decorated ex-Marine, told reporters after his release, "I've slept in a lot worse foxholes than that place."[32]

Archer only had to wait eleven days to hear his fate before Judge Suttle—ironically, appointed by Lyndon Johnson. Suttle asked if he had anything to say. "I know I did the legal work," Parr said. "I did perform the legal services."

"Of course," Judge Suttle replied, "the verdict of the jury was to the contrary."[33]

After having listened during the trial about corruption and graft by a Duval County judge and not liking what he heard, Suttle imposed a severe sentence. Archer received two consecutive five-year prison terms on the first two counts to run concurrent with five-year sentences on the other four counts. To demonstrate an unforgiving disdain for Archer, Suttle even recommended he be sent to Leavenworth—one of the toughest maximum-security prisons in the federal prison system. Archer was also ordered to pay $10,000 in fines on each of the six counts (the maximum penalty) and $3,810 in court costs. He was permitted to remain free on bond, pending appeal, only if he posted the $63,810 in cash for the fines and court costs, which Clint Manges paid, bringing his total outlay to keep his friend at liberty to $185,000.[34]

Archer's conviction didn't deter him from venting his displeasure on Jody, who was still struggling to obtain a divorce. Succumbing to physical and emotional exhaustion, Jody checked in to a hospital to avoid further contact with her estranged husband, but Archer wouldn't leave her alone. Visiting in her hospital room, he told Jody she would be thrown back in jail on February 19 to serve her sentence. Upon leaving the hospital, Jody learned Judge Smith had scheduled her contempt of court hearing for February 19, prompting her to ask: "How does [Archer] know in advance that I'm going to jail?"[35]

When the court of civil appeals ruled that the appointment of a receiver by Judge O. P. Carrillo in the divorce action was invalid, Judge Smith terminated the receivership and appointed a new one, former Alice municipal court judge Werner A. Gohmert. The new receiver had his hands full from the start. Jody dismissed her bankruptcy case, and the federal judge ordered her furs and jewelry returned to her. Gohmert now had to go after the valuables before Jody could sell them. The battle was getting costly—not only for the couple, but for the county as well. The dozen suits in state and federal courts had already cost Duval County close to twenty-five thousand dollars in fees from outside legal advice and the end was not in sight.[36]

Meanwhile, Archer was applying more pressure by encouraging vendors and banks he owed to file against the assets of the couple's community property. The Alamo Lumber Company sought $8,534 for lumber Archer had bought, and Clint Manges sued for notes of $20,000, $50,000 and $30,000, all signed by Archer and secured by property belonging to him and Jody. The First State Bank of San Diego added their claim for two notes totaling $125,000 signed by Archer, both secured by livestock and ranching equipment, which the bank now wanted from the community property funds being gathered by the court-appointed receiver.[37]

Judge Smith, of whom Jody said, "can't cross the street or go to the bathroom without Archer Parr telling him to," ignored a civil appeals court ruling throwing out the contempt charge and issued a bench warrant for her arrest on contempt charges stemming from Jody's assault on the original court-appointed receiver. Smith also ordered the townhouse Jody had been living in to be sold and deeds on four houses she sold to her sister to be voided. Defiant as ever, Jody told reporters Smith "can go to hell." She planned to barricade herself in the townhouse "and anyone trying to get me or my home will get shot."[38]

Jody filed for a habeas corpus hearing before the Texas Supreme Court to have the contempt charge set aside. While she was waiting at the Austin courthouse, two Texas Rangers served the warrant for her arrest and brought her back to the Nueces County jail in Corpus Christi. The following day, she was transferred to the Jim Wells County jail in Alice. Jody had virtually no assets remaining and was resigned to the fact she would probably remain in jail. "I'm going to get 90 days in jail and they're going to stack eight or nine charges against me and I'll get about two or three years in jail," she told reporters. Judge Smith gave Jody the ninety days she had predicted, but after serving four days of her sentence, she was released by order of the Texas Supreme Court.[39]

Although her attorney had gotten her released on a habeas corpus writ and even put up the five-thousand-dollar bond with his own money, Jody still felt her circumstances were hopeless. Mounting court costs (twenty-five thousand dollars was required to get her jewelry and furs back) and the aggravation caused by Duval County courts, which was being ignored by the higher courts, all seemed to be too much to handle. All she wanted was a divorce, but Archer was making her life unbearable.

Jody returned to her Corpus Christi townhouse, which had been stripped of almost all furnishings. One bedroom still had a single bed in it, where her sister, Bonnie White, slept. Jody stayed in the sun room, without furniture except for a folding metal cot. A table, a few chairs, and two portable TV sets were all that was left in the kitchen. The empty townhouse had taken on the appearance of a tomb, lonely and desolate, easily facilitating depression in Jody.

On the night of June 13, 1974, Jody sat at the kitchen table writing twenty-six letters to friends she felt had helped her during her troubles. She tried unsuccessfully to call Archer and then called her attorney, thanking him for his courageous efforts on her behalf in battling the powers of Duval, but she was resigned that nothing could be done. He tried keeping Jody on the phone as long as he could, attempting to cheer her up and encouraging her to keep fighting in the courts.[40]

In her handwritten letters, Jody maintained a lighthearted, pleasant tone, thanking people for their help and encouraging others to "keep up the good work, dig up the corruption—expose it & give 'em hell!" Newsmen, recent acquaintances, and even women inmates in the county jail where she stayed had letters addressed to them. Perhaps the letter she penned to her attorney Jack Pope may have been the last. "Maybe you can get some sleep now," she wrote, "and not have to work day and night with no pay on my case."[41]

Awake all night with her marathon letter writing, Jody went into the bedroom to ask Bonnie if she was going to work that morning. When her sister said she would be staying at the townhouse, Jody went into the sun room and lay down on the cot. At 7:15 in the morning a shot rang out. Bonnie rushed into the room and saw Jody lying on the cot; a .25-caliber pistol in her right hand rested on her stomach. Bonnie immediately called the police, but after seeing her sister was still breathing, she called for an ambulance. At 7:40 Jody was pronounced dead at Memorial Medical Center. Jody had found a way out. Ironically, a few hours after committing suicide, the postman delivered another contempt of court notice addressed to her.[42]

"The next judge she stands before, she will get justice and mercy," the minister atoned at Jody's funeral. Judge Smith, apparently feeling guilt over his involvement, went into seclusion for three days, refusing to offer a statement. Jack Pope, who admired Jody's courage in the face of both mental and physical abuse, told friends he was considering giving up law practice.[43] Archer, who had now won the divorce case by default, didn't attend the funeral—his victory was overshadowed by the prospect of spending several years in prison.

CHAPTER 25

DEATH OF THE DUKE

Political upheaval was expected in Duval County after the convictions of George and Archer, and observers were not disappointed as they watched them battle to maintain control against factions seeking to move in. In the middle was Clint Manges, who had amassed eighty-two thousand acres of prime cattle and oil-producing land in the county, along with majority control of two South Texas banks. He didn't care who won the struggle as long as he was on the winning side. He supported Old Party regulars but also contributed funds to those wanting to take over.

The Carrillos, led by eighty-year-old D.C. Chapa (born Carrillo, he had adopted his mother's name while hiding out in Mexico to avoid the World War I draft), had run Benavides with Parr's blessing, but now there was an opportunity to have it all. Manges supported the Carrillos with money and positions he doled out. He appointed O. P. and Ramiro Carrillo directors of his First State Bank and Trust Company of Rio Grande City and gave O. P. seven thousand dollars to purchase a new Cadillac. He also gave O. P. a low-cost grazing lease on property he owned.[1]

The rift between the Carrillos and the Parrs widened even more during the 1974 primary for state senator. Oscar Carrillo Sr. told George he would not seek the position but later changed his mind. Parr, in the meantime, had given his support to the incumbent John Andrew Traeger of Seguin. When Oscar had second thoughts and reentered the race, he accused Parr of abandoning the half-century alliance with the Carrillos. "He has deserted the people," Oscar Carrillo said. "I still represent the Old Party."[2] The power struggle was now in the open.

Parr scoffed at the suggestion of a split in the Old Party, but when reporters asked about Carrillo's comments, he said, "If you have one jackass braying and he is joined by another jackass, then you have two jackasses braying." The rift was real, and to illustrate his displeasure Parr had slips of paper distributed throughout Duval County. It was a simple message: "*Dice Choche Parr, No Cries Cuervos porque te Pican los Ojos.*" Roughly translated it meant "Parr says do not raise crows because they will pick (get) your eyes."[3]

It was the era of "dirty tricks" campaigning, and South Texas factions seemed to mimic Nixon's tactics. On February 25, a small airplane flew over Duval County scattering leaflets printed in Spanish reading: "Who controls Duval County, George Parr or the Carrillos?" Whoever was responsible for the air assault on the Old Party, O. P. Carrillo was quick to say the leaflet was "obviously put out by someone with money, and by someone trying to cause friction between the Parrs and the Carrillos." Denying his family was attempting a power move on the Parrs, O. P. Carrillo tried repairing the damage. "Politics have changed and people have changed. It is no longer possible to consider a takeover by any one group," he offered.[4]

To demonstrate their loyalty, O. P. and Ramiro made an appearance at a rally for the Old Party where George proudly announced, "They are with me." Evidently Oscar Carrillo Sr. didn't agree with his political family because shortly after the rally he held one of his own on the same spot, declaring, "Do we want an outsider running Duval County or do you want a Carrillo?"[5]

Both sides seemed to have a rebel in their midst. For George it was his niece Mary Elizabeth Thompson Ellis who helped stir the boiling political pot by having a black funeral wreath sent to Oscar Carrillo's home with a printed card reading: "Deepest sympathies" and a handwritten note: "My thoughts are with you, condolences and sympathy, Archer Parr." There had been no recent deaths in the Carrillo family, but after the wreath arrived, that night several shots were fired from a car passing by Oscar's home while he was celebrating victory in the Benavides school board election. "They are not going to scare me off," Carrillo declared. "These things have made me mad and I am going to run for office even harder now."[6]

It was Archer's turn to placate the opposition as he divorced himself from the tasteless act of his half sister. "It was a bad joke," he offered, "and it backfired." Although he vowed to continue the campaign, Oscar soon reconsidered and quietly stopped campaigning, but he did not withdraw from the race, claiming his worries were not "about my own safety, but I am concerned about the safety of the people."[7]

Hoping to salvage some respect and continue the power struggle over control of the Old Party, Oscar Carrillo focused his energy on the upcoming local elections in Benavides. Carrillo was backing incumbent mayor Octavio Saenz and city council candidate Barbara S. Gonzalez. The Parr faction was lead by Armando Garza for mayor and Ruben Chapa for city council. Beating one of the Parr candidates would lend credence to Carrillo's power; winning both seats would deal a serious blow to Parr. "This (city) election is a showdown," Carrillo declared, "and we're going to win it."[8]

When ballots were counted after the election, Barbara Gonzalez won by thirty-nine votes. The surprise was the mayoral race, which ended in a 350–350 tie. Immediately, district judge O. P. Carrillo ordered ballot boxes impounded. Not surprisingly, the Parr faction wanted the judge disqualified, since his brother backed the opposing candidate. "We never thought we would live to see the day that a Duval County election would end in a tie," an editorial in the *San Antonio Express* read. Noting it was "simply one political machine battling another," the editorial offered that "two machines are better than one—each serves as a brake on the other."[9]

At the request of both candidates, Judge O. P. Carrillo ordered a recount. An additional twenty-one votes, originally thrown out by an election judge, were added to the total. The Carrillo-backed candidate, incumbent Octavio Saenz, was declared winner by twenty-seven votes.[10] The city elections gave both factions a win, but the results only bolstered Oscar Carrillo Sr.'s claim that George Parr could be beaten at his own game.

Shifting alliances, gunfire, and pressure being applied to Duval County employees to vote for incumbent state senator John Traeger in the upcoming primary indicated all was not well behind the "Cactus Curtain" in Parr country. "It looks like the whole thing may blow up down there again," a Texas Ranger remarked.[11] No one wanted to admit the rift between the Parrs and the Carrillos was real, but the infighting was real. Jobs and management positions in the county were the focus of who was to maintain control.

The water district board was the first target. When three board directors resigned on April 11, 1974, Oscar Carrillo charged that George Parr was involved. "They resigned because there are a whole bunch of

Carrillos working for the water district," Parr said, "and they did not want to be involved in it." Parr announced that D.C. Chapa, patriarch of the Carrillos, agreed to step down within the month as water board director. "And all the Carrillos on the payroll won't get paid until he's off the board," Parr added. Oscar Carrillo Sr. charged that Parr people were intimidating schoolteachers, threatening to fire them if they sided with the Carrillos. "That stuff about teachers being threatened by us is a bunch of crap," Parr shot back.[12]

Playing the political game for George meant applying pressure on the opponent. Turning to the Duval County commissioners' court, headed by Archer Parr, George raised the stakes a notch by having all county road and bridge employees discharged and ordering all equipment returned to the San Diego central shop. The ruling was designed to "cut my brother out of any power in the county," Oscar said. Oscar filed for a temporary restraining order to halt the firing of any more employees. The petition was granted by the district court, which scheduled a hearing after the primary election. "It's getting hot down there," Oscar Carrillo Sr. commented. "They're using every type of tactic down here and everywhere else, Parr that is, to intimidate people."[13]

John Traeger won the primary against Oscar Carrillo Sr., breezing to victory by a two-to-one margin. Taking advantage of Carrillo's defeat and hoping to deal a crippling blow to takeover attempts of his political kingdom, Parr orchestrated a housecleaning. Five water district employees, all friends or relatives of Oscar Carrillo Sr., were fired by the board of directors. Two other Carrillo relatives had their pay reduced to the federal minimum wage of two dollars an hour. After two members of the water board resigned, the newly constituted directors voted to name Archer Parr's half sister, Mary Elizabeth Thompson Ellis, as general manager of the water district.[14] If Archer and George were headed for prison, at least one family member would be left in charge.

Not everyone under the Parr umbrella fared as well. Octavio Saenz, who won another term as Benavides mayor, still faced criminal charges. Unfortunately, George couldn't intervene on his behalf in the perjury trial that began on August 26, 1974, in San Antonio where Saenz faced Judge Suttle, as had Archer Parr.[15]

Like Archer, Saenz took the stand in his own defense to explain the $5,000 payment he told the grand jury was for years of dedicated service as Benavides mayor. Every Benavides city council member testified they hadn't authorized the compensation, which the jury evidently believed because they found him guilty on both counts. After posting a $10,000 bond, one week later Saenz was sentenced. Along with a five-year jail term he was fined $10,000 and $2,404.18 in court costs, both to be paid if he wanted to remain free pending appeal.[16]

When George Parr stood before Judge Cox to hear his sentence on May 3, 1974, Cox asked if he had anything to say. Parr declined the opportunity. Speaking on his behalf was a conglomeration of community leaders who pleaded for leniency and spoke of the good he had done for the poor.[17] Taking everything into consideration, the sentence was lighter than Archer had received. George received five years on each of four counts, but the second would run concurrent with the first and the last two were suspended. He would spend five years in prison and pay a fine of fourteen thousand dollars. Cox allowed him to remain free on a seventy-five-thousand-dollar cash bail pending appeal, which Clint Manges immediately provided, preventing his friend from having to spend the night in jail.[18]

With the main characters convicted, federal prosecutors went after the remaining supporting cast. Both school superintendents Eunice Powell and Bryan Taylor realized that if George and Archer couldn't escape prosecution, their own chances were slim. They each pleaded guilty to one count of tax evasion. Powell received one year in prison and Taylor two. Ramiro and O. P. Carrillo, along with Arturo Zertuche, were indicted on March 28, 1974, for filing false tax returns and conspiracy for obstruction to collect income taxes.

All the king's men began to fall as Barney Goldthorn, president of the First State Bank of San Diego, D.C. Chapa, head of the water district board, county judge Dan Tobin Jr., who had replaced Archer, and a handful of minor characters were all indicted by the state of Texas on a multitude of charges stemming from their involvement in depleting county and school district funds for personal use. "Every time we found something in the records that looked funny, we found five or six more people stealing," said assistant state attorney John Blanton, who was part of the team assigned to investigate Duval County on the state level.[19]

While awaiting the outcome of their federal appeals, George and Archer became targets of the Texas Bar Association. State law required

suspension of an attorney "upon . . . conviction of any felony involving moral turpitude." The state bar asked both Parrs be suspended from
practicing law during the appeal process—and disbarred upon their final
conviction.[20] As a delaying tactic, both Parrs hired state representative
Terry Canales to represent them because Texas law allowed for delays in
any case being handled by a state representative until thirty days after the
legislature adjourns.[21]

Even with federal conviction and disbarment proceedings hanging
over his head, George made sure everyone knew he was still in charge.
During a meeting of the Duval County commissioners' court, he strolled
into the courtroom, and without so much as uttering a word, summoned
Archer and three other commissioners for a meeting in an adjacent office.
Before entering the backroom conclave, one of the commissioners made
the sign of the cross.

No one ever learned what was discussed during the forty-five–minute
meeting, which technically was not legal. State law required such meetings to be open to the public, and as a private citizen Parr had no authority
to call the session. In addition, a new state law that had gone into effect
at the beginning of the year required that an executive session had to be
listed on the agenda to be legal. "So who's going to do anything about
it anyway?" asked a county official who asked not to be named. No one
would deny that George was still the boss. "Until someone special comes
along," another unnamed official noted, "it is going to be pretty hard to
unseat George Parr. He's still the Duke."[22]

In the interim George still collected "legal service" fees from the water
district board, and Archer was still Duval County judge, having been
recently reelected. The local district attorney filed a petition to have Archer
suspended from office, alleging that he was guilty of "incompetency, gross
carelessness and official misconduct." Acting on the complaint, district
court judge O. P. Carrillo ordered Archer temporarily suspended.[23]

On March 19, 1975, O. P. Carrillo met Clint Manges on the highway
between Benavides and San Diego. Manges told him, "Judge, you can't
go to the courthouse. George Parr is at the courthouse and he's going to
shoot you. He's dead serious about it." Carrillo knew his political adversary well enough to know the threat was real. Any doubts were removed
when Manges added he had seen Parr leaving home earlier that day "with
a machine gun, or something."[24]

The next morning the situation became tense when everyone entering the courthouse was searched for weapons, including the district judge. Acting as if it was just another day in his courtroom, Archer opened a session of inquiry dealing with county employees. At the same time, Judge Carrillo opened court and immediately issued a subpoena for Archer to appear before him. Exempted from the weapons search were two Texas Rangers, one of whom tried to serve Archer with the subpoena. Parr told him he could not be served while he was holding court.[25]

Defusing the situation, Archer agreed to appear before Judge O. P. Carrillo. "Are you going to obey the orders of this court and the State of Texas?" Carrillo asked. The packed courtroom suddenly fell hushed as everyone leaned forward to hear the answer. If Archer answered, "No," then Carrillo could find him in contempt and order him jailed. "Yes, sir," Archer answered, thus avoiding a confrontation. Observers were disappointed that the expected fireworks didn't occur. Outside the courthouse, Archer quipped with reporters. "Hey," he asked, "anybody know the address of the Texas Employment Commission?"[26]

Archer wasn't the only one in the unemployment line. Four Benavides school board members—all Parr supporters—were ousted by order of Judge Carrillo. The vacancies were then filled by men Carrillo personally selected. The removal action came as a result of a grand jury investigation uncovering a thousand-dollar-a-month payment, approved by the board, to school superintendent Eunice Powell while he was serving his prison term for tax evasion.[27] Adding salt to the wound of the Parr-Carrillo split, Judge Carrillo appointed Dan Tobin Jr. as the new Duval County judge, replacing Archer Parr.

Although Tobin claimed he was trying to remain neutral in the power struggle, George Parr felt it was Clint Manges who was pulling the strings. "Clinton (Manges) has put a bridle and rein on him (Tobin) and is telling him what to do," Parr said. "Danny was appointed because Manges ordered it." George didn't have a kind word for the new judge. "Danny double-crossed us one time and he's done it again," he said. "He's a double-crosser."[28]

When Oscar Carrillo Sr. accused Manges of attempting to become the new power in Duval, George dismissed the idea, calling it ridiculous. "Listen," he told reporters, "he can't any more take over Duval County than I can take wings and fly to heaven." Parr still considered Manges a friend. "The whole trouble comes from Oscar. He wants to dominate." But the following day, Parr had an afterthought. "Manges and I are still friends," he said, "but things may have to come to an end soon."[29]

George had filed an appeal with the Fifth District U.S. Court of Appeals in New Orleans, and on March 24, 1975, their decision was as expected—the conviction was upheld. The opinion delivered by circuit judge Thomas Gibbs Gee noted Carl Stautz's testimony was not refuted by Parr, who chose not to testify, leaving the jury with a "straight credibility choice" supported by evidence bolstering his testimony.[30] The U.S. Supreme Court could still review the case and overturn the sentence as it had in Parr's mail fraud case, but his chances of being heard by the highest court were slim. He could delay prison by petitioning the Supreme Court and remain free on bond, but federal prosecutors were concerned he might flee to Mexico. To prevent that, a motion was filed to revoke his bond and take him into custody, which Judge Cox reviewed and set a 4:00 P.M. hearing on March 31, 1975, to hear arguments.

Parr told reporters that facing incarceration again didn't worry him. "I've been before," he said. "I know. . . . It's just like a kid. You put him in jail one time and he's scared like to death. The next time, he says, 'I'll take my lunch with me because I know what's going to happen.'" But federal prosecutors were concerned about rumors that Parr was armed and seeking revenge against the Carrillos.[31]

With Parr being fluent in Spanish and living so close to the Mexican border, and with general speculation that he may have stashed hidden funds, the government worried that Parr was a flight risk. Judge Cox felt sufficient evidence had been shown to issue a show cause order and a U.S. marshal was ordered to arrest Parr and keep him in custody until his court appearance. Nago Alaniz, as George's attorney, petitioned Cox to allow Parr to voluntarily surrender, which was granted.

A meeting was arranged by Alaniz for Parr to meet at the Corpus Christi law office of Douglas Tinker at noon, only four hours before Parr was scheduled to appear before Judge Cox. Summoning Duval County deputy sheriff Rene Martinez to serve as his chauffeur, Parr arrived on time at Tinker's office where Alaniz and Tinker talked to him for over an hour on the best way to continue the legal battle after he was placed in custody. "What time do I have to show up?" Parr asked. They told him four o'clock and he said he would be there.[32]

After getting in the car, Parr told Martinez to head back to San Diego. "We stopped by the store and got some bananas, oranges and cantaloupe and ate all the way back," Martinez recalled. "He knew exactly what he was going to do and he was laughing and kidding about it."[33] On the way, Parr openly expressed his feelings to his driver. "I'm not going to jail and live like an animal. I'd rather just kill myself and stay right here, the place that I love."[34]

Parr was also contemplating murder. He confided to Martinez that Manges had "made a fool out of him," and he had ill-feelings toward the Carrillos, adding "he would like to see them suffer." Emotional and tearful, Parr kept talking. "He said he wanted to get Clinton Manges and O. P. Carrillo before he left," Martinez said. "Then he changed his mind and said he didn't want to go out as a murderer because people would remember him that way. His last orders he said, was for me to stop him."[35]

Arriving in San Diego, Parr instructed the deputy sheriff to stop at Alaniz's law office. Martinez would later give a written statement to the Texas Rangers that Parr returned to the car with a .45-caliber pistol in his hand. Nervous about the political boss holding a weapon openly and waving it around, Martinez pleaded for him to stop. Parr put the gun away but said he "would rather die at the ranch than die in jail." Arriving at Parr's mansion between two and three o'clock that afternoon, the deputy sheriff was told to go home. "You'll find me in the morning," was Parr's parting remark. The comment worried Martinez, who drove away before turning around a few minutes later to check on the Duke. George's wife, Eva, answered the door and Martinez's worst fears were confirmed when she said George just left the house with a rifle, telling her, "they wouldn't take him to jail, and that he was probably going to hurt somebody."[36]

According to the *Corpus Christi Caller-Times*, Before leaving the house, George had gone up to his bedroom, changed clothes, and left his ring and wallet behind. Still carrying his pistol, Parr asked Connie Garza Perez, his sister-in-law, for his AR-15 rifle.

"I've got to do something," he told her. "I'll be back, but if I don't come back, take care of Georgia."

Georgia, Parr's daughter, seeing her father distressed, grabbed his pants leg, crying and begging him not to go.

"I promise you, baby, I'll come back," he told her. "I wasn't coming back, but now I promise you I'll be back."[37]

When Nago Alaniz arrived at his office and was told by his secretary that Parr had walked out with the pistol, Alaniz immediately called Sheriff Raul Serna. The worried and concerned lawyer also reported the incident to the FBI and the U.S. Marshals Office. While Serna and his deputies began searching for Parr to prevent him from taking revenge on his enemies, George was spotted by a witness who saw him slowly driving past Oscar Carrillo's house around 3:30. "I had seen him mad," the witness said, "but I had never seen him that mad." John Blanton, part of the State of Texas team investigating Duval County, was previously a federal investigator with the Bureau of Narcotics. After firsthand observations of Parr's actions while in Duval County, he was convinced George was a methamphetamine user:

> George would be hyperactive for a couple of days at a time, and he'd do strange things, like demanding food from restaurants in San Diego at three or four o'clock in the morning, when every place in town was closed, and then he'd sleep around the clock and start over again. He had hallucinations too. He called the sheriff's office and told them he had killed his wife. When the deputies came rushing over to his house he said, "I killed Eva. See, there's the blood, right there on the floor," but nothing was there. He fired shots at imaginary enemies and real people, and he kept floodlights burning around his house all night. His behavior was bizarre. His neighbors were really afraid of him; they didn't know what he might do next.[38]

And now George Parr was on the loose, armed with a pistol and a rifle, and cruising around the community in his car looking for human targets.

After stopping at a gas station to fill his dark-blue Chrysler Imperial, Parr continued hunting for prey, driving by D.C. Chapa's house at a slow pace. Not finding anyone in his sights to wreak vengeance on, he circled back and headed to Oscar Carrillo's home but continued driving past the house, heading out of town towards his sister-in-law's (Mrs. Hilda Parr) ranch, Los Horcones.

At 4:00 P.M., both Nago Alaniz and Douglas Tinker were sitting in Judge Cox's Corpus Christi courtroom waiting for Parr to make his scheduled appearance. Sensing he wouldn't show, Cox asked the attorneys where their client was. "This is so unlike Mr. Parr," Alaniz told him. "The only reason he would not show up is because he is dead." He asked to approach the bench to offer an explanation without courtroom spectators listening. As an officer of the court, he was duty bound to tell the judge that Parr had taken the pistol from his law office but added his personal concern "that he might do away with his wife and his child."[39] Judge Cox said he had already known there might be a problem and had ordered the U.S. Marshals Office to find Parr and bring him in. Cox adjourned the proceedings for another hour to allow Parr the opportunity to make his appearance, but when he failed to show up at the end of the day, Cox ordered the appeal bond forfeited and issued a bench warrant for his arrest.[40]

The search team looking for the fugitive included FBI agents, U.S. marshals, Sheriff Raul Serna and his deputies, and a Texas Department of Public Safety helicopter. IRS agents had alerted U.S. Customs border stations in case Parr decided to flee to Mexico, while FBI agents interviewed Eva Parr. Apprehensive that George might be a danger to the community, she told them everything she knew, including a description of the weapon he was carrying—an M-15, thirty-round, automatic, assault rifle that was U.S. Infantry standard issue. Its sole purpose was to provide a rapid-firing, high-velocity, powerful rifle to kill the enemy in combat. Evening approached and knowing that Parr was heavily armed and an expert shot, no one wanted to continue searching at night, so plans were made to hunt for him the following morning.[41]

Law enforcement officials, local, state, and federal, gathered across the entrance to the ranch, accompanied by two reporters who wanted to be there for Parr's capture. The immense size of the ranch, coupled with lack of knowledge of the terrain and the awareness that they were searching for an armed and dangerous man, caused everyone to hesitate. The helicopter was brought in for a low-level aerial surveillance, guided by Deputy Sheriff Jose Israel Saenz, who was familiar with the ranch and friendly enough with the armed political boss to negotiate surrender when the time came. They began looking where Saenz felt Parr might be found—locations George frequently visited as his favorite spots on the ranch.

"I knew where to find him because that's where he went to meditate and relax," Saenz said. A windmill in an open area known as the Julian

Pasture was the best place to look. "One time about eight months ago, I was up on my windmill and I put my field glasses on George's windmill and there he was," Saenz said. "He had a board across the lower part of the windmill and was seated there." As the helicopter neared the windmill, Parr's Chrysler was spotted.[42]

As they circled around at a safe distance with observers focusing their attention on the Chrysler parked in the open pasture near the windmill, no movement was seen in the car. The site was in a shaded clearing on a slight knoll overlooking most of the ranch. A decision was made to land the helicopter far enough away from the car to allow FBI agent Ruben Martinez to approach on foot. Cautiously approaching, Martinez described what he observed:

> I walked up to the car. The car engine was running. I went to the passenger's side, looked in, and I could see Mr. Parr slumped to his right side. There was a bullet hole to the right side of his head with an exit wound on the left side. I walked over, shut off the engine, went back to the helicopter to alert the other agents and the other county officials that we had found Mr. Parr and to give them some possible directions on how to locate us. On the front seat of the vehicle was the AR-15. In addition, about eight magazines of loaded ammunition. The .45 was on Mr. Parr's lap. One spent round was found on the floorboard, I believe, of the vehicle.[43]

It was April 1, 1975, April Fool's Day, when George Parr, who had just turned seventy-four—political boss of Duval County for more than forty years—had taken his life rather than go to prison. Further investigation revealed that the rifle that had everyone concerned hadn't been fired.

CHAPTER 26

AFTER THE DUKE

Parr's suicide seemed to signal the end of a political regime that began with his father, continued for sixty years, interrupted at times by internal and external upheavals, but lasting until that day in a pasture when he took matters into his own hands. After medical attendants wrapped his body in a royal-blue blanket, Parr was taken from his car, placed on a gurney, and loaded into a waiting hearse. As the last reigning Duke of Duval was being transported to a funeral home, his attorneys were back in the Corpus Christi courtroom to inform Judge Cox of the unexpected turn of events. "I thought I knew the man," Alaniz said. "Now I know."[1]

Archer Parr, embittered over the death of his uncle and mentor, was vehement. "I have a statement: I hope the goddamned sons of bitches are satisfied," he told reporters.[2] Reflecting on what pushed his uncle over the edge, Archer blamed everyone except George. "It was his friends who stabbed him in the back, who lied to him, who gutted him," he said. "And it was the federal government. All this led to a situation that finally made him blow his bananas."[3]

As if he were a head of state, Parr's copper casket was placed in the sitting room at Los Horcones and surrounded by flowers. On the day of his funeral, the courthouse adjourned and schools were closed. Notice of his death was carried in the *New York Times*, the *Washington Post*, and *Time* magazine.[4] Flags flew at half-mast throughout Duval County, and the entourage accompanying the hearse from the ranch to the Benavides cemetery totaled more than 150 cars stretching for a half mile.

George's wife, Eva, and their eight-year-old daughter, Georgia, along with Archer, Givens, and Marie, represented the family during proceedings attended by former U.S. representative John Lyle Jr. and George's boyhood friend Walter Meek. Reached at his home in Telegraph, Texas, former governor Coke Stevenson said, "Everybody would know if I paid him a compliment I wasn't sincere about it." The Carrillo family, who hadn't attended the funeral, responded through Oscar as their spokesman. "On behalf of the family," he said, "I would like to say we are sorry. I don't think Mr. Parr had a better friend than my daddy." It may have been George Parr himself who coined a fitting epitaph. During a television interview several years before, he had said: "The Good Lord won't have me and the devil is afraid of me."[5]

Less than a month after Parr's death, the investigation by the Texas Rangers came to a close. "There is no doubt whatsoever that it was suicide," their report indicated. Five years later, the women Parr left behind expressed a different opinion. "George couldn't fire a weapon with his right hand. He couldn't even shake hands," Parr's sister-in-law Connie Garza Perez said. "He couldn't move the fingers on his right hand." According to her, Parr couldn't even zip up his own trousers. "We had to put a clip on them so he could zip them up and down."[6]

Parr's hand had given him trouble ever since he had surgery for skin cancer. He even started learning to shoot with his left hand because of the disability. Walter Meek, former Duval County auditor, and lifelong friend, disagreed with the extent of the incapacity of Parr's hand. Meek recalled an incident a few weeks before the suicide when Parr went to the courthouse, threatening to kill Judge O. P. Carrillo.

"I found him by himself in the hall walking up and down and he was tossing two or three .45 cartridge shells in his hands, and he was tossing them up one at a time," Meek said. "I said jokingly, 'George, do you have a . . . sling shot—to put those things in?' and quick as a flash he reached back and jerked out his .45 and said, 'This is my . . . shooter,' and that was all with his right hand."[7]

South Texas style politics continued after Parr's death. Four days after his suicide, Parr-backed candidates defeated the Carrillo faction in the Benavides school board election by a two-to-one margin. "It was a message to Manges," Archer commented. "It says he should stay the hell out of our politics." The defeat was the least problem for the Carrillos as O. P. and Ramiro were indicted by a federal grand jury on April 10, 1975, for filing false tax returns. Sensing an opportunity, Archer filed suit to have his removal as judge nullified.[8] What resulted was a civil trial to determine if Archer's removal from office was valid. Initially set for Rio

Grande City, to accommodate witnesses Judge Carrillo agreed to move the trial to Hebbronville, which was within the one-hundred-mile limit to subpoena witnesses.[9]

Throwing a monkey wrench into the proceedings, Archer filed suit in federal court asking for a permanent injunction to halt the civil removal trial. Naming Carrillo, Manges, and anyone else allied with the Carrillo family as defendants, he claimed they were all part of a "conspiracy" to take over the school district and the commissioners' court. He also claimed to being denied due process in the ouster. He wanted sixty-four thousand dollars in actual damages and thirty thousand dollars in exemplary damages. The petition was transferred to Corpus Christi for a ruling by federal judge Owen Cox.[10]

The ouster trial finally began in Hebbronville near the end of June 1975, but at the onset it had the markings of being an unusual court drama. Judge Carrillo refused to recuse himself, despite defense protests. Carrillo had been granted a delay to prepare his case for federal income tax charges, allowing him to continue presiding over the civil trial of his political enemy. Archer didn't want to attend his own trial and kept avoiding subpoena service. "You can change his name from the 'Duke of Duval' to 'King of the Road,'" quipped his attorney Marvin Foster.[11]

The normally isolated, sleepy town of Hebbronville was suddenly cast into the limelight and unprepared. "We don't get in the news very much here," a resident said, "but I guess we will be for a few days now." The proceedings drew a standing-room-only crowd on the second floor of the courthouse, which was not air-conditioned. Opening windows offered little relief, so electric fans were brought in. Because the watermelon and grain harvest was in full swing, overladen trucks roared through town, sometimes drowning out testimony. A loud speaker system was brought in from the local junior high school to allow the jury to hear the witnesses.[12]

"Things are done very informally in Duval County," testified county auditor Walter W. Meek. He was asked why a county budget was never drawn up, public hearings on the budget never held, and funds allowed for items not on the budget. "We don't pay much attention to the budget," Meek said.[13] Even if there were a budget, he said, it would be an "exercise in futility in Duval County." With no budget as a guide, Meek said he paid whatever bills were approved by the commissioners' court.[14]

One of the charges against Archer was negligence in his duty as chief budget officer for the county.

Duval County clerk Alberto Garcia Jr. testified that two utility firms in the county received substantial tax breaks in 1974. Reading from the minutes of the Duval County Board of Equalization (Archer Parr served as chairman), Garcia said Coastal States Gas Producing Company had its taxes cut by more than 50 percent. Central Power and Light Company had its taxes reduced during the same year by 15 percent. Both tax breaks were in the form of reduced property valuation.

In a scene straight out of a Hollywood movie, as Marvin Foster began objecting to board meeting minutes being introduced as evidence, the power went out. Although sufficient lighting was coming through windows, the outage stopped the fans, forcing Judge Carrillo to call a recess. What the jury hadn't heard, which the district attorney told reporters would be revealed in later testimony, was that Archer had been receiving legal retainer fees from both utilities when they received their tax breaks. The jury did hear that, while Archer headed the commissioners' court, Clint Manges had received a 75 percent tax reduction three years in a row for his ranch.[15]

According to the *Corpus Christi Caller*, Foster took exception to this last bit of evidence. With the Duval County clerk still on the stand, he asked Garcia if Dan Tobin was the commissioner who made the motion to have Manges's taxes reduced. Garcia answered, "Yes."

"Is that the same Dan Tobin who was appointed county judge by Judge Carrillo?"

"Yes."

"Is that the same Dan Tobin who is indebted to Manges' bank in Rio Grande City for $30,000?"

When the district attorney objected, Carrillo sent the jury out of the room. Foster said he was proving a conspiracy existed to remove Archer from the bench. The district attorney countered that Carrillo had already ruled out conspiracy when he refused to recuse himself. When Foster threatened to ask for a mistrial if Carrillo didn't overrule the district attorney's objection, the judge said that even if a conspiracy existed, it was not a defense.

"Your remedy," Carrillo told Foster, "is to bring out impeachment proceedings."

"I think somebody else already has that in mind," Foster countered, alluding to hearings being conducted against Carrillo by the Texas House of Representatives.

When Carrillo threatened to hold him in contempt of court for interrupting, Foster shot back: "You've been wanting to hold me in contempt of court since we started this trial."

"Sit down!" Carrillo ordered as he banged his gavel. "If you interrupt this court one more time, I'm not going to put up with it."[16]

Archer continued evading the subpoena for his own trial. The district attorney had had enough. In open court he set a time for Foster to have his client appear before the county clerk in San Diego to make his sworn statement. Parr never showed up. Instead, Foster announced to Judge Carrillo that Parr would agree to answer questions, but only at the office of his attorney James Gillespie, who represented Archer in the federal perjury trial. To resolve the issue, Carrillo offered to allow Parr to appear in the Hebbronville court, plead the Fifth, and leave.[17]

When he still failed to appear, the district attorney asked for an instructed verdict against Archer. Carrillo hesitated on taking such a harsh step. "I'm going to take my time; I'm not going to rush to judgment," he said. Another option would be to arrest Archer and bring him into court to show cause why he shouldn't be held in contempt. Carrillo instructed both sides to submit briefs on the contempt option, and he would take the directed verdict motion under advisement. The contempt motion wasn't even discussed when court resumed. Carrillo had made up his mind. He granted the motion for a directed verdict making Archer Parr's ouster permanent.[18]

An appeal was filed with the Texas Fourth Court of Civil Appeals in San Antonio. Foster asked the three-judge panel to void Carrillo's directed verdict on the ground it was illegal. He argued that under Texas law a jury is required to make such a determination on its own. Parr wasn't concerned. "The voters are going to straighten out this mess next April," he said. "I'll let the courts take care of it. If not by the courts, I'll guarantee the voters will put me back in."[19]

In the meantime, the Texas State Bar still wanted to consider Parr's disbarment. Archer avoided the matter by hiring state representative Terry Canales as his attorney. Considered a do-nothing representative, Canales rarely made an appearance in the legislature. Absent from almost every roll call, he was applauded by other representatives when he strolled into the house chamber one day to register his presence with the clerk. The Capitol Press Corps placed Canales on their "Top 10 Dumb" house members list, but that didn't faze him. "I may be," he quipped, "but there's no way for them to tell because I'm never here."[20]

As long as the legislature remained in session, Canales could postpone the case, but the question of whether the legislature was still in session was now the focal point. The Texas House of Representatives was conducting impeachment hearings against Judge Carrillo, but counsel for the State Bar of Texas, Davis Grant, argued the "impeachment proceeding is not the House in session."[21] It was a valid argument, but events in San Antonio overshadowed the matter of Archer being permitted to still practice law.

While having lunch at Jerry's Diner in San Diego, Archer was arrested by two Texas Rangers. They had been sent to pick him up by order of U.S. District Judge D. W. Suttle because there was concern Archer might jump bond and flee to Mexico. That was when Archer learned his federal perjury conviction had just been upheld by the U.S. Court of Appeals in New Orleans. In the unanimous opinion delivered by Judge Wisdom, the evidence presented in the lower court trial was reviewed in a twenty-page summation: "The record compels this Court to conclude that Archer Parr's perjury impeded the grand jury's attempt to determine whether the activities of George and Archer Parr violated federal law. Archer Parr could ask for money from the District 'when [he] needed it.' A petit jury could reasonably conclude that the payments to Archer Parr were not for legal services or any other legitimate purpose; that Archer Parr perjured himself in his testimony before the grand jury."[22] After accompanying Archer to his ranch to pick up some clothing, the rangers took him to the Bexar County jail to await a hearing before Judge Suttle.[23]

Placed alone in a cell in the first-floor hospital area, Archer received more bad news. Clint Manges had filed a motion to "exonerate and release" the $121,500 cash bond he had put up for Archer. If this motion was granted, Archer would have a difficult time getting out of jail. Born in Mexico, Archer might claim Mexican citizenship, contended U.S. Attorney John Clark. Because Mexico hadn't extradited any of its citizens since 1900, it was likely Archer could remain there indefinitely. "I believe the Mexican government would take a dim view of a man who served twice in the U.S. Marine Corps, claiming Mexican citizenship," Archer's attorney countered.[24] Nevertheless, Archer remained in jail until his bond hearing could be held.

While briefs were readied for the bond hearing, Archer received more bad news. The Texas Supreme Court refused to consider overruling Judge Carrillo's order that Archer be removed as Duval County judge. Archer seemed to be taking events in stride. "Presently he just sits there and reads magazines, books, talks to the guards," a jail spokesman said. "He's in good spirits." Although locked in the hospital area, Archer wasn't taking any medication. He had no work assignment except for sweeping and mopping out his own cell.[25]

In San Antonio, Judge Suttle listened to the government's plea to have bail revoked. It was claimed Archer was a potential flight risk because he might be considered a Mexican national and the Mexican Code of Criminal Procedure provided "no Mexican may be extradited to a foreign state." Archer was also shown to have substantial hidden assets, cited as forty-seven thousand acres of property held by his half sister, Lillian Parr Moffett, who was described by the court as Archer's "Swiss Bank." Records showed Archer still possessed real property totaling $640,000 and personal property amounting to $763,166. Archer may have given the court concern of his influence in Duval when he told reporters he "can run the County from federal prison if necessary." After reviewing twenty-eight findings of fact in the matter, Judge Suttle revoked Archer's bail and Manges received his money back.[26]

No sooner had Manges received his money when Parr's attorney presented a $121,500 check as a substitute bond. The new money came from Praxedis Canales, rancher and father of state representative Terry Canales. Judge Suttle said he would take the substitute bond under advisement, but he reminded Parr's attorney "There's no constitutional right to bail after conviction." On August 20, 1975, Judge Suttle made his ruling. Calling Archer a "danger to the community," he denied bond.[27]

During the proceedings Archer was planning to wed again. Syleta (Lita Mae) Hawn, the forty-five-year-old owner of Bell, Book and Candle, an Alice boutique, had been with Archer for fifteen years during three of his four marriages.[28] Arriving at the county jail with a marriage license, Syleta learned her husband-to-be had been moved to an undisclosed location. "I would suspect that this is the first time a bride has been left waiting at the jailhouse steps," she told reporters.[29]

Although the sentencing judge recommended that Archer serve his time at Leavenworth, he was sent to the federal penitentiary at Terre Haute, Indiana. Two weeks later he was moved to the maximum security federal prison at Marion, Illinois, where such notables as Andrew Daulton Lee, the "Snowman" of the "Falcon and the Snowman" duo, and John Gotti did their time. While in prison, Archer learned a summary judgment had been granted barring him from practicing law. The ruling would become permanent whenever Archer exhausted his appeals.[30]

Judge O. P. Carrillo and his brother Ramiro went on trial in September 1975 for their federal tax charges. After a sixteen-day trial, both were found guilty on all counts. Ramiro received four years in prison and a twenty-thousand-dollar fine; O. P. Carrillo received five years and a twenty-two-thousand-dollar fine. O. P. Carrillo's legal problems came not only from the federal government but also from the State of Texas. He was convicted of felony theft and sentenced to four years in prison. The indictment stemmed from his purchase of a station wagon, paid for by the water district. Claiming twenty-one grounds of error in the trial, O. P. Carrillo appealed the decision, but the court of criminal appeals of Texas affirmed the judgment.[31] The Texas legislature decided in August 1975, by a 128–16 vote on ten articles of impeachment against Judge Carrillo, and on January 23, 1976, the senate convicted him.[32]

Key players in Duval County politics had been convicted one after another. A minor cast of characters remained, and the Duval grand jury soon took action. Indictments poured out as smaller players faced charges for official misconduct and theft. Marvin Foster, Archer's attorney in the ouster trial, was convicted of accepting a three-thousand-dollar check from the school district for work he did not do. He received nine years in prison. Duval County treasurer Manuel C. Solis pleaded guilty to charges of official misconduct, was fined five thousand dollars and ordered to pay ten thousand dollars in restitution. Former president of the First State Bank of San Diego Barney O. Goldthorn was found guilty of stealing thirty-two thousand dollars from the water district and given ten years' probation.[33]

Nago Alaniz, acquitted twenty years earlier as an accomplice in the Buddy Floyd murder, was on trial again—this time for the break-in and theft of water district records. School superintendent Bryan Taylor testified he had helped Alaniz hide the records on a ranch outside of town, and another witness testified he observed Alaniz carrying boxes from the water district office late at night. Despite their testimony Alaniz proved again he was the "Teflon lawyer" when the jury returned with a not guilty verdict.[34]

After spending fourteen months in prison, Archer returned to South Texas. He was not a free man; he was back to face state charges. Four charges of official misconduct for using county employees to work on his ranch and one for theft of a tractor belonging to Duval County had brought him back "on loan" from the federal government. Escorted by two Texas Rangers, Archer was dressed in dark slacks, shirt, and a maroon windbreaker. Having shed 40 pounds since being in prison, he was down to 150, but the deep lines on his face showed his age.

At his arraignment in San Diego, Archer told the judge he hadn't yet hired an attorney. Instead of returning him to the county jail, the rangers treated Archer to lunch at Jerry's Diner, his favorite hangout. Friends and family sat quietly at a nearby table. He described his prison job as a civil servant clerk. "I go to work in the morning, do my job, and go about my business." Asked about his dramatic weight loss, he didn't blame it on the prison food. "You must realize that our social life is a little restricted," he joked, "which means no beer."[35]

Archer was finally arraigned after hiring a lawyer. He pleaded "Not Guilty," and pretrial hearings were scheduled for the following month. Before heading back to county jail, Archer was permitted to stop off in county judge W. C. McDaniel's chambers where Syleta Hawn waited with marriage license in hand. With a Texas Ranger as best man, Archer married for the fifth time; it was Syleta's third marriage. After the five-minute ceremony, Archer was taken to his cell.[36]

While he was awaiting trial, Archer was sued for child support by his ex-wife Anne Furman Dunn. He was ordered to pay three thousand dollars of back support for his daughter, Anne Claire Parr, and the judge also set future monthly payments at $250. Archer opposed the ruling, saying he was incarcerated and had no assets or means of income. Archer had no money, but his lawyer had more to add.

"Archer Parr is insane," Nelson Sharpe, attorney from Kingsville, said of his client, "and he's a pauper." Not only is he insane now, the motion read, but he was insane in 1974 when the alleged offenses occurred. Sharpe asked for Archer to be hospitalized and given "complete psychiatric, psychological and neurological examinations," and because his client was a pauper, the state should pick up the tab. The following day, the motion was dropped as Archer changed his plea to guilty. Prosecutors agreed to the plea bargain, recommending Archer receive a ten-year probationary sentence to run concurrently with his ten-year federal sentence.[37]

After reading the pre-sentencing report, Judge Darrell "Hang 'em High" Hester refused to accept the plea bargain, saying, "ten years is no punishment at all." Hester said Archer was "less than cooperative" in the investigation and even misled investigators. He scheduled a hearing to allow Archer to withdraw the guilty plea and stand trial. Hester also ordered him moved from the county jail to a federally approved facility "commensurate with and appropriate to a prisoner under a felony conviction and in federal custody."[38]

According to Hester, "special privileges" had been accorded Archer in the county jail. He said Archer had been "permitted to marry after such request was denied by federal authorities." Special food, unmonitored visits with his new wife, and receiving "a number of highly unusual visitors" rounded out the complaints.[39] After moved to a Brownsville jail, Archer stood before Judge Hester and withdrew his guilty plea. His attorney wasn't ready to go to trial, so Archer was sent back to federal prison at Marion, Illinois, to await his return to Texas.

When it was learned that the Federal Bureau of Prisons had a policy of not returning an inmate more than once to face state charges, the Duval grand jury reindicted Archer on a single charge of "theft of more than $10,000 in services of county employees while he was a county judge." The charge stemmed from Archer using county employees to work on his ranch.[40]

After returning to the Marion prison, Archer was transferred to Terre Haute, Indiana, and then to the federal prison at Sandstone, Minnesota. During a routine physical examination at Sandstone it was discovered he had tuberculosis. The illness was serious, requiring him to be transferred to the federal prison hospital in Springfield, Missouri, for treatment. The

Texas trial was put on hold until Archer had recovered sufficiently before facing the rigors of a trial.

Failing to respond to three months of treatment, Archer underwent further tests. In examining the x-rays, doctors discovered Archer may have developed a malignant tumor in one lung. In a letter to Judge Hester explaining this newest complication, U.S. Attorney James R. Gough wrote he had discussed Archer's condition with the doctors. "My opinion from the conversation," he wrote, "is that they do not ever expect Mr. Parr to be able to stand trial."[41]

After nearly a year in the prison hospital, Archer began showing signs that medication had finally arrested the tuberculosis. No longer considered contagious, he was transferred to a medium-security prison in Texarkana, Texas. On December 6, 1978, after serving a little more than three years and four months of his ten-year sentence, he was granted parole. However, he was not a free man. Waiting for him outside the prison were two Texas Rangers with a bench warrant on state charges still pending.[42]

Almost immediately there was talk that Archer might try to reopen his old plea bargain for probation. According to the *Corpus Christi Caller* on December 10, 1978, Duval officials were more concerned about his plans if the deal went through. "They think Archer will come back and rally up the old party," said Walter Meek. "But he's not in the mood for it." Times had changed, Meek observed. Although the Old Party would relish a chance to revitalize the almost dead political machine, Archer wasn't the man for the job.

"Archer is different from George," Meek said. "With George politics was the whole ball of wax. That's what he lived for. For Archer it was just a sideline.

"Now if George was coming back. . . ."[43]

The state had every intention of taking Archer to trial, but at the last minute a closed-door session was held between the prosecutors and Archer's attorneys so as to hammer out a plea bargain. They emerged with a deal. More importantly, it had been accepted by Judge Hester, who had previously refused to agree to a compromise.

The plea agreement was unusual in that, if Archer pleaded guilty, his federal parole would be jeopardized. To avoid that situation, he pleaded guilty to one charge, was ordered to pay twenty-five thousand dollars in restitution, and given ten years' probation. Because Judge Hester deferred making a formal ruling, technically, Archer would not be convicted. There were provisions in the agreement, however, which Hester took care to explain in no uncertain terms—Archer was prohibited from living in Duval County, from participating in politics, and from holding a public servant job.

"This means that you cannot even hold a job as a courthouse custodian," Hester warned him. "You are not to even set one foot in Duval County." If approached by any of his old political cronies seeking to get him involved in any type of political activity, Hester advised Archer to tell them to "get lost."[44] With Archer sidelined, Clint Manges attempted to flex his political muscles in South Texas.

Manges was not only having difficulty in implementing his influence in Duval politics, he was also having problems getting back the money he had provided for George Parr's bond. The government wanted the seventy-five thousand dollars Manges had paid to be forfeited because Parr failed to make his court appearance. In addition, Eva Parr, executrix of George's estate, contended "the transaction was in substance a loan from Manges to Parr," and the money should be paid to the estate where Manges could take his place among the other creditors for any reimbursement. Because George Parr could not be punished, the government wanted Manges to pay. They felt the court should consider damage Parr had caused in the expense for the search and the fines his estate was no longer liable for. The lower court ordered thirty-five thousand dollars remitted to Manges and the remaining forty thousand dollars to be forfeited to the government. Eva was left to look for help in another court. The U.S. Court of Appeals set aside the decision and suggested the district court "take another look" at the pleadings.[45]

Judge Owen Cox received the case again in his Corpus Christi courtroom, delineating two issues to be resolved. Was George Parr insane when he killed himself? What were the costs of the government's manhunt, and should they be reimbursed? After a two-hour hearing, Cox laid the first question to rest. "I don't think there's anything in the evidence to even raise the issue of insanity," he concluded.[46]

On May 3, 1978, Cox ruled that the FBI and the marshals' services should be reimbursed two thousand dollars for their expenses in looking for George Parr after he failed to make his court appearance. The court then took up the matter of the fourteen thousand dollars in fines levied against Parr as part of his sentence but determined that "his death abated the liability for the fine." Using its discretionary power, the court again ordered forty thousand dollars to be forfeited to the government and thirty-five thousand dollars returned to Manges.[47]

Manges appealed, asking to have the district court overturned again and set the amount of remittance he should receive. The court of appeals determined the forfeiture granted by the district court was "an abuse of discretion." They ordered ten thousand dollars forfeited and the remaining sixty-five thousand dollars given to Manges. Eva Parr's claim was ruled "title to the funds deposited by Manges did not pass to Parr."[48] It had taken Manges four years after George Parr's death to get his bond money returned and it still cost him ten thousand dollars plus attorney's fees.

Archer lived a quiet life, staying out of politics as ordered by Judge Hester, but he didn't live up to the terms of his probation. In 1981 he was called to testify in a civil trial between the First State Bank of San Diego and Duval County concerning overcharges when the county was issuing time warrants. As luck would have it, the case was heard before Judge Hester. According to the *Corpus Christi Caller*, after the jury left the courtroom Hester turned to Parr and asked, "Where did you say you were living?"

"About five miles west of San Diego, your honor."

Although shocked to learn this, Hester said that if there was any violation of probation it was "between him and his probation officer." Actually, Archer's probation officer had given him permission to live in Duval County "on a very temporary basis." Archer was there to make arrangements for his daughter to attend school in San Diego. He also received permission to work at a ranch owned by the estate of his late aunt, Lillian Parr Moffett. The following week, Hester signed a written order canceling the probation officer's permission. Archer would now have to ask for a court hearing for any reason he wanted to enter Duval County.[49]

In September 1987 Archer was arrested for driving while intoxicated. Judge Hester ordered him picked up for violating probation and held without bond. After nineteen days in county jail, he was released. He received a ninety-day suspended sentence for the DWI charge. After that,

Archer kept out of sight and was seldom seen by anyone. In a rare public appearance, he attended the funeral of Norman Ransleben, George Parr's personal accountant, who died on January 3, 1999. Archer served as an honorary pallbearer.[50]

Suffering from health problems, Archer was rushed to the Alice Regional Hospital emergency room on November 2, 2000, where he died at 3:00 P.M. He had finished his ten-year probation and was living on his sixty-seven-hundred-acre ranch, *La Muralla* (The Rampart) just north of San Diego. His return to Duval County for his final years had been marked with bitterness over the terms of his probation. "I'm the only son of a bitch that was treated that way," he told a reporter. "Of all the people (who faced corruption charges), I was the only guy who was exiled from his hometown."[51] Despite his bitterness, Archer readily admitted to another reporter that his family was responsible for corruption in Duval County. "You can't run a political machine without illegal activity . . . without some hanky-panky," he confessed. "There were a hell of a lot of funerals paid for."[52]

Hundreds attended the funeral to pay final respects for the man considered the last Duke of Duval. The procession stretched for more than a mile as his coffin was taken to the family plot at Benavides Cemetery. An ex-Marine, Archer received a service with military honors. According to the *Corpus Christi Caller-Times*, Houston millionaire oilman Oscar Wyatt Jr. gave the eulogy at the graveside, praising Archer and George Parr for what they did for their country. "Without these people," he said, "Lyndon Johnson would never have been president."

When services ended, friends and family remained at the cemetery to remember the human side of the man. "He was serious about serious things," a longtime friend recalled, "but when it was party time, he was ready." Former Texas state representative Hugo Berlanga may have summed up Archer's life better than anyone. "We've seen the passing of an era," he said. "He was obviously legendary in a lot of ways and visionary in a lot of ways. Like it or not, like the song says, he did it his way."[53]

The Duval County Museum in Alice dedicated a room with artifacts from George Parr's life, including his last will and testament, his driver's license, and the cowboy hat he wore when he took his life. "The centerpiece of this room was the guest bedroom suite of George Parr," said museum director Maggie G. Rangel, "but the commissioners' court had a fight, and it was taken away." Rangel had personal ties to Parr. "His men killed my uncle. They shot him to death in a fight over whether to remove the courthouse to Benavides." It has been difficult for residents to forget their history. "A lot of things have never changed here," former San Diego mayor Alfredo E. Cardenas said. "It's the kind of town where you don't leave history behind."[54]

Texans will never forget George Parr. Even several decades after his death there is still talk of how he pulled off the shrewd maneuver to propel LBJ on his way to the White House. He is regarded as a folk hero, much as Missourians consider Frank and Jesse James. Even the whereabouts of the tin box from Precinct 13 is still debated. Stories abound as to whatever happened to it. Some say it's being hidden by private citizens of Alice; others say it may have been sold at a sheriff's auction; while another claims it was thrown into the Rio Grande years ago.[55]

George Parr's widow, Eva, remarried and continued living at the mansion in San Diego. The couple lived downstairs, leaving the upstairs bedroom almost as it was when George lived there. A portrait of George and Eva remained hanging over the bed, and Parr's hats were still kept in a plastic hanging bag in the next room. The blood-stained Chrysler where Parr had shot himself was cleaned and parked in the garage amid hundreds of deer heads mounted on walls. The ghost of George Parr seemed to be present everywhere, unwilling to let go of the past.[56]

A five-part television mini-series based on Duval County and the life of George Parr was planned in 1984. Starring Clint Walker and Lee Meriwether, "Summit County" was to have a segment based on Ballot Box 13. Although financed with a $250,000 budget, the series never aired.[57]

As long as candidates seek votes, they will always curry favor from those who exert control over the ballot box—it is an ingrained condition of the democratic process. But the time of the old-fashioned ward heeler has passed, replaced by political action committees. George Parr was a dinosaur roaming the South Texas landscape, unaware that his effectiveness had ebbed but continuing to carry on business as usual. When his time came, he refused to "go gentle into that good night," preferring to do what he had always done—take matters into his own hands. He died penniless, although there are rumors he salted away substantial funds, but as one observer noted in the 1950s: "He considers his political power a property right. He would almost rather lose all his money than to lose his political power."[58] An evil, power-hungry tyrant or a benevolent patrón, the paradox will never truly be understood, but George Parr remains a part of South Texas history and his legacy is still felt by those who remember him.

NOTES

CHAPTER 1

1. "Twenty-Nine Are Seeking Senate Seat in Election on June 28," *Fort Worth Star-Telegram*, May 29, 1941.

2. Horace Busby Oral History, 22.

3. "Return of Fergusonism Looms if Late Strange Vote Pile Elects W. Lee," *Austin Statesman*, July 4, 1941; Caro, *Path to Power*, 733.

4. Heard and Strong, *Southern Primaries*, 177.

5. James H. Rowe Jr., quoted in Miller, *Lyndon*, 88.

6. Heard and Strong, *Southern Primaries*, 182.

7. Handbook of Texas Online, s.v. "Duval County."

8. Murphy Givens, "Cowboy from Matagorda Founded Political Dynasty," *Corpus Christi Caller*, August 31, 2011.

9. Kahl, *Ballot Box 13*, 80–81; Anders, *Boss Rule in South Texas*, 173; Clark, *Fall of the Duke*, 26–27; Hailey, "Breaching the Mesquite Curtain," 8–9.

10. Anders, "Origins of the Parr Machine," 122.

11. Lynch, *Duke of Duval*, 12, labels Cleary a Republican and suggests suspicions of Archie's involvement arose at the time. Hailey, "Breaching the Mesquite Curtain," 11, has Cleary as a county judge; Anders, *Boss Rule*, 174, has him as county tax assessor; Clark, *Fall of the Duke*, 27, has him as tax collector.

12. "John D. Cleary Assassinated," *Corpus Christi Weekly Caller*, December 27, 1907; "Might Have Prevented a Foul Murder," *San Antonio Light*, December 27, 1907.

13. "Is Shot in the Back," *Houston Daily Post*; "Tax Assessor Killed," *Dallas Morning News*; "Assessor of Duval County Is Shot Dead," *San Antonio Daily Express*; all dated December 22, 1907.

14. "No Clue to Assassin of Cleary," *Corpus Christi Weekly Caller*, January 3, 1908.

15. "The Lawsons Released," *Corpus Christi Weekly Caller*, April 24, 1908; Anders, "Bosses under Siege," 477.

16. Julie Silva, "Politics Loom over 1912 San Diego Slayings," *Corpus Christi Caller*, June 4, 2012.

17. "Duval Endorsed Bailey," *Corpus Christi Weekly Caller*, May 15, 1908; "The Democratic Clans Are Gathering," *Houston Daily Post*, May 26, 1912; photo caption, "Oldest Member State Democratic Committee," *Houston Daily Post*, September 7, 1912.

18. Tom Finty Jr., "What Is Matter with Zapata County?" *Dallas Morning News*, August 19, 1911; Anders, *Boss Rule*, 176. See also Clark, *Fall of the Duke*, 29.

19. "Duval Murder Cases Transferred Here," *Austin Daily Statesman*, July 6, 1912.

20. Armando Villafranca, "A Tragic Tie to History," *Corpus Christi Caller-Times*, February 19, 1990; "Three Met Death in Political Quarrel," *Houston Daily Post*, May 19, 1912;

"Three Killed in Election at San Diego," *San Antonio Light*, May 18, 1912; "Election Trouble in Duval County Ends in 3 Killed and 3 Arrested," *Houston Chronicle and Herald*, May 18, 1912; "Three Men Killed in San Diego Fight," *Dallas Morning News*, May 19, 1912.

21. Quite often one quotation will be found in more than one newspaper; in this case "Three Men Are Killed in a Pistol Duel," *Austin Daily Statesman*, May 19, 1912; "Tragedy at San Diego," *Alice Echo*, May 23, 1912; "Three Slain in Pistol Duel over Border Election," *Fort Worth Star-Telegram*, May 18, 1912.

22. Schendel, "Something Is Rotten," 14.

23. "Duval Murder Cases Transferred Here," *Austin Daily Statesman*, July 6, 1912; Lynch, *Duke of Duval*, 14. See also "Grand Jury Indicts Three at San Diego," *San Antonio Light*, June 13, 1912; "San Diego Killings before Grand Jury," *Houston Chronicle and Herald*, June 10, 1912; "San Diego Killings," *Houston Chronicle and Herald*, June 13, 1912; "Duval Murder Cases to Be Changed Again," *Fort Worth Star-Telegram*, September 29, 1912; "Duval County Cases May Be Transferred from Travis County," *Houston Chronicle and Herald*, September 29, 1912; "Transferred to Richmond," *Corpus Christi Caller and Daily Herald*, October 3, 1912; "Duval County Murder Cases Will Be Tried in Fort Bend County," *Houston Chronicle and Herald*, October 2, 1912; "Frank Robinson Was Acquitted Murder Charge," *Corpus Christi Weekly Caller*, April 24, 1914.

24. "Three Killed in Fight at San Diego," *San Antonio Express*, May 19, 1912.

25. "County Taxes Not to Be Paid till Audit Is Made," *San Antonio Express*, January 7, 1914 (quote); "Duval County District Court Promises to Be Spicy Session," *Corpus Christi Caller and Daily Herald*, January 11, 1914.

26. "Petitions Filed in Court Excite Duval County," *San Antonio Express*, January 15, 1914. See also "Proposed Audit of County Books Stirs Citizens," *San Antonio Express*, January 13, 1914.

27. Citizens of Duval County, "Remarkable Conditions in Duval County," 16–18.

CHAPTER 2

1. "Many Testify in Duval Case," *San Antonio Express*, June 18, 1914; "Judge Says He Refused Auditor Access to Books," *San Antonio Express*, June 19, 1914; Citizens of Duval County, "Remarkable Conditions in Duval County," 24; "Duval County Audit Holding," *Houston Chronicle*, July 8, 1914; "Findings of Judge Hopkins in the Celebrated Duval County Audit Case," *Corpus Christi Caller and Daily Herald*, July 8, 1914.

2. "People Win Fight; Duval Officers Quit under Fire," *San Antonio Express*, July 17, 1914.

3. "Archie Parr for Senator," *Corpus Christi Weekly Caller*, April 10, 1914.

4. "Archie Parr Defeats Perkins for Senator," *Corpus Christi Weekly Caller*, July 31, 1914.

5. "Duval County Court House Burns to Ground," *Houston Chronicle*, August 11, 1914; "Courthouse at San Diego Destroyed," *Corpus Christi Caller and Daily Herald*, August 12, 1914; "Courthouse of Duval County Is Burned," *San Antonio Light*, August 11, 1914; Lynch, *Duke of Duval*, 17.

6. "Duval Officials Indicted," *Austin Daily Statesman*, January 23, 1915; "Arrest Duval Co. Officials," *Austin Daily Statesman*, January 28, 1915.

7. Rowe, "The Mesquite Pendergast," 9.

8. "New District Court Bill Will Become Effective on Its Passage," *Corpus Christi Caller*, February 4, 1915.

9. "Archie Parr Sprang Surprise, Changing District Court Bill," *Corpus Christi Caller*, February 26, 1915; "Archie Parr Plan for Division Twenty-Eighth Judicial District Accepted by Dunn; Bill Passed," *Corpus Christi Caller*, March 5, 1915.

10. "Ferguson Names Voll M. Taylor District Judge," *Corpus Christi Caller*, March 13, 1915; Anders, *Boss Rule*, 186.

11. "Duval County Audit Case to Texas Supreme Court," *Corpus Christi Caller*, February 14, 1915; "Books of Duval County to Be Audited Shortly," *Corpus Christi Caller and Daily Herald*, June 13, 1915.

12. "Duval Officials Again Enjoined," *San Antonio Express*, September 4, 1915; "Injunction Trial Today," *San Antonio Express*, October 27, 1915; "Injunction against Duval County Judge," *Corpus Christi Caller*, September 4, 1915.

13. Anders, *Boss Rule*, 90–91.

14. *Lasater et al. v. Lopez, County Treasurer, et al.*, Court of Civil Appeals, San Antonio, 202 S.W. 1039 (March 27, 1918).

15. "Federal Probers to Report Today on Duval County," *San Antonio Express*, September 24, 1915; "Grand Jury Thursday Morning Recessed until September 24," *Corpus Christi Caller*, September 17, 1915; Clark, *Fall of the Duke*, 33; Anders, *Boss Rule*, 188–89.

16. "Jury Foreman Says That Parr Took Evidence," *Houston Chronicle*, February 8, 1919; "Books Taken from Grand Jury Room," *Houston Daily Post*, December 11, 1915; "Books Are Taken from Grand Jury in Duval County," *San Antonio Express*, December 11, 1915.

17. "Archie Parr and A. W. Tobin Fined by Judge Taylor," *Corpus Christi Caller*, December 14, 1915; "State Senator and Sheriff Go to Jail," *Dallas Morning News*, December 14, 1915.

18. "The Duval County Cases Are on Trial," *Houston Daily Post*, December 30, 1915.

19. "Experts Testify at Ouster Trial in Duval County," *San Antonio Express*, December 31, 1915; "Expenditures of County Discussed," *Houston Daily Post*, December 31, 1915.

20. "Testimony in Duval Case," *Dallas Morning News*, January 1, 1916.

21. "Ended Testimony in Duval Co. Case," *Houston Daily Post*, January 2, 1916; "End Draws Near in Case against Duval Officials," *San Antonio Express*, January 2, 1916.

22. "Court Ousts Four Accused Officers of Duval County," *Fort Worth Star-Telegram*, January 10, 1916; "Four Commissioners Ousted," *Dallas Morning News*, January 11, 1916; "New Commissioners for Duval County," *Austin Statesman and Tribune*, January 11, 1916.

23. "Duval County Voters $100,000 Road Bonds," *Corpus Christi Caller*, July 16, 1916; Anders, "Origins of the Parr Machine," 122.

24. Northcott, "A Death in Duval," 5.

25. Lasater, *Falfurrias*, 117–18n.

26. Clark, *Fall of the Duke*, 34.

27. "Glasscock Defeats Parr for Senator," *Corpus Christi Caller*, July 30, 1918.

28. "Duval County Vote Not Reported to State Committee," *Corpus Christi Caller*, August 14, 1918; "Parr and His Lieutenants to Fight Nomination of Glasscock," *Corpus Christi Caller*, August 24, 1918.

29. "Rival Conventions Name Glasscock and Parr as Candidates," *San Antonio Light*, August 25, 1918; "Glasscock Nominated as State Senator of Twenty-Third District," *Corpus Christi Caller*, August 25, 1918.

30. "Platform Is Agreed Upon by Democrats," *San Antonio Light*, September 4, 1918; "Texas Democrats Repudiate A. Parr," *Corpus Christi Caller*, September 4, 1918; "Parr Is Scorched by Democrats," *Corpus Christi Caller*, September 5, 1918.

31. "Parr Application to Be Heard by Judge Taylor on Sept. 30," *Corpus Christi Caller*, September 13, 1918; "Glasscock Will Be Certified as Senate Nominee," *Corpus Christi Caller*, September 22, 1918.

32. "Temporary Writ Is Issued in Parr Glasscock Case," October 2, 1918; "Senatorial Case at Edinburg May Terminate Today," October 3, 1918; "A. Parr Gets Decision from Judge Chambliss in Case at Edinburgh," October 9, 1918; all *Corpus Christi Caller*.

33. "For Clean Politics on the Rio Grande," *Alice Echo*, October 24, 1918.

34. "Glasscock and Childers Triumph," November 6, 1918; Editorial, "Revolution at Home," November 8, 1918; "Government Agents Are Investigating Election Held in Border Section," November 8, 1918; "Federal and State Officers Investigate Election of Last Tuesday in Border Counties," November 9, 1918; all in *Corpus Christi Caller*.

35. "Mexican Voters Swing Majority for Parr in Race for State Senator," *Corpus Christi Caller*, December 6, 1918.

36. Harry T. Warner, "Texas Legislature Faces Big Task," *Houston Post*, January 12, 1919; "Senate to Hear Glasscock-Parr Seat Contest." *Houston Chronicle*, January 12, 1919; "Seat Parr, But Committee Will Hear Opponent," *Fort Worth Star-Telegram*, January 14, 1919; "Twenty-Third District Contest," *Austin Statesman*, January 14, 1919.

37. "Senate Considers Parr-Glasscock Tilt for Senatorial Seat," *Austin Statesman*, January 17, 1919; Harry T. Warner, "Report Favorably on Suffrage and Prohibition," *Houston Post*, January 17, 1919; Harry T. Warner, "Glasscock Winner of One Point," *Houston Post*, January 19, 1919.

38. "Glasscock-Parr Probe to Be Deep," *Corpus Christi Caller*, January 19, 1919; "Parr-Glasscock Case Attracting Much Attention," *Houston Post*, January 14, 1919; "Clash between Glasscock and Parr Averted," *San Antonio Light*, January 19, 1919.

39. "Defer Action on Glasscock-Parr Contest," *Houston Chronicle*, January 20, 1919.

40. "Rangers May Be Used to Gather State Witnesses," *Houston Chronicle*, January 24, 1919.

41. "Parr-Glasscock Fight for Seat Costly Business," *Houston Chronicle*, January 27, 1919; Harry T. Warner, "Three Big Issues Pending before Texas House," *Houston Post*, January 27, 1919; Editorial, "The Glasscock-Parr Contest," *Houston Post*, January 30, 1919.

42. "Parr-Glasscock Controversy Is before Senate," *Houston Chronicle*, February 6, 1919.

43. Harry T. Warner, "Counsel for Parr Alleges Rangers Played Politics," *Houston Post*, February 5, 1919.

44. "Parr-Glasscock Controversy Is before Senate," *Houston Chronicle*, February 6, 1919; Harry T. Warner, "Glasscock-Parr Contest Develops Novel Sidelights," *Houston Post*, February 6, 1919.

45. Montejano, "A Journey through Mexican Texas," 114–15.

46. "Parr Begins His Case Presenting Many Witnesses," *Corpus Christi Caller*, February 19, 1919; "Parr Attempts to Show Up Election in Webb County," *Corpus Christi Caller*, February 26, 1919; "Parr Introduces First Witnesses," *Houston Post*, February 19, 1919; "Parr Witnesses Tell of Rangers Election Methods," *Houston Post*, February 22, 1919.

47. Harry T. Warner, "Witness for Parr Attacks Schemes to Get Control," *Houston Post*, March 1, 1919; "Wells Tells of His Efforts in Behalf of Parr," *Corpus Christi Caller*, March 1, 1919.

48. "Senate Sitting as Committee of Whole Seats Archie Parr," *Corpus Christi Caller*, March 11, 1919; "Archie Parr Wins in Committee by Vote of 14 to 12," *Houston Post*, March 11, 1919.

49. Harry T. Warner, "Glasscock-Parr Vote to Be Taken by Senate Today," *Houston Post*, March 12, 1919.

50. Harry T. Warner, "Seat in Senate Awarded to Parr by Vote 16 to 14," *Houston Post*, March 14, 1919; "Parr Wins in Contest Case by Lone Vote," *San Antonio Light*, March 13, 1919; "Parr Seated as Senator from Twenty-Third District," *Corpus Christi Caller*, March 14, 1919.

51. Lynch, *Duke of Duval*, 22; Hailey, "Breaching the Mesquite Curtain," 15.

52. "Would Erase Records of Impeachment," *San Antonio Light*, January 18, 1923.

53. "Confusion Prevails When Senate Tries to Restore Citizenship to Ferguson," *Corpus Christi Caller*, February 10, 1923.

54. McKay and Faulk, *Texas after Spindletop*, 87–88; "Try to Exonerate James E. Ferguson," *Dallas Morning News*, February 10, 1923.

55. Silliman Evans, "Senate Votes Pardon to Ferguson; Revokes Action in 30 Minutes," *Fort Worth Star-Telegram*, February 10, 1923.

56. "Parr Explains His Handling of Resolution," *Houston Chronicle*, February 12, 1923; "Parr Apologizes to Senate for Action in Ferguson Case," *Austin Statesman*, February 12, 1923; "Oil Is Poured on Waters in Senate," *Dallas Morning News*, February 13, 1923.

CHAPTER 3

1. Martin, "Tyrant in Texas," 20.

2. Lynch, *Duke of Duval*, 3.

3. Ibid., 25.

4. Givens, "Cowboy from Matagorda Founded Political Dynasty."

5. "Senators Probing A. & M. Hazing," *Fort Worth Star-Telegram*, February 17, 1921.

6. "Probe of Alleged Hazing Ordered," *San Antonio Express*, February 9, 1921; "Inquiry of A. & M. Hazing Finished," *Dallas Morning News*, February 19, 1921.

7. "Paddling Favorite Method of Hazing at A. & M. College," *Austin Statesman*, February 17, 1921; "Cadet Hit on Head, Others Whipped in Hazings, Testified," *San Antonio Express*, February 17, 1921.

8. Dr. Tex Leo Kassen, comp., *Southwestern Football Historical Review*; Lynch, *Duke of Duval*, 32–33.

9. Lynch, *Duke of Duval*, 33.

10. Rowe, "Mesquite Pendergast," 23.

11. "Judge Parr—Only Twenty-Four Years of Age," *Houston Post*, January 16, 1916.

12. Lynch, *Duke of Duval*, 26, 32.

13. Handbook of Texas Online, s.v. "Parr, George Berham"; "Humor in Duval County Carries a Barbed Thrust," *Houston Chronicle*, March 7, 1954.

14. "Parr: Duke Different Things to Different People," *San Antonio Express*, May 5, 1974.

15. *United States v. Archer Parr*, 399 F. Supp. 883, August 21, 1975.

16. Steinberg, *Sam Johnson's Boy*, 26.

17. Lynch, *Duke of Duval*, 37.

18. Clarence J. LaRoche, "Tax Man Tells of 'Slip' by Parr," *San Antonio Express*, October 18, 1955; "Duval County Judge Sentenced," *San Antonio Express*, May 22, 1934; Lynch, *Duke of Duval*, 39; "Valley Politics Leads to Sixteen U.S. Indictments," *Dallas Morning News*, March 5, 1932.

19. Schendel, "Something Is Rotten," 68 (quote); Haley, *A Texan Looks at Lyndon*, 30.

20. "Duval County Judge Sentenced," *San Antonio Express*, May 22, 1934.

21. Flora Rheta Schreiber and Stuart Long, "What Are Odds on Nixon Dumping Agnew?" *Deseret News*, July 19, 1971.

22. Smith Oral History, 6.

23. James Rowe, "Income Tax Evasion Brought Stay in Prison in 1930s," *Corpus Christi Caller*, April 7, 1975; "Duval Judge Fined $5000 in Tax Case," *Houston Post*, May 22, 1934.

24. Kahl, *Ballot Box 13*, 85; Rowe, "Mesquite Pendergast," 14; James Rowe, "Income Tax Evasion Brought Stay in Prison in 1930s," *Corpus Christi Caller*, April 7, 1975 (quote).

25. "Archie Parr Is Attacked by Seabury," *Corpus Christi Caller*, June 13, 1934.

26. Kahl, *Ballot Box 13*, 86; Lynch, *Duke of Duval*, 41.

27. Murphy Givens, "Eleven Individuals Who Made a Difference in Corpus Christi," *Corpus Christi Caller-Times*, January 2, 2000.

28. "Hug-the-Coast Highway to Pass through Kenedy," *Alice Echo*, September 21, 1933; "Deeds for Coast Road Are Secured by Senator Parr," *Alice Echo*, June 21, 1934; "Archie Parr Is Attacked by Seabury," *Corpus Christi Caller*, June 13, 1934 (quote); "Federal and State Funds Now Available for Road through Kenedy County," *Corpus Christi Caller*, June 24, 1934; Rowe, "Mesquite Pendergast," 10.

29. Lynch, *Duke of Duval*, 43.

30. "State, Senate Races in Doubt," *San Antonio Express*, July 31, 1934; "Deeds on Gap in Kenedy Co. Road Signed," *Houston Chronicle*, August 15, 1934.

31. "Neal Defeats Archie Parr," *Houston Post*, August 27, 1934; "Four Ex-Governors of Texas Endorse Sen. Archie Parr," *Alice Echo*, August 23, 1934.

32. "Archer Parr Goes Down to Defeat in Voting Battle," *San Antonio Express*, August 27, 1934; "Parr District Rumor Rapped," *San Antonio Express*, September 4, 1934; "Parr, Mathis Beaten; Purl Is Trailing," *Fort Worth Star-Telegram*, August 27, 1934 (quote); Byron C. Utecht, "Bill May Save Senate Seat for Parr," *Fort Worth Star-Telegram*, August 31, 1934.

33. Heard and Strong, *Southern Primaries*, 137, 139. For the pardon see Bailey, "Breaching the Mesquite Curtain," 41.

34. Schendel, "Something Is Rotten," 68.

35. FBI Report of Special Agent George N. Denton, File No. 73-58, November 22, 1943, Office of the Pardon Attorney Archives; Clark, *Fall of the Duke*, 313.

36. "Parr Must Serve Two-Year Sentence," *San Antonio Express*, June 4, 1936; Lynch, *Duke of Duval*, 45 (quote).

37. Schendel, "Something Is Rotten," 68; also "Duval County Judge Ordered to Prison," *Fort Worth Star-Telegram*, June 3, 1936.

38. Haley, *A Texan Looks at Lyndon*, 31; Schendel, "Something Is Rotten," 68.

39. "Mrs. Sevier Asks Clemency for Parr," *Houston Post*, June 3, 1936; "Parr May Receive Executive Clemency; Removal Is Delayed," *Alice Echo*, July 2, 1936; "Governor Explains Stand on Review of George Parr Case," *Alice Echo*, July 16, 1936.

40. Lynch, *Duke of Duval*, 47.

41. U.S. Attorney General Tom C. Clark to President Harry S. Truman, February 13, 1946, File No. 69–65–15001, Office of the Pardon Attorney Archives.

CHAPTER 4

1. James W. Mangan, "Vote Fraud Put LBJ into Office," *San Antonio Express News*, July 31, 1977; also Kahl, *Ballot Box 13*, 88.

2. Schendel, "Something Is Rotten," 71.

3. Mangan, "Vote Fraud Put LBJ into Office"; also Kahl, *Ballot Box 13*, 89.

4. Caro, *Path to Power*, 722; Martin, "Tyrant in Texas," 45 (quote).

5. Snow, "The Poll Tax in Texas," 79 (quote), also 1, 4, 13–15, 22.

6. "Archie Parr, Pioneer Rancher and Political Leader, Dies Sunday in Corpus Christi," *Alice Echo*, October 22, 1942.

7. Political advertisement, "So You Want a Job?" *Alice Echo*, May 28, 1942.

8. "Parr Promises Henchmen that Supporters Will Be Kept on Airport Payroll," *Alice Echo*, June 4, 1942.

9. FBI Report of Special Agent George N. Denton, 9–10, File No. 73-58, November 22, 1943, Office of the Pardon Attorney Archives.

10. Ibid., 3, January 18, 1944.

11. Clark, *Fall of the Duke*, 63.

12. "Reported Duval Five-Cent Beer 'Tax' May Face Probe," *Houston Chronicle*, September 11, 1948; Schendel, "Something Is Rotten," 15; Caro, *Means of Ascent*, 185.

13. Rowe, "Mesquite Pendergast," 22.

14. FBI Report of Special Agent George N. Denton, 6, File No. 73-58, November 22, 1943, Office of the Pardon Attorney Archives.

15. Schendel, "Something Is Rotten," 68; Dugger, *The Politician*, 325 (quote).

16. Northcott, "A Death in Duval," 6.

17. Clark, *Fall of the Duke*, 109–10; Rowe, "Mesquite Pendergast," 23.

18. Mary Lee Grant, "Duval's Sport of Kings," *Corpus Christi Caller-Times*, March 14, 1999.

19. "Heart Attack Kills Richard Kleberg, Sr.," *Corpus Christi Caller*, May 9, 1955.

20. "Attempt to Smear Dick Kleberg Collapses, False Charge Caused Great Indignation in Alice," *Alice Echo*, June 8, 1944; "Big Things in the News of the Week," *Alice Echo*, July 13, 1944.

21. Judith Ann Sutherland, "W. E. Pope Fought Parr Machine, Vote Fraud," *Corpus Christi Caller*, September 13, 2011.

22. Dallek, *Lone Star Rising*, 330; James Rowe, "Income Tax Evasion Brought Stay in Prison in 1930s," *Corpus Christi Caller*, April 7, 1975.

23. Clark, *Fall of the Duke*, 42; Schendel, "Something Is Rotten," 15.

24. Application for Executive Clemency, August 7, 1943, Record 69, Page 65-15001, Office of the Pardon Attorney Archives.

25. Caro, *Means of Ascent*, 461n.

26. Lyndon B. Johnson to James Rowe, Assistant to the U.S. Attorney General, August 4, 1943, Office of the Pardon Attorney Archives.

27. FBI Report of Special Agent George N. Denton, 15–16, File No. 73-58, November 22, 1943, Office of the Pardon Attorney Archives.

28. George B. Parr to Daniel M. Lyons, Pardon Attorney, February 28, 1945, Office of the Pardon Attorney Archives.

29. Clark, *Fall of the Duke*, 45.

30. Caro, *Means of Ascent*, 168.

31. Ibid., 190.

32. "An Open Letter," *Laredo Times*, February 3, 1943.

33. Lynch, *Duke of Duval*, 56.

34. Miller, *Lyndon*, 125–26.

35. "Parr Says Duval County Voted for Lyndon 'Because He Is Our Friend,'" *Austin Statesman*, September 7, 1948; Lynch, *Duke of Duval*, 59.

CHAPTER 5

1. "Steam Sizzles from Senate Caldron as Johnson, Peddy Land on Coke," *Austin American*, June 8, 1948.

2. Miller, *Lyndon*, 126.

3. "Salas Regrets It All Today," *San Antonio Express-News*, July 31, 1977.

4. Caro, *Means of Ascent*, 188; Mangan, "Vote Fraud Put LBJ into Office."

5. Kahl, *Ballot Box 13*, 89; James W. Mangan, "Riddle of LBJ's 'Landslide' Unlocked," *Dallas Morning News*, July 31, 1977.

6. Miller, *Lyndon*, 125 (quote); Caro, *Means of Ascent*, 185.

7. Dugger, *The Politician*, 323; George B. Parr to Lyndon B. Johnson, August 29, 1941, Pre-Presidential Confidential File, George B. Parr File, Box 4, LBJ Library; Dugger, *The Politician*, 323.

8. Caro, *Means of Ascent*, 191.

9. Phipps, *Summer Stock*, 306–7.

10. "Stevenson Regains Lead in See-Saw Senate Race," *Fort Worth Star-Telegram*, August 30, 1948; Heard and Strong, *Southern Primaries*, 182.

11. "Stevenson Increases Lead Slightly in Senate Race; 1,016,106 Votes Counted," *Fort Worth Star-Telegram*, July 26, 1948; "Coke's Margin Increases Slightly in Latest Count," *Austin Statesman*, July 26, 1948 (quote).

12. John B. Connally Oral History, 26; Rowe, "Mesquite Pendergast," 25.

13. Dugger, *The Politician*, 325; Caro, *Means of Ascent*, 305.

14. Busby Oral History, 32.

15. Dallek, *Lone Star Rising*, 661n.

16. Kahl, *Ballot Box 13*, 91.

17. Schendel, "Something Is Rotten," 70.

18. Kahl, *Ballot Box 13*, 93 (quote); Caro, *Means of Ascent*, 264.

19. Mangan, "Riddle of LBJ's 'Landslide' Unlocked."

20. James H. Rowe Jr., quoted in Miller, *Lyndon*, 88.

21. Banks, *Money, Marbles and Chalk*, 85 (Connally); Busby Oral History, 22 (Parr).

22. Rowe, "Mesquite Pendergast," 26.

23. Dugger, *The Politician*, 326; Green, *The Establishment in Texas Politics*, 114.

24. "Ex-Official Says He Stole 1948 Election for Johnson," *New York Times*, July 31, 1977.

25. Al Learkin, "LBJ May Have Lost '41 Election through Fraud, Kearns Says," *Boston Sunday Globe*, August 7, 1977; "Salas Reaffirms His Story of 'Stolen' Votes in Box 13," *San Antonio Express*, August 5, 1977.

26. "'48 Johnson Victory Debated Anew in Texas as Fraud Issue Is Revived," *New York Times*, August 15, 1977; Byers Oral History, 36.

27. Kahl, *Ballot Box 13*, 96.

28. Ibid.; Caro, *Means of Ascent*, 393.

29. Grubin, "LBJ: Part One, Beautiful Texas," *The American Experience* (Connally); Reston, *The Lone Star*, 145, 632.

30. Dugger, *The Politician*, 328; "Johnson Memo Denies Charges of Vote Fraud," *New York Times*, August 4, 1977; "Memo Denies LBJ Knew of Vote Changes," *San Antonio Express*, August 4, 1977.

31. Kahl, *Ballot Box 13*, 97; Clark, *Fall of the Duke*, 60. See also "Texan Denied Involvement in '48 Johnson Vote Case," *New York Times*, August 30, 1977.

32. Editorial, "Good Senator by Bad Margin," *Dallas Morning News*, September 2, 1948.

33. Caro, *Means of Ascent*, 317.

34. "Spotlight Turns on South Texas," *Corpus Christi Caller*, September 4, 1948 (quote); "The Story of Eighty-Seven Votes That Made History," *U.S. News & World Report*, April 6, 1964, 46–50.

35. Lynn Landrum, "Thinking Out Loud: El Patron," *Dallas Morning News*, September 3, 1948.

36. "Let's Clear Texas' Good Name," *Dallas Morning News*, September 4, 1948; "FBI 'Proper Agency' for Election Probe: Johnson," *Austin Statesman*, September 4, 1948; "Sure, Let the FBI Investigate," *Dallas Morning News*, September 5, 1948. See also Dawson Duncan, "Coke Sees Attempt to Count Him Out," *Dallas Morning News*, September 4, 1948; Dawson Duncan, "Johnson Says Battle Is Won," *Dallas Morning News*, September 5, 1948.

37. Shomette quoted in James Rowe, "Foe of Parr Says Duval Count Right," *Corpus Christi Caller*, September 9, 1948.

38. "'Didn't Buy Votes,' Johnson Declares," *Dallas Morning News*, September 7, 1948.

39. "Vote Fraud Checkup Invited by Johnson," *Corpus Christi Caller*, September 7, 1948 (quote); Miller, *Lyndon*, 126.

40. "Parr Says Duval County Voted for Lyndon 'Because He Is Our Friend,'" *Austin Statesman*, September 7, 1948 (quote); Hailey, "Breaching the Mesquite Curtain," 52–53.

41. Pycior, *LBJ and Mexican Americans*, 65.

42. Jerry Deal, "'They Told Us to Get Out,'" *San Antonio Express-News*, August 7, 1977.

43. According to Dallek, *Lone Star Rising*, 332, Stevenson went to Alice with Hamer and Gardner. Caro, *Means of Ascent*, 323, has Gardner going with Dibrell and Graham on Tuesday; Callan Graham agrees with Caro. Graham Oral History, 16. Testifying under oath, B. M. Brownlee said he was with Stevenson at the bank and that the others present included Homer Dean and Dibrell, "Johnson Barred Pending Checkup in South Texas," *Corpus Christi Caller*, September 23, 1948.

44. Graham Oral History, 18; Miller, *Lyndon*, 127.

45. Schendel, "Something Is Rotten," 70; "Demo County Chairman Issue Puzzles Jim Wells," *Corpus Christi Caller*, September 9, 1948 (quote).

46. Graham Oral History Interview, 19–20.

47. Ibid., 23.

48. Ibid., 25–26.

49. Dugger, *The Politician*, 330.

50. Kahl, *Ballot Box 13*, 118.

51. Garth Jones, "'One Mob, One Ranger' Story Is Still True," *Corpus Christi Caller-Times*, September 9, 1956.

52. Kahl, *Ballot Box 13*, 120, 121. See also Frost and Jenkins, *Frank Hamer*, 280.

53. Miller, *Lyndon*, 128.

54. Rowe cited from a letter to Sidney Blumenthal, Book Review Editor, *New York Times*, March 31, 1991.

55. Graham Oral History, 34.

56. Program transcript, *The American Experience*, Grubin, "LBJ, Part One: Beautiful Texas" (quote); also "Johnson Barred Pending Checkup in South Texas," *Corpus Christi Caller*, September 23, 1948.

57. Mangan, "Riddle of LBJ's 'Landslide' Unlocked."

58. Ibid.

59. E. L. Wall, "Politics Out in Duval Talks with Strangers," *Houston Chronicle*, September 7, 1948. See also "Johnson Barred Pending Checkup in South Texas," *Corpus Christi Caller*, September 23, 1948; Caro, *Means of Ascent*, 329.

60. Allen Duckworth, "U.S. Court Bars Johnson from Ballot until Inquiry," *Dallas Morning News*, September 23, 1948; "Johnson Barred Pending Checkup in South Texas," *Corpus Christi Caller*, September 23, 1948.

CHAPTER 6

1. "No Joy in Seven Sisters because Papa Returned," *Dallas Morning News*, October 19, 1948. The original version omitted Johnson's name.

2. Quoted from both "Coke Claims Proof of Jim Wells Vote Fraud," *Alice Daily Echo*, September 10, 1948; "Coke Stevenson Claims Fraud in South Texas Precinct Vote," *Dallas Morning News*, September 11, 1948.

3. "Court Halts Recanvass of Jim Wells Returns," *Austin Statesman*, September 11, 1948.

4. "Johnson Raps Coke, 'Pistol-Packing Pal,'" *Houston Chronicle*, September 11, 1948; "Senate Fight Approaches Climax," *Houston Chronicle*, September 12, 1948.

5. "Stevenson's Lawyers Urge Court to Throw out Johnson Injunction," *Austin Statesman*, September 13, 1948; "Judge Broeter Rules for Johnson," *Alice Daily Echo*, September 13, 1948.

6. "Parr Says He'll Be in Fort Worth Today," *Houston Post*, September 14, 1948.

7. Leonard Mohrmann, "Parr Guffaws at Report of Eighteen-County Control," *Corpus Christi Caller*, September 14, 1948.

8. Phil North, "Stevenson-Johnson Clash Due for Convention Floor," *Fort Worth Star-Telegram*, September 14, 1948; Ray Osborne, "Injunction Bars Check of Jim Wells Co. Votes," *Dallas Morning News*, September 14, 1948.

9. Dave Cheavens, "Subcommittee Checking Each County's Returns," *Austin Statesman*, September 13, 1948; "Member of Vote Group Collapses," *Fort Worth Star-Telegram*, September 13, 1948.

10. Jack Guinn, "Executive Committee O.K.'s Johnson," *Houston Post*, September 14, 1948.

11. Caro, *Means of Ascent*, 348. Another version was that Bill Kitrell had found Gibson in his hotel room—drunk. Throwing him into a cold shower, Kitrell hustled Gibson down to the ballroom. Reston, *The Lone Star*, 151.

12. Dallek, *Lone Star Rising*, 336; Editorial, "Field Day for Johnson," *Houston Post*, September 15, 1948. Dugger, *The Politician*, 333, wrote that a photograph (never found) was taken of Parr and Johnson. He quotes John Cofer, Houston attorney and supporter of Johnson: "I saw it taken. I was standing back of the photographer." Dugger, *The Politician*, 459n. E. L. Wall reported that it was chairman Tom Tyson who had called Parr to the stage. "I'm not asking him to make a speech," Tyson said. "I just want to tell him that if I ever run for office I want him on my side." E. L. Wall, "Johnson's Certification Enjoined," *Houston Chronicle*, September 15, 1948.

13. "Precinct 13 Vote Basis for Federal Court Injunction Granted Coke," *Alice Daily Echo*, September 15, 1948.

14. Green, *The Establishment in Texas Politics*, 116.

15. Allen Duckworth, "Court to Air Plea by Coke Next Tuesday," *Dallas Morning News*, September 16, 1948.

16. Reston, *The Lone Star*, 154–55 (Dibrell); Joe Bell, "U.S. Court Blocks Johnson Certifying," *Fort Worth Star-Telegram*, September 15, 1948.

17. "Court Says Lyndon's Suit Is Unnecessary," *Corpus Christi Caller*, September 17, 1948 (quote). See also Margaret Mayer, "Johnson Takes Ballot Plea to Supreme Court,"

Austin Statesman, September 16, 1948; "New Court Order Filed to Block Brown Putting Johnson on Ballot," *Austin Statesman*, September 17, 1948; William M. Thornton, "Top Court Refuses Johnson's Petition," *Dallas Morning News*, September 17, 1948.

18. Davidson, *Memoirs of Judge T. Whitfield Davidson*, 103.

19. "Court's Jurisdiction Still Argued in Senatorial Case," *Corpus Christi Caller*, September 22, 1948.

20. Caro, *Means of Ascent*, 358; Steinberg, *Sam Johnson's Boy*, 267.

21. *Johnson et al. v. Stevenson*, 170 F.2d 108 (October 7, 1948).

22. "Johnson Barred Pending Checkup in South Texas," *Corpus Christi Caller*, September 23, 1948.

23. "Judge Orders Vote Probe Report Oct. 2," *Fort Worth Star-Telegram*, September 25, 1948.

24. Smith Oral History, 2–3.

25. Haley, *A Texan Looks at Lyndon*, 45; also in Kahl, *Ballot Box 13*, 180, and Dallek, *Lone Star Rising*, 344.

26. Fortas Oral History, 4–6. See also Murphy, *Fortas*, 92.

27. Dugger, *The Politician*, 335, has Parr meeting with Truman in a hotel; Schendel, "Something Is Rotten," 71, and Steinberg, *Sam Johnson's Boy*, 269, both place the meeting on the train.

28. Miller, *Lyndon*, 135 (Mangan); Stevenson from "No Wonder, Coke Says," *Corpus Christi Caller*, September 28, 1948. See also "Truman to Start Texas Swing at El Paso Sept. 25," *Fort Worth Star-Telegram*, September 16, 1948.

29. James Rowe, "Jim Wells Ballot Boxes Opened by Investigator," *Corpus Christi Caller*, September 29, 1948; Ray Osborne, "U.S. Court Impounds All Boxes in Jim Wells," *Dallas Morning News*, September 28, 1948 (quote).

30. Bill Mason, "Street Scene," *Alice Daily Echo*, September 29, 1948 (quote); Kahl, *Ballot Box 13*, 192.

31. Caro, *Means of Ascent*, 379.

32. "The Duke Delivers," *Time* 52 (September 27, 1948): 24.

33. Mangan, "Riddle of LBJ's 'Landslide' Unlocked."

34. James Rowe, "Jim Wells Ballot Boxes Opened by Investigator," *Corpus Christi Caller*, September 29, 1948.

35. Ray Osborne, "Vote Fraud Quiz Goes on Despite Nod for Johnson," *Dallas Morning News*, September 29, 1948 (quote); Kahl, *Ballot Box 13*, 198.

36. "Black's Rule Puts Johnson on Ballot," *Corpus Christi Caller*, September 29, 1948.

37. Lewis Wood, "Texas Ballot Writ Is Stayed by Black," *New York Times*, September 29, 1948.

38. Lois Felder, "Official in Duval Discloses Failure to Report Returns," *Corpus Christi Caller*, September 29, 1948.

39. Poage, *Politics*, 122. Poage was representative to Congress at the time. See also Dugger, *The Politician*, 333–34.

40. "US Court Halts Vote Fraud Quiz," *Alice Daily Echo*, September 29, 1948.

41. Rowe, "Mesquite Pendergast," 37 (quote); Hailey, "Breaching the Mesquite Curtain," 58.

42. Ray Osborne, "Coke Throws His Support to GOP Senate Candidate," *Dallas Morning News*, October 13, 1948; "Johnson Calls Foe Turncoat," *Austin Statesman*, October 13, 1948; "Parr's Sister Comes Out for Jack Porter," *Alice Daily Echo*, October 26, 1948.

43. "Grand Jury Spanks Vote Officials," *Alice Daily Echo*, November 16, 1948.

44. Busby Oral History, 32–33.

45. Wick Fowler, "Outside Criticism Strengthens His Control, Duval's Duke Says," *Dallas Morning News*, October 31, 1948. See also "Seized Ballots Will Be Taken to Washington," *Fort Worth Star-Telegram*, October 26, 1948; "Senate Seizes Jim Wells Records," *Alice Daily Echo*, October 26, 1948; Claude Ramsey, "Duval Courthouse Janitor Frustrates US Senate by Burning up All Ballots," *Austin Statesman*, October 28, 1948.

46. Grubin, "LBJ, Part One: Beautiful Texas."

CHAPTER 7

1. Pycior, *LBJ and Mexican Americans*, 60–61.

2. Rowe, "Mesquite Pendergast," 24.

3. James Rowe, "Deputy Held in Death of Alice Newscaster," *Corpus Christi Caller*, July 30, 1949; Warren, *Memoirs of Earl Warren*, 85.

4. *Alice Daily Echo*, July 10, 1953; "Rangers Patrol Alice after Slaying," *Houston Chronicle*, July 30, 1949; Sparks, "Murder of a Broadcast Journalist," 10.

5. *Smithwick v. State*, Court of Criminal Appeals of Texas, 234 S.W.2nd 237 (October 4, 1950).

6. "Mason Pounded; Officer Is Fined," *Alice Daily Echo*, January 28, 1949; "Rangers Patrol Alice as Feeling Rises after Killing," *Fort Worth Star-Telegram*, July 30, 1949 (quote).

7. "Girls Being Held in Alice Inquiry," *San Antonio Express*, August 6, 1949; James Rowe, "Rancho Alegre Operator Switches to Grocery Store," *Corpus Christi Caller-Times*, August 14, 1949. See also "Special Jury May Be Called to Investigate Mason Slaying," *Corpus Christi Caller*, August 2, 1949; Rowe, "Mesquite Pendergast," 42.

8. "Records of Mason Broadcasts May Be Used in Murder Trial," *Corpus Christi Caller*, August 12, 1949.

9. All quotes from two sources: William C. Barnard, "Hundreds Attend Rites for Slain Radioman," *Houston Chronicle*, August 1, 1949; William C. Barnard, "Slain Radio Man's Final Program Told of Threat," *Fort Worth Star-Telegram*, August 1, 1949.

10. "Witness Describes Slaying of Mason," *Austin Statesman*, January 23, 1950. See also "Jailed Deputy Back as Bill Mason Buried," *Houston Post*, August 1, 1949; Hailey, "Breaching the Mesquite Curtain," 62.

11. "Deputy Held in Death of Alice Newscaster," *Corpus Christi Caller*, July 30, 1949; "Alice Deputy Sped to Corpus Haven," *Houston Post*, July 31, 1949.

12. "Deputy Held in Death of Alice Newscaster," *Corpus Christi Caller*, July 30, 1949.

13. "Rangers Patrol Tense Alice; Officers Move Accused Killer," *San Antonio Light*, July 31, 1949.

14. "Gunmen Blast Dance Hall Hit by Slain Critic," *Chicago Sunday Tribune*, July 31, 1949.

15. James Rowe, "Rancho Alegre Operator Switches to Grocery Store," *Corpus Christi Caller-Times*, August 14, 1949. See also "Smithwick, Spirited Away, Held at Corpus Christi," *Alice Daily Echo*, July 31, 1949; "Arson Attempt Made upon Alice Night Club," *San Antonio Express*, August 15, 1949.

16. "Deputy Spirited from Alice," *Houston Chronicle*, July 31, 1949. See also "Burt Mason Plans Radio Broadcasts," *Alice Daily Echo*, August 3, 1949; "Slain Radio Man's Son in Hospital after Beating," *Fort Worth Star-Telegram*, August 15, 1949.

17. "Mason under Treatment after Houston Assault," *Corpus Christi Caller*, August 16, 1949.

18. "Son of Slain Man Is Beaten," *San Antonio Express*, August 16, 1949 (quote); "Mason Closes Broadcast," *Alice Daily Echo*, August 19, 1949.

19. "Mason Gives Up Radio Show," *Corpus Christi Caller*, August 20, 1949.

20. "Burt Mason Is Held on Burglary Charge," *Alice Daily Echo*, February 9, 1950; "Burt Mason Given Suspended Sentence," *Alice Daily Echo*, March 31, 1950.

21. James Rowe, "Eyewitness Describes Shooting of Mason," *Corpus Christi Caller*, August 3, 1949.

22. James Rowe, "Full Mason Case Inquiry Called," *Corpus Christi Caller*, August 5, 1949. See also James Rowe, "Martineau Judge of Court for Mason Death Inquiry," *Corpus Christi Caller*, August 30, 1949; Rowe, "Mesquite Pendergast," 43.

23. "Grand Jury Opens Investigation into Slaying of Bill Mason at Alice," *All Valley Morning Express*, September 8, 1949 (all quotes); "Special Panel May Dig into Coke-Lyndon Vote," *Austin Statesman*, September 10, 1949.

24. "Grand Jury May Go into Election Case," *Alice Daily Echo*, September 11, 1949; "Seven More Subpoenaed in Jim Wells Vote Probe," *Houston Chronicle*, September 14, 1949.

25. James Rowe, "Further Study of Alice Vote Is Indicated," *Corpus Christi Caller*, September 14, 1949.

26. "More Witnesses Called in Ballot Box Inquiry," *Fort Worth Star-Telegram*, September 16, 1949; "Grand Jury Hears Martens in Probe of Jim Wells Vote," *Houston Chronicle*, September 15, 1949; "Box 13 Inquiry to Resume," *Corpus Christi Caller*, September 13, 1949; James Rowe, "Alice Grand Jury to Resume Vote Inquiry Today," *Corpus Christi Caller*, September 15, 1949.

27. "Reporter Can't Write His Story," *Corpus Christi Caller*, September 22, 1949; "Alice Grand Jury Ends Vote Probe," *Houston Chronicle*, September 24, 1949.

28. Salas quoted from Mangan, "Riddle of LBJ's 'Landslide' Unlocked."

29. "DA in Smithwick Trial Ambushed," *Houston Post*, January 24, 1950; Thomas E. Turner, "Effort Made to Kill Belton Prosecutor," *Dallas Morning News*, January 24, 1950.

30. Martha Cole, "Smithwick Says Mason Grabbed Gun and He Shot." *Alice Daily Echo*, January 24, 1950. See also Martha Cole, "Smithwick Found Guilty, Sentenced to Life Term," *Corpus Christi Caller*, January 26, 1950; Haley, *A Texan Looks at Lyndon*, 51.

31. Mabel Gouldy, "He Cursed Me, I Shot Him, Smithwick Says," *Fort Worth Star-Telegram*, January 24, 1950.

32. Dean from "Smithwick 'Broke Officer Code,'" *San Antonio Light*, January 25, 1950; Skelton from Martha Cole, "Heated Exchange Marks Smithwick Arguments," *Alice Daily Echo*, January 25, 1950.

33. "Smithwick Gets Life for Murder of Mason," *Houston Post*, January 26, 1950.

34. Dawson Duncan, "Prison Letter Reveals 1948 Election Evidence," *Dallas Morning News*, May 25, 1952.

35. Lynch, *Duke of Duval*, 64. See also "Smithwick's Son Charges Father Killed in Prison," *Corpus Christi Caller*, May 28, 1952; Dugger, *The Politician*, 340.

36. "Sen. Johnson Brushes Off Disclosure," *Dallas Morning News*, May 26, 1952 (quotes); Dugger, *The Politician*, 465n.

37. Schendel, "Something Is Rotten," 71.

CHAPTER 8

1. Lynch, *Duke of Duval*, 65 (quote); "Jester Dies from Heart Attack; Shivers Prepares to Take Office," *Austin Statesman*, July 11, 1949.

2. James Rowe, "Trouble in the Dukedom: Parr Has Parting of Ways with Ex-Gov. Shivers," *Corpus Christi Caller*, April 9, 1975.

3. "Broeter on Appeals Bench," *San Antonio Light*, January 4, 1950.

4. William H. Gardner, "Boss Parr without Candidate for Governor," *Houston Post*, April 8, 1950.

5. Rowe, "Mesquite Pendergast," 49.

6. James Rowe, "Sample Ballot May Be Clue to Favorite Duval Candidates," *Corpus Christi Caller*, July 14, 1950; "Corpus Christi Paper Is Sued," *Fort Worth Star-Telegram*, August 24, 1950.

7. James Rowe, "Trouble in the Dukedom: Parr Has Parting of Ways with Ex-Gov. Shivers," *Corpus Christi Caller*, April 9, 1975.

8. James Rowe, "Jim Wells Official Asks Ranger Protection during Primary Vote," *Corpus Christi Caller*, July 21, 1950.

9. "Box 13 In; Three Runoffs Sure in Jim Wells County," *Corpus Christi Caller*, July 25, 1950.

10. Hailey, "Breaching the Mesquite Curtain," 74; Clark, *Fall of the Duke*, 65.

11. James Rowe, "Jim Wells Ballots Impounded," *Corpus Christi Caller*, August 30, 1950.

12. "Write-In Voting in Area Reported," *Alice Daily Echo*, November 7, 1950.

13. "Reams Election as Judge Indicated," *Alice Daily Echo*, November 8, 1950.

14. "Vale Ousts Reams in Judge's Post," *Alice Daily Echo*, November 13, 1950; Schendel, "Something Is Rotten," 71.

15. "Reams Certified as District Judge," *Alice Daily Echo*, November 22, 1950; Schendel, "Something Is Rotten," 71. See also "Vote Contest Still Looms," *Alice Daily Echo*, November 20, 1950.

16. "Reform Party in Duval Is Formed," *Alice Daily Echo*, March 28, 1952.

17. "Fair Elections in County Promised," *Alice Daily Echo*, March 20, 1952.

18. Lynch, *Duke of Duval*, 67; Rowe, "Mesquite Pendergast," 78 (quote).

19. "Parr Named Duval Sheriff," *Alice Daily Echo*, April 4, 1952; James Rowe, "Study of 1950 Duval County Voting Asked," *Corpus Christi Caller*, May 10, 1952.

20. "Gov. Shivers Orders Rangers into Duval," *Corpus Christi Caller*, May 6, 1952.

21. "Duval Spots Raided Again," *Alice Daily Echo*, January 25, 1951.

22. Rowe, "Mesquite Pendergast," 72–74.

23. *Corpus Christi Caller-Times*, July 1, 1952; Hailey, "Breaching the Mesquite Curtain," 80 (quote).

24. "No Verdict in Wheeler Death," *Alice Daily Echo*, July 9, 1952 (quotes); "Tip on Wheeler Foul Play from Alice," *Alice Daily Echo*, July 10, 1952.

25. James Rowe, "Parr Charges Plot to Oust His Friends," *Corpus Christi Caller*, May 14, 1952.

26. Schendel, "Something Is Rotten," 71.

27. "Freedom Party Opens Duval Campaign," *Alice Daily Echo*, June 8, 1952.

28. Northcott, "A Death in Duval," 6; "San Diego Bus Depot Change Is Protested," *Alice Daily Echo*, June 4, 1952; "Politics Charge over San Diego Bus Site Over-Ruled," *Alice Daily Echo*, July 8, 1952.

29. Northcott, "A Death in Duval," 5.

30. "Freedom Party Rally Hits Parr," *Corpus Christi Caller*, July 7, 1952; James Rowe, "Growing Anti-Parr Faction May Deal Boss Real Misery," *Corpus Christi Caller-Times*, July 13, 1952.

31. Jim Greenwood, "Uneasiness Reigns throughout Duval," *Corpus Christi Caller*, July 28, 1952. See also "Eleven Rangers to Patrol Duval Area," *Corpus Christi Caller*, July 25, 1952; "Judge Orders Seating of Duval Freedom Party Supervisors," *Corpus Christi Caller*, July 26, 1952.

32. Jim Greenwood, "Uneasiness Reigns throughout Duval," *Corpus Christi Caller*, July 28, 1952.

33. Rowe, "Mesquite Pendergast," 83.

34. James Rowe, "Violence at Polls Marked 1950 Runoff Election in Duval," *Corpus Christi Caller*, April 10, 1975.

CHAPTER 9

1. Unless otherwise noted, Floyd's testimony on the conversation with Alaniz comes from *Mario Sapet alias Mario Sapet Arteaga v. State,* Court of Criminal Appeals of Texas, 159 Tex.Crim. 620; 266 S.W.2d 154 (January 20, 1954). It also appears in "Starr County Party Blamed for Floyd Plot," *Alice Daily Echo*, September 17, 1952. See also Clark, *Fall of the Duke*, 66–68; Hailey, "Breaching the Mesquite Curtain," 89–94; Rowe, "Mesquite Pendergast," 92–99.

2. Bill Hitch, "Ranger Captain Slaps Sapet Defense Attorney," *Fort Worth Star-Telegram*, March 19, 1953.

3. "Floyd Says Accused Killer Admitted Ballot 'Fix,'" *Austin Statesman*, September 18, 1952.

4. "Alaniz Denied Bond in 'Error' Shooting," *Dallas Morning News*, September 18, 1952.

5. Ibid.

6. Quotes from both "Starr County Party Blamed for Floyd Plot," *Alice Daily Echo*, September 17, 1952; Bill King, "Floyd Calls Sapet Killer Leader," *San Antonio Express*, March 19, 1953.

7. "Rangers Probe Threat to Kill Victim's Father," *San Antonio Express*, September 10, 1952.

8. James Rowe, "Floyd Says He Was Told Sapet Led 'Killers,'" *Corpus Christi Caller*, March 19, 1953.

9. Ibid.

10. Antonio Bill, "Tragedy on East Fourth Street," guest column, June 20, 2012, available at http://alice24-7.com/, accessed on August 17, 2015 (no longer available).

11. James Rowe, "Alice Youth Fatally Wounded in Ambush," *Corpus Christi Caller*, September 10, 1952.

12. "Seek Sapet-Mystery Man Link," *San Antonio Light*, March 20, 1953 (quote); Curtis Vinson, "Slaying Probe Boils to Climax," *Houston Chronicle*, September 12, 1952.

13. James Rowe, "Alaniz, Sapet May Waive JP Examining Trial Today," *Corpus Christi Caller*, September 17, 1952.

14. Frederick Hodgson, "Ballots, Bullets, Beatings, Booty: That's The Story of Duval County," *Bastrop Advertiser*, January 10, 1957.

15. Curtis Vinson, "Death Plot Informer Charged," *Houston Chronicle*, September 11, 1952 (quote); "Police Locate Auto Sought in Shooting," *Dallas Morning News*, September 13, 1952.

16. James Rowe, "Justice Fuller Refuses Sapet Bail in Floyd Case," *Corpus Christi Caller*, September 19, 1952 (quote); James Rowe, "Brownwood Trial Opens for Sapet," *Corpus Christi Caller*, March 17, 1953.

17. Letter quoted in full in both "Parr Regrets Floyd's Death," *Corpus Christi Caller*, September 12, 1952, and "My Conscience Is Absolutely Clear," *Houston Chronicle*, September 12, 1952.

18. Gladwin Hill, "Murder Accents Texas Vendetta," *New York Times*, February 6, 1954.

19. "Barons of the Court," *Texas Monthly*, November 1974, 79.

20. Don Hinga, "Alice Slaying Plotted in Tavern?" *Houston Chronicle*, September 15, 1952; "Young Nephew of George Parr Is New Sheriff," *Alice Daily Echo*, October 1, 1952.

21. Hailey, "Breaching the Mesquite Curtain," 98. See also James O. Holley, "Spurgeon Bell Sent to Alice," *Houston Post*, September 13, 1952; "Parr Called by Grand Jury in Jim Wells," *Corpus Christi Times*, October 11, 1952.

22. Hailey, "Breaching the Mesquite Curtain," 100.

23. Wilbur Martin, "Jake Floyd Tells of Bitter Political Strife at Mario Sapet Murder Trial," *Houston Chronicle*, March 19, 1953.

24. Bill Hitch, "Ranger Captain Slaps Sapet Defense Attorney," *Fort Worth Star-Telegram*, March 19, 1953; Allen Duckworth, "Ranger Slaps Sapet Lawyer," *Dallas Morning News*, March 20, 1953.

25. James Rowe, "Sapet Says He Learned of Slaying while in Jail," *Corpus Christi Caller*, March 20, 1953.

26. "Sapet Case Defense Under Way," *San Antonio Light*, March 21, 1953.

27. Wilbur Martin, "No Witnesses for Sapet's Defense!" *Houston Chronicle*, March 21, 1953.

28. Lynch, *Duke of Duval*, 72. See also James O. Holley, "Sapet's Fate Is Weighed by Jurors," *Houston Post*, March 22, 1953; Allen Duckworth, "Sapet Given Ninety-Nine Years for Death Conspiracy," *Dallas Morning News*, March 23, 1953.

29. "Divorcee's Testimony Is Wanted," *Austin Statesman*, May 22, 1954.

30. Tony Slaughter, "Woman Says She Has Papers Important in Floyd Probe," *Fort Worth Star-Telegram*, July 1, 1954; "Floyd Believes Others Involved in Son's Slaying," *Fort Worth Star-Telegram*, May 31, 1954. See also "Florida Says It Will Free Mrs. Bushey," *Austin Statesman*, May 25, 1954.

31. "'No Deals,' Burris Says," *Alice Daily Echo*, May 25, 1954 (quote); "Mrs. Bushey Goes before Duval Jury," *Corpus Christi Times*, June 28, 1954.

32. "Atty. Gen. Shepperd Wants Corpus Woman to Testify on Duval," *San Antonio Express*, May 22, 1954 (quotes). See also "Parr Labels Woman 'Stoolie' for Rangers," *Corpus Christi Times*, May 21, 1954.

33. Caro Brown, "Street Scene," *Alice Daily Echo*, June 29, 1954.

34. Tony Slaughter, "Woman Says She Has Papers Important in Floyd Probe," *Fort Worth Star-Telegram*, July 1, 1954 (quote); "Betty Bushey Not Due Call in Alaniz Trial," *Austin Statesman*, October 1, 1954.

35. Bill Haworth, "Parr 'Friend' in Jail with Trouble Aplenty," *Fort Worth Star-Telegram*, February 10, 1955 (quotes); "Self-Styled Ex-Girl Friend of Parr Due Sentencing Today," *Fort Worth Star-Telegram*, February 21, 1955.

36. "Romance Shattered by Death of Attorney," *Fort Worth Star-Telegram*, April 5, 1955.

37. "Ideas Differ on Cause of Morris Death," *Fort Worth Star-Telegram*, April 6, 1955; "Widow Cleared of Charge in Car Leap Death of Husband," *Fort Worth Star-Telegram*, April 8, 1955.

38. "Alaniz Trial Is Delayed by Appendectomy," *Fort Worth Star-Telegram*, July 5, 1954; "Alaniz Trial Slowed Down by Argument," *Austin Statesman*, October 4, 1954.

39. "Sixth Juror Selected for Trial of Alaniz," *Corpus Christi Times*, October 5, 1954.

40. Thomas Turner, "Jury Nearly Completed for Nago Alaniz Trial," *Dallas Morning News*, October 6, 1954; "Jury Picked in Trial of Nago Alaniz," *Austin Statesman*, October 6, 1954.

41. Thomas Turner, "Defense Pictures Nago Alaniz as Risking His Life for Floyd," *Dallas Morning News*, October 7, 1954.

42. "State Shows Gun It Says Killed Floyd to Jury," *Fort Worth Star-Telegram*, October 7, 1954.

43. Thomas Turner, "Defense Pictures Nago Alaniz as Risking His Life for Floyd," *Dallas Morning News*, October 7, 1954.

44. "State Shows Gun It Says Killed Floyd to Jury," *Fort Worth Star-Telegram*, October 7, 1954 (quotes); "Not Alaniz 'Benefactor' Floyd Insists on Stand," *Houston Post*, October 7, 1954.

45. Wilbur Martin, "Wife Testifies Alaniz Tried to Save Life," *Corpus Christi Times*, October 9, 1954.

46. "Jury Begins Deliberations on Fate of Nago Alaniz," *Fort Worth Star-Telegram*, October 10, 1954.

47. Caro Brown, "Waco Jury Finds Alaniz Innocent," *Alice Daily Echo*, October 11, 1954; "Alaniz Found Innocent of Part in Murder Plot," *San Antonio Express*, October 11, 1954; Thomas Turner, "Jury at Waco Acquits Alaniz," *Dallas Morning News*, October 11, 1954.

48. Cervantes told an acquaintance he met in Guadalajara the story of what had happened that night. "I heard the telephone ring, that was my sign. I stepped into the garage and waited. Then I saw my man go out and get into a taxicab. I saw the job had been loused up, so I started to go. I stumbled on the step. I started to get up. Then that boy came charging out of the house. I thought he was coming at me. I got up and shot him. I didn't want to shoot him, but I had to." Rowe, "Mesquite Pendergast," 98.

49. Martin, "Tyrant in Texas," 51 (quote); "State Attempts to Link Alaniz to Floyd Killers," *Houston Post*, October 9, 1954.

50. "Accused Killer Still Concealed in Old Mexico," *Alice Daily Echo*, April 9, 1958; "Cervantes Extradition Hope Seen," *Corpus Christi Caller*, June 16, 1960.

51. "Buddy Floyd Ambush Slaying Suspect Caught in Mexico," *Corpus Christi Caller*, June 14, 1960 (quote). See also "Action Due on Floyd 'Trigger Man,'" *San Antonio Light*, February 4, 1954; "Mexican Police Nab Cervantes," *Alice Daily Echo*, June 14, 1960; "Accused Killer Still Concealed in Old Mexico," *Alice Daily Echo*, April 9, 1958; "Extradition Battle Shaping in Mexico," *Corpus Christi Caller*, June 15, 1960.

52. "Cervantes Extradition Hope Seen," *Corpus Christi Caller*, June 16, 1960; "Mexico Judge Rules against Extradition," *Alice Daily Echo*, August 7, 1960.

53. "William Bradford Huie Writes a Letter to President Kennedy about a Murder in Texas," *Cavalier*, August 1961, 10 (quote); "Mexico Denies Extradition in Mistake Killing," *Houston Chronicle*, January 4, 1961.

54. Larry Allen, "Suspect Facing Mexican Court in Jacob Floyd Murder Case," *Houston Chronicle*, August 31, 1964; "Parr Opponent in Duval Dies," *Houston Chronicle*, February 27, 1964.

55. "Cervantes Gets Thirty Years for Buddy Floyd Murder," *Alice Daily Echo*, November 30, 1964.

CHAPTER 10

1. "Alice Mothers Backing Up Write-In Drive," *Corpus Christi Times*, October 27, 1952 (quote). See also "Write-In Drive for Reams Started," *Corpus Christi Times*, October 21, 1952; "Parr to Have Foe in Sheriff's Race," *Corpus Christi Times*, October 28, 1952.

2. "Parr to Have Foe in Sheriff's Race," *Corpus Christi Times*, October 28, 1952. See also Hailey, "Breaching the Mesquite Curtain," 102; Martin, "Tyrant in Texas," 52.

3. Rowe, "Mesquite Pendergast," 76.

4. Quoting from James Rowe, "Duval Ballots, Stubs Burned by Officials," *Corpus Christi Caller*, September 28, 1952. See also "Judge Yet to Post Bond in Two Charges," *Alice Daily Echo*, December 30, 1952.

5. "Shivers to Invite Jurors to Austin," *Fort Worth Star-Telegram*, March 4, 1953; "Parr's Judge Laughlin Quashes Sixty-Eight Bills; Shivers Pledges Study," *Houston Chronicle*, March 11, 1953.

6. Hailey, "Breaching the Mesquite Curtain," 105–6.

7. "Laughlin Accused of Reprehensible Conduct in Office," *Alice Daily Echo*, April 26, 1953 (quote); Hailey, "Breaching the Mesquite Curtain," 109.

8. "Eleven Lawyers of Seventy-Ninth Sign Bill," *Alice Daily Echo*, July 10, 1953; Texas State Constitution (adopted February 15, 1876), Article XV, Section 6, available at http://www.constitution.legis.state.tx.us/.

9. Hailey, "Breaching the Mesquite Curtain," 114.

10. "Laughlin Decides Custody of Sheriff's Child Today," *Corpus Christi Caller*, March 14, 1953; "Laughlin Warns Attorney, Reporter at Custody Case," *Corpus Christi Caller-Times* March 15, 1953; "Garza Gets Suspended Sentence at Alice," *Corpus Christi Caller*, March 31, 1953.

11. Hailey, "Breaching the Mesquite Curtain," 115–16, 119.

12. Tom Mulvaney and Don Hinga, "Parr Pistol-Whipped Them, Duval Men Say," *Houston Chronicle*, February 17, 1954.

13. Hailey, "Breaching the Mesquite Curtain," 119; "Suspension of Laughlin Is Denied," *Fort Worth Star-Telegram*, January 7, 1954. See also Mac Roy Rasor, "Judge Raymond Takes Stand," *Alice Daily Echo*, September 8, 1953.

14. Henry Alsmeyer Jr., "Parr and Rangers in Scuffle at Alice," *Corpus Christi Caller*, January 19, 1954.

15. Newsletter, Bob Mullen, Candidate for Congress, undated, Pre-Presidential Confidential File, George B. Parr, Box 4, LBJ Library; Martin, "Tyrant in Texas," 52.

16. Wilbur Martin, "May Charge Rangers in Parr Brawl," *Houston Chronicle*, January 19, 1954 (Bridge); "Rangers Start Parr Hunt," *San Antonio Light*, January 18, 1954.

17. "Boss Parr Belted by Ranger," *Houston Post*, January 19, 1954.

18. Caro Brown, "Reporter Tells How Ranger Cuffed South Texas Kingpin," *Houston Chronicle*, January 19, 1954. See also "Boss Parr Belted by Ranger," *Houston Post*, January 19, 1954; "Rangers to Be Charged, Alice Hears," *Fort Worth Star-Telegram*, January 19, 1954.

19. Quoted from Caro Brown, "Reporter Tells How Ranger Cuffed South Texas Kingpin," *Houston Chronicle*, January 19, 1954.

20. Quoted from "Pistol Toting Charged," *San Antonio Light*, February 23, 1954.

21. Caro Brown, "Reporter Tells How Ranger Cuffed South Texas Kingpin," *Houston Chronicle*, January 19, 1954.

22. Martin, "Tyrant in Texas," 54.

23. Quoted from "Parr Says 'Gun' He Had Was His Binoculars," *San Antonio Express*, January 20, 1954.

24. "Ranger Foes of Parr Indicted," *Houston Post*, February 4, 1954 (quote); "Laughlin Threatens Allee with Jail for Refusing Jury Order," *Corpus Christi Caller-Times*, January 24, 1954.

25. Clarence J. LaRoche, "Even Kids Well Versed on Duval County Politics," *San Antonio Express*, June 17, 1954.

26. "Allee Claims Life Periled; Has Scuffle with Norris," *Corpus Christi Caller*, February 10, 1954.

27. Caro Brown, "Allee Says His Life Threatened," *Alice Daily Echo*, February 10, 1954. See also Tom Mulvany, "Parr Vs Rangers in Closing Battle," *Houston Chronicle*, February 24, 1954.

28. Quoting from "Allee Claims Life Periled; Has Scuffle with Norris," *Corpus Christi Caller*, February 10, 1954. See also "Ranger Whips Duval DA; Bares Plot to Kill Him," *Austin American*, February 10, 1954.

29. Tom Mulvany, "State Asks Dismissal of Parr Suit," *Houston Chronicle*, February 23, 1954.

30. "Parr Seeks Order against Two Rangers," *Dallas Morning News*, February 17, 1954; John Ruckman, "Fearful Parr Sues Two Rangers," *San Antonio Light*, February 16, 1954; "Duke Cries 'Help,' Rangers after Him," *Austin Statesman*, February 16, 1954; "Parr Asks Federal Court Order against Rangers," *Corpus Christi Caller*, February 17, 1954.

31. Steve Richard, "Parr Case Not for ACLU, Says Hays," *Houston Post*, February 19, 1954; "Arthur G. Hays, Noted Attorney Dies at Age Seventy-Three," *Corpus Christi Times*, December 14, 1954.

32. Fritz Harsdorff, "Hays Confirms Report He'll Represent Parr in Civil Rights Case," *Corpus Christi Caller*, February 19, 1954.

33. "Hays Denies Acting for Rights Body," *Dallas Morning News*, February 19, 1954.

34. Tom Mulvany, "Duval Group Slaps Parr in Own Civil Rights Plea," *Houston Chronicle*, February 19, 1954.

35. Louis Hofferbert, John Gurwell, and George Wysatta, "Parr Wins First Round! Judges Throw Out Freedom Party Suit," *Houston Press*, February 22, 1954.

36. Ibid.

37. Quoted from two sources: Wilbur Martin and Max B. Skelton, "Intervenors Denied by Court," *Alice Daily Echo*, February 22, 1954; "Judges Deny Five Right to Intervene in Parr Suit," *Fort Worth Star-Telegram*, February 22, 1954.

38. Louis Hofferbert, John Gurwell, and George Wysatta, "Parr Wins First Round!" *Houston Press*, February 22, 1954.

39. "Judges Deny Five Right to Intervene in Parr Suit," *Fort Worth Star-Telegram*, February 22, 1954.

40. Tom Mulvany, "Parr Wins in Skirmish; Citizen Suit Ruled Out," *Houston Chronicle*, February 22, 1954; "Parr Foes Denied Part in 'Death Threat' Action," *Austin Statesman*, February 22, 1954.

41. Tom Mulvany, "Parr Wins in Skirmish; Citizen Suit Ruled Out," *Houston Chronicle*, February 22, 1954.

42. Wilbur Martin and Max B. Skelton, "Parr Tells Federal Court of Trouble with Rangers," *Corpus Christi Caller*, February 23, 1954.

43. Tom Mulvany, "State Asks Dismissal of Parr Suit," *Houston Chronicle*, February 23, 1954.

44. Lynch, *Duke of Duval*, 79.

45. Wilbur Martin, "Allee, Son and Grandson of Rangers, Holds Tongue about Parr's Charges," *Fort Worth Star-Telegram*, February 18, 1954.

46. All quotes in this cross-examination are from "Capt. Allee Denies He Threatened to Kill Parr," *Fort Worth Star-Telegram*, February 23, 1954.

47. Ibid.

48. "Two Rangers Deny Threatening Parr," *Corpus Christi Caller*, February 24, 1954.

49. Marshall Verniaud, "Parr, Rangers Near Last Wire," *Houston Post*, February 24, 1954.

50. "No Fast Decision Seen in Parr Injunction Bid," *Corpus Christi Caller*, February 25, 1954.

51. "Parr Bloodshed Warning," *San Antonio Light*, February 24, 1954.

52. Quoting from "No Fast Decision Seen in Parr Injunction Bid," *Corpus Christi Caller*, February 25, 1954. See also "Three Judges Consider Parr Case," *Houston Post*, February 25, 1954.

53. "U.S. Judges Deny Parr Injunction," *New York Times*, March 4, 1954.

54. Editorial, "Three-Judge Injunction Ruling," *Houston Post*, March 5, 1954; Northcott, "A Death in Duval," 7.

55. Marshall Verniaud, "Parr-Allee ACLU Chapter for South Texas Suggested," *Houston Post*, February 25, 1954.

56. "Freedom Party Makes Bid for Parr's Lawyer," *Alice Daily Echo*, March 5, 1954.

CHAPTER 11

1. Caro Brown, "Parr Guilty in Gun-Carrying Case." *Alice Daily Echo*, March 24, 1954.

2. Martin, "Tyrant in Texas," 54.

3. Bill Woods, "Parr: 'Old Politicians Never Die; They Just Fade Away,'" *La Verdad*, February 5, 1954.

4. "Ding Dong Daddy of Duval Chided," *San Antonio Express*, April 25, 1954.

5. Gladwin Hill, "Pistols, Rangers, Indictments Mix in Old-Time Texas Political Row," *New York Times*, February 5, 1954; Gladwin Hill, "Murder Accents Texas Vendetta," *New York Times*, February 6, 1954; Gladwin Hill, "Parr Power Ebbs in Texas Politics," *New York Times*, February 7, 1954. See also "Shepperd Sees Parr's Downfall," *Corpus Christi Caller*, January 22, 1954; "Shivers Reaffirms Duval Cleanup Plan," *Fort Worth Star-Telegram*, February 3, 1954.

6. "Shepperd Pressed for Duval Details," *Austin Statesman*, February 4, 1954.

7. Newsletter, Bob Mullen, Candidate for Congress, undated, Pre-Presidential Confidential File, George B. Parr, Box 4, LBJ Library.

8. Donahue quoted from John Moore, "Parr Men Take the Offensive," *Houston Post*, February 5, 1954.

9. Gresham quoted from William H. Gardner, "Oaths Back Duval Fund Charges," *Houston Post*, February 3, 1954.

10. Heras quoted from Bill Woods, "Parr: 'Old Politicians Never Die; They Just Fade Away,'" *La Verdad*, February 5, 1954.

11. Heras quoted from William H. Gardner, "Oaths Back Duval Fund Charges," *Houston Post*, February 3, 1954.

12. Dawson Duncan, "Refusal by Shepperd Brings Jury Accusation," *Dallas Morning News*, February 6, 1954.

13. "Duval Tiff Becomes Battle-by-Telegram," *Austin Statesman*, February 6, 1954.

14. Don Politico, "Johnson Eyed in Duval Row," *San Antonio Light*, February 11, 1954; Caro Brown, "Street Scene," *Alice Daily Echo*, February 5, 1954.

15. Clarence J. LaRoche, "Parr Political Fat Fries at Tiny Café," *San Antonio Express*, February 21, 1954.

16. Caro Brown, "Street Scene," *Alice Daily Echo*, February 9, 1954; Parr to Schendel from Rowe, "Mesquite Pendergast," 163.

17. Martin, "Tyrant in Texas," 45.

18. Gladwin Hill, "Parr Power Ebbs in Texas Politics," *New York Times*, February 7, 1954; Murphy Givens, "Eleven Individuals Who Made a Difference in Corpus Christi," *Corpus Christi Caller-Times*, January 2, 2000.

19. James Rowe, "George Parr, under Cross-Fire, Appears a Scared and Angry Man," *Corpus Christi Caller-Times*, February 7, 1954.

20. Wallace H. Smith, "Supreme Court Ruling Boosts Parr Return to Duval Control," *Alice Daily Echo*, June 17, 1960.

21. Paul Thompson, "Packing of Juries Is Charged," *San Antonio News*, February 16, 1954.

22. Martin, "Tyrant in Texas," 51; James Rowe, "Investigation of Duval Finances Months in Building up Steam," *Corpus Christi Caller-Times*, February 7, 1954.

23. "Parr Fires Back at Shepperd," *Alice Daily Echo*, February 11, 1954; Wilbur Martin, "Publicity, Probe Is Labeled by Parr," *Houston Post*, February 11, 1954.

24. John Ruckman, "Political Crown Contested," *San Antonio Light*, February 10, 1954.

25. "Judge Orders Duval Records Saved," *Austin Statesman*, February 10, 1954 (Ninedorf); Sam Kinch, "Visiting Judge Ties Up Duval School Records," *Fort Worth Star-Telegram*, February 10, 1954.

26. Dawson Duncan, "State Impounding Records in Duval," *Dallas Morning News*, February 11, 1954 (Parr); James Rowe, "County, School Financial Files Impounded in Duval," *Corpus Christi Caller*, February 11, 1954.

27. Sam Kinch, "Laughlin Indicates He'll Sit at Hearing on Order," *Fort Worth Star-Telegram*, February 11, 1954 (Laughlin); O. B. Lloyd Jr., "Laughlin Hints Fight for Records," *Austin Statesman*, February 11, 1954.

28. Clarence J. LaRoche, "George Parr Dealt Out by Duval School Board," *San Antonio Express*, February 12, 1954.

29. Dawson Duncan, "Foes Offer Trade, Says George Parr," *Dallas Morning News*, February 13, 1954.

30. Don Hinga, "'I'm Not Making Deals,' Storms Boss of Duval," *Houston Chronicle*, February 12, 1954; Dawson Duncan, "Foes Offer Trade, Says George Parr," *Dallas Morning News*, February 13, 1954; "McDonald Blasts at Parr," *Alice Daily Echo*, February 15, 1954.

31. "Grand Jury Calls Parr in Quizzing," *San Antonio Express*, February 16, 1954.

32. Wilbur Martin, "Shepperd Leaves Duval, Sees 'Rebirth of Justice,'" *Corpus Christi Caller*, February 12, 1954.

33. Dallek, *Lone Star Rising*, 448–49.

34. Dugger, *The Politician*, 463n.

35. "The Land of Parr," *Time* 63 (February 15, 1954): 20–21.

36. Lynch, *Duke of Duval*, 83; Dallek, *Lone Star Rising*, 448.

37. C. H. Cavness, State Auditor's Report to Attorney General on Special Examination of Records Made Available Under Order No. 6049: Seventy-Ninth Judicial District Court of Duval County, Texas, February 17, 1954, Texas State Library.

38. Quoting from "Rangers Guard Parr Banks after Data Ordered Kept," *Houston Chronicle*, February 19, 1954. See also "Rangers Guarding Parr's Two Banks," *Dallas Morning News*, February 19, 1954.

39. Advertisement, Opening of Texas State Bank of Alice, *Alice Echo*, April 17, 1941.

40. "County May Ask for New Depository Bids," *Alice Daily Echo*, February 16, 1949. See also "County Asks New Bids on Keeping Funds," February 18, 1949, and "Texas State Bank Named County Funds Depository," May 9, 1949, both in *Alice Daily Echo*.

CHAPTER 12

1. "Rangers Guarding Parr's Two Banks," *Dallas Morning News*, February 19, 1954; Marshall Verniaud, "Two Banks of Parr Guarded," *Houston Post*, February 19, 1954.

2. Tom Mulvany, "Parr Wins Fight over Duval Jury; Battle Moves Here," *Houston Chronicle*, February 21, 1954.

3. "Parr Banks Told to Save All Records," *San Antonio Light*, February 26, 1954.

4. "Rangers Ask Quash of Parr's Charges," *Houston Post*, March 2, 1954; Henry Alsmeyer, "Rangers Lose Court Action," *Corpus Christi Caller-Times*, March 7, 1954; "Change of Venue Asked for Trial of Rangers," *Houston Post*, March 9, 1954; "Norris Prepares Ranger Case Orders," *Corpus Christi Times*, March 16, 1954.

5. "Ousted Judge Pays $3,079 Suit Costs," *Dallas Morning News*, April 4, 1954; "Judge Laughlin Removed Effective at Noon Today," *Austin Statesman*, March 17, 1954; "Supreme Court Removes Laughlin as District Judge at Noon Today," *Alice Daily Echo*, March 17, 1954.

6. "State Ousts Laughlin as Boss Parr's Judge," *Houston Chronicle*, March 17, 1954.

7. "Court Removes Parr's Judge," *San Antonio Light*, March 17, 1954. See also Don Politico, "Ousted Judge's Aid Plans All-Out Appeal," *San Antonio Light*, March 17, 1954; "Laughlin's Last Act Puts Parr Aide In," *Austin Statesman*, March 18, 1954.

8. "Action in Duval Awaits New Judge," *Houston Chronicle*, March 19, 1954.

9. E. L. Wall, "Retired Judge May Get Laughlin's Job," *Houston Chronicle*, March 19, 1954.

10. Mac Roy Rasor, "Court Naming of Duval Judge Takes Pressure off Shivers," *Corpus Christi Times*, March 20, 1954; Editorial, "The Court Picks a Judges' Judge," *Dallas Morning News*, March 21, 1954.

11. "Duval District Gets Judge of Old School," *Houston Chronicle*, March 21, 1954; "New Judge Takes Over at Alice," *Austin Statesman*, March 29, 1954.

12. "Judge Broadfoot Takes Over Laughlin Bench," *Fort Worth Star-Telegram*, March 29, 1954.

13. "Parr's State Bank Ordered to Cease Illegal Payments," *San Antonio Express*, March 30, 1954; "Duval School Board Election Ballots Ordered Impounded," *Fort Worth Star-Telegram*, April 1, 1954.

14. "Duval's New Judge Ousts Jury Panels," *Dallas Morning News*, April 1, 1954.

15. "Duval Jury Report," *Corpus Christi Caller*, April 3, 1954.

16. Henry Alsmeyer, "Shepperd Hit by Duval Jury," *Corpus Christi Caller*, April 3, 1954; "Duval Grand Jurors Fail to Find Evidence," *Fort Worth Star-Telegram*, April 3, 1954. See also "'Dissolved' Duval Jury to Attempt to Report," *Houston Chronicle*, April 2, 1954; "Duval County Grand Jury Ready to Make Its Report," *Corpus Christi Caller*, April 2, 1954.

17. Martin, "Tyrant in Texas," 54.

18. "Parr's Slate Wins School Board Posts," *Houston Post*, April 4, 1954; "Anti-Parr Men 'Encouraged,'" *San Antonio Express*, April 5, 1954. See also "Boss Parr's Three Men Win," *New York Times*, April 5, 1954.

19. "Judge Names New Auditor for Duval," *Corpus Christi Caller*, April 6, 1954.

20. "New Auditor Still Trying in Duval," *Austin Statesman*, April 9, 1954. See also "Duval Auditor Receives Oath," *Corpus Christi Times*, April 7, 1954; "County Court Fails to Act on Thomason," *Corpus Christi Caller*, April 10, 1954; Henry Alsmeyer, "Duval Commissioners Ask Opinion on New Auditor," *Corpus Christi Caller*, April 13, 1954.

21. "Broadfoot Says He'll Name New Duval Auditor," *Corpus Christi Times*, May 14, 1954; "Foe of Parr Nominated as Duval Auditor," *Fort Worth Star-Telegram*, May 26, 1954; Caro Brown, "Duval Funds Frozen," *Alice Daily Echo*, May 30, 1954.

22. "Broadfoot Calls Four into Court," *Austin Statesman*, May 27, 1954.

23. Quoting from "Commissioners Again Deny Serna," *Alice Daily Echo*, July 12, 1954. See also "Walter Meek Named Duval Commissioner," *Corpus Christi Times*, April 2, 1954.

24. "Serna Granted Injunction," *Alice Daily Echo*, July 23, 1954 (quote); also Henry L. Alsmeyer Jr., "Serna Plans Court Move to Get Auditor's Post," *Corpus Christi Times*, July 12, 1954.

25. "Ranger's Trial Is Set," *New York Times*, March 30, 1954; "Allee Drops Plea to Send Hearing Back," *Austin Statesman*, April 15, 1954.

26. Wilbur Martin, "Testimony to Begin in Allee Trial," *Alice Daily Echo*, April 19, 1954 (quote); Caro Brown, "Street Scene," *Alice Daily Echo*, April 20, 1954.

27. "Trial of Capt. Allee Called Off as Parr Drops Assault Charge," *Corpus Christi Caller*, April 20, 1954; Rowe, "Mesquite Pendergast," 141.

28. "Judge Broadfoot Says Help Needed," *Dallas Morning News*, April 9, 1954.

29. "Ousted Jury in Duval Wants Back," *Houston Post*, April 6, 1954 (quotes); "Duval Jury's Seating Asked," *Fort Worth Star-Telegram*, April 5, 1954.

30. "Reinstatement of Duval Jury Asked," *Corpus Christi Times*, April 12, 1954.

31. "Suit on Duval Jury Ouster under Fire," *Corpus Christi Times*, April 27, 1954 (quote); "Hearing on Duval Jury Ouster Set," *San Antonio Express*, April 13, 1954.

32. "Court Okays Broadfoot Duval Move," *Austin Statesman*, May 26, 1954.

33. Sam Kinch, "Dismissal of Duval County Grand Jury Upheld by Court of Appeals," *Fort Worth Star-Telegram*, May 26, 1954.

34. "Judge Calls 4 for New Duval Jury Commission," *Corpus Christi Times*, May 27, 1954; "New Duval Jury to Get 'Lot of Work,'" *Austin Statesman*, May 28, 1954.

35. "Shepperd to Appear before Jury in Duval," *Corpus Christi Times*, June 1, 1954 (quote); "Curb on Duval Jury Denied," *San Antonio Express*, June 1, 1954.

36. "New Duval Grand Jury Starts Work," *Austin Statesman*, June 2, 1954.

37. "Jury Rejects Services of Norris, Luna," *Corpus Christi Times*, June 2, 1954.

38. "MacDonald Talks to Jury," *Alice Daily Echo*, June 3, 1954; "Duval Jury to Probe Offices of Attorneys," *Fort Worth Star-Telegram*, June 3, 1954.

39. "Jury Demands End of Poll 'Guards,'" *Alice Daily Echo*, June 4, 1954; "Parr Charges New Jury Is Hand-Picked," *Fort Worth Star-Telegram*, June 4, 1954.

40. James Rowe, "Duval Jury Seems Set to Make Indictments," *Corpus Christi Times*, June 4, 1954; "Parr Indicted on Assault to Murder Count," *San Antonio Express*, June 6, 1954.

41. "Parr Jests While Awaiting Arrest on Assault Charge," *Fort Worth Star-Telegram*, June 6, 1954; "Parr Out on Bond after Indictment," *Corpus Christi Caller-Times*, June 6, 1954; Wilbur Martin, "Parr Awaiting Service on Assault Indictment," *Corpus Christi Times*, June 5, 1954 (last quote from all three sources).

42. "Judge Takes under Study Motion to Dismiss Parr," *Austin Statesman*, June 9, 1954. See also "Parr, Stansell Face Charges," *Alice Daily Echo*, June 6, 1954; "Parr Seeks Dismissal of Indictment," *Fort Worth Star-Telegram*, June 8, 1954; "Parr Told to Keep Handy until Trial Can Be Set," *San Antonio Express*, June 8, 1954.

43. "Jury Hears Bruni Teacher," *Alice Daily Echo*, June 7, 1954; "Duval Jury Calls School Witnesses," *Corpus Christi Times*, June 9, 1954.

44. "Adame's Removal Asked," *Alice Daily Echo*, April 2, 1954; "Luna Reveals Plan to Oust Schools Head," *Alice Daily Echo*, April 8, 1954; "Injunction Restrains School Head of Duval," *Corpus Christi Times*, May 8, 1954; "Duval Jurors Indict Couple in School Quiz," *Corpus Christi Times*, June 12, 1954.

45. "Parr Forces Press for Court Redress," *Fort Worth Star-Telegram*, June 10, 1954.

46. Quoting from "Duval Grand Jurors Resume Investigation," *Corpus Christi Times*, June 11, 1954. See also "Pre-trial Hearing for Parr Scheduled Friday," *Corpus Christi Times*, June 16, 1954.

CHAPTER 13

1. Caro Brown, "Street Scene," *Alice Daily Echo*, June 16, 1954.

2. "Raeburn Norris Gets Suspension in Duval Trial," *San Antonio Express*, June 19, 1954.

3. Ibid.

4. Caro Brown, "Court 'Friends' Battle Monday over Parr Case," *Alice Daily Echo*, June 20, 1954.

5. "Judge Bars Norris from Parr's Case," *San Antonio Express*, June 23, 1954 (quote); Henry Alsmeyer, "Norris Thrown Out as Parr Case Prosecutor," *Corpus Christi Times*, June 22, 1954.

6. Caro Brown, "Karnes City Lawyer Replaces Norris," *Alice Daily Echo*, June 25, 1954.

7. "Attorney Files for Laughlin's Ex-Post," *Austin Statesman*, April 23, 1954; "Heath Will Seek Seventy-Ninth Judgeship," *Corpus Christi Caller*, April 28, 1954; "Burris, Mullen Announce," *Alice Daily Echo*, April 30, 1954.

8. "Laughlin Joins Parr in Seventy-Ninth Race," *Alice Daily Echo*, May 3, 1954.

9. Gladwin Hill, "Parr Fights Back on Texas Charges," *New York Times*, August 1, 1954; "South Texas Boss to Run for Judge," *San Antonio Express*, May 3, 1954; "Laughlin to Run for Job He Lost," *Corpus Christi Times*, May 3, 1954.

10. "Laughlin to Run for Job He Lost," *Corpus Christi Times*, May 3, 1954 (quote); "Laughlin Joins Parr in Seventy-Ninth Race," *Alice Daily Echo*, May 3, 1954.

11. Sam Kinch, "Parr Ineligible for Judge Race," *Fort Worth Star-Telegram*, May 3, 1954.

12. Caro Brown, "Archer Parr, Grimes Oppose Mullen," *Alice Daily Echo*, May 4, 1954.

13. "Parr Withdraws, Backs Laughlin for Judgeship," *Fort Worth Star-Telegram*, June 28, 1954.

14. Caro Brown, "Father, Two Sons Indicted in Duval," *Alice Daily Echo*, July 1, 1954.

15. James Rowe, "Parr Forced out of Alice, San Diego Banks," *Corpus Christi Times*, July 6, 1954.

16. "Parr Case Reported Under Way," *Austin Statesman*, July 8, 1954; "South Texas Justice Seen by Shepperd," *Austin Statesman*, July 9, 1954.

17. Caro Brown, "Street Scene," *Alice Daily Echo*, July 9, 1954.

18. "Legal or Illegal, Grand Jury Active," *Alice Daily Echo*, July 11, 1954.

19. "Rumors of Big News Spreading in Duval," *Corpus Christi Times*, July 17, 1954; "Duval Witness Will Talk about $750 School Check," *Austin Statesman*, July 14, 1954.

20. "Parr, Thirteen Others Indicted in School Funds Scandal," *Fort Worth Star-Telegram*, July 18, 1954.

21. "Parr 'Dishes It Out' at Duval Barbecue," *Corpus Christi Times*, July 12, 1954.

22. Caro Brown, "Street Scene," *Alice Daily Echo*, July 18, 1954; "'Retired' Judge Is Duval Case Witness," *Fort Worth Star-Telegram*, July 15, 1954.

23. Henry Alsmeyer Jr., "$200,000 a Year 'Missing' in Duval," *Corpus Christi Times*, July 16, 1954.

24. Henry L. Alsmeyer Jr., "Hearing on Forty Duval Indictments Set July 27," *Corpus Christi Times*, July 19, 1954.

25. Caro Brown, "Parr Henchman Implicates 'Duke' in Misdeeds," *Alice Daily Echo*, July 20, 1954.

26. Clarence J. LaRoche, "Parr Sees 'Easy' Victory in Vote," *San Antonio Express*, July 25, 1954; "Parr Candidates Lead in Duval by 2–1 Count," *Alice Daily Echo*, July 25, 1954.

27. "Burris In; Laughlin, Mullen Ahead," *Alice Daily Echo*, July 26, 1954.

28. "Jury Indicts Duval County Tax Collector," *Austin Statesman*, July 28, 1954.

29. "Duval County Officer-Elect Is Indicted," *Fort Worth Star-Telegram*, July 28, 1954; Henry L. Alsmeyer Jr., "Shepperd Denies Duval Conspiracy," *Corpus Christi Times*, July 28, 1954.

30. Both quotes from "Parr's Charge Dismissed as Double Jeopardy Case," *Austin Statesman*, July 31, 1954; also "Assault to Murder Charge against Parr Dismissed as Double Jeopardy," *Fort Worth Star-Telegram*, July 31, 1954.

31. Henry Alsmeyer Jr., "Duval Jury Indictments Are Upheld," *Corpus Christi Caller-Times*, August 1, 1954; Henry L. Alsmeyer Jr., "Duval Trial Sites Moved to Three Towns," *Corpus Christi Times*, August 2, 1954.

32. "Ex-Duval Sheriff Weds at Corpus," *San Antonio Express*, August 13, 1954; "Archer Parr Resigns as Duval Sheriff," *Houston Post*, August 4, 1954; "Jury to Get Parr Income Tax Case," *Austin Statesman*, August 17, 1954.

33. "Broadfoot Resigns Post," *Fort Worth Star-Telegram*, August 31, 1954; "Seventy-Ninth Again without Judge," *Alice Daily Echo*, September 12, 1954; "Duval Tax Officer Indicted Thursday," *Alice Daily Echo*, September 3, 1954; "Duval Attorney Luna Charged with Theft," *Alice Daily Echo*, September 5, 1954; "Judge Winborn Assigned to Court at Alice," *Houston Chronicle*, September 13, 1954; Henry Alsmeyer Jr., "Judge Tobin Indicted for Theft," *Corpus Christi Caller-Times*, October 3, 1954.

34. Robbie Robinson, "Fifty-One Indictments Transferred out of Duval," *Alice Daily Echo*, October 6, 1954.

35. "Suit Seeks Disbarment of Laughlin," *Houston Post*, September 23, 1954; James Rowe, "Laughlin Can't Serve if Disbarred by Court," *Corpus Christi Times*, September 23, 1954.

36. "Parr Friend Fails to Get on Ballot," *Dallas Morning News*, October 1, 1954; "DA Battle Not Over Yet," *Alice Daily Echo*, October 1, 1954 (Burris).

37. "High Court Favors Weatherly," *Alice Daily Echo*, October 6, 1954. See also "Court to Hear Parr District Ballot Plea," *Fort Worth Star-Telegram*, October 4, 1954; "Fulgham Blasts Law as Court Gives Weatherly Ballot Spot," *Houston Post*, October 7, 1954.

38. "Governor, Laughlin Confer on Judgeship," *Houston Post*, October 15, 1954; "Keep Laughlin off Duval Bench—Shepperd," *Houston Chronicle*, October 16, 1954.

39. Ben Bradford, "Bar Opposes Laughlin Move," *Dallas Morning News*, October 17, 1954 (quote); Caro Brown, "Laughlin Files Disbarment Answer," *Alice Daily Echo*, October 18, 1954.

40. Henry L. Alsmeyer Jr., "Laughlin Trial Set; Two Judges Enter Case," *Corpus Christi Times*, October 18, 1954.

41. "Rep. Vale Will Oppose Laughlin's Judge Bid," *Austin Statesman*, October 26, 1954; Laughlin quoted from Clarence J. LaRoche, "Parr, Laughlin in Break," *San Antonio Express*, October 30, 1954.

42. "Floyd Partner Charges Write-In 'Parr Trick,'" *Corpus Christi Times*, November 2, 1954; Clarence J. LaRoche, "Parr Plays for All in Vote Today," *San Antonio Express*, November 2, 1954. See also "Perkins Says Trick Involved in Use of Name," *Alice Daily Echo*, November 2, 1954.

43. "Laughlin, Burris Definite Victors," *Alice Daily Echo*, November 4, 1954; "Laughlin Loses First Court Round," *Alice Daily Echo*, April 18, 1955.

44. "Laughlin Acquittal Will Be Taken to High Court," *Fort Worth Star-Telegram*, April 20, 1955.

CHAPTER 14

1. "U.S. Jury Calls Parr's Ex-Wife," *Fort Worth Star-Telegram*, September 25, 1954; "Witnesses from Duval Shuffled," *Houston Chronicle*, September 29, 1954.

2. "Parr's Ex-Wife Queried in His Tax Probe," *Houston Chronicle*, October 5, 1954; "Grand Jurors Quiz Parr's Former Wife," *Dallas Morning News*, October 6, 1954. See also "Four Called Today in Parr Tax Case," *Houston Chronicle*, October 4, 1954.

3. "Grand Jury Studies Parr's Oil Activities in Tax Case," *San Antonio Express*, October 5, 1954 (quote); "Parr Tax Probe Given Trunk of Bank Records," *Houston Chronicle*, October 6, 1954.

4. Moselle Jacobs, "'Ghost' Rankled by Free Press," *Houston Chronicle*, October 6, 1954.

5. "Parr Is Indicted on Tax Charges," *Fort Worth Star-Telegram*, November 15, 1954; "Bond of $10,000 Posted by Parr on Tax Charges," *Corpus Christi Times*, November 16, 1954.

6. "Parr, Ex-Wife Facing New Taxes Claim," *Austin Statesman*, November 29, 1954.

7. Al McCulloch, "Parr Arraigned; Pleads Not Guilty," *Corpus Christi Times*, December 1, 1954; "Parr Pleads Not Guilty in Tax Case," *Houston Post*, December 2, 1954.

8. Caro Brown, "Adame Case Opens Today," *Alice Daily Echo*, December 9, 1954; "Adame Guilty on Theft Count," *Fort Worth Star-Telegram*, December 12, 1954; "Duval School Head Quits; Wife Named," *Houston Post*, December 15, 1954.

9. "Court Throws Out Duval Indictments," *Austin Statesman*, October 5, 1955; Sam Kinch, "Ex-Duval School Man's Conviction Is Reversed," *Fort Worth Star-Telegram*, October 5, 1955.

10. "Court Ruling No Surprise to Duval Duke," *San Antonio Express*, October 6, 1955.

11. "Shepperd Urges Duval Case Ruling Reversal," *Houston Post*, November 3, 1955 (quote); "Court Snubs Duval Move by Shepperd," *Austin Statesman*, November 9, 1955.

12. Henry Alsmeyer, "Indictment Says Parr Removed Bank Files," *Corpus Christi Caller*, October 19, 1955. See also "Adame, Six Others Face Tax Charges," *Corpus Christi Caller*, December 13, 1955; "Thirty-One Reindictments Returned in Duval," *Fort Worth Star-Telegram*, November 10, 1955.

13. "Defense in Adame Trial Due Today," *Fort Worth Star-Telegram*, March 28, 1956; "Adame Gets Five Years at Del Rio," *Alice Daily Echo*, March 29, 1956; "Ex-Duval Official R.L. Adame, Dies," *Corpus Christi Caller*, September 21, 1956.

14. "Parr's Clamp on Duval Broken, Shepperd Says," *Dallas Morning News*, October 28, 1954.

15. Caro Brown, "Controversial Grand Jury to Conclude Term," *Alice Daily Echo*, October 31, 1954; Caro Brown, "New Duval Grand Jury 'In,'" *Alice Daily Echo*, November 1, 1954; "Shepperd Steps out of Duval County Inquiry," *Corpus Christi Times*, December 30, 1954.

16. Rowe, "Mesquite Pendergast," 4.

17. It was a strict school and Caro was expelled for missing curfew, when she stayed out one night with friends at a Fort Worth nightclub. "As you get older, your behavior will get

worse," the Dean of Women said. Robert Jones and Louis K. Falk, "Caro Brown and the Duke of Duval: The Story of the First Woman to Win the Pulitzer Prize for Reporting," *American Journalism* (winter 1997): 40.

18. Ibid.

19. Shortly after the Floyd murder, her youngest son drowned in a swimming accident. "I stayed away from work five days and I felt the best thing to do was to get back," she said. Beasley and Harlow, *Voices of Change*, 32.

20. Jones and Falk, "Caro Brown and the Duke of Duval," 46–47; Lynwood Abram, "Deaths: Brown, Small-Town Reporter, Pulitzer Prize Winner, Ninety-Three," *Houston Chronicle*, August 7, 2001.

21. "*Echo* Nominated for Pulitzer Prize," *Alice Daily Echo*, December 23, 1954.

22. "Editors Say Duval, Politics Top Stories," *Houston Post*, December 19, 1954; "Echo Nominated for Pulitzer Prize," *Alice Daily Echo*, December 23, 1954.

23. Jones and Falk, "Caro Brown and the Duke of Duval," 44 (quote); "Caro Brown Wins Pulitzer Award," *Alice Daily Echo*, May 3, 1955.

24. "Immunity Plea Due to Delay Parr's Trials," *Austin Statesman*, January 5, 1955.

25. "Chapa, Son's Trial Delayed," *Corpus Christi Caller*, January 25, 1955; "Prosecutors of Duval Cases Plan Conclave," *Alice Daily Echo*, January 30, 1955.

26. "Duval Jury Returns More Indictments," *Fort Worth Star-Telegram*, February 5, 1955; "Pair Post Bond after Night in Jail," *Alice Daily Echo*, September 28, 1955; "De La Garza Says He's Out of Chapa, Carillo Cases," *Corpus Christi Caller*, September 30, 1955.

27. "Chapa on Trial in Tyler," *Alice Daily Echo*, November 14, 1955.

28. "Chapa Case Motions Overruled," *Corpus Christi Caller*, November 16, 1955.

29. "More Chapa Jurors Sought," *Fort Worth Star-Telegram*, November 17, 1955; "Chapa Trial Judge Calls New Venire," *Corpus Christi Caller*, November 18, 1955; Jake Lewis, "Tyler Recess May Halt Hearings Here," *Alice Daily Echo*, November 20, 1955.

30. "$69,853 BISD Shortage Reported," *Alice Daily Echo*, November 29, 1955. See also "Chapa Defense Produces Missing School Minutes," *Corpus Christi Caller*, November 26, 1955; "Chapa Jury Hears Local Auditor," *Corpus Christi Caller-Times*, November 27, 1955.

31. "State Says Check Submitted in Trial Spent by Chapa," *Corpus Christi Caller*, December 1, 1955 (quote); "Bank Cashier Testifies Signatures Not Chapa's," *Corpus Christi Caller*, December 3, 1955.

32. "Roach on Stand as Football Recess Called," *Alice Daily Echo*, December 4, 1955.

33. "Chapa Defense Started," *Alice Daily Echo*, December 5, 1955.

34. "Ex-Board Member Says No One Checked Chapa," *Corpus Christi Caller*, December 7, 1955.

35. "Judge in Chapa Case Gives Two More Hours to Defense, State," *Corpus Christi Caller*, December 8, 1955.

36. "Duval School Tax Man Is Acquitted," *Fort Worth Star-Telegram*, December 10, 1955; "Burris Says State to Press Duval Cases," *Alice Daily Echo*, December 14, 1955.

37. "T-Men Probe Duval Records Again Today," *Alice Daily Echo*, February 23, 1955.

38. "U.S. Says Parr Owes More Taxes," *Corpus Christi Caller*, March 13, 1955; "Claims against Duval Leader Extended to '51," *Alice Daily Echo*, June 8, 1955.

39. "Change of Venue Asked by Attorneys for Parr," *Houston Post*, January 4, 1955.

40. "Affidavits for Parr Are Received only in Local U.S. Court," *Corpus Christi Caller*, February 8, 1955.

41. "U.S. Says Parr Plea Is Unique," *Corpus Christi Caller*, February 17, 1955; "Ninety-Seven Affidavits Offered against Transfer of Parr's Tax Trial," *Corpus Christi Caller*, March 30, 1955.

42. Quote is from *United States v. George B. Parr*, 17 F.R.D. 512 (April 27, 1955). See also "Parr Trial Transfer Denounced by Mullen," *Corpus Christi Caller*, April 30, 1955; copy of decision in Everett L. Looney to Senator Lyndon B. Johnson, May 3, 1955, Pre-Presidential Confidential File, George B. Parr Tax Case, 1955, Box 4, LBJ Library.

43. "U.S. Seeks New Parr Trial Site," *Corpus Christi Caller*, May 5, 1955; Editorial, "Site for Parr Trial," *Corpus Christi Caller*, May 6, 1955.

44. "One Parr Indictment Dismissed," *Corpus Christi Caller*, May 17, 1955; "George Parr Posts New Bond in Tax Case," *Alice Daily Echo*, May 19, 1955.

45. "U.S. Completes Its Reply to Parr Dismissal Plea," June 16, 1955; "Parr Attorneys Move to Delay Arraignment," May 27, 1955; "Parr Case Removal Pleaded," June 25, 1955; all in *Corpus Christi Caller*.

46. Everett L. Looney to Senator Lyndon B. Johnson, May 3, 1955, Pre-Presidential Confidential File, George B. Parr Tax Case, 1955, Box 4, LBJ Library. See also "Parr Tax Trial Set in Austin July 18," *Corpus Christi Caller*, June 30, 1955; *George B. Parr v. United States*, 225 F.2d 329 (July 22, 1955); Abe Fortas to Senator Lyndon B. Johnson, September 14, 1955, Pre-Presidential Confidential File, George B. Parr Tax Case, 1955, Box 4, LBJ Library.

47. "High Court to Rule on Parr Case," *Fort Worth Star-Telegram*, October 17, 1955.

48. Brief for the Respondents in Opposition, September 1955, Pre-Presidential Confidential File, George B. Parr Tax Case, 1955, Box 4, LBJ Library. See also *Parr v. United States*, 350 U.S. 861 (October 17, 1955).

49. *Parr v. United States*, 351 U.S. 513 (June 11, 1956); Editorial, "No Decision at All," *Corpus Christi Caller*, June 15, 1956.

50. "Early Court Setting of Parr Tax Trial Is Sought," *Houston Post*, June 12, 1956. See also "Trial of Parr Awaits Ruling," *Fort Worth Star-Telegram*, June 15, 1956; "Tax Charge Is Upheld," *New York Times*, October 9, 1956.

CHAPTER 15

1. "County Judge Tobin, 6 Ex-Commissioners Indicted in Duval," *Corpus Christi Caller*, June 21, 1955; "Boss George Parr, 13 Others Named in 11 New Indictments in Duval County," *Fort Worth Star-Telegram*, July 17, 1955; "Raeburn Norris Is Indicted in Duval," *Alice Daily Echo*, July 19, 1955.

2. "Three Commissioners under Indictment in Duval Resign," *Fort Worth Star-Telegram*, July 24, 1955.

3. Quoting from "Foreman Presses Grand Jury Probe," *Alice Daily Echo*, July 26, 1955. See also "Judge Slates Action Saturday on Quash Motions in Duval," *Alice Daily Echo*, July 27, 1955.

4. Jake Lewis, "Judge Denies Duval Quash Motion," *Alice Daily Echo*, July 31, 1955; "New Charges Facing Parr," *Corpus Christi Caller*, September 2, 1955.

5. "State May Be Facing Civil Liberties Charge," *Alice Daily Echo*, October 6, 1955.

6. "Defendants May Plead Limitations Law," *Alice Daily Echo*, October 9, 1955.

7. "May Ask Judge Be Disqualified," *Houston Chronicle*, October 9, 1955; "Judges Applaud Jackson Thrust at Court Blast," *Fort Worth Star-Telegram*, October 14, 1955.

8. "Shepperd's Remark No Slur, He Says," *Corpus Christi Caller*, October 14, 1955 (telegram); Richard M. Morehead, "Shepperd Says He Won't Ask Disqualification of Davidson," *Dallas Morning News*, October 18, 1955.

9. "State Bar Plans Shepperd Probe," *Alice Daily Echo*, October 23, 1955 (quote); "Closed Hearing for Shepperd," *Fort Worth Star-Telegram*, October 28, 1955.

10. "Lawyers Take No Action in Shepperd Case," *San Antonio Express*, October 29, 1955.

11. "Ten Witnesses Invoke Immunity to Testify," *Alice Daily Echo*, October 14, 1955; "Parr Won't Answer Grand Jury," *Corpus Christi Caller*, October 14, 1955.

12. "Duval Investigator Gets California Pardon," *Corpus Christi Caller*, October 18, 1955.

13. "Parr Indicted Again over Bank's Records," *Alice Daily Echo*, October 19, 1955 (quote); "Duval Jury Reindicts Ex-Auditor," *Corpus Christi Caller*, October 22, 1955.

14. Jake Lewis, "Skepticism Greets Duval 'Split,'" *Alice Daily Echo*, August 12, 1955 (quote); Jake Lewis, "Duval Machine Shows Internal Cracks," *Alice Daily Echo*, October 20, 1955.

15. "Duval Official Is Suspended," *Corpus Christi Caller*, October 27, 1955.

16. "Charges Fly at Duval Ouster Quiz," *Corpus Christi Caller*, November 17, 1955; "Luna Denies He's Afraid of Anyone," *Corpus Christi Caller*, November 18, 1955.

17. "Hearing on Tobin Ouster Set on January 2 by Judge Laughlin," *Alice Daily Echo*, December 4, 1955.

18. "Parr Aide's Ouster in Duval Is Upheld," *Fort Worth Star-Telegram*, December 14, 1955; "Court Rules Out Appeal to Disbar Judge," *Fort Worth Star-Telegram*, December 29, 1955; Henry Alsmeyer Jr., "Confusion Reigns after Treasurer Quits in Duval," *Corpus Christi Caller*, December 20, 1955.

19. "Anti-Parr Factions Make Merger Talk," *Alice Daily Echo*, December 15, 1955; "Anti-Parr Factions Slate Third Meet to Unite Forces," *Alice Daily Echo*, February 12, 1956.

20. Henry L. Alsmeyer Jr., "Talks Leading to Anti-Parr Merger Fail," *Corpus Christi Times*, February 20, 1956 (quote); "Judge Tobin Disavows Plan for New Party," *Alice Daily Echo*, February 22, 1956.

21. "Youthful Parr Employee Shot," *Austin Statesman*, December 15, 1954; Clark, *Fall of the Duke*, 314.

22. Clark, *Fall of the Duke*, 314.

23. "Parr Charged with Pulling Pistol in San Diego Scuffle," *Houston Post*, November 24, 1955.

24. Bill Wallace, "JW Jury Declares George Parr Guilty, Assesses $1500 Fine," *Alice Daily Echo*, September 19, 1956.

25. Ibid.; *George B. Parr v. State*, 164 Tex. Crim. 424; 299 S.W. 2d 940 (March 20, 1957).

26. Bill Wallace, "Testimony Continues in Parr Trial," *Alice Daily Echo*, September 18, 1956; Bill Wallace, "JW Jury Declares George Parr Guilty, Assesses $1500 Fine," *Alice Daily Echo*, September 19, 1956. See also Jake Lewis, "Ranger Disarms Duval Politico," *Alice Daily Echo*, July 12, 1956.

27. "Three Rangers Assigned to Keep Duval Quiet," *Houston Post*, July 13, 1956. See also "$7500 Peace Bond for Parr," *San Antonio Light*, July 15, 1956; Spencer Pearson, "Parr Convicted, Gets $1,500 Fine," *Corpus Christi Caller*, September 19, 1956; *George B. Parr v. State*, 164 Tex. Crim. 424; 299 S.W. 2d 940 (March 20, 1957).

28. "Parr Charged with Carrying Gun into Café," *Fort Worth Star-Telegram*, March 19, 1957.

29. "George Parr Arrested on New Assault Count," *Corpus Christi Caller-Times*, May 5, 1957.

30. "Parr Bond Revocation Is Sought," *San Antonio Express*, June 15, 1957 (quote); Rowe, "Mesquite Pendergast," 174–75.

31. Tex McCord, "Parr Convicted Fined $25 in Assault Case," *Alice Daily Echo*, July 14, 1958.

32. Ibid.

33. Rowe, "Mesquite Pendergast," 175–76.

34. "Grand Jury Report Rakes Duval Offices," *Corpus Christi Caller*, November 8, 1955.

CHAPTER 16

1. *George B. Parr v. Sam H. Burris ex rel. Duval County Texas et al.*, 292 S.W. 2d 146 (June 13, 1956).

2. "New Recovery Suit Leveled at Parr," *Alice Daily Echo*, July 3, 1955.

3. *Estella G. Garcia et al. v. State of Texas et al.*, 290 S.W. 2d 555 (April 4, 1956); *George B. Parr v. Victor Leal ex rel. Duval County, Texas et al.*, 290 S.W. 2d 536 (May 9, 1956).

4. J. Frank Dobie, "Ranch Involved in George Parr Suit Once Owned by Dobie's Kin," *Fort Worth Star-Telegram*, December 30, 1956.

5. "Amended Suit Filed in Dobie Ranch Case," *Alice Daily Echo*, July 21, 1955; "Parr Asks Change of Venue," *Alice Daily Echo*, July 28, 1955.

6. "Commissioners Again Asked to Enter Suit," *Alice Daily Echo*, August 8, 1955 (quote); "Duval Commissioners Act on Klein Report," *Alice Daily Echo*, August 7, 1955.

7. Jake Lewis, "Burris Labels Duval Report 'Ruse,'" *Alice Daily Echo*, August 14, 1955 (quotes); "Court Favors New Action against Parr," *Houston Post*, August 13, 1955.

8. "Duval Action Questioned," *Fort Worth Star-Telegram*, August 17, 1955; "Duval Citizens Seeking to Void Klein Contract," *Alice Daily Echo*, August 23, 1955.

9. "Court at Odds as Parr Case Lawyer Quits," *Houston Post*, August 26, 1955 (quote); "Legal Battle Looms to Gain Control of Parr Recovery Suits," *Alice Daily Echo*, August 24, 1955.

10. Jake Lewis, "Tobin Affirms Suits Sought to Aid Parr," *Alice Daily Echo*, August 25, 1955.

11. "Duval Commissioners Hire Laredo Lawyer as Chief Counsel," *Alice Daily Echo*, August 26, 1955.

12. "Donald on Stand in Hearing," *Alice Daily Echo*, August 29, 1955.

13. *George B. Parr v. Sam H. Burris ex rel. Duval County, Texas et al.*, 292 S.W. 2d 146 (June 13, 1956).

14. Henry Alsmeyer Jr., "Duval Recovery Suits against Parr Halted," *Corpus Christi Caller*, September 2, 1955; "Parr, Ex-Wife Up for Trial on October 31," *Austin Statesman*, September 7, 1955.

15. "State Gets Green Light in Parr Recovery Suit," *Alice Daily Echo*, September 11, 1955 (quote); Henry Alsmeyer Jr. "Split Apparent on Duval Court," *Corpus Christi Caller*, September 13, 1955.

16. "Gibson Plans Appeal of Injunction Ruling," *Alice Daily Echo*, September 16, 1955; "State Confident Recovery Suit Will Be Tried," *Alice Daily Echo*, September 19, 1955; "Parr Jurisdiction Petition Studied," *Fort Worth Star-Telegram*, October 3, 1955.

17. "High Court Studies Parr Suit Question," *Corpus Christi Caller*, October 4, 1955; "Plea to Delay Suit against George Parr Is Overruled," *Houston Chronicle*, October 10, 1955.

18. "$3 Million in Parr Law Suits on Tap," *San Antonio Express*, October 13, 1955 (quote); "Judge Reinstates Injunction; State Can't Sue Parr," *Corpus Christi Caller*, October 22, 1955.

19. "Local Lawyer, Parr Indicted by Duval Jury," *Corpus Christi Caller*, October 27, 1955.

20. "State Handed Parr Suit Job," *San Antonio Express*, October 28, 1955.

21. "Gibson Seeks to Reinstate Pact in Duval," *Alice Daily Echo*, October 30, 1955 (quote); "Curb Sought on State in Parr Suits," *Austin Statesman*, November 2, 1955.

22. "Parr Sets Appeal of Court's Ruling," *Austin Statesman*, December 13, 1955; "Parr Loses Round in Recovery Suits." *San Antonio Express*, December 15, 1955.

23. "Appeal Court Holds Key to Litigation to Recover Funds," *Alice Daily Echo*, February 3, 1956.

24. *John B. Shepperd, Attorney General of Texas et al. v. George B. Parr et al.*, 287 S.W.2nd 204 (February 16, 1956); "Parr, Wife Released from Injunction Here," *Alice Daily Echo*, February 26, 1956.

25. "Deposition in Parr Suit Concludes Here," *Alice Daily Echo*, March 1, 1956.

26. Jake Lewis, "$500,000 Was Loan from Duval—Parr," *Alice Daily Echo*, March 2, 1956.

27. "Parr's Counsel Meets Defeat in Waco Court," *Alice Daily Echo*, March 4, 1956; "Recovery Suit against Parr Slated May 14," *Alice Daily Echo*, March 5, 1956; Henry Alsmeyer Jr., "Summary Order Asked against Parr," *Corpus Christi Caller*, March 23, 1956.

28. "Hearing April 20 on Duval Claims," *Corpus Christi Times*, March 24, 1956; Henry Alsmeyer Jr., "Summary Judgment Asked against Parr in Ranch Suit," *Corpus Christi Caller*, April 12, 1956; "Parr Hearing Slated Friday to Be Delayed," *Alice Daily Echo*, April 19, 1956.

29. "Parr Deeds Ranch to Duval County," *San Antonio Express*, April 20, 1956.

30. "Parr Returns Dobie Ranch to Duval County; Claims, Damages Released," *Alice Daily Echo*, April 20, 1956; "Parr Suits to Be Tried despite Release Agreement," *Fort Worth Star-Telegram*, April 23, 1956.

31. Jake Lewis, "Court Upholds Suits against Parr," *Alice Daily Echo*, May 16, 1956. See also Jake Lewis, "Parr Loses Two Court Decisions," *Alice Daily Echo*, May 11, 1956; "Court Gives Parr Trial Sites Its OK," *Fort Worth Star-Telegram*, May 16, 1956.

32. "Hearing Set in Parr Case," *Corpus Christi Times*, May 19, 1956; "Parr Hearing to Be Delayed," *Corpus Christi Times*, May 24, 1956; "Luna Files Suit Here for Dismissal of Suit," *Alice Daily Echo*, May 23, 1956.

33. "Bank Asks Lien against Land Owned by Parr," *Corpus Christi Caller*, May 24, 1956; "Bank Suit against Parr Moved to Court Here," *Corpus Christi Times*, June 7, 1956.

34. "Parr Hearing Postponed, New Defendants Named," May 25, 1956. See also "Parr Asks Rehearing on Appeals," May 24, 1956; "Parr Loses Rehearing Request," June 14, 1956; all in *Corpus Christi Caller*.

35. "Three Defendants Added to Parr Suit in Cotulla," *Alice Daily Echo*, May 25, 1956.

36. "Resolution on Parr Suit Is Up Tuesday," *Houston Post*, May 27, 1956; "Duval Kills Parr's Liability Release," *Corpus Christi Caller*, June 20, 1956; "Three Duval Officials Seek to Join Parr Suit," *Alice Daily Echo*, July 9, 1956.

37. Quote from both "Duval Gets Parr's Ranch," *San Antonio Express*, July 14, 1956, and "Judge Gives Parr Ranch to Duval," *Corpus Christi Caller*, July 14, 1956.

38. "Judge Gives Parr Ranch to Duval," *Corpus Christi Caller*, July 14, 1956.

39. Henry Alsmeyer Jr., "Judge Denies Duval Motion against Parr," *Corpus Christi Caller*, July 21, 1956.

40. Jake Lewis, "Jury to Settle Issues in Parr Suit," *Alice Daily Echo*, July 22, 1956; "Tobin Denies Ranch Suit Summons Served," *Corpus Christi Caller*, July 24, 1956.

41. "Court Contempt Charged to Parr," *Fort Worth Star-Telegram*, July 29, 1956 (quote); "State Moves to Set Aside Webb Court Judgment," *Alice Daily Echo*, August 1, 1956.

42. "Dobie Ranch Hearing Slated by Judge Barrow," *Alice Daily Echo*, September 2, 1956; "Duval Wins $688,000 from Parrs," *Corpus Christi Caller*, September 5, 1956.

43. Jake Lewis, "Duval County Given Full Dobie Ranch Possession," *Corpus Christi Caller*, October 13, 1956.

44. "Boy Scouts, FFA Invited to Camp at Dobie Ranch," *Corpus Christi Caller*, October 26, 1956; "Motion for New Dobie Trial Is Overruled," *Alice Daily Echo*, October 30, 1956.

45. "Ranch Is Sold to Pay Claim against Parr," *San Antonio Express*, January 3, 1957.

46. "Dobie Ranch Public Auction Set in Cotulla," *Alice Daily Echo*, February 15, 1957; *George B. Parr et al. v. Duval County*, 304 S.W.2nd 957 (July 19, 1957).

47. "Duval County Given Go-Ahead on Dobie Sale," *Alice Daily Echo*, September 18, 1957; "Parr Should Be Retried on $500,000 Dobie Deal," *Alice Daily Echo*, January 15, 1958.

48. "Duval County Gets Additional $65,000 from Dobie Ranch," *Corpus Christi Caller*, May 21, 1957; "Mrs. Parr Pays Down on Court Judgment," *Alice Daily Echo*, August 12, 1957.

CHAPTER 17

1. Jim Mathis, "Parr Backs Sen. Daniel for Governor," *Corpus Christi Caller,* July 7, 1956.

2. "Green Moffett Called in Parr Jury Inquiry," *Corpus Christi Times,* January 24, 1956; "Mail Fraud Case on Parr Due for Airing," *Alice Daily Echo,* January 22, 1956.

3. "Investigation of Parr to Resume Monday," *Fort Worth Star-Telegram,* January 26, 1956; see also "Five Duval Witnesses Heard in Mail Fraud Inquiry," *Corpus Christi Caller,* February 1, 1956.

4. "Parr Indicted for Mail Fraud," *San Antonio Express,* March 7, 1956.

5. "Parr Files Four Motions Here," *Houston Post,* June 16, 1956; "Parr Trial Date on Mail Fraud Set in Houston, Nov. 5," *Alice Daily Echo,* August 7, 1956.

6. "Parr Suit Testimony Being Sought in Duval," *Corpus Christi Caller,* October 5, 1956 (quote); "Parr Data Fills Two Mail Carts," *Corpus Christi Caller,* September 25, 1956.

7. "Thirty Witnesses Subpoenaed in Duval Mail Fraud Trial," *Fort Worth Star-Telegram,* October 20, 1956; "103 Called by U.S. for Parr Trial," *Houston Post,* November 7, 1956; "Parr Trial Reset after Election," *Houston Post,* October 19, 1956.

8. Dorman, *King of the Courtroom,* xi–xii, 1 (quote).

9. "Parr Trial Attorneys Flare Up," *Corpus Christi Caller,* December 8, 1956; "Parr Trial to Bare Kingdom," *Austin Statesman,* November 9, 1956.

10. "Two Heard in Parr Fraud Case," *Corpus Christi Caller,* November 9, 1956.

11. Isabel Brown, "Parr Trial Is Started in Flurry of Objections," *Houston Post,* November 9, 1956; "Parr Jury Told One Hundred on Pay List Unknown," *San Antonio Express,* November 10, 1956.

12. "Check Payees 'Not Known' at Post Offices," *Fort Worth Star-Telegram,* November 10, 1956 (Heras); "Postal Officials Testify in Parr School Tax Case," *Austin Statesman,* November 10, 1956 (Williams).

13. "Duval Banker Spending Much Time in Court," *Houston Chronicle,* November 12, 1956.

14. "No Work Done for Checks, Banker Tells Parr Jurors," *San Antonio Express,* November 13, 1956.

15. "Bank Teller Testifies in Parr Trial," *Fort Worth Star-Telegram,* November 14, 1956.

16. "Nun, Nurse Home Head Testify in Trial of Parr," *Houston Post,* November 15, 1956.

17. Moselle Jacobs, "Bank Records Used in Parr Fraud Trial," *Houston Chronicle,* November 15, 1956.

18. "Parr Suit Witness Says Official Used District's Gasoline Card," *Corpus Christi Caller,* November 16, 1956.

19. "Moffett Says School District Paid $15,000 for No Work," *Corpus Christi Caller,* November 17, 1956; "Court Told of Thirty Cent Charge on School Fund," *Houston Post,* November 17, 1956.

20. Isabel Brown, "Fifty-Three Checks Deposited to Saenz Account Listed," *Houston Post,* November 20, 1956.

21. Isabel Brown, "Witness Identifies Sixteen Checks as Going to Parr," *Houston Post,* November 21, 1956.

22. "Witness Took Checks 'for Safety,'" *Corpus Christi Caller*, November 22, 1956.

23. Isabel Brown, "Verbal Exchanges Mark Twelfth Day of Parr Trial," *Houston Post*, November 22, 1956.

24. "Parr Quoted: Duval County under Control," *Dallas Morning News*, November 24, 1956; Moselle Jacobs, "Parr's Ex-Auditor Peppery Witness," *Houston Chronicle*, November 24, 1956 (Benson). See also Moselle Jacobs, "$220,000 Loss Claimed in Parr Trial," *Houston Chronicle*, November 23, 1956.

25. "Nope, Good Honest Graft Ain't Stealing, Says Duval Witness," *San Antonio Express*, November 24, 1956.

26. "Former Auditor Denies Sharing Benavides Graft," *Houston Post*, November 24, 1956; "Boss Parr's Income Set at $50,000," *Dallas Morning News*, November 27, 1956.

27. "Parr's Defense Starts Today," *Houston Chronicle*, November 28, 1956 (Williams); "Parr Jury Hears Writing Expert," *Houston Chronicle*, November 27, 1956; "'Lost Link' Cited in Parr Trial," *San Antonio Express*, November 27, 1956.

28. "Parr Trial Witness Branded 'Drunkard,'" *San Antonio Express*, November 29, 1956; "Bartender Testifies in Defense of Parr," *Dallas Morning News*, November 29, 1956.

29. "Parr Trial Witness Gives Differing Testimony Now," *Corpus Christi Caller*, December 4, 1956; Isabel Brown, "Witness in Trial of Parr 'Can't Remember,'" *Houston Post*, December 4, 1956.

30. Moselle Jacobs, "Witness Says Post Office Box Easy to Open," *Houston Chronicle*, December 4, 1956.

31. "Parr Mail Fraud Trial Enters Last Phase; Final Arguments Due," *Houston Chronicle*, December 6, 1956.

32. Isabel Brown, "Pleading Begins in Parr Trial," *Houston Post*, December 7, 1956.

33. "Foreman Says Shepperd Persecuting George Parr," *Houston Post*, December 8, 1956.

34. "Parr Trial Attorneys Flare Up," *Corpus Christi Caller*, December 8, 1956.

35. "Foreman Says Shepperd Persecuting George Parr," *Houston Post*, December 8, 1956.

36. "Parr Trial Attorneys Flare Up," *Corpus Christi Caller*, December 8, 1956.

37. "Foreman Says Shepperd Persecuting George Parr," *Houston Post*, December 8, 1956.

38. "Parr Trial Attorneys Flare Up," *Corpus Christi Caller*, December 8, 1956.

39. "Foreman Says Shepperd Persecuting George Parr," *Houston Post*, December 8, 1956.

40. "Shivers Blamed for Trial of Parr," *Dallas Morning News*, December 11, 1956.

41. Isabel Brown, "Jury to Get George Parr Mail Fraud Case Today," *Houston Post*, December 11, 1956.

42. "Parr Jury Recesses Overnight," *Corpus Christi Caller*, December 12, 1956; "Parr Jury Sent Home Second Night without Verdict," *Houston Post*, December 13, 1956; "Jury to Hear Charge Again in Parr Trial," *Dallas Morning News*, December 14, 1956.

43. "Parr Jury Foreman Indicates Progress," *Corpus Christi Caller*, December 15, 1956.

44. Isabel Brown, "Parr Jury Indicates Deadlock," *Houston Post*, December 18, 1956.

45. "Parr Mail Fraud Jury Dismissed," *Alice Daily Echo*, December 19, 1956.

46. Moselle Jacobs, "Jurors Unable to Agree on Parr, Eight Others," *Houston Chronicle*, December 19, 1956; "Parr Jury Split 11–1; Dismissed," *Fort Worth Star-Telegram*, December 19, 1956.

47. "Parr's U.S. Trial Reset," *Corpus Christi Caller*, January 8, 1957.

CHAPTER 18

1. "Parr Case Limitations Status Asked of Court," *Fort Worth Star-Telegram*, April 4, 1956; "Court Refuses Parr Ruling," *San Antonio Express*, April 6, 1956.

2. "Absent Lawyer, Witnesses Delay Start of Norris Trial," *Corpus Christi Caller*, May 1, 1956; "Duval County Case Delayed," *Fort Worth Star-Telegram*, May 2, 1956; "Norris Runs for District Attorney Post," *Corpus Christi Times*, May 8, 1956.

3. Quoting from both "Chandler Issues Statement Today on Parr Complaint," *Alice Daily Echo*, May 15, 1956, and "Official Cites Parr Indictments," *Houston Post*, May 16, 1956.

4. Henry Alsmeyer Jr., "Parr Complaint Names Chandler," *Corpus Christi Caller*, May 15, 1956 (quote); "Parr Trial Set June 18," *Fort Worth Star-Telegram*, May 18, 1956.

5. "Parr Forces Sweep Duval City Election," *Alice Daily Echo*, April 4, 1956.

6. "Two Parr Men Beaten in San Diego Elections for School Trustees," *Corpus Christi Caller-Times*, April 8, 1956; "Parr Bloc Faces Slightly Tougher Vote Test Today," *Corpus Christi Times*, April 7, 1956; Henry L. Alsmeyer Jr., "Anti-Parr Forces Nearing Coalition," *Corpus Christi Times*, April 19, 1956.

7. Jake Lewis, "Duval Parties Combine Candidates," *Alice Daily Echo*, April 26, 1956; "George Parr Candidate for Duval Sheriff Post," *Corpus Christi Caller-Times*, April 29, 1956.

8. Sam Kinch, "Shivers Chides Johnson over Parr Promise of Duval Machine Backing," *Fort Worth Star-Telegram*, April 25, 1956; "Parr Backs Johnson, Paper Says," *Corpus Christi Times*, April 24, 1956.

9. Sam Kinch, "Shivers Digs at Parr's Voting Bloc for Johnson," *Fort Worth Star-Telegram*, May 2, 1956.

10. "Tobin, Parr Line up to Support Johnson," *Corpus Christi Caller-Times*, May 6, 1956.

11. Jake Lewis, "Duval Demos Split in Two Groups," *Alice Daily Echo*, May 9, 1956.

12. "Split Duval Forces Gain Equal Rights," *Alice Daily Echo*, May 22, 1956.

13. Jim Mathis, "Daniel Heads 'Ticket' Which Parr Is Backing," *Houston Post*, July 7, 1956.

14. Editorial, "Support Not Wanted," *Fort Worth Star-Telegram*, July 10, 1956; "Parr Backing Unwelcomed," *Austin Statesman*, July 9, 1956.

15. "Parr Backing Sparks Governor's Race Row," *Houston Post*, July 10, 1956.

16. "Haley Says Bexar Vote Denied," *San Antonio Light*, July 12, 1956; "DA Raps Politicians' Use of Duval Trouble," *San Antonio Express*, July 12, 1956. See also "Parr Backing Sparks Governor's Race Row," *Houston Post*, July 10, 1956.

17. Dawson Duncan, "Haley Thanks Parr for 'Endorsement,'" *Dallas Morning News*, July 19, 1956.

18. "Tobin Raps Parr's Bid for Sheriff," *Alice Daily Echo*, July 8, 1956; Editorial, "Duval Awakening," *Corpus Christi Caller-Times*, August 5, 1956.

19. "Parr, Some of Backers Face Runoffs, Defeat," *Houston Post*, July 30, 1956; Henry Alsmeyer, "Parr Wins without Runoff," *Corpus Christi Caller*, July 30, 1956; Henry Alsmeyer Jr., "Closed Door Check on Duval Votes Held," *Corpus Christi Caller*, August 2, 1956.

20. Jake Lewis, "Parr Election Challenged," *Alice Daily Echo*, August 10, 1956; Bill Walraven, "State Acts to Keep Parr off Ballot," *Corpus Christi Caller*, August 22, 1956; Bill Walraven, "Laughlin Won't Halt Duval Nominations," *Corpus Christi Caller*, August 23, 1956.

21. Bill Wallace, "Parr, Mrs. Adame Ruled Nominees," *Alice Daily Echo*, August 28, 1956; "Parr Foes Pick Two for Write-In Race," *Corpus Christi Caller*, September 20, 1956.

22. "Parr Will Be Sheriff if He Stays out of Jail," *Austin Statesman*, November 8, 1956.

23. Jake Lewis, "Duval Sheriff, Clerk Vote Canvass Barred," *Corpus Christi Caller*, November 13, 1956.

24. "Parr Attempting to Spur Action on Sheriff Appeal," *Corpus Christi Caller*, December 31, 1956; "Parr Denied Sheriff's Job in Duval," *San Antonio Express*, January 2, 1957.

25. Quoting from "Appeals Court Hears Parr, Others Argue for Posts in Duval," *Corpus Christi Caller*, January 10, 1957. See also "Boss Parr Wins Request for Trial," *San Antonio Light*, January 30, 1957.

26. "D.C. Chapa Trial Enters Second Day," *Alice Daily Echo*, June 6, 1956.

27. "Witnesses for State 'Scared,' Prosecutor in Chapa Trial Says," *Corpus Christi Caller*, June 7, 1956 (Burris); "Checks Were Cashed, Chapa Hearing Told," *Fort Worth Star-Telegram*, June 8, 1956.

28. "Benson Testifies in D.C. Chapa Trial," *Alice Daily Echo*, June 8, 1956 (quote); "Chapa Trial Bares Check Handling," *Alice Daily Echo*, June 7, 1956.

29. "More Defense Witnesses Talk in Chapa Trial," *Corpus Christi Times*, June 9, 1956; "Chapa's Trial Nearing Close," *Fort Worth Star-Telegram*, June 12, 1956; "Chapa Jury Continues Deliberation," *Fort Worth Star-Telegram*, June 13, 1956.

30. "Chapa Given Five Years," *San Antonio Express*, June 14, 1956.

31. "Chapa to Appeal Five-Year Term," *Corpus Christi Times*, June 14, 1956.

32. "Norris Jury Completed; Four Cleared," *Corpus Christi Caller*, September 11, 1956.

33. "Tobin Can't Recall Okay on Check," *Corpus Christi Caller*, September 12, 1956.

34. "Norris Attorney Reveals Appeal," *Alice Daily Echo*, September 18, 1956.

35. "Fifty-One of 108 Veniremen Dismissed," *Alice Daily Echo*, October 22, 1956.

36. "Duval School Fund Theft Trial Starts," *Corpus Christi Caller*, October 24, 1956; "Check 'Recipients' Deny Payment in Duval Case," *Austin Statesman*, October 25, 1956.

37. "Witness Tells about Checks," *Fort Worth Star-Telegram*, October 26, 1956; "State Rests in Donald Trial," *Alice Daily Echo*, October 26, 1956.

38. "Theft Conviction Handed First of Parr Case Trio," *Austin Statesman*, October 27, 1956; "Parr Trial Is Reset Today in New Braunfels," *Alice Daily Echo*, December 10, 1956.

39. "Chapa Seeks Reversal of Conviction," *San Antonio Express*, January 3, 1957.

40. "DA Vows to Continue Duval Fight," *Alice Daily Echo*, March 14, 1957 (quote); "Chapa Wins New Trial in School Fund Case," *Corpus Christi Times*, March 13, 1957.

41. "Norris, Parr Appeal to Austin Court," *Alice Daily Echo*, February 20, 1957.

42. *Raeburn Norris v. State of Texas*, 302 S.W.2d 135 (April 24, 1957); "New Trial Ruled for Alice Lawyer," *Fort Worth Star-Telegram*, April 24, 1957.

43. "Burris Blasts Appeals Court," *Alice Daily Echo*, April 24, 1957.

44. *B. F. Donald Jr. v. State*, 165 Tex. Crim. 252; 306 S.W.2d 360 (June 19, 1957); "New Reversal May Help Parr," *Corpus Christi Caller*, June 20, 1957 (Burris).

45. Dorman, *King of the Courtroom*, 233.

CHAPTER 19

1. Jake Lewis, "Parr Trial Scheduled for Alice," *Corpus Christi Caller*, January 12, 1957.

2. "Parr Jury Selection Under Way," *Austin Statesman*, January 21, 1957.

3. "Witnesses Places Parr at School Board Meetings," *Houston Post*, January 23, 1957; "Witness Calls Parr Part of Conspiracy," *Dallas Morning News*, January 24, 1957.

4. "Parr Case Witness Tells of Checks," *Fort Worth Star-Telegram*, January 25, 1957.

5. "Contractor Takes Stand against Parr," *Austin Statesman*, January 25, 1957.

6. "Testifies Parr O.K.'d Stealing School Funds," *Houston Chronicle*, January 26, 1957.

7. "Signing Names to Checks Told," *San Antonio Light*, January 27, 1957; "State Rests Case as George Parr Trial Nears Jury," *Alice Daily Echo*, January 27, 1957.

8. "Testimony in Parr Trial to Resume," *Houston Post*, January 28, 1957; "Bankruptcy for Parr Accepted," *Corpus Christi Caller*, January 29, 1957.

9. "Parr Aide Due to Curb His Witness," *Austin Statesman*, January 28, 1957.

10. "Parr Convicted of Theft; Gets Five Years," *Fort Worth Star-Telegram*, January 29, 1957.

11. "Stay Order against Sale of Parr's Ranch Issued," *Corpus Christi Caller*, February 2, 1957.

12. "Duval County Asking Bids on Dobie Ranch," *Corpus Christi Caller*, February 15, 1957.

13. "Parr Alters Bankruptcy Petition," *Corpus Christi Caller*, February 19, 1957; "Suit against Parr May Open Here Thursday," *Alice Daily Echo*, March 4, 1957.

14. "Attorney Contends Parr Has Some More Assets," *Corpus Christi Times*, March 5, 1957.

15. "Parr Accuses Burris of Buying Court Decision," *Alice Daily Echo*, March 6, 1957; "Parr's Appeal in Ranch Case Opens Today," *Corpus Christi Caller*, April 16, 1957.

16. "Thelma Parr to Pay $60,000 on $388,000 Debt," *Alice Daily Echo*, May 21, 1957; "Dobie Judgments May Reduce Taxes," *Corpus Christi Caller*, May 4, 1957.

17. "Order Issued to Liquidate Parr Property," *Houston Chronicle*, June 2, 1957; "Parr Oil Stock Put on Block," *Corpus Christi Caller*, June 30, 1957; "Parr Interest in Oil Firm Purchased for $216,000," *San Antonio Express*, July 2, 1957.

18. "Sale of Parr Holdings Brings Suit," *San Antonio Express*, July 12, 1957; "Objection to Parr Sale Is Withdrawn," *Corpus Christi Caller*, July 12, 1957; "Delaney Group Buys Parr Leases," *Corpus Christi Caller*, August 7, 1957.

19. "Parr Says He's Living on Loans," *Corpus Christi Times*, September 16, 1957.

20. "Parr Auto Agency Sale Negotiated," *Corpus Christi Caller*, November 13, 1957; "Receiver Asked for Duval Motor Company in SD," *Alice Daily Echo*, February 20, 1958.

21. Garth Jones, "Parr Aides Win Duval Row," *Alice Daily Echo*, March 30, 1958.

22. "Duval Demos Okay Plan to Compromise," *Alice Daily Echo*, May 11, 1958; "New Faces Are Due in Duval Courthouse," *Alice Daily Echo*, July 28, 1958.

23. Tex McCord, "Old Party Candidates Are Better Qualified, Duval Judge Tobin Says," *Alice Daily Echo*, August 4, 1958; "Duval County Attorney Raps Judge Tobin," *Alice Daily Echo*, August 6, 1958.

24. "Grand Jury to Continue Probe on Duval Voting," *Alice Daily Echo*, September 8, 1958.

25. "Burris Brands Charges as 'Lie,'" *Alice Daily Echo*, November 6, 1958.

26. "Court Action Returns Parr Case to Duval," *Fort Worth Star-Telegram*, April 17, 1957. Quotes from Tex McCord, "Parr's Bid for Sheriff's Job to Be 'Open Book' Case," *San Antonio Express*, June 8, 1957.

27. "Summary Judgment for Parr Is Sought," *Corpus Christi Caller*, August 15, 1957; Jake Lewis, "Parr Will Appeal Court Rejection of Bid for Sheriff," *Corpus Christi Caller*, August 28, 1957; Jake Lewis, "Judge Still Hearing Parr's Sheriff Suit," *Corpus Christi Times*, August 26, 1957.

28. *Amando Garcia, Jr., and George B. Parr v. Daniel Tobin, Jr., et al.*, 307 S.W.2d 836 (November 27, 1957).

29. Tex McCord, "Duval Sheriff's Post Poses Legal Problem," *Alice Daily Echo*, February 6, 1958.

30. "Mother of George Parr Dies at Ninety-One," *Alice Daily Echo*, April 24, 1958; Rowe, "Mesquite Pendergast," 176.

31. *Daniel Tobin, Jr., et al. v. Amando Garcia, Jr., and George B. Parr*, 159 Tex. 58 (April 30, 1958).

32. Tex McCord, "Plans Revealed in Efforts to Certify Parr for Sheriff," *Alice Daily Echo*, August 8, 1958.

33. "Duval Court Passes Order in 3–2 Vote," *Alice Daily Echo*, October 13, 1958.

34. Tex McCord, "Court Order Halts Parr Sheriff Bid," *Alice Daily Echo*, October 14, 1958.

35. Tex McCord, "Duval Sheriff Still in Doubt" *Alice Daily Echo*, October 17, 1958.

36. "Hearing Friday on Ouster Suit," *Alice Daily Echo*, November 20, 1958.

37. "New Hearing Set in Complex Duval Suit," *Alice Daily Echo*, December 4, 1958; *J. P. Stockwell et al. v. George B. Parr et al.*, 319 S.W.2d 779 (December 10, 1958).

38. "Vidal Garcia Named as Duval Sheriff; County Workers Fired," *Alice Daily Echo*, January 2, 1959.

39. "Vidal Garcia Still Sheriff of Duval Co.," *Alice Daily Echo*, January 13, 1959; *George B. Parr et al. v. J. P. Stockwell et al.*, 159 Tex. 440; 322 S.W.2d 615 (April 8, 1959).

40. *J. P. Stockwell et al. v. Vidal Garcia et al.*, 325 S.W.2d 405 (May 20, 1959); "George Parr Sues Duval for Back Pay," *Alice Daily Echo*, July 29, 1959; "Court Decision Is against Parr in Salary Suit," *Alice Daily Echo*, May 30, 1961.

CHAPTER 20

1. "Mistrial in Parr Case Is Declared," *Corpus Christi Times*, March 12, 1957; "Parr Mistrial Ruled; Ex-Convict on Jury," *Fort Worth Star-Telegram*, March 20, 1957.

2. "Government's Attempts to Convict Parr Costly," *Alice Daily Echo*, March 25, 1957.

3. "Postal Men Witnesses in George Parr Trial," *Fort Worth Star-Telegram*, May 8, 1957.

4. "Teller Says 'Bundles' Cashed," *Corpus Christi Caller*, May 9, 1957; "Freer School Official Witness in Parr Trial," *Alice Daily Echo*, May 10, 1957.

5. "Parr Trial Enters Second Week in Houston," *Alice Daily Echo*, May 13, 1957; "Parr's Brother-in-Law Tells of Monthly Pay," *Austin Statesman*, May 14, 1957.

6. "Oil Checks Identified in Parr Trial," *Corpus Christi Caller*, May 14, 1957.

7. "Mistrial Asked in Parr Trial," *Alice Daily Echo*, May 16, 1957.

8. "Parr Trial Resumes Tomorrow," *Corpus Christi Caller-Times*, June 2, 1957; "Records at Parr Bank Missing," *San Antonio Light*, June 3, 1957.

9. "'Politics' Charged by Foreman in Parr Case," *Houston Post*, June 4, 1957.

10. "Audit Called 'Impossible,'" *Houston Post*, June 5, 1957.

11. "Parr Lawyers Score Point," *San Antonio Express*, June 5, 1957.

12. "Heras Tells about Writing Fictitious Checks, Giving Money to George Parr," *Alice Daily Echo*, June 6, 1957.

13. "High Court's Ruling Enters Parr Fraud Trial," *Houston Post*, June 6, 1957.

14. "False Check Testimony Given Again," *Corpus Christi Caller*, June 6, 1957.

15. "Parr Judge Orders FBI Statement," *Corpus Christi Caller*, June 7, 1957.

16. "Defense Wins Major Point in Trial of George Parr," *Dallas Morning News*, June 8, 1957.

17. Quoting from "Heras Denies Being Granted 'Immunity,'" *Alice Daily Echo*, June 10, 1957. See also C. W. Skipper, "Parr's Defense Given Two FBI Reports on Witness," *Houston Post*, June 8, 1957.

18. "Parr Fraud Trial Enters Fifth Week," *Houston Chronicle*, June 11, 1957.

19. "Diego Heras Is Accused of 'Stealing,'" *Corpus Christi Caller*, June 11, 1957.

20. "Diego Heras Questioned on Deposits," *Corpus Christi Caller*, June 12, 1957.

21. "Diego Heras Again Denies Immunity," *Corpus Christi Caller*, June 13, 1957.

22. "Foreman to Claim Immunity Granted Parr Trial Figure," *Dallas Morning News*, June 13, 1957.

23. "Judge Voices Displeasure at Slowness," *Houston Post*, June 14, 1957.

24. "Defense Wins Right to Use Names in Parr Case," *Houston Post*, June 15, 1957.

25. "Heras Denies Delivering Money to FBI Man Here," *Corpus Christi Caller*, June 15, 1957.

26. "Auditor Says Parr Scoffed at Warning," *Corpus Christi Caller*, June 18, 1957.

27. "Benson Describes Tax Returns," *Alice Daily Echo*, June 18, 1957; "Parr's Ex-Aide Denies Pressuring Educator," *Corpus Christi Caller*, June 19, 1957.

28. "Parr Defense Contends Check Payees Are Real," *Houston Post*, June 20, 1957; "Expert Says Parr Signed Checks," *Corpus Christi Caller*, June 22, 1957.

29. "FBI Agent Testifies in Trial of Parr," *Houston Post*, June 25, 1957.

30. "Parr Trial Prosecution Statements Demanded," *Houston Post*, June 21, 1957; "Open-File Order Again Benefits Parr Defense," *Houston Chronicle*, June 22, 1957.

31. "New Mistrial Motion Rejected in Parr Trial," *Alice Daily Echo*, June 26, 1957.

32. "Defense Forbidden to Keep Documents," *Corpus Christi Caller*, June 26, 1957.

33. Quoting from "New Mistrial Motion Rejected in Parr Trial," *Alice Daily Echo*, June 26, 1957. See also "Defense Forbidden to Keep Documents," *Corpus Christi Caller*, June 26, 1957.

34. "Wilkey Denies Politics in Prosecution," *Alice Daily Echo*, June 27, 1957.

35. "Parr Calls Federal DA," *San Antonio Express*, June 27, 1957 (quote); Heras's sworn affidavits are reported exactly the same in two sources: "Wilkey Denies Politics in Prosecution," *Alice Daily Echo*, June 27, 1957; "U.S. Attorney Is Made Witness in Parr Trial," *Corpus Christi Caller*, June 27, 1957.

36. Testimony concerning Heras's sworn affidavits is from Dorman, *King of the Courtroom*, 244.

37. "Heras' Testimony Is Target for Parr Defense Witnesses," *Corpus Christi Caller*, June 28, 1957; "Parr Trial Witness Says School Office Rifled, Searched," *Corpus Christi Caller*, June 29, 1957.

38. "Jurors in Parr Trial Raised to $10 a Day," *Houston Post*, June 29, 1957.

39. Dorman, *King of the Courtroom*, 246.

40. "Attorneys and Judge Study Two Hundred Charges to Parr Trial Jury," *Corpus Christi Caller*, July 9, 1957; "Foreman Describes Heras as a 'Talking Machine,'" *Alice Daily Echo*, July 11, 1957.

41. "Parr and Eight Others, Two Banks Adjudged Guilty," *Houston Post*, July 18, 1957 (quote); "Parr Is Convicted of Fraud in Texas," *New York Times*, July 18, 1957.

42. "Parr Given Ten Years in Pen, Fined $20,000," *Houston Post*, July 31, 1957 (quote); "Sentencing Set for Parr," *San Antonio Express*, July 30, 1957.

43. Dorman, *King of the Courtroom*, 249.

44. "Parr Sentenced to Ten-Year Term," *New York Times*, July 31, 1957.

45. "Parr Is Given Ten-Year Term," *Corpus Christi Caller*, July 31, 1957; Dorman, *King of the Courtroom*, 250. See also *George B. Parr v. United States*, 265 F.2d 894 (April 6, 1959).

46. "Parr Income Tax Trial to Be Delayed," *Fort Worth Star-Telegram*, August 1, 1957 (quote); Jake Lewis, "Burris Plans Parr Prison Term Offer," *Corpus Christi Caller*, August 2, 1957.

47. "U.S. Drops Tax Charge against Parr's Ex-Wife," *Dallas Morning News*, August 9, 1957.

48. *George B. Parr v. State of Texas*, 307 S.W.2d 94 (November 20, 1957); "State-Court Parr Case Tossed Out," *Houston Post*, November 21, 1957.

49. "Parr Accused Again," *New York Times*, March 11, 1958.

50. "Dispute over Parr Loan to Continue Today," *Alice Daily Echo*, October 21, 1958.

51. "Parr Tax Hearing Continues in CC," *Alice Daily Echo*, October 23, 1958; "Cross Examination of Heras Continues," *Alice Daily Echo*, October 24, 1958.

52. "Resigned for $20,000, Says Ex-Sheriff," *Fort Worth Star-Telegram*, October 25, 1958.

53. "Missing Bank, County Records Cited by Agent," *Alice Daily Echo*, October 28, 1958.

54. "Agreement in Parr Tax Case," *Alice Daily Echo*, October 29, 1958; "Parr Income Tax Debates Resume Monday," *Alice Daily Echo*, June 18, 1959.

55. "U.S. Over-Billed Parr $1.24 Million Is Ruling," *Houston Chronicle*, April 14, 1961; "Legal Battle Looms on Parr Tax Ruling," *Alice Daily Echo*, April 14, 1961.

56. *In the Matter of George B. Parr, Bankrupt*, 205 F. Supp. 492 (May 31, 1962).

57. "Agreement Reached on Parr Tax Claims," *Alice Daily Echo*, November 10, 1963.

58. "Two More Months Needed to Finish Records for Appeal of Parr Case," *Alice Daily Echo*, January 3, 1958; "Parr Trial Transcript Completed," *Alice Daily Echo*, March 5, 1958; "Appeal Filed in Parr Case," *Alice Daily Echo*, July 31, 1958; "Fifth U.S. Court Here Hears Parr Appeal" *Fort Worth Star-Telegram*, November 6, 1958.

59. *George B. Parr v. United States*, 265 F.2d 894 (April 6, 1959). See also *Parr v. United States*, 268 F.2d 959 (August 12, 1959).

CHAPTER 21

1. Douglas Martin, "Malcolm Wilkey, Noted Judge, Dies at Ninety," *New York Times*, September 19, 2009. It is interesting to note that when Wilkey was appointed as U.S. Assistant Attorney General of Office of Legal Counsel, his confirmation was temporarily held up by the leader of the Senate, Lyndon Johnson.

2. "Justice Department Attacks Parr Appeal," *Alice Daily Echo*, November 16, 1959. See also "Parr Files Appeal," *New York Times*, September 16, 1959; "Texan to Get Hearing," *New York Times*, December 8, 1959.

3. Dallek, *Lone Star Rising*, 561 (quote); Murphy, *Fortas*, 105.

4. *Parr et al. v. United States*, 361 U.S. 912, 80 S.Ct. 254 (December 7, 1959); "Parr Files Appeal," *New York Times*, September 16, 1959.

5. John Harris, "Prosecutor of Parr Admits Trial Error," *Houston Chronicle*, April 29, 1960; "Wilkey Admits Error in Parr Fraud Case," *Alice Daily Echo*, April 29, 1960.

6. Clark, *Fall of the Duke*, 84; *Parr et al. v. United States*, 363 U.S. 370; 80 S.Ct. 1171 (June 13, 1960).

7. *Parr et al. v. United States*, 363 U.S. 370; 80 S.Ct. 1171 (June 13, 1960).

8. "High Court Tosses out Parr's Fraud Conviction," *Houston Post*, June 14, 1960; "Dismissal of Twenty-Count Parr Indictment Asked," *Houston Chronicle*, December 20, 1960.

9. "Heart Attack Claims Freedom Party Chief at Benavides Rally," *Alice Daily Echo*, May 4, 1960; "Duval Voters Asked to Vote for Canales," *Alice Daily Echo*, May 5, 1960.

10. "Absentee Vote Aids Old Party," *Alice Daily Echo*, May 9, 1960; "Parr Party in Victory," *San Antonio Express*, June 5, 1960.

11. "Late Reports Verify Parr Wins in Duval," *Alice Daily Echo*, November 10, 1960; "Quietest State Election Looms," *Houston Chronicle*, February 2, 1960.

12. "Court Says Parr Wins Demo Rule," *Corpus Christi Caller*, June 9, 1960.

13. Wallace H. Smith, "Irregularities in Duval Voting Aired," *Alice Daily Echo*, June 8, 1960.

14. *Santiago Cantu et al. v. George B. Parr et al.*, 338 S.W.2d 182 (August 10, 1960); *George B. Parr et al. v. Santiago Cantu et al.*, 161 Tex. 296; 340 S.W.2d 481 (November 30, 1960).

15. "Duval County Will Sell Dobie Ranch," May 24, 1959; "Meeting Clears Way to Dobie Ranch Sale," July 31, 1960; "Dobie Ranch to Be Sold Tuesday," November 14, 1960; all in *Alice Daily Echo.*

16. Clark, *Fall of the Duke*, 85. See also Olen Clements, "$100,000 Ante, and the Sky's the Limit," *Houston Chronicle*, November 16, 1960; "Dobie Ranch Sale Is Center of Interest," *Alice Daily Echo*, November 16, 1960.

17. "$172,500 Suit against Parrs Is Dismissed," *Alice Daily Echo*, March 31, 1961.

18. Rowe, "Mesquite Pendergast," 181–82.

19. "Parr Resigns His Post on BISD Board," *Alice Daily Echo*, April 12, 1962.

20. "Bob Kennedy Asked to Aid in Duval Issue," *Alice Daily Echo*, May 4, 1962.

21. Editorial, "An Editorial," *Alice Daily Echo*, May 20, 1962.

22. "Sixty-One Indictments Are Dismissed in Duval," *Alice Daily Echo*, April 5, 1960; "Government Seeks to Drop Income Tax Charge Filed in '55," *Alice Daily Echo*, March 28, 1963; Clark, *Fall of the Duke*, 86.

23. "Bills Introduced to Create Water District in Duval Co.," *Alice Daily Echo*, March 15, 1963.

24. "$2.5 Million Duval Bond Election Carries Handily," *Alice Daily Echo*, April 13, 1965.

25. Teletype, SAC, Jacksonville to FBI Director, FBI Record Number 124-10012-10237, Agency File Number 62-109060-1190, November 25, 1963, JFK Assassination Archives, National Archives.

26. Unsigned FBI notes, CIA Record Number 104-1006-10029, Agency File Number 201-289248, November 27, 1964, JFK Assassination Archives, National Archives.

27. Memorandum, SC William H. Schmidt to SAC, San Antonio, FBI Record Number 124-10180-10139, Agency File Number 89-67-737, July 31, 1967, JFK Assassination Archives, National Archives.

28. "Activities of Oswald before the Death of President," *New York Times*, November 30, 1963.

29. "Oswald Interviewed for a Job by KOPY," *Alice Daily Echo*, November 27, 1963 (quotes). See also Memorandum, John M. Kemmy to SAC, San Antonio, FBI Record Number 124-10178-10419, Agency File Number 89-67-131, November 26, 1963; Memorandum, SAC, Houston to Director, FBI, FBI Record Number 124-10018-10241, Agency File Number 62-109060-1543, November 27, 1963, JFK Assassination Archives, National Archives; *Official Warren Commission Report*, 666.

30. Memorandum, SAC, San Antonio to Chief Clerk, FBI Record Number 124-10180-10167, Agency File Number 89-67-801, 802, 803, 804, February 4, 1977, JFK Assassination Archives, National Archives.

31. "George Parr Is Elected," *Houston Chronicle*, April 5, 1964; "Parr Resigns as Duval Demo Head; King Appointed," *Alice Daily Echo*, April 19, 1964.

32. "Parr Hunting Charge May Be Transferred," *Corpus Christi Caller*, October 29, 1969.

33. "A Misunderstanding in Duval County," *Texas Observer*, January 23, 1970.

34. *Elizabeth Frances Parr et al. v. George Hamilton, Judge of the Court of Domestic Relations, Nueces County, Texas et al.*, 437 S.W.2d 29 (December 31, 1968).

35. Lynch, *Duke of Duval*, 104. See also John Depue, "Duval Judge Parr Is Top Buyer at Beefmaster Breeder Auction," *Corpus Christi Caller-Times*, October 26, 1969; Clark, *Fall of the Duke*, 240, 86.

36. Lynch, *Duke of Duval*, 105.

CHAPTER 22

1. Clark, *Fall of the Duke*, 93.

2. Ibid., 96.

3. Ibid., 96.

4. "Telephone Threats Told by Witness in Parr Tax Trial," *Houston Post*, March 9, 1974.

5. Clark, *Fall of the Duke*, 102–4.

6. Ibid., 111.

7. "Parr Linked to Fee at Duval Consultant," *Dallas Morning News*, March 7, 1974.

8. Lynch, *Duke of Duval*, 106.

9. Joe Coudert and Spencer Pearson, "Checks for $16,185 Endorsed by Duval Official," *Corpus Christi Caller*, November 30, 1973; *Ex Parte Jody Martin Parr*, 505 S.W.2d 242 (February 6, 1974).

10. "San Diego Bank Sells to Investment Banker," *Alice Daily Echo*, April 6, 1966.

11. *United States v. Archer Parr*, 516 F.2d 458 (July 24, 1975); *United States v. George B. Parr*, 509 F.2d 1381 (March 24, 1975).

12. Clark, *Fall of the Duke*, 117, 120.

13. "U.S. Move to Obtain Parr Records Dropped," *Corpus Christi Caller*, May 19, 1972.

14. Clark, *Fall of the Duke*, 131–40, 147.

15. Clark, *Fall of the Duke*, 133 (quote), 134–35.

16. Ibid., 135.

17. Ibid., 136.

18. Ibid., 138–40.

19. Ibid., 142.

20. Ibid., 147.

21. "U.S. Move to Obtain Parr Records Dropped," *Corpus Christi Caller*, May 19, 1972.

22. Clark, *Fall of the Duke*, 161.

23. "Parr Pocketed $60,000, Man Claims," *San Antonio Express*, March 8, 1974.

24. On May 29, 1979, Wood was assassinated by Charles Harrelson, father of actor Woody Harrelson.

25. Clark, *Fall of the Duke*, 171.

26. Ibid., 173.

27. Ibid., 175–76.

28. Wilson McKinney, "George Parr Case Records 'Missing,'" *San Antonio Express*, July 14, 1972.

29. Clark, *Fall of the Duke*, 186–88.

30. Ibid., 195.

31. Ibid., 197.

CHAPTER 23

1. David Pickering, "Tale of Mysterious Records Spun during Parr Hearing," *Corpus Christi Caller,* January 4, 1974; Clark, *Fall of the Duke*, 203.

2. *United States v. George B. Parr,* 509 F.2d 1381 (March 24, 1975); *United States v. Archer Parr,* 516 F.2d 458 (July 24, 1975); Clark, *Fall of the Duke*, 205–6.

3. Clark, *Fall of the Duke*, 210.

4. Ibid., 213–14, 217.

5. Ibid., 219.

6. CBS, *60 Minutes,* vol. 8, no. 5, "The Duke of Duval," January 4, 1976, produced by Richard Clark.

7. Clark, *Fall of the Duke*, 228–29.

8. Ibid., 236.

9. *United States v. George B. Parr,* 509 F.2d 1381 (March 24, 1975).

10. Clark, *Fall of the Duke*, 237 (quote); CBS, *60 Minutes,* vol. 8, no. 5, "The Duke of Duval," January 4, 1976.

11. Clark, *Fall of the Duke*, 238.

12. *United States v. Archer Parr,* 516 F.2d 458 (July 24, 1975).

13. Clark, *Fall of the Duke*, 257, 259.

14. Ibid., 248, 253, 257, 260, 266, 298.

15. Ibid., 274.

16. To clarify the family relations here: the father was David Carrillo, however, he preferred using the name D.C. Chapa. He had three sons, all of whom preferred using the name Carrillo. They were Ramiro Carrillo, a Benavides city councilman and a county commissioner; O. P. Carrillo, a district judge; and Oscar Carrillo Sr., a state representative and board member of the BISD.

17. John Lumpkin, "New Charge against George Parr," *Houston Chronicle,* April 7, 1973; "Two Officials Indicted for Perjury," *Dallas Morning News,* November 7, 1973.

18. Nicholas—unlike his law partner of more than fifty years, Roy Barrera, who had been kicked out of the University of Texas Law School at Austin—received his license to practice law a year *before* graduating from the same law school.

19. Elaine Ayala, "Nicholas Was Half of a Legendary Legal Duo," *San Antonio Express-News,* May 11, 2011; "George Parr Re-Elected," *San Antonio Express,* April 8, 1973; "Parr, Schoolmen Indicted on Taxes," *Dallas Times Herald,* April 7, 1973.

20. "Parr's Empire Was Crumbling," *San Antonio Express,* April 2, 1975; Dave McNeely, "Duval County Rulers Have a Way with Law," *Dallas Morning News,* August 24, 1974.

21. "Others Named in Parr Investigation," *Houston Post,* April 11, 1973.

22. "Tax Evasion Case Invalid, 'Political Boss' Parr Says," *Dallas Morning News,* April 26, 1973; "Parr Tax Charges Dismissed," *Alice Echo-News,* May 3, 1973.

23. "Parr, Two Others Again Indicted on Tax Charges," *San Antonio Express*, June 15, 1973; "Parr Plea Entered in Tax Case," *Dallas Morning News*, July 31, 1973.

24. "Position as Deputy Resigned by Parr," *Corpus Christi Caller*, June 6, 1973; "Jury Declines to Indict Parr," *Corpus Christi Caller*, August 7, 1973; "Grand Jury Reindicts S. Texas Political Boss," *Alice Echo-News*, June 15, 1973.

25. Joe Coudert, "San Diego Auto Firm's Water Still Off," June 6, 1973; Joe Coudert, "Firm's Water Cutoff Poses Puzzle," June 7, 1973; "Duval Dispute on Water Panel Agenda," June 8, 1973; Joe Coudert, "Water Flows Again for Duval Firm," June 13, 1973; all in *Corpus Christi Caller*.

26. *White v. Parr*, 538 S.W.2d 234 (June 9, 1976).

27. Joe Coudert, "Mrs. Parr Says Duval Pays Ranch Help," *Corpus Christi Caller*, August 11, 1973.

28. Ibid.; Joe Coudert, "Duval Courthouse Observers Predict More Activity in Parr Divorce Cases," *Corpus Christi Caller*, August 13, 1973.

29. Bob Coombes, "Attorneys Argue Point on Parr Case Subpoenas," *Alice Echo-News*, August 21, 1973.

30. Joe Coudert, "Carrillo Removal from Parr Case Due Hearing," *Corpus Christi Caller*, August 24, 1973 (quote); Joe Coudert, "Carrillo to Preside at Hearing Today," *Corpus Christi Caller*, August 25, 1973.

31. Bill Hester, "Parr Loses Fight to Keep Wife from Testifying," *Corpus Christi Caller*, September 7, 1973 (quote); Joe Coudert, "Mrs. Parr Subpoenaed for Grand Jury," *Corpus Christi Caller*, August 28, 1973.

32. Joe Coudert, "$2-Million Suit Filed in Parr Case," *Corpus Christi Caller*, August 30, 1973.

33. Joe Coudert, "Parr Divorce Case Gets Continuance," *Corpus Christi Caller*, September 5, 1973.

34. Brooks Peterson, "Parr Battle," *Corpus Christi Caller*, September 9, 1973.

35. Ibid.

36. Lynch, *Duke of Duval*, 109 (quote); Joe Coudert, "Mrs. Parr Sentenced to Ninety-Day Jail Term," *Corpus Christi Caller*, October 20, 1973.

37. Spencer Pearson, "Jody Loses Ground in Divorce Suit," *Corpus Christi Caller*, September 22, 1973 (quote); Joe Coudert, "Receiver Files Suit against Mrs. Parr," *Corpus Christi Caller*, September 12, 1973.

38. Joe Coudert, "Carrillo Quits Parr Case," *Corpus Christi Times*, September 24, 1973; Joe Coudert, "Archer Parr Divorce Action Judge Assigned," *Corpus Christi Caller*, October 2, 1973.

39. *Ex Parte Jody Martin Parr*, 505 S.W.2d 242 (February 6, 1974).

40. Joe Coudert, "Mrs. Parr Sentenced to Ninety-Day Jail Term," *Corpus Christi Caller*, October 20, 1973.

41. Joe Coudert, "Civil Rights Lawsuit Is Filed by Mrs. Parr," *Corpus Christi Caller*, October 28, 1973; "Petition for Bankruptcy Is Filed by Jody Martin Parr," *Corpus Christi Times*, October 30, 1973.

42. "Jody Martin Parr Sentenced to Jail," *Alice Echo-News*, October 31, 1973; Mary Alice Davis, "Mrs. Parr Denied Restraining Order to Halt Jailing, Property Disposition," *Corpus Christi Caller*, October 31, 1973; "Mrs. Parr Loses Jailing Halt Bid," *San Antonio Express*, October 31, 1973.

43. Joe Coudert, "Duval Told to Treat Mrs. Parr Well," *Corpus Christi Caller*, November 2, 1973; Joe Coudert and Spencer Pearson, "Mrs. Parr Has Striking Presence," *Corpus Christi Caller*, November 28, 1973. See also Joe Coudert and Guile Gonzalez, "Nueces Refuses to Jail Mrs. Parr," *Corpus Christi Caller*, November 1, 1973; "Court Frees Judge's Wife," *Dallas Times Herald*, November 4, 1973.

44. "Judge Parr, Mayor Indictment Made," *San Antonio Express*, November 7, 1973.

CHAPTER 24

1. Joe Coudert and Spencer Pearson, "Duval County Vehicle Maintenance Bills Double Nueces," *Corpus Christi Caller*, November 29, 1973; Joe Coudert, "Duval Approves Budget despite Strong Protests," *Corpus Christi Caller*, December 1, 1973.

2. Joe Coudert, "Taxpayers Crowd Duval Courthouse," *Corpus Christi Caller*, November 27, 1973 (quote). Joe Coudert and Spencer Pearson, "High Officials of Duval County on Delinquent Tax Rolls," *Corpus Christi Caller*, November 26, 1973; "Parr Has Unlimited Credit for Car," *Corpus Christi Caller*, November 30, 1973.

3. Clark, *Fall of the Duke*, 300 (quote); Mary Ann Cavazos and Fanny S. Chirinos, "Lawyer Tinker, Seventy-Four, Dies of Brain Tumor," *Corpus Christi Caller-Times*, November 10, 2008.

4. Clark, *Fall of the Duke*, 300; David Pickering, "Phone Official Denies Tale of Parr Wiretap," *Corpus Christi Caller*, January 5, 1974; "Government Denies Parr Bugging," *Corpus Christi Caller*, October 19, 1973; "Lists of White House 'Enemies' and Memorandums Relating to Those Named," *New York Times*, June 28, 1973.

5. "Archer Parr Says State Demos Target of GOP Conspiracy," *Corpus Christi Caller*, December 4, 1973; Jim Wood, "Tower Denies Parr Claim of Enemies List," *Corpus Christi Caller*, December 8, 1973.

6. Jencks was president of Local 890, International Union of Mine, Mill & Smelter Workers. The National Labor Relations Act required all union officials to sign an affidavit that they were not members of the Communist Party. Jencks falsely stated he was not a member and was convicted. During his trial, two paid undercover agents for the FBI testified they had submitted oral and written reports to the FBI. A motion to produce these reports was denied. The U.S. Supreme Court reversed the conviction and ruled that Jencks "is entitled to inspect the reports to decide whether to use them in his defense," adding that "criminal action must be dismissed when the Government, on the ground of privilege, elects not to comply." *Jencks v. United States*, 353 U.S. 657, 77 S.Ct. 1007 (June 3, 1957).

7. Spencer Pearson, "Testimony Due in George Parr Trial," *Corpus Christi Caller*, March 5, 1974.

8. "Jurors in Parr Income Tax Trial Here Live in Howard Hughes Type Seclusion," *Corpus Christi Caller*, March 10, 1974.

9. "'Duke of Duval' Accused of Misusing Public Funds in Tax Evasion Trial," *Houston Chronicle*, March 6, 1974; "Parr Linked to Fee at Duval Consultant," *Dallas Morning News*, March 7, 1974.

10. "Parr Witness Testifies He Got Phoned Threats," *San Antonio Express-News*, March 9, 1974 (quote); "Austin Man Testifies," *Austin American-Statesman*, March 7, 1974.

11. Spencer Pearson, "Defense Attacking Payoff Testimony," *Corpus Christi Caller*, March 8, 1974; Spencer Pearson, "Builder Tells of Threatening Calls," *Corpus Christi Caller*, March 9, 1974.

12. "Parr's Brother Linked to Payment by Water District," *Houston Chronicle*, March 13, 1974.

13. "Parr Employee Allegedly Got Public Funds," *Austin American-Statesman*, March 14, 1974; Spencer Pearson, "Parr Receiving $5,000 a Month, Water District Official Testifies," *Corpus Christi Caller*, March 14, 1974.

14. "Testimony Cites Parr Windfall," *Dallas Times Herald*, March 15, 1974.

15. "Parr Got Tax Aid, Jury Told," *San Antonio Express*, March 16, 1974.

16. "Dallas Banker Denies Parr Retained Bonds," *Dallas Morning News*, March 16, 1974; "Prosecution Rests in Parr Tax Case," *Austin American-Statesman*, March 17, 1974; "George B. Parr Rests Defense in Tax Case," *Alice Echo-News*, March 18, 1974.

17. Spencer Pearson, "George Parr Guilty of Evading Income Taxes," *Corpus Christi Caller*, March 20, 1974.

18. "Parr Convicted on All Eight Counts," *Rio Grande Herald*, March 21, 1974.

19. "Parr Found Guilty of Evading Taxes," *Houston Post*, March 20, 1974.

20. Clark, *Fall of the Duke*, 307.

21. "Jury to Ignore Chapa Testimony," *Alice Echo-News*, May 1, 1974.

22. "Testimony of Witness Taken Again in Parr Trial," *Dallas Morning News*, May 2, 1974; Spencer Pearson, "Chapa Testifies Archer Parr Has Reputation for Truth," *Corpus Christi Caller*, May 1, 1974.

23. "Prosecution Witness Refutes Parr's Claim," *Alice Echo-News*, May 2, 1974. See also Spencer Pearson, "Duval Board Minutes Trial Evidence," *Corpus Christi Caller*, May 2, 1974; Spencer Pearson, "Parr Work on Budget Denied," *Corpus Christi Times*, May 2, 1974.

24. Spencer Pearson, "Archer Parr Prosecution Reads Testimony, Rests Case," *Corpus Christi Caller*, May 3, 1974.

25. John Lumpkin, "Parr Trial Recesses Early Due to Illness," *San Antonio Express*, May 4, 1974; "Parr Trial Resumes Today," *Dallas Morning News*, May 7, 1974.

26. "'Underpaid,' Archer Parr Says," *Corpus Christi Caller*, May 8, 1974.

27. "Final Arguments Open in Archer Parr's Trial," *Alice Echo-News*, May 9, 1974; Clark, *Fall of the Duke*, 308–9.

28. *United States v. Archer Parr*, 516 F.2d 458 (July 24, 1975).

29. "Couldn't Find Files, Parr Says," *San Antonio Express*, May 9, 1974.

30. John Lumpkin, "Prosecution Lawyer Says Archer Parr Liar," *Corpus Christi Times*, May 9, 1974; Clark, *Fall of the Duke*, 310; "Duval County Judge Parr Convicted," *Houston Chronicle*, May 10, 1974.

31. "Archer Parr Convicted on Six Perjury Counts," *Dallas Times Herald*, May 10, 1974.

32. "Parr Freed, Jokes after Night in Jail," *Houston Post*, May 11, 1974.

33. "Bar Suspension," *Corpus Christi Caller*, May 22, 1974; "Appeal Set in A. Parr Conviction," *Dallas Times Herald*, May 22, 1974.

34. *United States v. Archer Parr*, 516 F.2d 458 (July 24, 1975); "Archer Parr Gets Thirty Years, $60,000 fine," *Corpus Christi Caller*, May 21, 1974.

35. Joe Coudert, "No Action Is Taken in Parr Divorce Case," *Corpus Christi Caller*, February 20, 1974.

36. Joe Coudert, "Parr Cases Cost Duval $23,755," February 9, 1974; Joe Coudert, "Parr Receivership Dissolved," March 8, 1974; Joe Coudert, "New Receiver Named in Parr Divorce Case," March 27, 1974; Joe Coudert, "Mrs. Parr, Sister Facing Charges," April 6, 1974; all in *Corpus Christi Caller*.

37. *Jody Martin Parr et al. v. First State Bank of San Diego, Texas et al.*, 507 S.W.2d 579 (February 27, 1974).

38. Joe Coudert, "Rulings against Jody Snowball," *Corpus Christi Caller*, June 4, 1974.

39. Joe Coudert and Ray Caballero, "Jody Transferred to Jim Wells Jail," *Corpus Christi Caller*, June 7, 1974 (quote). See also "Jody Parr Arrested in Austin," *San Antonio Express*, June 7, 1974; "Jody Is Becoming Authority on Jails," *Alice Echo-News*, June 9, 1974; Joe Coudert, "Jody Treated like the Rest, Jailers Say," *Corpus Christi Caller*, June 11, 1974; "Parr's Wife Free?" *San Antonio Express*, June 13, 1974.

40. Bill Hester, "Jody's Death Came Only Hours before a New Citation Arrived," *Corpus Christi Caller*, June 14, 1974.

41. "Pen Shows Little Venom," *Dallas Times Herald*, June 16, 1974.

42. "Wife of Duval County Judge Dies of Gunshot Wound," *Fort Worth Star-Telegram*, June 13, 1974; Spencer Pearson, "Farewell Letters," *Corpus Christi Caller*, June 14, 1974.

43. Joe Coudert, "Roloff Lauds Jody's Courageous Fight," *Corpus Christi Caller*, June 17, 1974 (quote); Lynch, *Duke of Duval*, 115.

CHAPTER 25

1. Dave McNeely, "Duval County Rulers Have a Way with Law," *Dallas Morning News*, August 24, 1974.

2. Joe Coudert, "Carrillo Breaks with Parr," *Corpus Christi Caller*, March 28, 1974.

3. "Parr Says He'll Keep Power," *Corpus Christi Caller*, March 29, 1974.

4. "Leaflets Question Duval Power," *Corpus Christi Caller*, February 26, 1974; "Carrillo Denies Split between Family, Parrs," *Corpus Christi Caller*, February 27, 1974.

5. Joe Coudert, "Carrillo, Parr Swap Accusations," *Corpus Christi Caller*, April 4, 1974.

6. Joe Coudert, "Shots Follow Carrillo Wreath," *Corpus Christi Caller*, April 8, 1974.

7. Joe Coudert, "Archer Parr Disclaims Part in Wreath Gift," *Corpus Christi Caller*, April 9, 1974; "Carrillo Cites 'Serious Matters' in Race," *Corpus Christi Caller*, April 19, 1974.

8. "Power Struggle Rages in Duval," *San Antonio Express*, April 9, 1974.

9. "Benavides Mayor Race Ends in Tie Vote," *Corpus Christi Caller*, April 9, 1974; Editorial, "Duval County's Political Gain," *San Antonio Express*, April 13, 1974.

10. Joe Coudert, "Benavides Canvass Scheduled for Today," *Corpus Christi Caller*, April 10, 1974; "Extra Votes in Benavides Recount Are Accounted For," *Corpus Christi Caller*, April 12, 1974.

11. K. Mack Sisk, "Politics May End Control by Parr," *Dallas Morning News*, April 25, 1974.

12. "Parr: My Hands Off Resignations," *Corpus Christi Caller*, April 20, 1974.

13. Joe Coudert, "Duval Discharges Road Employees," *Corpus Christi Caller*, April 26, 1974; "Duval Gets Order," *Alice Echo-News*, April 28, 1974.

14. Nell Fenner Grover, "Traeger Breezing 2–1 over His Rival Carrillo," *San Antonio Express*, May 5, 1974; "Duval County Fires Carrillo Supporters," *Dallas Morning News*, May 9, 1974; "Duval Job in Family," *Austin American-Statesman*, May 23, 1974.

15. "Benavides Mayor's Trial Set," *Dallas Morning News*, August 26, 1974.

16. "Jury Convicts Mayor Tied to Parr Probe," *Dallas Morning News*, August 30, 1974; Clark, *Fall of the Duke*, 312–13.

17. "'Duke of Duval' Sentenced to Five Years in Prison," *Austin American-Statesman*, May 4, 1974; Nick Jimenez, "George Parr Sentenced to Five Years," *Corpus Christi Caller*, May 4, 1974.

18. "Parr Gets Five-Year Sentence," *San Antonio Express*, May 4, 1974; "George Parr's Bond Posted by Manges," *Corpus Christi Caller*, May 10, 1974.

19. Clark, *Fall of the Duke*, 322–23.

20. "Parrs to Face Bar Committee," *Austin American-Statesman*, June 3, 1974.

21. Lynn Faivre, "George Parr's Bar Standing Lagging," *San Antonio Express*, May 23, 1974; "Parrs Get Legislative Continuance," *Alice Echo-News*, December 17, 1974.

22. Joe Coudert, "George Parr Still Calls the Signals," *Corpus Christi Caller*, September 24, 1974.

23. "Judge Parr Re-elected," *Alice Echo-News*, November 7, 1974; "Judge Parr Ordered Suspended from Office," *Dallas Morning News*, March 25, 1975.

24. Gary Garrison, "Carrillo to Stay with Trial of Parr," *Corpus Christi Times*, June 17, 1975.

25. "Parr Agrees to Step Aside in Duval County Struggle," *Dallas Morning News*, March 29, 1975.

26. Joe Coudert, "Archer Parr Obeys Carrillo's Order to Cease and Desist Acting as Judge," *Corpus Christi Caller*, March 29, 1975.

27. "Parr, Carrillo Clans Split over Election," *Dallas Morning News*, March 23, 1975; "Political Storm Gathering over Duval County," *Dallas Morning News*, March 27, 1975.

28. "George B. Parr Says Manges Causing Duval Rift," *Alice Echo-News*, March 26, 1975.

29. Gary Garrison, "Parr Chuckles about 'Takeover,'" *Dallas Morning News*, March 27, 1975; K. Mack Sisk, "Parr Family Dynasty 'Appears' to Be Crumbling," *Alice Echo-News*, March 28, 1975.

30. *United States v. George B. Parr*, 509 F.2d 1381 (March 24, 1975).

31. CBS, *60 Minutes*, vol. 8, no. 5, "The Duke of Duval," January 4, 1976.

32. Nick Jimenez, "Parr's Hearing Held for Record," *Corpus Christi Caller*, April 2, 1975.

33. Dave Montgomery, "Parr Hinted to Family End Was Near," *Dallas Times Herald*, April 2, 1975.

34. Dave Montgomery, "Parr Considered Murder, Says Deputy," *Dallas Times Herald*, April 5, 1975.

35. Ibid.

36. Clark, *Fall of the Duke*, 6–7 (quotes); *United States v. George B. Parr*, 451 F.Supp. 190 (May 3, 1978).

37. Gary Garrison, "George Parr's Kin Dispute Circumstances of His Death," *Corpus Christi Caller-Times*, April 20, 1980.

38. Clark, *Fall of the Duke*, 9, 334.

39. Nick Jimenez, "George Parr Skips Court; Arrest Ordered," *Corpus Christi Caller*, April 1, 1975; Clark, *Fall of the Duke*, 14.

40. "Deputies Scouring Ranch to Arrest George Parr," *Houston Chronicle*, April 1, 1975.

41. Clark, *Fall of the Duke*, 17–18.

42. "Town Salutes 'Patron' Parr," *San Antonio Express*, April 3, 1975.

43. Clark, *Fall of the Duke*, 20.

CHAPTER 26

1. "Buddies the Winners," *San Antonio Light*, April 2, 1975.

2. "G. B. Parr Found Dead on Ranch," *Houston Post*, April 2, 1975.

3. Dave Montgomery, "Parr Hinted to Family End Was Near," *Dallas Times Herald*, April 2, 1975.

4. "Texas Politician Dead; Ruled Suicide," *New York Times*, April 2, 1975; "Political Boss Dead," *Washington Post*, April 2, 1975; "Death of a Duke," *Time* 105 (April 14, 1975): 30.

5. K. Mack Sisk, "Fiefdom Won't Fall, Archer Vows," *San Antonio Light*, April 4, 1975; Dave Montgomery, "Parr Hinted to Family End Was Near," *Dallas Times Herald*, April 2, 1975. See also "Ex-Gov. Stevenson Declines to Comment," *Corpus Christi Caller*, April 2, 1975.

6. Joe Coudert, "Parr's Death Ruled Suicide," *Corpus Christi Caller*, April 25, 1975; Gary Garrison, "George Parr's Kin Dispute Circumstances of His Death," *Corpus Christi Caller-Times*, April 20, 1980.

7. Joe Coudert, "Friend Says Parr Had Full Use of Hands before Suicide," *Corpus Christi Caller-Times*, April 20, 1980.

8. "Duval Is Still 'Parr Country,'" *San Antonio Express*, April 7, 1975 (quote). See also "Carrillos Indicted on Taxes," *Austin American-Statesman*, April 11, 1975; "Judge Rules Archer Parr Must Wait Turn for Suit," *Alice Echo-News*, April 15, 1975; "Archer Parr Loses in Bid to Regain Duval Judgeship," *Dallas Morning News*, April 17, 1975.

9. Spencer Pearson, " . . . and Parr Trial Goes Back to Square One," *Corpus Christi Caller*, June 21, 1975; Gary Garrison, "Carrillo to Stay with Trial of Parr," *Corpus Christi Times*, June 17, 1975.

10. Nick Jimenez, "Parr-Carrillo Battle Spreads to New Arenas," *Corpus Christi Caller*, June 24, 1975.

11. Spencer Pearson, "Parr's Attorney Gaveled Down," *Corpus Christi Caller*, July 4, 1975 (quote); "O.P. Carrillo Gets Own Trial Delayed," *Alice Echo-News*, July 1, 1975.

12. "Parr Spotlight Touches Hebbronville," *Corpus Christi Caller*, June 29, 1975.

13. "Duval County Does 'Things Informally,'" *Alice Echo-News*, June 29, 1975.

14. Spencer Pearson, "Duval County Auditor Testifies," *Corpus Christi Times*, July 1, 1975.

15. Spencer Pearson, "Lack of Witness Halts Parr Trial," *Corpus Christi Times*, July 2, 1975; "Duval County Cuts Taxes for Manges," *Alice Echo-News*, July 3, 1975.

16. Spencer Pearson, "Parr's Attorney Gaveled Down," *Corpus Christi Caller*, July 4, 1975.

17. "Parr Fails to Appear," *Alice Echo-News*, July 7, 1975; Nick Jimenez, "Parr Will Answer—If," *Corpus Christi Times*, July 7, 1975.

18. Nick Jimenez, "Carrillo Threatens Contempt, Arrest for No-Show Parr," *Corpus Christi Caller*, July 8, 1975 (quote); Nick Jimenez, "Carrillo Makes Parr Ouster Permanent," *Corpus Christi Times*, July 9, 1975.

19. "Archer Parr Says Carrillo and Manges Out to Get Him," *Alice Echo-News*, July 17, 1975.

20. "Terry Canales Has Key Role," *Alice Echo-News*, August 4, 1975.

21. "Parr's Disbarment Sought," *Corpus Christi Caller*, July 19, 1975.

22. *United States v. Archer Parr*, 516 F.2d 458 (July 24, 1975).

23. Spencer Pearson, "Parr Arrested, Conviction Upheld," *Corpus Christi Caller*, July 25, 1975.

24. Spencer Pearson, "Motion to Postpone Parr Hearing Granted," *Corpus Christi Times*, July 28, 1975 (quote); "Manges Asks Bail Back He Put Up for Archer Parr," *Alice Echo-News*, July 27, 1975.

25. "Parr Catches Up on Reading," *Alice Echo-News*, August 3, 1975 (quote); "Court Refuses to Reinstate Parr," *Alice Echo-News*, July 30, 1975.

26. *United States v. Archer Parr*, 399 F.Supp. 883 (August 21, 1975).

27. "Midland Jail Parr's Home until Aug. 20," *Corpus Christi Caller*, August 9, 1975; "Parr Bond Denied; Called 'Danger to Community,'" *Corpus Christi Caller*, August 21, 1975. See also "Duval Saga Is a Moveable Feast," *Corpus Christi Times*, August 8, 1975.

28. Joe Coudert, "Parr Divorce Case Gets Continuance," *Corpus Christi Caller*, September 5, 1973.

29. Joe Coudert, "Still Waiting at Jailhouse Door," *Corpus Christi Caller*, August 23, 1975.

30. Spencer Pearson, "Parr Moved to Top Security Prison," *Corpus Christi Caller*, September 11, 1975; "Archer Parr Disbarred," *Corpus Christi Caller*, February 3, 1976.

31. "Carrillos Guilty," *Austin American-Statesman*, October 2, 1975; "O.P., Ramiro Carrillo Sentenced," *Alice Echo-News*, November 25, 1975; *O.P. Carrillo v. The State of Texas*, 566 S.W.2d 902 (May 10, 1978).

32. "Impeachment Resolution Approved," *Alice Echo-News*, August 5, 1975.

33. Gary Garrison, "Foster Sentenced to Jail," *Alice Echo-News*, December 11, 1975; "Duval Treasurer 'Guilty,'" *Alice Echo-News*, December 16, 1975; Joe Coudert, "Archer Parr Changes His Plea to Guilty," *Corpus Christi Caller*, November 25, 1976.

34. Joe Coudert, "Ex-Duval Employee Says George Parr Ordered Stolen Records Burned," *Corpus Christi Caller,* July 3, 1976; Clark, *Fall of the Duke,* 325.

35. Joe Coudert, "A Slimmer Parr Hasn't Lost Humor," *Corpus Christi Caller,* September 26, 1976 (quotes); Spencer Pearson, "Arraignment Delayed; Parr Visits Friends," *Corpus Christi Caller,* September 25, 1976.

36. Billy Newton, "Parr Weds after Year of Waiting," *Corpus Christi Caller,* October 16, 1976.

37. "Parr Must Pay Child Support," November 11, 1976; "Lawyer: Archer Parr Is Insane," November 24, 1976; Joe Coudert, "Archer Parr Changes His Plea to Guilty," November 25, 1976; all in *Corpus Christi Caller.*

38. Joe Coudert, "Plea Change Sends Parr Back North," *Corpus Christi Caller,* January 19, 1977; Joe Coudert and Billy Newton, "Parr Changes Jails, but Treatment Hassle Remains," *Corpus Christi Caller,* January 18, 1977; Joe Coudert and Billy Newton, "Judge Orders Parr Moved to New Jail," *Corpus Christi Caller,* January 15, 1977.

39. Joe Coudert and Billy Newton, "Judge Orders Parr Moved to New Jail," *Corpus Christi Caller,* January 15, 1977.

40. Joe Coudert, "Duval Jury Indicts Parr on New Count," *Corpus Christi Caller,* April 27, 1977.

41. "Illness May Halt Trial of Parr," *San Antonio Express,* July 20, 1977; Spencer Pearson, "TB Puts Parr into Hospital," *Corpus Christi Caller,* May 4, 1977; "Lung Tumor May Keep Archer Parr from Trial," *Corpus Christi Caller,* July 20, 1977.

42. "Parr Moved to Texarkana Cell after Hospitalization," *Corpus Christi Caller,* May 20, 1978; "Parr to Be Released Tomorrow," *Corpus Christi Caller,* December 5, 1978.

43. "Duval Crony Insists Parr Wants No Part of Politics," *Corpus Christi Caller,* December 10, 1978.

44. Joe Coudert, "Parr Gets Ten-Year Probation Term," *Corpus Christi Caller,* December 13, 1978; Ken Herman, "Parr Exiled; Judge Hopes Duval Can Grow," *Corpus Christi Times,* December 13, 1978; Joe Coudert, "Parr Gets Ten-Year Probation Term," *Corpus Christi Caller,* December 13, 1978.

45. *United States v. George B. Parr, Clinton Manges Movant-Appellant, Evangelina P. Parr, etc., Intervenor-Appellant,* 560 F.2d 1221 (October 14, 1977).

46. Peter Cawley, "Insanity Out as Issue in Parr Case," *Corpus Christi Caller,* April 6, 1978 (quote); Lloyd Grove, "Hearing on Parr Sanity Set," *Corpus Christi Caller,* January 28, 1978.

47. *United States v. George B. Parr,* 451 F.Supp. 190 (May 3, 1978).

48. *United States v. George B. Parr, Mary Elizabeth Ellis Saenz, Intervenor-Appellant, Clinton Manges, Surety, Movant-Appellant,* 594 F.2d 440 (May 3, 1979).

49. Joe Coudert, "Ex-Judge Archer Parr Living in Duval County," *Corpus Christi Caller,* April 30, 1981 (quotes); Joe Coudert, "Parr Probation Order Special Permits Cancelled," *Corpus Christi Caller,* May 5, 1981.

50. Joe Coudert, "Archer Parr Jailed; No Bond," *Corpus Christi Caller,* November 11, 1986; Darla Morgan, "Archer Parr Gets Suspended Ninety-Day Sentence," *Corpus Christi Caller,* January 28, 1987; Obituary listing, "Ransleben," *Corpus Christi Caller-Times,* January 5, 1999.

51. John Tedesco and Veronica Flores, "Last 'Duke of Duval' Dies at Seventy-Five," *San Antonio Express-News*, November 3, 2000.

52. Pauline Arrillaga, "Last Duke of Duval Now Prefers Cattle to County Politics/ Archer Parr Still Irked over Ten-Year Exile," *Houston Chronicle*, April 28, 1996.

53. Chris Neely, "Archer Parr Laid to Rest with Honors," *Corpus Christi Caller-Times*, November 7, 2000.

54. Mary Lee Grant, "Duval County Museum Reveals Little-Known Tales through Anecdotes," *Corpus Christi Caller-Times*, March 23, 1998.

55. San Attlesey, "Whereabouts of 'Box 13' a Mystery, Fifty Years Later," *Arlington Morning News*, August 9, 1998.

56. Mimi Swartz, "A Legacy of Evil," *Texas Monthly* (September 1988): 167.

57. Darla Morgan, "TV Mini-Series Planned on Legendary Duke of Duval," *Corpus Christi Times*, February 11, 1984.

58. Editorial, "Duval County," *Corpus Christi Caller*, February 5, 1954.

BIBLIOGRAPHY

BOOKS AND ARTICLES

Anders, Evan. *Boss Rule in South Texas*. Austin: University of Texas Press, 1982.

———. "The Origins of the Parr Machine in Duval County, Texas." *Southwestern Historical Quarterly* (October 1981): 119–38.

Banks, Jimmy. *Money, Marbles and Chalk: The Wondrous World of Texas Politics*. Austin: Texas Publishing, 1971.

"Barons of the Court." *Texas Monthly*, November 1974.

Beasley, Maurine H., and Richard R. Harlow. *Voices of Change: Southern Pulitzer Winners*. Washington, DC: University Press of America, 1979.

Caro, Robert A. *Means of Ascent*. New York: Knopf, 1990.

———. *The Path to Power*. New York: Knopf, 1982.

Clark, John E. *The Fall of the Duke of Duval: A Prosecutor's Journal*. Austin: Eakin Press, 1995.

Dallek, Robert. *Lone Star Rising: Lyndon Johnson and His Times, 1908–1960*. New York: Oxford University Press, 1991.

Davidson, T. Whitfield. *The Memoirs of Judge T. Whitfield Davidson*. Waco: Texian Press, 1972.

"Death of a Duke." *Time* 105 (April 14, 1975): 30.

Dorman, Michael. *King of the Courtroom: Percy Foreman for the Defense*. New York: Delacorte Press, 1969.

Dugger, Ronnie. *The Politician: The Life and Times of Lyndon Johnson*. New York: Norton, 1982.

"The Duke Delivers." *Time* 52 (September 27, 1948): 24.

Frost, H. Gordon, and John H. Jenkins. *"I'm Frank Hamer": The Life of a Texas Peace Officer*. Austin: Pemberton Press, 1968.

Green, George Norris. *The Establishment in Texas Politics: The Primitive Years, 1938–1957*. Westport, CT: Greenwood Press, 1979.

Haley, J. Evetts. *A Texan Looks at Lyndon: A Study in Illegitimate Power*. Canyon, TX: Palo Duro Press, 1964.

Heard, Alexander, and Donald S. Strong. *Southern Primaries and Elections, 1920–1949*. Tuscaloosa: University of Alabama, 1950.

Huie, William Bradford. "William Bradford Huie Writes a Letter to President Kennedy about a Murder in Texas." *Cavalier*, August 1961.

Jones, Robert, and Louis K. Falk. "Caro Brown and the Duke of Duval: The Story of the First Woman to Win the Pulitzer Prize for Reporting." *American Journalism* (Winter 1997): 40–53.

Kahl, Mary. *Ballot Box 13: How Lyndon Johnson Won His 1948 Senate Race by Eighty-Seven Contested Votes*. Jefferson, NC: McFarland, 1983.

Kassen, Tex Leo, comp. *Southwestern Football Historical Review: 1908–1950*. Georgetown, Texas, 2000.

"The Land of Parr." *Time* 63 (February 15, 1954): 20–21.

Lasater, Dale. *Falfurrias: Ed C. Lasater and the Development of South Texas.* College Station: Texas A&M University Press, 1985.

Lynch, Dudley. *The Duke of Duval: The Life and Times of George B. Parr.* Waco: Texian Press, 1976.

Martin, Harold H. "Tyrant in Texas." *Saturday Evening Post* 226, June 26, 1954.

McKay, Seth Shepard, and Odie B. Faulk. *Texas after Spindletop.* Austin, TX: Steck-Vaughn, 1965.

Miller, Merle. *Lyndon: An Oral Biography.* New York: G. P. Putnam's, 1980.

"A Misunderstanding in Duval County." *Texas Observer* (January 1970).

Murphy, Bruce Allen. *Fortas: The Rise and Ruin of a Supreme Court Justice.* New York: William Morrow, 1988.

Northcott, Kaye. "A Death in Duval." *Texas Observer,* April 25, 1975, 5.

Official Warren Commission Report on the Assassination of President John F. Kennedy. Garden City, NY: Doubleday, 1964.

Phipps, Joe. *Summer Stock: Behind the Scenes with LBJ in '48.* Fort Worth: Texas Christian University Press, 1992.

Poage, W. R. *Politics—Texas Style.* Waco: Texian Press, 1974.

Pycior, Julie Leininger. *LBJ and Mexican Americans: The Paradox of Power.* Austin: University of Texas Press, 1997.

Reston, James Jr. *The Lone Star: The Life of John Connally.* New York: Harper and Row, 1989.

Schendel, Gordon. "Something Is Rotten in the State of Texas." *Collier's* 127, June 9, 1951.

Steinberg, Alfred. *Sam Johnson's Boy.* New York: Macmillan, 1968.

"The Story of Eighty-Seven Votes That Made History." *U.S. News and World Report* 14 (April 6, 1964): 46–50.

Swartz, Mimi. "A Legacy of Evil." *Texas Monthly,* September 1988.

Walker, Donald R. "Attacking the Texas Tammany: Caro Brown vs. George B. Parr of Duval County." *Texas Gulf Historical and Biographical Record* (November 1998): 21–33.

Warren, Earl. *The Memoirs of Earl Warren.* Garden City, NY: Doubleday, 1977.

NEWSPAPERS

Alice Daily Echo. September 10, 1948–April 6, 1966.

Alice Echo. May 23, 1912–July 13, 1944.

Alice Echo-News. May 3, 1973–December 16, 1975.

All Valley Morning Express. September 8, 1949.

Amarillo News-Globe. January 25, 1976.

Arlington Morning News. August 9, 1998.

Austin American. June 8, 1948, February 10, 1954.

Austin American-Statesman. March 7, 1974–October 2, 1975.

Austin Daily Statesman. May 19, 1912–January 28, 1915.

Austin Statesman. January 14, 1919–May 14, 1957.

Austin Statesman and Tribune. January 11, 1916.

Bastrop Advertiser. January 10, 1957.

Boston Sunday Globe. August 7, 1977.

Chicago Sunday Tribune. July 31, 1949.

Corpus Christi Caller. February 4, 1915–June 4, 2012.

Corpus Christi Caller and Daily Herald. October 3, 1912–June 13, 1915.

Corpus Christi Caller-Times. October 1, 1948–November 10, 2008.

Corpus Christi Times. October 11, 1952–February 11, 1984.

Corpus Christi Weekly Caller. December 27, 1907–July 31, 1914.

Dallas Morning News. December 22, 1907–July 31, 1977.

Dallas Times Herald. April 7, 1973–April 5, 1975.

Deseret News. July 19, 1971.

Fort Worth Star-Telegram. May 18, 1912–June 13, 1974.

Houston Chronicle. July 8, 1914–August 7, 2001.

Houston Chronicle and Herald. May 18, 1912–October 2, 1912.

Houston Daily Post. December 22, 1907–January 2, 1916.

Houston Post. January 16, 1916–April 2, 1975.

Houston Press. February 22, 1954.

Laredo Times. February 3, 1943.

La Verdad. February 5, 1954.

New York Times. September 29, 1948–September 19, 2009.

Rio Grande Herald. March 21, 1974.

San Antonio Daily Express. December 22, 1907.

San Antonio Express. May 19, 1912–August 5, 1977.

San Antonio Express-News. March 9, 1974–May 11, 2011.

San Antonio Light. December 27, 1907–April 4, 1975.

San Antonio News. February 16, 1954.

Washington Post. April 2, 1975.

UNPUBLISHED SOURCES

Anders, Evan Marcus. "Bosses under Siege: The Politics of South Texas during the Progressive Era." PhD thesis, University of Texas, Austin, Texas, 1978.

Busby, Horace. Oral History Interview, July 29, 1988, by Michael L. Gillette. Transcript. Internet Copy, LBJ Library.

Byers, Bo. Oral History Interview, December 8, 1983, by Michael L. Gillette. Transcript. LBJ Library.

Cavness, C.H. State Auditor's Report to Attorney General on Special Examination of Records Made Available Under Order No. 6049: 79th Judicial District Court of Duval County, Texas, February 17, 1954. Texas State Library.

Citizens of Duval County. "Remarkable Conditions in Duval County: Protest by Citizens against Proposed Division." Petition to the Thirty-Fourth Texas Legislature. Pamphlet, 1915.

Clark, Richard, producer. "The Duke of Duval." Transcript. CBS *60 Minutes*, vol. 8, no. 5, January 4, 1976.

Connally, John B. Oral History Interview, November 28, 1969, by Joe B. Frantz. Transcript. Internet Copy, LBJ Library.

Fortas, Abe. Oral History Interview, August 14, 1969, by Joe B. Frantz. Transcript. Internet Copy, LBJ Library.

Graham, Callan. Oral History Interview, August 10, 1978, by Michael L. Gillette. Transcript. LBJ Library.

Grubin, David, producer. "LBJ: Part One, Beautiful Texas." *The American Experience.* Program transcript. Available at http://www.pbs.org/wgbh/americanexperience/features /transcript/lbj-transcript/.

Hailey, James Lamar. "Breaching the Mesquite Curtain: A Study of George Berham Parr." Master's thesis, Texas A&I University, Kingsville, Texas, 1988.

Handbook of Texas Online. s.v. "Duval County." University of Texas at Austin.

Handbook of Texas Online. s.v. "Parr, George Berham." University of Texas at Austin.

Montejano, David. "A Journey through Mexican Texas, 1900–1930: The Making of a Segregated Society." PhD thesis, Yale University, New Haven, Connecticut, 1982.

Parr, George B. Pardon File. U.S. Department of Justice, Office of the Pardon Attorney.

Rowe, James M. "The Mesquite Pendergast." Unpublished manuscript. Photocopy. Corpus Christi Public Library.

Smith, William Robert. Oral History Interview, November 9, 1983, by Michael L. Gillette. Transcript. LBJ Library.

Snow, Laura. "The Poll Tax in Texas: Its Historical, Legal, and Fiscal Aspects." Master's thesis, University of Texas, Austin, 1936.

Sparks, Mary K. "A Look at Factors Leading to the Murder of a Broadcast Journalist." Paper submitted to the Seventy-Fifth Annual Meeting of the Association for Education in Journalism and Mass Communication, August 5–8, 1992. Montreal, Quebec, Canada.

Texas State Constitution. Adopted February 15, 1876. Available at http://www.constitution .legis.state.tx.us/.

INDEX

Page numbers in *italics* refer to illustrations.

Printed in the USA
CPSIA information can be obtained
at www.ICGtesting.com
LVHW041659091123
763265LV00035B/1113/J